LICENTIOUS FICTIONS

Licentious Fictions

NINJŌ AND THE NINETEENTH-CENTURY
JAPANESE NOVEL

Daniel Poch

Columbia University Press
New York

Columbia University Press wishes to express its appreciation for assistance given by the
Wm. Theodore de Bary Fund in the publication of this book.

Columbia University Press
Publishers Since 1893
New York   Chichester, West Sussex
cup.columbia.edu
Copyright © 2020 Columbia University Press
All rights reserved

Library of Congress Cataloging-in-Publication Data
Names: Poch, Daniel (Daniel Taro), author.
Title: Licentious fictions : ninjō and the nineteenth-century Japanese novel / Daniel Poch.
Other titles: Ethics of emotion in nineteenth-century Japanese literature
Description: New York : Columbia University Press, [2020] | Revised and expanded version
of the author's thesis (doctoral)—Columbia University, 2014 titled Ethics of emotion in
nineteenth-century Japanese literature : Shunsui, Bakin, the political novel, Shôyô, Sôseki. |
Includes bibliographical references and index.
Identifiers: LCCN 2019018560 (print) | LCCN 2019981050 (ebook) | ISBN 9780231193702 (cloth) |
ISBN 9780231550468 (ebook)
Subjects: LCSH: Japanese fiction—19th century—History and criticism. | Emotions in literature. |
Ethics in literature.
Classification: LCC PL747.53.E36 P63 2020 (print) | LCC PL747.53.E36 (ebook) |
DDC 895.63/3093538—dc23
LC record available at https://lccn.loc.gov/2019018560
LC ebook record available at https://lccn.loc.gov/2019981050

Columbia University Press books are printed on permanent and durable acid-free paper.
Printed in the United States of America

Cover design: Milenda Nan Ok Lee

Cover art: Image based on black-and-white illustration from chapter 6 of *Ōshū kiji: Karyū
shunwa* (illustrator unknown; published by Sakagami Hanshichi in Tokyo, 1878).
Courtesy of Waseda University Library.

CONTENTS

CONTENTS

ACKNOWLEDGMENTS

Completing this book would not have been possible without the help of many individuals and institutions. My greatest debt of gratitude goes to Haruo Shirane and Tomi Suzuki. Without their unconditional support over many years, too great to capture in words, this project would never have materialized, from its initial conception to its publication in these pages. I thank them for their unstinting advice, patience, energy, and trust—for providing me with an ideal mentorship that I consider myself extremely fortunate to have received. I am also deeply thankful to David Lurie and Satoru Saito for their incisive feedback. Their detailed comments and advice were invaluable in my revision process. I am greatly indebted as well to Nan Ma Hartmann, Christina Yi, and Tom Gaubatz for reading my entire manuscript and providing detailed and helpful feedback.

I would like to express my heartfelt gratitude to Toeda Hirokazu and Ikezawa Ichirō for graciously facilitating longer stays of research at Waseda University, Tokyo, at different stages of my project. Both Professor Toeda and Professor Ikezawa were wonderful hosts and warm mentors to me. My research and writing would not have been possible without generous financial support from Columbia University, Waseda University, the Canon Foundation in Europe, the Japan Foundation, the Japan Society for the Promotion of Science, and a General Research Fund–Early Career Scheme grant awarded by the Research Grants Council of Hong Kong. The University of Hong Kong also provided generous funding for my research and the publication of this book.

I would like to thank my former mentor at the University of Heidelberg, Wolfgang Schamoni, whose scholarship and careful training in reading Japanese literary texts initially enabled me to embark on the future study and research culminating in this monograph. I am also grateful to the following scholars for their insightful advice, encouragement, questions, or invitations to present my work: David Atherton, Rebecca Copeland, Wiebke Denecke, Bettina Gramlich-Oka, Irmela Hijiya-Kirschnereit, Ken K. Ito, Su Yun Kim, Kōno Kimiko, Haiyan Lee, Munakata Kazushige, Saitō Mareshi, Jan Schmidt, Ariel Stilerman, Shiho Takai, J. Keith Vincent, Jeremy A. Yellen, and Eve Zimmerman. I am also thankful to Pau Pitarch Fernández, Jenny Guest, Matthew Mewhinney, Arthur Mitchell, Nate Shockey, Charles Woolley, Hitomi Yoshio, and Chi Zhang. I would like to thank my colleagues at the University of Hong Kong, who provided me with a supportive environment for research and teaching. I would like to name in particular Adam Jaworski, Kendall A. Johnson, Charles Schencking, and my colleagues in the Department of Japanese Studies Janet Borland, Timothy Unverzagt Goddard, Yoshiko Nakano, Izumi Nakayama, Victor E. Teo, and Daniel Trambaiolo. I am grateful to the University of Hong Kong for allowing me to take the research leave necessary for writing this book, and my special thanks go to Derek Collins, the dean of the Faculty of Arts, for his support.

At Columbia University Press, Christine Dunbar and Christian Winting provided professional and always gracious support throughout the publication process. I am also grateful to Leslie Kriesel and to Mike Ashby for their meticulous help in copyediting the manuscript. I am indebted to Angelo Yeuk Wong for his careful proofreading of my translations and references. I thank Anne Holmes and Rob Rudnick for creating the index. Many thanks also go to Milenda Nan Ok Lee for designing the wonderful book cover. Last but not least, the feedback, criticism, and advice of my three anonymous reviewers were tremendously important in tackling the final revisions. I also thank them for pointing out embarrassing mistakes in the manuscript. Needless to say, all remaining inaccuracies and weaknesses are my responsibility alone.

An earlier version of parts of chapter 6 appeared in "Measuring Feeling as Theory of Literature: Romanticism and the Performance of Genre in Natsume Sōseki's *Kusamakura* and Critical Writings," *Monumenta Nipponica* 73, no. 1 (2018): 1–26. An earlier version of a short portion of chapter 3 was originally published in "Translation, Human Emotion, and the *Bildungsroman* in Meiji Japan: Narrating Passion and Spiritual Love in the Novel *Karyū shunwa*," *Japanese Language and Literature* 53, no. 1 (2019): 63–93. I am grateful to Waseda University Library and the National Diet Library, Tokyo, for kindly granting me permission to reproduce visual materials from their collections.

Finally, I would like to thank Dietrich Bollmann, Nan Ma Hartmann, Martin Hell, Peter Nejkov, Jan Schmidt, and Robin Weichert, whose friendship has been a continuous source of strength extending over the years and continents. I am deeply grateful to Akiko Nishiyama for being there in Berlin and for her tireless support in proofreading; to my family in Japan; to Su Yun Kim for companionship, love, and for bearing with me; and to Gösta Poch for carrying much of the emotional cost throughout my journey while being himself on an intellectual journey of much greater significance than mine. This book is dedicated to him and to the memory of my mother.

ABBREVIATIONS

KBHT	Kindai bungaku hyōron taikei
MBZ	Meiji bungaku zenshū
NBKSS	Nihon bungaku kenkyū shiryō sōsho
NKBT	Nihon koten bungaku taikei
NKiBT	Nihon kindai bungaku taikei
SNKBT	Shin Nihon koten bungaku taikei
SNKBTM	Shin Nihon koten bungaku taikei Meiji-hen
SNKBZ	Shinpen Nihon koten bungaku zenshū

LICENTIOUS FICTIONS

INTRODUCTION

Readers of novels in this world must see them with utmost precaution! Novels are like morphine: one must love them, but also fear them.

—TSUBOUCHI SHŌYŌ, *IMOTOSE KAGAMI*

In his seminal treatise of 1885–1886, *Shōsetsu shinzui* (*The Essence of the Novel*), the literary critic, translator, and novelist Tsubouchi Shōyō (1859–1935) famously defined the fundamental objective of the novel thus: "The main focus of the novel is on *ninjō* [human emotion]. Social customs come next in importance."[1] This often-cited declaration has been read as the programmatic formulation of a new understanding of the novel, focusing on the emotional interiority of the modern private subject and the mimetic representation of social customs. Shōyō's emphasis on human emotion—male-female love and desire—came to be seen as the discursive origin of the modern novel in Japan, for which the depiction of emotion was a major signifier. It is striking, however, that Shōyō, throughout his treatise, defines the key word *ninjō* in predominantly negative terms, such as vulgar passion (*retsujō*). The true novel (*makoto no shōsetsu*) that Shōyō envisions should didactically demonstrate how the protagonist fights his or her vulgar passion, for instance through reason.[2] It is by depicting the plot of such a struggle that the novel, for Shōyō, can confer its social "benefits," including the ability to elevate and civilize the readers' feelings and thus free them from devastating passion. In seemingly paradoxical fashion, Shōyō highlights as the novel's main focus an element—*ninjō*—that is immoral or, from the viewpoint of Meiji-period (1868–1912) enlightenment ideology, uncivilized. Only through the novel's didactic framework, which lies in writing the struggle with and control of vulgar passion, can it contain the danger of *ninjō* and deploy its social, civilizational, and moral significance.

A bit more than twenty years after the publication of *Shōsetsu shinzui*, in 1907, Natsume Sōseki (1867–1916) defined the literary genre of sketch prose (*shaseibun*) as one that would allow for more affective distance from the "human emotions" of the depicted fictional characters than the novel.[3] Whereas the novelist, Sōseki argues, passionately cries with the emotions of his or her characters—their love, for instance—the sketcher, while not necessarily cold, is humorously detached from those emotions. In Sōseki's famous analogy, the sketcher is like a parent who does not cry with his or her child but distantly, and gently, observes its tears. What brings together Shōyō's and Sōseki's literary projects is their common understanding of the novel as a genre focusing on *ninjō* as something problematic. Sōseki's exploration of sketch prose precisely hinges on his interest in a type of narrative that still relates to *ninjō* like the novel but is less exposed to its potential dangers.

About seventy years prior to Sōseki's reflection on sketch prose, in the mid-1830s, the popular author Tamenaga Shunsui (1790–1843) defined the type of narrative fiction he called *ninjōbon* (books of human emotion) as one that would predominantly focus on *ninjō*—male-female love. Shunsui's view of *ninjō* was positive because he claimed, in line with previous Edo-period (1600–1868) discussions, that an understanding of emotion, to be brought about by his writings, could promote empathy in his readers and allow for stronger social cohesion. However, contemporary discourses of which Shunsui was well aware also decried his writings as licentious because of their emphasis on *ninjō*. The critical view of Shunsui's *ninjōbon* as licentious writing was the outcome of prior eighteenth- and early nineteenth-century discussions of narrative fiction; at the same time, the label of licentiousness became attached to the novel more broadly, thus branding it for its problematic depiction of *ninjō* well across the Edo-Meiji divide. Shōyō's equation, in *Shōsetsu shinzui*, of *ninjō* with vulgar passion must be seen in the context of this broader historical awareness of the novel's licentiousness.

Licentious Fictions explores and historicizes the central significance of *ninjō* in the nineteenth-century Japanese novel, and in discourses surrounding it, from the Edo period to the Meiji period. *Ninjō* was an important key word in traditional criticism that, while literally meaning "human emotion," was often used primarily in reference to amorous sentiment (love) and sexual desire. It was seen as a powerful moral agent that could reinforce the social order, by inspiring empathy, for example. At the same time, it became an object of mistrust as a force that could be dangerously excessive, to the point of breaking social and ethical norms. Most important, *ninjō* was seen as what literary writing was meant to represent and convey— and what made it potentially suspect. Traditional critical discussions defined poetry as a medium that could channel and represent unregulated emotions and desires. But beginning in the eighteenth century, a strong awareness of *ninjō* started to shape a broader spectrum of Japanese genres, including *jōruri* puppet plays and particularly narrative fiction. The exploration of love and desire also lay at the heart of the early-modern Chinese vernacular novel. This book argues that Edo-period narrative genres beginning in the early nineteenth century, especially *ninjōbon* and *yomihon* (books for reading), continued and extended this exploration. It also demonstrates how the Meiji novel, instead of superseding earlier discourses and narrative practices related to *ninjō*, complicated them, for instance by integrating them into the cultural and literary concepts brought about by Western texts and translation—concepts such as realism and passionate love. An important goal is to historicize the Meiji-period novel in its interconnection not only to modern Western models but also to early-modern (and premodern) critical views and narrative practices spurred by cultural anxieties about literary writing, emotion, and desire.

On the one hand, *Licentious Fictions* presents a discursive history. It examines the continuity of discourses on poetry and, starting in the mid-eighteenth century, the novel (*shōsetsu*) as textual media that were thought not only to represent emotion and desire but also to dangerously convey them to the reader—to "teach licentiousness and incite to desire" (*kaiin dōyoku*), as the often-repeated early-modern catchphrase had it. I contextualize the continuity of these discussions within broader shifting discursive and epistemological frameworks across the early modern–modern divide—from a Confucian ethical framework in the late Edo period, for example, to the dominant discourses of civilization and enlightenment in the early to mid-Meiji. The primary historiographical objective, however, is not to reassert epistemological divides as they are often identified with regard to the Edo-Meiji transition. Instead, I examine, across the sometimes radical permutations in the discursive, sociocultural, and literary environment of nineteenth-century Japan, the continuous concern with the novel as problematic and licentious because of the emotions that it contained and generated in readers.

On the other hand and most important, this study closely analyzes narrative practices surrounding *ninjō* in the Japanese novel. These practices—involving, among other aspects, dynamics of plot and gendered representation—negotiate a fundamental ambivalence inherent in the novel. This ambivalence derives, for one, from the writers' critical awareness of not only representing emotion and desire but also dangerously conveying them to the reader and thus potentially disrupting the social order. The other side of the novel's ambivalence is its claim to moral, social, political, or (in the context of Meiji Japan) civilizational value—its ambition, for instance, to contain the licentiousness of *ninjō*. The ascription of social and political significance to literary writing, including narrative fiction, was traditionally reflected in notions of didacticism that sought to legitimate and, to a certain extent, elevate literature as moral teaching or as a medium that could "promote virtue and chastise vice" (*kanzen chōaku*). In the Meiji period, the social benefit of the novel, in turn, was largely defined by its ability to elevate society to civilization and progress. These didactic ascriptions contrasted and sometimes clashed with the novel's perceived lowly entertainment value and, more fundamentally, with its awareness of being a genre representing and producing in the reader licentious emotions and desire. The ambiguity produced by the contrast between the novel's licentiousness and ascribed didactic value was the motor for complex narrative practices surrounding the nature and value of the novel as literary writing that this book brings to light and disentangles.

Licentious Fictions describes the nineteenth century as a coherent literary and discursive space held together by an intensified critical and narrative awareness of emotion. The anxiety about the licentiousness of *ninjō* in literary writing was a traditional one, greatly predating the nineteenth century, but with the emergence of mass-produced popular genres—in particular *yomihon* and *ninjōbon*—in the early nineteenth century, the tension produced by the need to both represent licentious *ninjō* and assert the social-didactic value of literary fiction engendered narrative practices of an unprecedented complexity. This complexity continued to mark the Meiji novel, even within its new epistemological parameters. Japan's nineteenth-century modernity was an intermediate and hybrid literary-historical space, where the traditional concern with *ninjō* and its licentiousness underwent an unparalleled intensification within the new medium of the novel, *before* these concerns were ultimately superseded in the early twentieth century. We must get away from narratives that have described the emergence of modern literature in Meiji Japan by a new emphasis on, or even the liberation of, emotion as the prerogative of modern interiority and its realist representation, defined against the alleged didacticism of premodern genres. Major narrative works across the Edo-Meiji divide were in fact both didactic and emotional, engaging with and negotiating in various ways the problematic character of emotion and desire.

NINJŌ AND THE NINETEENTH-CENTURY JAPANESE NOVEL

My use of the term "novel" closely follows the historical concept of *shōsetsu* (Ch. *xiaoshuo*) that, in the early nineteenth century, started to gain broader currency and defined an important literary continuity across the Edo-Meiji transition.[4] The Chinese term *xiaoshuo* (literally, "small talk"), and the largely synonymous *baishi* (Jp. *haishi*, "unofficial or petty history"), was originally associated with the historiographical tradition. Popular gossip or the "small talk" on the streets was collected by low-ranking "petty officials" (Ch. *baiguan*, Jp. *haikan*) and compiled, for the ruler to peruse, into unofficial histories of a more private, fictional, and morally dubious nature than that of official history.[5] This understanding of *xiaoshuo* as "petty" historiographical writing at the bottom of the genre hierarchy prevailed throughout the premodern period in China. But beginning in the seventeenth century, the term also came to increasingly refer to the long vernacular masterworks of the Ming (1368–1644) and Qing dynasties (1644–1911), including historical works like *The Romance of the Three Kingdoms* (*Sanguozhi yanyi*) and *The Water Margin* (*Shuihuzhuan*) or the erotic classic *The Plum in the Golden Vase* (*Jinpingmei*).[6] While constituting "lowly" fictional entertainment, these works had important literary, intellectual, and moral ambitions. It was in the context of the reception and study of these works and other vernacular and classical narrative Chinese texts in the eighteenth century that the concept of *shōsetsu* became more broadly disseminated in Japan. However, only with the emergence of the new genre of the *yomihon*, often written as adaptations of Ming-Qing vernacular works and culminating in Kyokutei Bakin's (1767–1848) oeuvre in the early nineteenth century, did the term *shōsetsu* start to refer more specifically to Japanese fiction.[7]

The early nineteenth century in Japan witnessed a boom in new vernacular genres, subsumed under the label of *gesaku* (playful writing). The notion of *gesaku*, which originated in the eighteenth century, by the early nineteenth century comprised all varieties of popular, widely read, and often mass-produced Japanese fiction in various material and narrative formats, including *yomihon, ninjōbon, kokkeibon* (books of humor), and heavily illustrated genres such as *kusazōshi* (picture books) and *gōkan* (bound books). The term *shōsetsu*, however, came to refer almost exclusively to works of vernacular Chinese fiction and Japanese *yomihon*, especially those by Bakin, who was the unrivaled master of the genre. The latter stood out among all other *gesaku* genres by their stylistic sophistication, their extreme degree of literacy as adaptions of sometimes multiple Chinese works and sources (both classical and vernacular), and by a "serious" moral and didactic ambition best summarized by Bakin's key slogan of "promoting virtue and chastising vice."[8] By modeling his *yomihon* on the long masterworks of Chinese vernacular fiction, Bakin firmly established the Japanese *shōsetsu* within the genealogy of the Chinese vernacular novel.

The tremendous impact of Bakin's *yomihon* in defining the nature of *shōsetsu* in nineteenth-century Japan cannot be underestimated. There was a continuous sense of the canonicity and superior value of these works. Tsubouchi Shōyō, who avidly consumed all types of popular fiction as a youth, states in one of his memoirs how, as a young reader, he awoke to the great superiority of Bakin over all other authors of popular fiction.[9] An important reason for the ascription of value to Bakin's *yomihon* was certainly the inherent quality of the writing—the stylistic and thematic sophistication of his works—but of particular relevance was the great extent to which Bakin made moral didacticism, crystallized in the slogan *kanzen chōaku*, the major structural and thematic paradigm of his long novels. This didacticism is what Shōyō defined as Bakin's writing of "idealist novels" (*aidiaru noberu*), and he also significantly notes that with Bakin the novel could, for the first time, be enjoyed by readers belonging to the "intellectual class."[10] Although Shōyō, in *Shōsetsu shinzui*, famously criticized Bakin's *yomihon* for their one-sided didacticism, a strong admiration for Bakin's "idealism" also continuously marked his project of the novel's reform.

Another important, but hitherto little-discussed, aspect of Bakin's novels was their strong awareness of *ninjō*—amorous emotion and erotic desire—that derived from the reception, in the early nineteenth century, of so-called licentious books (*insho*) from China. These were vernacular erotic novels like the *Jinpingmei* or scholar and beauty fiction (Ch. *caizi jiaren xiaoshuo*, Jp. *saishi kajin shōsetsu*) that foregrounded the devastating and titillating power of desire while also emphasizing, as especially the scholar and beauty genre did, virtuous chastity as desire's equally titillating antipode. Bakin wrote adaptations of both the *Jinpingmei* and scholar and beauty novels, and his masterwork *Nansō Satomi hakkenden* (Eight dog chronicle of the Nansō Satomi clan, 1814–1842) engages in narrative practices that subtly negotiate the novel's didactic idealism against the writing of desire or, more fundamentally, the novel's desire-inspiring nature.

Bakin's *yomihon*, however, were not seen as licentious books. This label came to refer to another genre that was of particular importance in a longer nineteenth-century perspective: the *ninjōbon* that were especially associated with their "founder," Tamenaga Shunsui.[11] *Ninjōbon* presented narratives of an often mildly erotic nature that focused on male-female amorous interactions involving pleasure-quarter courtesans and geisha.[12] Like other genres of *gesaku* fiction, *ninjōbon* were more lowbrow than Bakin's sophisticated historical novels, and Shunsui rarely refers to his writings as *shōsetsu*.[13] However, I argue that *ninjōbon* must also be contextualized in the broader nineteenth-century reception of Chinese vernacular fiction—especially the chaste scholar and beauty genre—and Bakin's novels. In his masterwork *Shunshoku umegoyomi* (*Spring-Color Plum Calendar*, 1832–33), Shunsui explicitly highlights the virtuous chastity of his courtesan heroines, emphasizing the didactic mission of his writing as *kanzen chōaku*. At the same time, surrounding discussions consistently condemned the *ninjōbon* as licentious for their representation of *ninjō*. This was tremendously important because such discussions were instrumental in the broader criticism, across the Edo-Meiji transition, of the *shōsetsu* as a problematic and dangerous genre.

The early to mid-nineteenth century in fact witnessed a broadening of the *shōsetsu* concept toward a wider array of vernacular Japanese genres, including *ninjōbon*. In 1849, Kimura Mokurō (1774–1856), a senior samurai official and friend and disciple of Bakin's, wrote a treatise titled "Kokuji shōsetsu tsū" (A guide to the novel in native script) that offered a comprehensive chart of the *shōsetsu* as Mokurō understood it. In addition to classical Japanese works like *The Tale of Genji*, the chart subsumed under this generic label works of Ming-Qing vernacular fiction and, notably, all contemporary Japanese writings that belonged to *gesaku*, including *yomihon*, *ninjōbon*, and the heavily illustrated *kusazōshi* and *gōkan*.[14] Mokurō's chart was strictly hierarchical. An admirer of Bakin's *yomihon* for their moral value and literary sophistication, Mokurō saw the *ninjōbon* in particular as the novel's most dangerous and vulgar subfield, on the same level as reprehensible Chinese licentious works like the *Jinpingmei*. At the same time, his chart outlined the *shōsetsu*'s broader conceptual scope that would be of great relevance in a longer nineteenth-century perspective. Significantly, in *Shōsetsu shinzui*, Tsubouchi Shōyō largely adopted the historical and semantic range of the *shōsetsu* that had been delineated in Mokurō's treatise. He also subsumed works of Western fiction under the conceptual umbrella of the *shōsetsu*. However, Shōyō's exposure to the Western contemporary novel was extremely limited and largely restricted to works by specific English authors. These works had a strong similarity to genres of *gesaku* fiction, of which Shōyō was aware.[15] In this fashion, *Shōsetsu shinzui* performed only a gradual—and not a radical—transformation of the *shōsetsu* concept in Japan.

Licentious Fictions relies on the genealogy of the *shōsetsu* from the eighteenth-century reception of specific vernacular Chinese works across the Edo-Meiji transition. In particular, I retrace the genealogy of the *shōsetsu* that revolved around discourses and narrative practices of *ninjō*, negotiating what I previously called the novel's ambivalence: its critical awareness of inciting potentially licentious emotions in the reader, along with its claim to moral, social, and (in the Meiji period) civilizational value. In the first half of the nineteenth century, particularly *yomihon* and *ninjōbon*—and their paradigmatic authors Kyokutei Bakin and Tamenaga Shunsui, respectively—were of paramount importance in shaping the discourses and narrative practices surrounding *ninjō* that would have a great impact on notions of the novel in the Meiji period. As already discussed, *yomihon* and *ninjōbon* were antithetical genres that seemed to embody opposed qualities of the *shōsetsu*: the *yomihon*'s moral and didactic value and the *ninjōbon*'s desire-inducing licentiousness. Taken together, both genres defined the ambiguous range of the *shōsetsu* in nineteenth-century Japan, but they also, in different ways, negotiated the novel's ambiguity within their own generic formats.

Important recent studies have provided a much more nuanced understanding of the new Meiji novel from a variety of analytical and thematic angles, and there is no doubt about the tremendous transformations—sociopolitical, ideological, stylistic—that Japanese writing underwent during the Meiji period, sometimes conceptualized as a moment of a radical epistemological break. My study, however, proposes a different model for the Edo-Meiji transition, highlighting the constitutive critical awareness of what could be called the *gesaku* classics—especially Bakin's *yomihon* and Shunsui's *ninjōbon*—for the reform of the novel in the mid-Meiji period. Specific *gesaku* works were canonized as paradigmatic for their respective subgenres in the early Meiji period. The "scholar of the West" (*yōgakusha*) and later journalist Fukuchi Ōchi (1841–1906), for example, identified as early as 1875 the following "four masterworks of the novel" (*shidai kisho*) in Japan that were all produced in the first half of the nineteenth century: Bakin's *Hakkenden* for the *yomihon*, Shunsui's *Shunshoku umegoyomi* for the *ninjōbon*, Ryūtei Tanehiko's (1783–1842) *Nise Murasaki inaka Genji* (*A Country Genji by a Commoner Murasaki*, 1829–1842) for the bound picture books (*gōkan*), and Jippensha Ikku's (1765–1831) *Tōkaidōchū hizakurige* (*Travels on the Eastern Seaboard*, 1802–1809) for the books of humor (*kokkeibon*).[16] These works are still considered today as representative masterpieces, included in most anthologies and literary histories of late Edo-period *gesaku* literature. This in itself is an important demonstration of the *longue durée* historicity of the literary canon for certain works, which complicates assumptions about the canon as a simple modern construction.[17]

Even more important, the early canonization of these *gesaku* classics helps us see the Edo-Meiji transition in a new conceptual light. In *Shōsetsu shinzui*, Bakin's *Hakkenden* and Shunsui's *Shunshoku umegoyomi* are by far the most-cited literary references, not only in quantity but also in quality. Two conclusions must be drawn from this fact. First, more than any prior works, the early nineteenth-century *gesaku* classics—particularly Bakin's *yomihon* and Shunsui's *ninjōbon*—were references of primary importance for the newly emerging Meiji novel. There is a continuous literary space of the nineteenth-century Japanese novel. Second, it is legitimate to discard, at least for the purposes of this discussion, the many minor *gesaku* works and authors that proliferated, from the *bakumatsu* period well into Meiji times, in the shadow of the *gesaku* classics—authors and works that Shōyō, in *Shōsetsu shinzui*, dismisses as the "dregs of Bakin and Tanehiko." Instead, I seek to make visible the important genealogy of the Japanese novel directly linking the *gesaku* classics to Shōyō's reform or, to be more precise, to the early translations from Western fiction in the late 1870s and early 1880s. These works for the first time challenged the model of *gesaku* fiction and paved the way for Shōyō's literary reform and the subsequent Meiji novel.

In the late 1870s and 1880s, *ninjō* became a key concept in discourses of the novel's reform. These were partly triggered by new Western translations, in particular the highly acclaimed novel *Karyū shunwa* (Spring tale of flowers and willows, 1878–1879), the abridged translation of Edward Bulwer-Lytton's (1803–1873) novel *Ernest Maltravers* (1837) and its sequel *Alice* (1838). Translations like *Karyū shunwa* provided a new model for the representation of *ninjō* where passion (translated as *jō*)—a new Meiji term for sexualized love and desire, also used in reference to *ninjōbon*—could be integrated into a narrative that emphasized the moral and civilized control of passion and desire. This new type of narrative reflected Meiji civilizational and enlightenment concerns that aimed at the suppression of unenlightened practices, including the type of licentious love associated with the *ninjōbon*, but it also gestured back to the moral didacticism of Bakin's *yomihon*. New translations like *Karyū shunwa* allowed for the representation of a new type of male protagonist, who was subject to licentious *ninjōbon* passion but could also subject this passion to civilized and moral control, for instance by integrating it into a monogamous marriage. New Western notions of sexualized passion and married love, predicated on the control of passion, were translated into a narrative format that combined elements of the *ninjōbon* and *yomihon* while responding to new Meiji enlightenment parameters.

Shōyō's *Shōsetsu shinzui* needs to be contextualized in the new literary space opened up by translations like *Karyū shunwa* that allowed for the discursive and narrative reconfiguration of *ninjōbon* and *yomihon* elements. I examine Shōyō's reform discourse and his novels produced during the 1880s in great detail because his literary project not only synthesized the earlier *gesaku* tradition but also shaped the subsequent Meiji novel, which became defined primarily in reference to its representation of *ninjō*. In this sense, Shōyō's project of literary reform lies at the heart of the nineteenth-century space of the Japanese novel. In *Shōsetsu shinzui*, Shōyō defined the (male) protagonist of the reformed novel as subject to "vulgar passion," which Meiji discourses associated with the licentious *ninjōbon*. But he also integrated Bakin's didacticism into his discussion of *ninjō* by postulating the novel's protagonist as a good person (*zennin*) able to control passion through enlightened reason. Shōyō thus conceived of the novel as a moral-didactic and civilizing agent that could divert readers from their own uncivilized passions.

Shōyō's own novels written in the late 1880s, however, dramatize in various ways how the realist depiction (*mosha*) of *ninjō* "as it is" (*ari no mama*) in Japan was not reconcilable with the novel's moral-didactic and civilizing ambition—what Shōyō called, in reference to Bakin, its idealism. Shōyō's novels engaged in complex narrative practices—dynamics of plot and gender—that again brought to the fore the traditional anxiety about the novel as a medium representing uncontrollable lust. Shōyō's new notion of realism here significantly came to stand for the depiction of *ninjō* "as it is," mirroring the licentious reality of Japanese emotions and social customs (*setai fūzoku*)—an anxiety that was inherent in contemporary civilizational discourse and overlapped with the more traditional concern about the licentiousness of the novel. Shōyō's novels deconstruct the criticism of *Shōsetsu shinzui*, highlighting the difficulty of integrating the novel's realist representation of *ninjō* with an assertion of its moral and civilizational value. It is no surprise, then, that Shōyō ultimately abandoned the novel and its reform.

In the wake of Shōyō's demise as a novelist, critical discussions continued to denounce the novel for its depiction of licentious passion and for failing to promote moral and social ideals. At the same time, the critical notion of the realist depiction of *ninjō* became constitutive of the new Meiji novel in the wake of Shōyō's reform. *Ninjō* also became identified as the privileged content of the new notion of literature (*bungaku*). Beginning in the late 1890s, critical discussions—for example, in the context of Japanese naturalism (*shizenshugi*)—promoted an increasingly unproblematic understanding of literature as imaginative writing focusing on emotion and erotic passion while moral-didactic and civilizational anxieties regarding the licentiousness of *ninjō* seemed to recede into the background. However, in the first decade of the twentieth century, Natsume Sōseki again self-reflexively questioned various genres—sketch prose, poetry, the novel—as literary media representing, expressing, or conveying emotion. One of the fundamental intellectual movements in Sōseki's literary and theoretical project was to problematize and critically deconstruct *ninjō* as the affective core of the novel and literature more broadly. Sōseki's literary writing and theory thus still belonged to the broader nineteenth-century space of the Japanese novel that revolved around *ninjō* as a licentious, or at least inherently problematic, aspect of the novel and literary writing. *Licentious Fictions* delineates this space and the complexity of the literary projects— Bakin's, Shōyō's, or Sōseki's—it engendered over time and across the Edo-Meiji transition.

EMOTION, LITERATURE, AND NINETEENTH-CENTURY MODERNITY

A key word in this study is the Japanese historical term *ninjō* or, synonymously, *jō* (emotion) as well as cognates of it such as *jōyoku* (erotic desire). In her recent work on the history of emotion, Barbara Rosenwein has emphasized the analytical importance of what she calls emotion words.[18] These are words used in the historical record to denote specific emotions and shared by historical groups of users, which she labels "emotional communities." While a historical concept, *ninjō* probably does not exactly match Rosenwein's definition, because the term mostly did not denote a specific emotion but was an umbrella term subsuming various emotions and erotic desire. One of the earliest historical definitions of *ninjō* is probably the following excerpt from the Chinese *Record of Rites* (*Liji*), which had been compiled by the first century AD: "What are the human emotions [Ch. *renqing*, Jp. *ninjō*]? They are joy, anger, sadness, fear, love, disliking, and desire [Ch. *yu*, Jp. *yoku*]. These seven feelings belong to men without their learning them."[19] This definition remained highly influential over the centuries in China and Japan, often quoted as a set phrase. In many historical discussions, however, *jō* or *ninjō* became, explicitly or implicitly, reduced semantically to the meaning of amorous emotion or love, often including sexual desire. It was through this semantic reduction that the term became most controversial in historical discourses and narratives, and it is with this narrower meaning that I am primarily concerned.

I outline in detail the discursive history of *ninjō* in chapter 1; suffice it to note here that the term continuously served as a key word in discourses on literary writing. Of particular significance, a critical consciousness of *ninjō* is inherent in nineteenth-century Japanese narrative writings. Note Bakin's conscious use of the term *jōyoku* in the context of his writing of sexual desire, Shunsui's dramatization of love as exemplification of his key concept of *ninjō*, or Shōyō's and Sōseki's critical awareness of *ninjō* in conceiving of their narrative plots. These authors, who dramatized *ninjō* as part of their narratives, were at the same time often the critics who reflected on the significance of emotion and desire in the novel. Nineteenth-century Japanese novels, in their plots and narrative representations of gender and sexuality, engaged with the parameters of literary discourse, sometimes exceeding and complicating them in various ways. In this respect, the textual practices surrounding *ninjō* I describe differ from melodrama or sentimentalism. In his seminal study, Peter Brooks has defined melodrama as a "mode of excess" characterized by "high emotionalism"—that is, the staging of strong emotions, often produced by stark moral conflicts and excessive to the extent of producing cathartic effects in viewers of plays or readers of books.[20] The textual practices I describe, however, do not elicit excessive emotions or tears—another important motif in melodrama—from readers, protagonists, or even authors. Instead, they reflect the novel as an ethically and socially problematic genre focusing on love and desire. A major portion of my textual analysis precisely examines how novelistic texts critically—even intellectually—negotiate their writing of problematic feelings and desires against their self-assertion of moral, social, cultural, and civilizational value.

A theoretical objective here is to reexamine and complicate historical narratives that have emphasized the significance of emotion—including love and desire—for the history of modernity, in Japan and globally. The following discussion engages with two major theoretical paradigms that have influenced the way emotion has been conceptualized for the context of Japanese modernity but that have also problematically obscured a critical awareness of the discourses and narrative practices connected to *ninjō*.

One important paradigm that I critique is the history of the "civilizing process," in line with Norbert Elias's (1897–1990) study originally published in German in 1939 (*The Civilizing Process*; *Über den Prozeß der Zivilisation*). Elias conceptualizes the history of modernity as a civilizing process that leads to the increasing restraint and control of emotions and their expression, especially those emotions deemed "uncivilized," including aggressiveness and sexual desire.[21] For Japan, especially the work of cultural historian Saeki Junko, while not explicitly engaging with Elias, has yielded comparable insights. In her seminal study *"Iro" to "ai" no hikaku bunkashi* (A comparative cultural history of "lust" and "love," 1998), Saeki argues that the promotion of a new Western model of chaste, spiritual, and Christian love (*ren'ai*) in Meiji Japan led to the discursive devaluation and, ultimately, the demise of early-modern or premodern Japanese notions and practices epitomized by the terms *iro, koi,* and *nasake*—all denoting an erotic and often elegant type of romance. Saeki's point is that Meiji authors often negotiated between the ideality of a new standard of spiritual, chaste love based on Western translation and the tenacity of prior conceptions and practices of erotic love inscribed in their aesthetic sensibilities. The general history of modernity that she outlines, however, is one of an increasing restraint of cultural practices of erotic love and desire.[22]

Saeki's well-documented analysis is thought-provoking, but it does not entirely avoid the romanticizing narrative of the premodern or early-modern age as one of sexual diversity and freedom, eclipsed by the civilizing and disciplining impulses of (Western) modernity. According to Saeki, *iro*, before it became devalued as pure physical lust in Meiji discourses, was synonymous with the premodern cultural practices surrounding *irogonomi*—the elegant pursuit of erotic romance—or the aesthetic universe of the pleasure quarter in the Edo period.[23] *Iro* thus principally belonged to the realm of what Foucault, in the first volume of *The History of Sexuality* (*Histoire de la sexualité*, 1976), labeled *ars erotica* and, in a surprising gesture of orientalism, restricted to the non-Western civilizations and the West's premodern antecedents. Only Western modernity could produce discursive regimes of *scientia sexualis* focused on the production of knowledge and discipline instead of pleasure. (Foucault of course later complicated his historical vision by turning the focus of inquiry to the multilayered disciplinary discourses on sexuality in ancient Greece and Rome.) For the context of Japan, Gregory Pflugfelder has provided an important corrective in precisely highlighting the "disciplinary" nature of Edo-period practices of male-male love (*nanshoku*), thus complicating the prevalent image of these practices as primarily concerned with the production of pleasure.[24] As my study demonstrates, moreover, early-modern narrative genres in Japan were greatly invested in the didactic containment of amorous desire and emotion. Note, for instance, the obsessive interest in chastity and virginity in Chinese scholar and beauty fiction, which was important for the production of the early nineteenth-century *yomihon* and *ninjōbon* interest in chaste virtue and, as its flip side, licentious desire. Shunsui's *ninjōbon*, although often seen as the epitome of the world of *iro*, in fact carefully avoided the depiction of obscenity, promoting chastity as virtuous restraint, especially for women. While I do not deny the importance and reality of sophisticated erotic cultures in the Edo period, I intentionally do not frame this study around concepts like *iro* or Kuki Shūzō's (1888–1941) *iki* (erotic elegance).[25] These notions, highlighting the production of pleasure as a cultural practice, conceal the prevalent anxiety about and attempts to control licentious desire in the novel. This anxiety and the ambiguous tension between the representation and didactic containment of emotions and desire came to the fore primarily in narrative practices focused on *ninjō*.

The Meiji period, as Saeki argues, certainly witnessed, in the context of its civilization and enlightenment ideology, the emergence of new discourses of chaste spiritual love that relegated sexual desire—derogatively labeled by Shōyō as vulgar passion—to the unenlightened past and the *ninjōbon* tradition. However, amorous feeling and desire, as epitomized by the traditional *ninjō* concept, continued to be an integral part of the Meiji novel and even merged with the new Western notion of passion. The novel continued to be seen as problematic and licentious because of its representation of passion. Meiji discourses and narratives, while couched in the new idiom and sociocultural concerns of civilization and enlightenment, were not necessarily more disciplinary and restrictive than Edo discourses, but they continuously engaged, in critical or didactic fashion, with the novel's licentiousness.

I should note here that my study investigates primarily the critical significance of *ninjō* as male-female love and desire. Male-male love (*nanshoku*) was certainly an important practice described in the Edo-period textual record that came under restrictions in the sociopolitical context of Meiji Japan, often described as increasingly heteronormative. Recent important scholarship has investigated how the Meiji novel produced narrative strategies that marginalized, suppressed, or redirected the representation of male-male love and male homosocial desire.[26] However, while not suppressed, representations of male-male love were also highly contextualized and by no means ubiquitous in pre-Meiji literary texts. This book relies on the observation that major late Edo-period narrative genres with a strong impact on the Meiji novel, in particular Shunsui's *ninjōbon* and Bakin's *yomihon*, were concerned mainly with male-female love and desire.[27] There is a significant continuity of heteronormative—or, if this term is ahistorical for the period prior to Meiji, predominantly male-female—narrative representations and practices related to *ninjō* in the novel throughout the nineteenth century. The demarcation between heteronormativity and *nanshoku* culture therefore appears to have been not only historical, mirroring an increasing suppression of male-male desire brought about by Meiji modernity, but also, especially prior to Meiji, highly contingent on textual genre and sociocultural context.[28]

The second major historical narrative of modernity that I seek to complicate revolves around the notion of modern literature as an inherently emotionalized and interiorized textual practice. A classical formulation of this influential paradigm for the context of western Europe was provided by Jürgen Habermas in his epoch-making study *The Structural Transformation of the Public Sphere* (*Strukturwandel der Öffentlichkeit*, 1962). Habermas's work retraces the emergence of the modern private subject as an active and articulate agent in what he calls the public sphere, a discursive space of rational exchange on political and economic interests. For Habermas, the development of the modern (predominantly male) subject as an active agent in the public sphere correlated with—in fact was not possible without—the concurrent development of his private subjectivity, an inner emotionalized realm that relied on the new intimacy of the married couple, the home, and the family. This realm, in Habermas's model, finds expression in modern literature, whose modernity derives from its serving as the privileged medium of representation for the private subjectivity and emotionality of the inner—but at the same time necessarily public—modern subject.[29]

Narratives of Japanese modernity have similarly stressed, although not necessarily in connection to Habermas, the intricate relationship of modern literature, emotion, and the emergence of the modern private (and inner) subject. An important case in point are the seminal essays, titled *Nihon seiji shisōshi kenkyū* (Studies in the history of Japanese political thought), written by the political philosopher Maruyama Masao (1914–1996) in the early 1940s, predating Habermas's work. Maruyama's ultimate interest lies in what he identifies as the beginnings of a modern "public" (and potentially democratic) political awareness in eighteenth-century Japan, especially in the writings of eminent Confucian scholar Ogyū Sorai (1666–1728). In correlation to the new public discourse, however, Maruyama also highlights the emergence of a new private domain in Japanese writings, focused on *ninjō*. What Maruyama has in view are eighteenth-century Confucian and so-called nativist (*kokugaku*) writings on classical poetry that evaluated *ninjō* as poetic core content much more positively than earlier (especially neo-Confucian) discussions, which viewed emotion as the origin of social turmoil and evil.[30] In these eighteenth-century Japanese texts, Maruyama sees a protomodern liberation of literature (*bungei*) as the medium of expression of a new, emotionalized private subjectivity. This liberation remained protomodern insofar as it was not yet complete, still retaining remnants of premodern Confucian morality that had to be overcome while also containing the seeds for a modern order.

In his recent study on eighteenth-century Japanese discussions on poetry and emotion, Peter Flueckiger provides a helpful critical reevaluation of Maruyama's approach. He shows that these discussions, rather than liberating a new private sphere of literature, continue to be motivated by Confucian moral concerns about the management of community and the social order. Flueckiger argues that eighteenth-century Confucian thinkers continued to view *ninjō* in moral and political terms as a means to bring about social cohesion—like Ogyū Sorai, who saw an important function of poetry in its potential to provide the ruler with knowledge of his subjects' emotions that could aid his government. Flueckiger rejects the validity of modernization narratives, like Maruyama's, that postulate the emergence of literature as an independent cultural field, liberated from the shackles of Confucian morality and focused on the emotions of the private subject. Instead, he sees eighteenth-century discussions on poetry and *ninjō* as part of a "series of reconfigurations of the relationship between emotions and the social order" that ultimately does not exceed the meaning structure of traditional Confucian moral and political discourse.[31]

Flueckiger offers a helpful historicization of the significance of *ninjō* in eighteenth-century scholarly discussions of poetry. However, the question remains: how to conceptualize the continuous importance of *ninjō* in the nineteenth century and particularly in the context of narrative fiction. Meiji discussions, including Shōyō's important emphasis on *ninjō* as the main focus of the novel, lent themselves much more convincingly to narratives of a liberation of emotionality as the private inner sphere of the modern subject. Such narratives are not entirely unjustified, as Shōyō's views were indeed informed by new notions of interiority and psychology derived from Western sources. At least since the early twentieth century, literary scholarship in Japan relied on Shōyō's notion of the novel's "realist depiction" of *ninjō* to define the nature of modern literature as a psychological realism centered on the representation of the inner and private self. Precisely for this reason, discourses from the turn of the century started to produce *Shōsetsu shinzui* as the origin of modern Japanese literature.[32] From the 1920s well into the postwar period, moreover, Marxist criticism posited *Shōsetsu shinzui* as the historical starting point of a literature concerned with the representation of capitalist bourgeois interiority and individualism. In a 1930 essay, for example, Marxist critic Senuma Shigeki (1904–1988) argued that modern literature (*kindai bungaku*), defined by psychological realism (*shinri mosha*), had emerged in Japan with *Shōsetsu shinzui*. He notes that this new type of literature, "having destroyed the shackles of [Confucian] feudalism, relied on the development of the capitalist economic structures newly fostered by the modern bourgeoisie. Its worldview was shaped by the conceptual forms of individualism, liberalism, and subjectivism."[33]

However, Shōyō's interest in the novel's realist representation of *ninjō*, rather than aiming to create a literature of the psychological and bourgeois individual, was closely linked to moral, civilizational, and political concerns. As we saw, Shōyō claims that the novel's protagonist who controls his vulgar passion is a good person—a seemingly trivial statement that, however, leads to complex narrative practices, in Shōyō's own novels, surrounding the morality of the protagonist subject to licentious passion. These narrative practices derived from Shōyō's awareness of Bakin's didacticism as well as of contemporary enlightenment concerns regarding the regulation of uncivilized emotions and social practices. These concerns were also intimately tied to the civilizational ambitions of contemporary political discourse, connected in particular to the Constitutional Reform Party (Rikken Kaishintō).

Shōyō's critical interest in *ninjō* thus certainly does not belong anymore to what Flueckiger calls, with regard to the eighteenth-century writings he examines, a "series of reconfigurations of the relationship between emotions and normative conceptions of the social order" *within* Confucian literary discourse. Unlike pre-1868 discussions, Shōyō's ideological agenda was closely tied to Meiji civilizational and enlightenment concerns. To conceptualize the difference between the parameters of Shōyō's discourse and earlier Confucian discussions, Haiyan Lee's historiographical approach in *Revolution of the Heart* (2007) can provide a helpful comparative model. In this study of the iterations of "love" in early twentieth-century Chinese culture and literature, Lee identifies what she calls, in reference to Raymond Williams's term, "structures of feeling." Lee's (and Williams's) use of the term is similar to Foucault's "episteme"—the overarching discursive configuration structuring the production of knowledge (discourses) in a given historical period—but a structure of feeling also differs from Foucault's term in that it more strongly relates to lived and "felt" everyday life experience (for instance, the experience of love) than to knowledge and thought. Lee differentiates between what she calls a "Confucian structure of feeling" in early-modern China until the early twentieth century and an "enlightenment structure of feeling" after the May Fourth period.[34] She argues that the representation of love in these different structures of feeling serves their dominant ideological and discursive concerns—the Confucian moral order (virtue) in the former and the enlightenment ideology of freedom and individualism in the latter. Indeed, as Lee remarks, "discourses of sentiment are not merely representations or expressions of inner emotions, but articulatory practices that participate in (re)defining the social order and (re)producing forms of self and sociality. Emotion talk is never about emotion pure and simple, but is always about something else, namely, identity, morality, gender, authority, power, and community."[35] Lee's approach has great merit in that it provides an alternative to the common modernization narrative that defined emotion as the prerogative of the new inner subject and literature as the representation or expression of this emotionality.[36] It also offers a historiographical model that takes into account the continuous relevance of emotion across the early modern–modern divide. It would in fact be possible to conceptualize Shōyō's critical and literary project within an "enlightenment structure of feeling"—or, in the Japanese context, perhaps more accurately a "civilizational structure"—that invests great (also political) interest in the civilizing regulation of emotions and desires.

My approach, however, differs from Lee's (and Flueckiger's) in that I do not see the role of emotion and literature primarily in (re)producing and (re)defining normative structures of feeling—Confucian morality or enlightenment values. Instead, I retrace how Japanese discourses and narrative practices constantly engaged with the social and moral instability of literature deriving from its representation of licentious *ninjō*. Major narratives across the Edo–Meiji divide dramatize *ninjō* as a force that dangerously exceeds the attempt to contain it didactically, thus destabilizing the social legitimacy of the novel. The continuous negotiation of this instability underlies the discursive and narrative production of the novel throughout the nineteenth century in Japan. My historiographical approach, moreover, emphasizes continuity, fluidity, and hybridity. I acknowledge the heuristic value in differentiating between epistemological configurations or structures of feeling, which is certainly helpful in conceptualizing the sometimes radical permutations in textual practices surrounding *ninjō* as well. At the same time, I highlight the continuous awareness, in the Meiji period, of earlier critical discussions and genres—particularly *ninjōbon* and *yomihon*, but also Chinese vernacular works like the erotic *Jinpingmei* and premodern discussions, which all revolved around the ethically subversive quality of *ninjō*.

Licentious Fictions thus contributes to the revision of narratives of modernity that saw the significance of emotion in the liberation of literature from a didactic paradigm. But the increasing importance of *ninjō* in eighteenth- and particularly nineteenth-century Japan—across the Edo-Meiji transition—is an undeniable fact that necessarily brings back the question of modernity. I therefore conceive of a specifically nineteenth-century literary modernity in Japan that relied on a continuous intensified awareness of emotion.[37] Underlying this interest were sociopolitical factors belonging to modernity in the broadest sense: urbanization, socioeconomic change, anxieties about social fragmentation, or an increasingly capitalist economy as well as, especially for the purpose of this study, the emergence of the novel as a mass-produced and mass-circulated textual medium that relied on an increasingly broad group of sufficiently educated readers as consumers.[38] I do not intend to establish a simplistic connection of cause and consequence between these admittedly broad factors of socioeconomic modernity on the one hand and discourses on *ninjō* and the novel in eighteenth- and nineteenth-century Japan on the other. But I believe that these factors underlay the production of the Japanese novel and contributed to the intensified anxieties surrounding its representation of disruptive emotions and desires. Anxieties about licentious *ninjō* in literary writing certainly predated the nineteenth century, but with the emergence of the novel as a mass-produced medium, they reached an unprecedented degree of intensity, producing variegated discourses and increasingly complex narrative practices in novelistic texts. My concept of the nineteenth-century modernity of the Japanese novel therefore relies not on epistemological shifts but, more fluidly and hybridly, on the appropriation and intensification—but, in this fashion, also the profound reconfiguration—of the traditional consciousness of literary writing and emotion as licentious and disruptive. This specifically nineteenth-century modernity was inherently transitory, though, given its erasure in the early twentieth century. To map its literary space and historiography is the project of this book.

OVERVIEW

Part 1 (chapters 1–2) retraces premodern and early-modern discourses and narrative practices of the novel. Chapter 1 starts by examining the discursive tradition in China and Japan that defined literary writing as expressive of *ninjō*. It covers traditional discourses on poetry but also the new spectrum of genres that, in the eighteenth century, came to be discussed in reference to *ninjō*: works like *The Tale of Genji* and especially the vernacular Chinese novel. I also examine the so-called cult of *qing* in late imperial China and its reception in Japan. "Cult of *qing*" refers to the great proliferation of writings about love and desire in late imperial Chinese culture that influenced works of vernacular fiction. While the intellectual discussions associated with the Chinese "cult" found relatively little resonance in Japan, vernacular works like the *Jinpingmei* and chaste scholar and beauty fiction were indeed received. I argue that the reception of these novels in Japan produced a specifically nineteenth-century aesthetic of *ninjō* representation highlighting virtuous chastity and faithfulness (often in women), but also evil desire and licentiousness. This aesthetic was particularly productive in the early nineteenth-century *yomihon* and *ninjōbon*. The chapter finally discusses the genesis of the *ninjōbon* and Tamenaga Shunsui's *Shunshoku umegoyomi*, which soon came to be seen as the paradigmatic masterwork of the genre. While Shunsui emphasized the chastity and faithfulness particularly of his heroines, surrounding critical discussions—what I call *ninjōbon* discourse—well into the Meiji period viewed the *ninjōbon* and the novel more broadly as licentious.

Chapter 2 discusses Kyokutei Bakin's *Nansō Satomi hakkenden*, the undisputed masterwork of the *yomihon* genre. Bakin's *yomihon* greatly differed from the *ninjōbon* by their much higher degree of literary sophistication, their focus on martial themes, and their thoroughly sustained ethical discourse that bespoke the genre's moral-didactic ambitions. My reading, however, highlights the great relevance of emotion and desire in *Hakkenden*, which derived from Bakin's awareness of Chinese vernacular works like the *Jinpingmei* and scholar and beauty fiction. As in that genre, Bakin often predicates virtue on the absence or control of amorous emotion, but his text also dramatizes how virtuous figures are ambiguously receptive to desire. *Hakkenden*'s narrative critically engages with the problematic ambiguity of literary fiction as a textual medium that promotes moral-didactic ends while representing desire and generating it in the reader.

Part 2 (chapters 3–5) moves to the early to mid-Meiji period, where *ninjō* became a key concept in the discourses and narrative practices related to literary reform. Chapter 3, after reviewing new Meiji discussions on gender, sexuality, and love, offers an in-depth reading of an important, though little-studied, novel: *Karyū shunwa*, the translation of Edward Bulwer-Lytton's *Ernest Maltravers* and its sequel, *Alice*. I argue that this novel was foundational in producing the literary space for 1880s novelistic reform, allowing for the integration of the representation of passion—a new Meiji term discursively associated with the *ninjōbon*—into a narrative that emphasized the control of passion, thus responding to both moral-didactic and new enlightenment (civilizational) concerns. Relying on a new bildungsroman format, *Karyū shunwa* stages a new type of masculinity that is subject to licentious passion but also able to subject this passion to civilized and moral control. The control of passion, moreover, connects to the new narrative themes of advancement through hard study and work (*risshin shusse*) as well as democratic political activity within the contemporary People's Rights Movement (Jiyū Minken Undō)—themes that transposed the exemplarity of *yomihon* masculinity into Meiji enlightenment discourse. I close this chapter with a discussion of Kikutei Kōsui's (1855–1942) novel *Seiro nikki* (Diary of getting on in the world, 1884), a rewriting of *Karyū shunwa* into a Japanese novel. This novel, more unambiguously than *Karyū shunwa*, combined the representation of erotic passion and its control with the new themes of *risshin shusse* and democratic activity.

Chapter 4 argues that Tsubouchi Shōyō's project of the novel's reform was closely connected to the new literary space produced in Japan by the translation *Karyū shunwa*. Shōyō's project initially developed out of his reception and translation of a highly limited body of English novels, primarily by Bulwer-Lytton and Walter Scott (1771–1832), in the wake of *Karyū shunwa*'s publication. These Western works allowed Shōyō to conceive of a new type of novel focusing on *ninjō* that critically engaged with previous Japanese genres, particularly Shunsui's *ninjōbon* and Bakin's *yomihon*. In *Shōsetsu shinzui*, Shōyō appropriates Bakin's moral-didactic discourse within his conceptualization of *ninjō*, thus integrating the representation of vulgar passion associated with the *ninjōbon* into a framework of the control of passion through reason. The chapter finally stresses the significance of Shōyō's model of literary reform within broader political and social discourse in the late 1880s and early 1890s, including the ideology of the Constitutional Reform Party. Shōyō's model most immediately resonated with Reform Party–inflected authors of political fiction, whose agenda was invested in what could be called the civilizational politics of *ninjō*.

Chapter 5 investigates Shōyō's own novels from the mid to late 1880s, including famous works like *Tōsei shosei katagi* (Characters of present-day students, 1885–1886) but also texts still largely unexamined. I argue that Shōyō's novels dramatize an aporia between the realist depiction of *ninjō* and what he calls idealism—the depiction of "good people"—a term referring to the moral didacticism of Bakin's *yomihon* but also an enlightened masculinity predicated on the control of uncivilized passion. Unlike *Shōsetsu shinzui*'s criticism, Shōyō's novels increasingly deconstruct such an ideal masculinity, revealing doubts about the civilized reality of Japan but also bringing back the traditional anxiety about the novel as a medium generating licentious desire in readers. The aporia between realism and idealism triggered Shōyō's ultimate abandonment of the novel. It also dramatized the novel's continuous instability—its inability to reconcile the representation of emotion with normative conceptions of the social order.

Part 3 (chapter 6) moves to the late Meiji period and in particular Natsume Sōseki's literary project, which I recontextualize within the literary space of the Japanese novel shaped by Shōyō's reform and newly emerging notions of literature (*bungaku*). Despite Shōyō's ultimate suspicion and abandonment of the "novel of human emotion and social customs" (*ninjō setai shōsetsu*), *ninjō*, in explicit reference to Shōyō's discourse, became the key word in discussions of the Japanese novel beginning in the 1890s.[39] This chapter starts by retracing the development of the Meiji novel in the wake of Shōyō's reform as well as of discourses that produced an increasingly naturalized understanding of literature grounded in the representation of emotion, primarily love and desire. I then examine how Sōseki explored so-called *shaseibun* and various poetic genres as emotionally detached literary media, thus questioning the contemporary novel and discourse on literature. This deconstructive exploration also complemented his theory of literature as a radical reinvestigation of literary emotionality. I thus resituate Sōseki's literary and critical project within the nineteenth-century literary space that continuously dramatized a suspicion of *ninjō*.

The epilogue briefly outlines the factors that led to the gradual demise, around the turn of the century, of the continuous genre memory that problematized the novel's writing of *ninjō*. It demonstrates how fundamental parameters of this memory—including social-didactic legitimation discourses of literary writing and the suspicion of *ninjō*'s licentiousness—were waning in the early twentieth century. This discussion historically delimits the nineteenth-century modernity of discourses and narrative practices of *ninjō* in the novel.

PART I

Ninjō and the Early-Modern Novel

Chapter One

FROM *NINJŌ* TO THE *NINJŌBON*

Toward the Licentious Novel

The "Fireflies" (Hotaru) chapter of *The Tale of Genji* contains a famous discussion—the first of its kind in Japan—about the dangers and benefits of tales (*monogatari*). The discussion is skillfully framed within a scene of seduction. The much older Genji has designs on the young woman Tamakazura, the long-lost daughter of his former lover, Yūgao, whom he has brought to his mansion under the pretext of caring for her like his own daughter. In the scene—a damp day during the midsummer rains—Genji finds Tamakazura engrossed in reading tales, her long hair wet and in a tangle owing to her excitement and the hot, humid air. To tease her, Genji severely criticizes the fictional tales as lies (*soragoto*), although he admits that their verisimilitude or force of deception can be strongly moving. Genji also smilingly notices the girl's entangled hair (*kami no midaruru*), an eroticized attribute usually associated with lovemaking. When Tamakazura accuses Genji of being a liar himself—she has a point, given his attempts at seduction under the pretext of fatherly care—he changes his rhetorical strategy and launches into a defense of fiction. Tales can fill in all the details (*kuwashiki koto*), Genji explains, that the official histories of Japan have left out. Tales can also allow an author to pass on to subsequent generations things that he or she has seen or heard about other people—things so emotionally moving that they cannot be kept shut in the author's heart.[1] Most important, tales can function like the Buddha's expedient means (Jp. *hōben*,

Sk. *upāya*), allegorical fictional parables that he tells his listeners. Although fictional untruths and delusions in themselves, these expedient stories can lead the unenlightened listener or reader, by the teaching they convey, to a realization of the Buddhist truth that is beyond the sensuous and fictional delusions of the world.[2]

Genji's discourse, like Murasaki Shikibu's tale, is unprecedented and exceptional, unparalleled by any extant contemporaneous discussions. In its ambivalence, however, it captures well some of the core ideas regarding literature and fiction that were influential in East Asia throughout the premodern period. On the one hand, it presents the negative view that literary tales are fictional and false—lies that captivate and entertain but also depict erotic desire and incite the reader to it. Tamakazura's wet, tangled hair is no coincidence in a scene that is set during the summer rains—a seasonal motif associated with boredom but also, especially in poetry, erotic longing. Even more unmistakably, Genji closes his discourse with an invitation to Tamakazura to create together "a tale that has never been told" and to "pass it on to the world."[3] His seductive intent is loud and clear. Subtler, though, is Murasaki Shikibu's exploration of the fine line between reality and fiction through Genji's words and the critical, self-referential reflection of *The Tale of Genji* itself. Genji and Tamakazura are already part of the tale being written and passed on to the world that captivates, moves, and tangles the hair of present and future (female) readers—in other words, that seduces them as much as Genji attempts to seduce Tamakazura. Genji's attempt at erotic seduction is an allegory of literary fiction. *The Tale of Genji*'s writing of love and desire involving, besides Genji and Tamakazura, innumerable other protagonists, both male and female, became the main point of criticism leveled against the tale over subsequent centuries. Especially in the early modern period, scholars and critics came to label the tale a licentious book (*insho*).

Genji's defense of fiction also ties in with important paradigms in traditional fiction discourse. The idea that fiction could complement official history (*seishi*) by filling in the left-out details, often of a more private and sometimes erotic nature, served as a commonplace legitimation of fiction writing in China, bringing it closer to the more canonical genre of history, sanctioned by factuality and truth.[4] Even more important is Genji's emphasis on the didactic potential of literature. Genji merely alludes to the Buddhist idea of the expedient quality of fiction. But in a similar vein, later readers also saw in *The Tale of Genji*, from a Confucian perspective, the potential for moral instruction that could show them, for instance, what they should avoid in their own behavior: especially the licentiousness of love.[5]

The primary concern of my book and this chapter is not with *The Tale of Genji* or Heian-period (794–1192) literature but with the nineteenth century. My motivation, however, in starting with Genji's ambivalent discourse on fiction is to point to the historical depth of the problem at stake and to the subtle connections of the *Genji* passage to some of the nineteenth-century writings discussed in my study. Tsubouchi Shōyō's 1886 novel *Imotose kagami* (Mirror of marriage), for example, contains an important scene of reading that subtly references Genji's "Fireflies" discussion. In Shōyō's novel, Tamakazura is a university-educated young male hero, the book that is read is a Western novel, and Shōyō's moralizing narrator, instead of Genji, delivers the discourse on fiction's benefits and dangers. Yet the scene's setting in the tedious (*tsurezure naru*) midsummer rainy season is similar, as is its theme: the ability of the novel, which for Shōyō must focus on love, to incite dangerous lust and the necessity to read it in the correct way, to see its didactic intent. Otherwise, Shōyō writes, "Novels [*haishi*] are like morphine: one must love them, but also fear them."[6] Besides *The Tale of Genji* and the Western novel (Edward Bulwer-Lytton's *Ernest Maltravers*), another important intertextual reference in Shōyō's discussion on fiction is to the *Jinpingmei*, the canonical Chinese erotic novel, often decried as licentious. This brings us closer to the problem of historical layers to be explored in this chapter. The example of Shōyō's novel, however, is a layer that looks forward to the late nineteenth century, a historical frame that the later chapters explore.

This chapter seeks to uncover historical layers by looking into the past and ultimately to reach forward to the late Edo period. The goal is to offer a new historical contextualization of the early nineteenth-century *ninjōbon* by outlining the literary and discursive history of *ninjō* that led to the view of this genre as the paradigm for the licentious novel well into the Meiji period. My objective is not so much to produce a linear history as to shed light on interlocked historical layers that informed the understanding of *ninjō* in the nineteenth-century Japanese novel. My discussion covers approximately three thousand years and jumps from the highbrow to the lowbrow (from the canonical and classical to the vulgar), from genre to genre (from poetry to the *shōsetsu*), and from China to Japan. Yet I contend that these historical layers fundamentally underlie not only the *ninjōbon* but also, more broadly, the narrative practices surrounding the licentiousness of *ninjō* discussed later in this book.

The oldest discursive layer comprises traditional discussions of Chinese poetry, especially the canonical poetry of the *Shijing* (*Classic of Poetry*), the oldest poetic anthology of China. Discourses on *Shijing* poetry identified emotion (Ch. *qing*, Jp. *jō*) and sometimes desire (Ch. *yu*, Jp. *yoku*) as what poetry expresses and stirs in the listener or reader, and they negotiated between the blatantly scandalous subjects of the poems—often licentious love and desire—and their purportedly moral significance in an anthology that was a venerated Confucian classic. These discourses produced the idea of literature as a type of textuality that expresses and communicates *ninjō* and therefore, in comparison with other types of writing (for example, history), is morally unstable—a type of writing that has didactic potential and, in the case of *Shijing* poetry or *The Tale of Genji*, can even be ascribed great high-cultural value, but that can also elicit socially destabilizing desire. I then move to the eighteenth century in Japan, which witnessed a broadening of literary discourses on *ninjō* from canonical Chinese poetry to lowbrow vernacular genres, including the novel. This development was closely interlocked with the new reception of Chinese vernacular fiction in Japan. Early-modern Chinese vernacular novels, especially of the seventeenth and early eighteenth centuries, presented new ways of representing emotion and desire and their didactic significance. The little-studied Japanese reception of so-called licentious books like the *Jinpingmei* and chaste scholar and beauty novels is an important case in point. Whereas, in the eighteenth century, notions of the novel's licentiousness, mediated by the reception of Chinese fiction, remained confined largely to scholarly discourse, by the nineteenth century they had come increasingly to define the broader literary imagination of popular fiction, especially in the genre of *ninjōbon* and the work of Kyokutei Bakin. This literary imagination, in a nutshell, pitched the representation of licentiousness against chastity. *Ninjōbon* often highlighted the chastity of female virtue while surrounding discourses decried them as immoral. This contradiction informed Tamenaga Shunsui's foundational *Shunshoku umegoyomi* and its sequels. Shunsui's works came to exemplify the *ninjōbon* genre and epitomized what readers and critics would refer to as licentious novels well into the late Meiji years.

BETWEEN MORALITY AND EXCESS: EARLY DISCOURSES ON EMOTION, DESIRE, AND LITERATURE

Since the highly influential "Great Preface" (Daxu) to the *Shijing*, traditional discourses in East Asia had identified "emotion" as the fundamental psychological driving force and content of poetic expression. This foundational text defined basic assumptions about the social meaning of poetry and literature throughout the premodern period in both China and Japan. The prefaces to the *Kokinshū* (*Collection of Ancient and Modern Poems*), the extremely influential early tenth-century imperially commissioned collection of *waka* (classical Japanese poetry), famously make reference to the "Great Preface." The short treatise presented in condensed form the theoretical position of the so-called Mao school of *Shijing* interpretation, which arose in the Former Han dynasty (206 BCE–9 CE).[7] This position assumes that poetry (Ch. *shi*, Jp. *shi*) is the linguistic product of a physiologically grounded emotional response to external stimuli: "The emotions are moved within and take form in words [poetry]. If words are inadequate, we speak them out in sighs. If sighing is inadequate, we sing them. If singing them is inadequate, unconsciously our hands dance and our feet tap them."[8] The compositional process of poetry is thus conceived of as natural and spontaneous, the extension of an emotional and physiological movement that, depending on its intensity, can involve the entire body.[9]

An important strategy of the "Great Preface" and the Mao tradition of *Shijing* exegesis was to define the nature of the external stimuli inducing the movement of emotion and the production of poetry—as well as the nature of poetic emotion itself—as political and moral. In this way, the erotic character of many poems in the anthology, especially in the "Airs of the States" (Guofeng) section, could be didactically redirected. For example, the famous first poem, titled "Fishhawk" (Guanju), could be read as a poem of male erotic longing for a young girl. These are the first and third stanzas:

The fishhawks sing *gwan gwan*
on sandbars of the stream.

Gentle maiden, pure and fair,
fit pair for a prince. . . .

Wanting, sought her, had her not
waking, sleeping, thought of her,
on and on he thought of her,
he tossed from one side to another.[10]

The Confucian tradition of the Mao commentary, however, viewed this poem as the expression of the "virtuous attainment" of the queen consort of King Wen of the Zhou dynasty (ca. 1046–256 BCE), who "delighted that pure and fair maidens had been found to be mated with the prince [King Wen]."[11] The poem thus expressed the queen consort's lack of jealousy, which in itself was seen as the result of the sage-king's civilizing influence. In this way, the "Great Preface" saw poetry as an emotional reaction to and comment on the moral nature of political government. When stirred by good government, such as the ideal rule of King Wen (under which the older corpus of *Shijing* poetry was allegedly composed), human emotions and the poetry that they generated were defined as "peaceful" and "happy." The emotions and poetry produced by morally degenerate government, however, were "bitter" and "angry." The "Great Preface" defined the emotions expressed in *Shijing* poetry, whether happy or angry, as ethical and correct.[12] Even the so-called mutated poetry produced under degenerate governance, after the decline of King Wen's civilizing influence, was not seen as immoral because it was allegedly composed by virtuous officials (the "historians of the states") lamenting the decline. The mutated poems in particular often had a strongly erotic quality.

By emphasizing the ethicality of the entire corpus of *Shijing* poetry, the "Great Preface" left untouched the morally problematic potential of emotion and the illicit amorousness of many poems. However, in the "Record of Music" (Yueji), a contemporary compilation with a textual and intellectual affinity to the "Great Preface," this dimension was more explicitly explored.[13] The "Record of Music" introduced the concept of desire (Ch. *yu*, Jp. *yoku*), which was more strongly immoral in comparison with emotion but also similar in being receptive to exterior stimuli—objects inciting desire—that could generate inner movement and outward expression. One prominent concern of the "Record of Music" was how to regulate desire, which, if uncontrolled, could have the power to lead human nature (Ch. *xing*, Jp. *sei*), defined as innately moral, to "depraved excess and turmoil." Important means to give "proper measure" to destructive desire were music and ritual. The "Record" did not discuss poetry, but its philosophical model was very close to that of the "Great Preface." Although the latter posited *Shijing* poetry as inherently ethical, poetry was also seen as the result of inner stirrings provoked by external stimuli and thus had, like the emotions it expressed, an implicit affinity to the power of desire. Yet unlike emotion, desire could never be the expression of moral feelings. It was seen as the result of strong physiological urges, including sexual ones.[14]

Neither the "Record of Music" nor the "Great Preface," however, explicitly defined key terms such as emotion, desire, or human nature or discussed how they would relate to one another.[15] These terms remained relatively unsystematized in early philosophical discourse but were brought together in a more coherent and unified model in the Song period (960–1276), in particular by Zhu Xi's (1130–1200) neo-Confucian philosophical system. Zhu Xi was also the first to comment on the ethically ambiguous nature of poetry, especially in connection to its expression of emotion and desire.

Although it is impossible here to provide a comprehensive overview of Zhu Xi's philosophical model, a short discussion of some essential tenets is necessary given the tremendous impact that neo-Confucian notions exerted on discourses of literature, including narrative fiction, in early-modern Japan.[16] Zhu Xi distinguishes between two fundamental states of the human mind: an original state of perfect tranquility and moral goodness that is the state of inborn human nature conforming to the cosmic moral order, or heavenly principle (Ch. *tianli*, Jp. *tenri*); and the state of the movement (Ch. *dong*, Jp. *dō*) of emotions and desires that are stirred by external stimuli and disrupt the tranquility of the mind, thus removing it from the absolute moral goodness of heavenly principle. Zhu Xi notes,

Nature [*xing*] is the state before activity begins, the feelings [*qing*] are the state when activity has started, and the mind [Ch. *xin*, Jp. *shin*] includes both of these states. For nature is the mind before it is aroused, while feelings are the mind after it is aroused. . . . Desire [*yu*] emanates from feelings. The mind is comparable to water, nature is comparable to the tranquility of still water, feeling is comparable to the flow of water, and desire is comparable to its waves. Just as there are good and bad waves, so there are good desires, such as when "I want humanity" [a reference to

Confucius' *Analects* (*Lunyu*)] and bad desires which rush out like wild and violent waves.[17] When bad desires are substantial, they will destroy the Principle of Heaven, as water bursts a dam and damages everything.[18]

Both emotions and desires could be good, as when Confucius presents the urge to enact virtues like humanity or benevolence (Ch. *ren*, Jp. *jin*) as a desire; they could also be bad if directed at less-noble objects—good food, luxurious clothes, or sex. Zhu Xi situates the origin of and possibility for moral evil in the movement of emotions and desires, which is the realm of material force or vital energy (Ch. *qi*, Jp. *ki*), the antipode of the good and calm heavenly principle, and is stirred by external stimuli. Martin Huang, who quotes and discusses the preceding passage, notes that Zhu Xi implies a "subtle hierarchical pattern of moral valorization" in his juxtaposition of human nature, emotion, and desire through the water metaphor.[19] While the mind, when in the state of its morally good inborn nature, is like still water, the movement of its emotions is like flowing water, and its desires are likened to violent waves. Although both emotions and desires produce movement, which can be the potential origin of evil, the movement induced by desires is stronger and more dangerous than the one produced by emotions. At the same time, emotions and desires form a continuum that stretches to the "good" tranquility of human nature. To make them good by harmonizing them with heavenly principle was precisely the goal of neo-Confucian self-cultivation.

This model, even if not necessarily on a theoretically explicit level, formed the discursive backdrop for cultural assumptions about emotion and desire in premodern East Asia and, more specifically, in early-modern and even Meiji-period Japanese literary texts. More directly, it also informed Zhu Xi's thinking about *Shijing* poetry. In the preface to his *Shijing* commentary, which draws on both the "Great Preface" and the "Record of Music," Zhu Xi defined human desire, stirred by external things, as the origin of poetic expression.[20] Poetry was the expression of the movement of emotion or desire, and it could be either good or bad. It could either conform to the Confucian Way or be removed from it, depending on the ethical quality of the emotion or the desire from which it originated. Nakamura Yukihiko has categorized the various approaches toward literary writing that Zhu Xi's model could generate in the early Edo period, the historical moment when neo-Confucianism became prevalent as an intellectual discourse in Japan.

Given the ethically ambiguous nature of poetry, neo-Confucian discourses spanned a seemingly contradictory spectrum of positions, ranging from the total rejection of poetic writing as useless and harmful to the view that poetry could serve as a medium to "transmit the Way" (*saidō*) if expressing good desires. The third possible and very influential view was that poetry could provide examples for good behavior to emulate and bad behavior to avoid—in other words, "promote virtue and chastise vice" (*kanzen chōaku*).[21]

The contradictory range of these positions demarcated the most basic assumptions about literary discourse, the long-lasting cultural anxieties about, but also the attempts to find social value in, poetic expression and literary writing, including, later, narrative fiction. On the one hand, literary writing—both poetry and fiction—could be condemned as a medium "teaching licentiousness and inciting to desire" (*kaiin dōyoku*), the often repeated formula about the danger of literary activity and consumption.[22] On the other hand, the didactic function of literature, for instance in "promoting virtue and chastising vice," always provided a means to legitimate its pursuit. These neo-Confucian views, often as popularized common sense, also complemented medieval Buddhist notions that were equally ambiguous. As Genji's discourse demonstrated, literature could be far removed from truth (enlightenment) by constituting a fictional lie, presenting delusions related to the phenomenal world that Buddhist doctrine thought to be grounded in desire; but it could also lead to truth as an "expedient means." In all these discourses, desire—particularly erotic desire—constituted the ethically problematic backdrop of literary writing in need of didactic containment.

BRANCHING OUT TO NEW GENRES: LITERATURE AND EMOTION IN THE EIGHTEENTH CENTURY

The eighteenth century witnessed the emergence of a new type of literary discourse in Japan that marked a departure from the neo-Confucian views prevalent in the earlier Edo period by stressing the intrinsic value of *ninjō* in poetic writing, regardless of the ethical or unethical character of a specific poem or literary text. As Peter Flueckiger has argued, though, the new valorization of *ninjō* in the writings of eighteenth-century Confucian thinkers such as Itō Jinsai (1627–1705) and Ogyū Sorai, or in the nativist (*kokugaku*) writings of Motoori Norinaga (1730–1801), had an essentially social and political motivation. For these writers, poetry and literary writing, by virtue of their emotional expressivity, could provide knowledge about the experience of other human beings and thus teach empathy, a quality of utmost importance for social cohesion and the political government of the state. Ogyū Sorai argued that poetry could aid a ruler in knowing the emotions of his subjects and thus contribute to benevolent government, which again implied a more efficient regulation and control of these emotions. Eighteenth-century discussions thus focused less than prior neo-Confucian discourses on the moral dangers of emotion and literary writing, but they still emphasized the ethical role of poetry in bringing about social cohesion and control.

Concurrently, the late seventeenth and eighteenth centuries witnessed a new valorization, within intellectual debates, of popular culture and vernacular literature, including theater and narrative fiction, as a unique repository of *ninjō*. Most previous discourse had been concerned mainly with the interpretation and status of classical poetry, particularly of the *Shijing*. As a Confucian classic, the latter enjoyed a high degree of orthodox canonicity that was also not entirely undisputed, given the morally unstable character of its poems.[23] In the eighteenth century, however, literary debates in Japan opened up to new genres and texts by integrating them into a discursive context and critical vocabulary that had previously been reserved for *Shijing* poetry.

One important new textual domain was the field of *Genji* criticism, revived in the context of Confucian discourse beginning in the late seventeenth century. Although less canonical than *Shijing* poetry, *The Tale of Genji* held a comparably ambiguous moral position as a literary classic. Highly valued for its literary quality and as a repository of the cultural ideals of the Heian court, *The Tale of Genji* was also morally problematic for the many illicit love affairs that it depicted, including Genji's infamous adulterous incursion (*mono no magire*) into the imperial bloodline. Intellectual discussions of the mid-Edo period aimed at rehabilitating the tale with discursive strategies derived from *Shijing* exegesis. Kumazawa Banzan's (1619–1691) *Genji gaiden* (*Discursive Commentary on* Genji, ca. 1673), for example, described Murasaki Shikibu's classic as a window onto the idealized past of the Heian court, in which Confucian ritual, music, and literature prevailed, as in the *Shijing* poetry allegedly produced under King Wen's civilizing influence. Banzan also argued that the tale provides the reader with knowledge about *ninjō*, good and bad, and thus aids the "Way of Government."[24] Andō Tameakira's (1659–1716) early eighteenth-century treatise on *The Tale of Genji*, moreover, argued that the human emotions and social customs (*ninjō setai*) depicted in it could serve as moral instruction (*fūyu*):

This tale portrays human emotions and social customs, depicting the manners and mores of the upper, middle, and lower levels of society. Without openly expressing either praise or blame, it allows readers, through the medium of the amours it depicts, to discern for themselves what is good and what is evil. Although the principal aim of the tale is said to be the moral instruction of women, it also contains much that serves naturally to admonish men.[25]

Andō subsequently qualifies the moral teaching that the reader can gain from the representation of human emotion and social customs in the tale as *kanzen chōaku*.[26]

Subsequent eighteenth-century *kokugaku* scholars and especially Motoori Norinaga denounced, in line with their nativist critique of Chinese philosophical influences, Buddhist and Confucian interpretations that had decried the scandalous licentiousness of the tale while emphasizing its didactic potential. Norinaga argued that illicit love was the necessary "fertilizer" (*ryō*) for the valued poetic sensibility of *The Tale of Genji* and classical *waka* poetry to develop, thus likening this sensibility to the beautiful lotus flower, which relies on mud, an allegory for licentious love, to grow.[27] Norinaga's emphasis on love (*koi*) as an indispensable and valuable component of *The Tale of Genji* opened up new discursive terrain. One of the significant innovations of Norinaga's discourse was the semantic reduction of the spectrum of *ninjō* to love—an outcome of his scholarly engagement with classical *waka*, where love was, besides the four seasons, the most important topic of poetic composition. Whereas previous Confucian discussions had only implicitly referred to *ninjō* as love, Norinaga made this connection explicit and also defended illicit love as valuable even if morally problematic. His goal, however, was not to liberate literature and love from Confucian morality. On the contrary, his views displayed a strong affinity with contemporary Confucian discussions, especially of the Jinsai and Sorai schools, which equally aimed at the normative construction of social and political community. Norinaga promoted a type of Japanese pro-tonational community, held together by the ability of "knowing the pathos of things" (*mono no aware o shiru*)—a deep sensitivity and empathy for others that the emotions expressed in *The Tale of Genji* and in classical *waka*, even if immoral from a Confucian viewpoint, could purportedly teach.[28]

The various positions of late seventeenth- and eighteenth-century *Genji* criticism did not all belong to the same intellectual context. Indeed, Andō Tameakira's neo-Confucian *kanzen chōaku* apology for the tale was different from Norinaga's emphasis on empathy and the intrinsic value of love, which more closely fit the intellectual climate of eighteenth-century Japan. Yet the possibility of discussing *The Tale of Genji* in terms previously reserved for the canonical *Shijing* or Sinitic poetry points to a new intellectual and discursive environment that broadened the scope of literature—and its discourse about *ninjō*—to new genres and texts.[29]

The most important intellectual center from the late seventeenth well into the eighteenth century that promoted a broader array of genres and cultural practices was the Kogidō (Hall of Ancient Meanings) Academy, founded in Kyoto by Itō Jinsai in 1662. Jinsai and his son Tōgai (1670–1736), an eminent scholar himself who followed his father in leading the academy, attracted more than three thousand students from various social backgrounds, including the merchant and samurai classes. Jinsai, who was from the merchant class, was the first scholar to radically push away from the orthodoxy of neo-Confucian discourse through his "emphasis on emotionality and on practical ethics cultivated by ordinary people in their everyday lives."[30] For Jinsai, literature like *Shijing* poetry had value insofar as it could teach the emotions of others, regardless of a person's class background, and thus ensure more empathetic and "considerate" social interactions in an everyday context.[31] A key word in his discourse was *zoku*—the common, everyday, or vulgar—and he famously stated, "*Shijing* poetry takes the common as good. The reason why the three hundred poems [the *Shijing*] are a Classic is because they are of the common."[32] The everyday life of the common people thus formed a repository of *ninjō*, and literature "of the common," for Jinsai, was the best medium to allow insight into it. This stance naturally opened up the range of genres able to provide such insight. Indeed, in his *Dōjimon* (Questions from children, 1707), a collection of essays on various topics, Jinsai encourages the reading of unofficial histories and novels (*yashi haisetsu*) as well as songs and dramas (*shikyoku zatsugeki*)—genres that had been seen as much more vulgar and socially lowbrow than *The Tale of Genji*, not to mention the *Shijing*.[33] Jinsai's insight was that all these genres, as literature, could provide knowledge of *ninjō* and thus have high moral value even though they did not explicitly discuss morality as did canonical Confucian texts.

The discourse about *ninjō* in the Kogidō Academy brought new attention to and influenced Japanese vernacular genres. Nakamura Yukihiko has pointed to Itō Baiu's (1683–1745) positive evaluation of Ihara Saikaku (1642–1693) as an author of narrative fiction "knowledgeable about human emotion" (*ninjō ni satoku*).[34] Baiu was another of Jinsai's sons. The most remarkable cross-fertilization, however, took place with Chikamatsu Monzaemon's (1653–1724) contemporary puppet (*jōruri*) theater. One important source is Hozumi Ikan's (1692–1769) preface to *Naniwa miyage* (*Souvenirs of Naniwa*, 1738), a commentary on Chikamatsu's puppet plays that is thought to overlap with Chikamatsu's own views on *jōruri* performance. Ikan for the first time discusses the puppet theater as a genre expressing *ninjō*. He argues that since *jōruri* relies on the performance of lifeless puppets, as opposed to the live play of human actors in kabuki, the playwright needs to make a particular effort to bring out the emotions of his figures and move the spectator. The words spoken by a puppet performing a woman, Ikan explains, should openly state the true emotions (*jitsujō*) of that woman even if, in real life, a woman would not openly utter her feelings for reasons of propriety. *Jōruri* in this way has to rely on artifice (*gei*), as opposed to the mimetic depiction of reality "as it is," in order to express true emotion and affectively reach the viewer.[35] Ikan was a Confucian scholar who had studied under Jinsai's son Tōgai at the Kogidō Academy. That the lowbrow genre of the puppet theater could catch Ikan's interest and be subjected to such a discourse on *ninjō* was a direct outcome of Jinsai's philosophical views.[36]

A brief word about Chikamatsu's own famous dramatization of *ninjō* versus *giri* (obligation or duty) is in order here. Chikamatsu's love suicide *sewamono* (contemporary life) plays memorably staged the ambivalence of *ninjō*. Works like *Shinjū ten no Amijima* (*The Love Suicides at Amijima*, 1721) emphasized, like Jinsai's philosophical writings, the profound ethicality of *ninjō* as empathy rooted in the awareness of the suffering of others—a quality that became especially associated with women. Note, for example, the strong mutual compassion (*nasake*) of the two women Koharu and Osan in the play, who should, by virtue of being, respectively, the lover and the wife of the same man, be the worst competitors. This empathy translates into the strongly ethical acts of these women supporting each other while suppressing their personal and less-noble emotions: jealousy (in Osan's case) and sexual love (in Koharu's). *Ninjō* and *giri* are not opposed here but similar in function. Through the mediation of empathy, emotion and ethicality essentially converge, thus conforming to Jinsai's ideas about the moral role of *ninjō* in everyday social life.[37] However, Chikamatsu also dramatizes *ninjō* as an excessive passion that defies Confucian social norms and finds gratification only in the act of double suicide (*shinjū*), the ultimate defiance of the social order. In *The Love Suicides at Amijima*, it is the male protagonist—the papermaker Jihei—who gives up not only his (Confucian) responsibility as a husband and father but also his socioeconomic position as an artisan for a passion that breaks moral duty (*giri*). As we shall see, the ambivalence in the representation of *ninjō*, doubled by the gender divide, anticipates the early nineteenth-century popular fiction of Tamenaga Shunsui's *ninjōbon*.

Most important, though, the Kogidō Academy and the broader intellectual network it formed was a, if not *the*, major venue through which Chinese vernacular fiction and fiction discourse were disseminated in eighteenth-century Japan. In the context of this reception, the *shōsetsu*, as a popular literary form, was increasingly discussed as a genre relating to *ninjō*. From Kumazawa Banzan's and Andō Tameakira's remarks on *The Tale of Genji* to countless prefaces and treatises in the eighteenth and nineteenth centuries, the novel was seen as representing *ninjō*, often in conjunction with *setai* (social customs), "as it is" (*ari no mama*). *Ninjō* and *setai* were mutually inclusive terms, indicating that emotion was conceptualized in connection to ideas of community and social norms. Banzan, for instance, notes that the depiction of *ninjō* in *The Tale of Genji* can teach about the importance of the five cardinal Confucian relationships as well as "good" and "bad" emotions in the vein of the Mao tradition of *Shijing* exegesis.[38] Even Norinaga writes that the knowledge about *ninjō* and *setai* that *The Tale of Genji* imparts is about "good" and "bad" deeds and people, about "everything there is in the world and in the depths of people's hearts"—knowledge intricately related to his vision of social community.[39] Once again, these discourses on *ninjō* and *setai* brought *The Tale of Genji* and the *shōsetsu* into the domain of literature and its more highbrow moral-didactic aims, previously reserved for Sinitic poetry or, more narrowly, the *Shijing*. The term *shōsetsu* emerged in Japan only in the eighteenth century in reference to Ming- and Qing-period vernacular works as well as their subsequent Japanese translations and adaptations—that is, *yomihon*. The vernacular Chinese novel, however, already possessed its own complex strategies of representing emotion and desire. To gauge these, a short detour via the world of late imperial Chinese fiction and its "cult of *qing*" is necessary because of the impact this world had on nineteenth-century Japanese literary texts and their narrative practices of *ninjō*.

THE CULT OF *QING* AND THE JAPANESE RECEPTION OF LICENTIOUS BOOKS

The "cult of *qing*" is a term coined by literary scholars and cultural historians of late Ming-period China to refer to a number of intellectual debates and literary works in the late sixteenth and early seventeenth centuries.[40] These debates and texts aimed at the rehabilitation and revalorization of emotion (*qing*), and to a lesser extent desire (*yu*), against the dominant neo-Confucian discourse characterized by a strong suspicion, if not outright rejection, of both. The intellectual ancestor of this new tendency in Ming discourse was Wang Yangming's (1472–1529) school of Confucianism, also influential in Japan beginning in the early Edo period. While the concept of *qing* in earlier Chinese discourses was used broadly and often did not refer to any specific emotion, late Ming-period discussions reduced the semantic range of *qing* to mean primarily the love and desire between a man and a woman, or husband and wife.[41] In this respect, what is called the cult of *qing* was more narrowly a cult of love.[42] Some late-Ming discourses, moreover, radically repositioned *qing* as the center and origin of all Confucian virtue. Whereas the husband and wife relationship had been seen as rather minor or, even worse, ethically suspicious in comparison with the traditionally more validated relationships between lord and minister or father and son, late-Ming commentators provocatively elevated it to the first place in the hierarchy of the Confucian cardinal relationships.[43] Their reason was the putative emotional intensity inherent in the matrimonial bond that surpassed the affective bonds of all other relationships. The scholar Li Zhi (1527–1602), for instance, claimed, "Husband and wife comprise the beginnings of human life. Only after there has been a husband-wife relation can there be a father-son relation . . . can there be a distinction between superior and subordinate. Should the relationship between husband and wife be proper, then all the relations among the myriads of living things and nonliving matters will also be proper. Thus it is evident that husband-wife is actually the beginning of all things."[44] Haiyan Lee, who discusses this passage and similar pronouncements by late-Ming literati, emphasizes the potentially iconoclastic radicalness of the cult of *qing* as a "counterdiscourse that valorizes the personal and the subjective." But she also argues that these new discourses eulogizing *qing* as a source of virtue and pillar of the social order were still essentially Confucian—hence her term Confucian structure of feeling.[45]

A limitation of Lee's term, however, is that it does not take into account the strong interest that some late-Ming intellectual debates and, especially, literary works invested in sexual love and desire precisely for their potential to undermine the Confucian moral order. As Martin Huang and other scholars have shown, works of literature, particularly vernacular theater and narrative fiction, started to explore to an unprecedented degree the various and sometimes contradictory implications of amorous emotion and desire. While *qing*, as Li Zhi claims, could be profoundly ethical and underlie all virtue, it could also be transgressive, radical, and sexual to the extent of undermining the social order. This reiterated the old neo-Confucian fear of emotion and desire, but a new body of late-Ming literary texts, often commercially published, explored this potentially rich literary topic—rich in ambiguities—for the sake of entertainment but also didactic moralism. Scholars have often singled out Tang Xianzu's (1550–1616) drama *The Peony Pavilion* (*Mudanting*) as an epoch-making work in China, depicting the transcendent power of sexual passion in overcoming the boundaries of life and death and in challenging social norms. The work had a tremendous success among contemporary and later readers in China, and it was cherished and commented on by men and women alike.[46] However, despite its tremendous importance in the Chinese context, it had (to my knowledge) no significant reception in early-modern Japan. This indeed exemplifies William Fleming's important observations about the lack or very limited path of dissemination that specific Chinese works, even if famous in China, would take in Edo-period Japan.[47]

The most radical late-Ming literary work in its depiction of erotic desire, with a strong and long-lasting impact in both China and Japan, was the novel *Jinpingmei*. Martin Huang has argued that this novel, depicting the private life and sexual escapades of the profligate male protagonist, Ximen Qing, in great graphic detail, constituted a turning point in the history of Chinese narrative. Among the traditional "four masterworks" of the Ming novel—*The Romance of the Three Kingdoms, The Water Margin, The Journey to the West (Xiyouji),* and the *Jinpingmei*—this last was written the latest (sometime in the late sixteenth or early seventeenth century) and marked an important shift in narrative focus that can, very broadly, be described as one from the public to the private.[48] While *The Romance of the Three Kingdoms* and *The Water Margin* focused predominantly on the world of the battlefield and the male homosocial and at times misogynistic bonds that undergirded it, the *Jinpingmei* for the first time shifted toward other, more private spaces of narrative—the bedchamber and the garden—and the male-female relationships that could fill them. This shift was foundational for the subsequent development of the vernacular novel that, from overtly erotic works to the chaste scholar and beauty fiction of the early Qing period and even extending to the eighteenth-century masterwork *Hongloumeng (The Dream of the Red Chamber),* continuously displayed a strong intertextual awareness of the *Jinpingmei* and its writing of desire.[49]

The *Jinpingmei* is a fundamentally ambiguous work that openly relishes the depiction of private desire—the sexual escapades of the male protagonist within and outside marriage—but also presents a starkly didactic framework that negatively judges such excesses. The male hero, Ximen Qing, dies a gruesome death resulting from his sexual overindulgence, and his once-prosperous household collapses. Huang notes that the ambiguous balance between transgression and punishment in the *Jinpingmei* became one of the most controversially discussed issues among subsequent readers and writers. Narrative fiction thus assumed its peculiar position as a "didactic genre that paradoxically focuses on transgression with the double aim of entertaining and educating."[50] Didacticism and transgressive licentiousness—these were the two contradictory pillars with which much of subsequent fiction and fiction discourse were concerned, reaffirming both the instructive and dangerous potential that neo-Confucian morality saw in the literary representation of emotions and desire. Subsequent literary works and genres negotiated the tension between the two pillars in various ways.

A case in point was the new early Qing-period genre of scholar and beauty fiction, which became popular in late eighteenth- and nineteenth-century Japan through various adaptations. Although stories of love between women and men of literary talent are extant from the Tang dynasty (618– 907) and even earlier, the genre of scholar and beauty fiction per se emerged only in the seventeenth century, after the *Jinpingmei*, with distinct generic characteristics.[51] The most significant is the obsessive concern with the virtue of chastity—the explicit attempt to desexualize *qing* and keep it in line with Confucian propriety. The novels usually end happily with the talented man's success in the imperial examinations and the lovers' marriage after overcoming various difficulties, but the protagonists' conscious rejection of erotic opportunities, often in spite of their desire, and their virginity at the moment of marriage constitute an important narrative concern, sometimes even involving devices like virginity tests. In the seventeenth-century novel *Haoqiuzhuan* (*The Fortunate Union*), a major text of the genre with a nineteenth-century Japanese adaptation by Bakin, the male and female protagonists remain chaste even after their marriage to demonstrate the Confucian propriety of their relationship in the face of various suspicions, an important motor of the novel's plot.[52] This excessive anxiety about chastity of course betrays an inverted obsession with sexuality and points to the genre's intertextual awareness of more openly erotic works such as the *Jinpingmei*.

I have discussed the cult of *qing* and specific Chinese works at some length to shed light on an understudied topic: the reception of the "cult" and of works like the *Jinpingmei* and scholar and beauty fiction in Japan as well as their impact on narrative practices of *ninjō* in Japanese texts. I do not believe that the discourses referred to as cult of *qing*—for instance, Li Zhi's remarks—had a considerable impact on literary developments in Japan. There was certainly no "cult of *jō*" in Edo-period culture in any way comparable to the phenomenon in the late Ming. It is true that *ninjō* was greatly validated in the eighteenth-century Confucian discourses of Itō Jinsai and Ogyū Sorai, who shared with the Chinese advocates of *qing* an intellectual affiliation with the anti–neo-Confucian criticism of the Wang Yangming school. Moreover, the simultaneous rise of intellectual interest in emotionality in both China and Japan with their world-historically and socioeconomically comparable contexts of early modernity—the Ming-Qing cultural efflorescence of the Jiangnan region (the breeding ground of the cult of *qing*) and eighteenth-century urban Japan—is certainly not a coincidence. An important difference from the Chinese cult, however, is that Jinsai's and Sorai's (and their schools') discourses on *ninjō* were not specifically on love. Although amorous emotion and desire constituted, as we saw, an important semantic subtext of *ninjō* in these discourses, they did not explicitly reduce the term to love. Norinaga's emphasis on love as the "deepest" emotion in classical literature echoes the Chinese discourse.[53] Yet his interest derived from research in the Japanese classics and *waka* poetry rather than from the discussions on *qing* in late imperial China.

However, Chinese novels like the *Jinpingmei* and early Qing-period scholar and beauty fiction were received in Japan. Jonathan Zwicker, relying on Ōba Osamu's foundational research, has emphasized the extent to which scholar and beauty fiction in particular was continuously imported in relatively high numbers throughout the eighteenth century—a fact confirmed by Bakin for the first half of the nineteenth century.[54] As Zwicker shows, scholar and beauty fiction clearly topped, by the numbers of imported books, the otherwise popular genres of historical fiction and military romance novels. Unlike for the other Ming-period "masterworks," no Japanese translation or adaptation of the *Jinpingmei* was produced until Bakin's successful *gōkan* version, titled *Shinpen Kinpeibai* (*The Plum in the Golden Vase* newly edited), was serialized between 1831 and 1847. This seeming lack of reception was a result of the *Jinpingmei*'s particular linguistic difficulty as a vernacular text.[55] However, beginning shortly after its publication in China, the *Jinpingmei* was continuously circulated in Japan and became, like other Chinese novels, the academic object of vernacular-Chinese studies (*tōwagaku*), especially in the eighteenth century. Specific passages were quoted in various dictionaries and a glossary of its vocabulary was privately compiled.[56]

We can gain an idea of how contemporary Japanese readers, aficionados of vernacular Chinese fiction, approached those texts from a limited number of critical pronouncements. One interesting source is a manuscript written by Katsube Seigyo (1712–1788), a doctor, Confucian scholar, and *haikai* (comic linked verse) poet from Nishinomiya in western Japan. Seigyo's teacher in Confucianism, the famous Uno Meika (1698–1745), had studied at Ogyū Sorai's Ken'en Academy in Edo, which, together with Jinsai's

Kogidō, was one of the most important centers advocating vernacular-Chinese learning and the reading of Chinese fiction in eighteenth-century Japan. Seigyo writes,

It is difficult to depict true emotions [*jitsujō*] in elegant language. For *waka* poetry, it seems difficult to express everyday content as *haikai* can do; and when a *waka* poem accomplishes this, it is exceptionally good. But the vernacular novels [*zokugo shōsetsu*] in China represent emotions in minute detail.

The Tale of Genji and *The Tales of Ise* are licentious books [*insho*], but since they are written in elegant language, they depict emotions less well than the books of the puppet theater or *hachimonjiya* books.[57] Because licentious books in Japan are written with literary flourish, they contain many lies. . . . The licentious books of China, however, depict things as they are. In the *Jinpingmei*, . . . the wanton women are all evil, and the men who are liked by women are all evil as well. This is different from the books in Japan. In the end, [these evil figures] are killed, and the principle of promoting virtue and chastising vice is truly effective. Chen Jingji [in the *Jinpingmei*] is an attractive young man, and although twice reduced to being a beggar, owing to his attractiveness he is helped by women and can redress himself; however, in the end he is killed. [The adulteress] Pan Jinlian is killed by Wu Song as in *The Water Margin*. *The Carnal Prayer Mat* [*Rouputuan*, 1657] is full of lasciviousness and indecent women, but in the end, [the protagonist] becomes a Zen monk. The *Salacious History of Emperor Yang* [*Yangdi yanshi*, 1631] abounds in cruelty and is unbearable throughout.[58] [The scholar and beauty novels] *Ping, Shan, Leng, and Yan* [*Pingshanlengyan*, 1680] and *Yu, Jiao, and Li* [*Yujiaoli*, ca. 1660] are also licentious books, but since they do not depict coarse things and do not contain sexually explicit details [*un'u no jō*], parents and their children can read them.[59] [In these novels,] men and women long for one another, but the women are chaste, and the men are talented scholars who become officials. This resembles *The Tale of Genji*. [These novels] are rather shallow in [illustrating] the principle of promoting virtue and chastising vice.[60]

Seigyo's remarks are noteworthy in several respects. First, they offer a glimpse of the contemporary Japanese reception of a number of Chinese vernacular novels that Seigyo labels as licentious, beyond the mainstream generally discussed as most popular in the Edo period—most importantly *The Water Margin*, certainly the most studied and commented on Chinese novel in Japan in the eighteenth and nineteenth centuries. Seigyo discusses various literary genres—Japanese poetry, the vernacular Chinese novel, the puppet theater, and literary classics like *The Tale of Genji*—in terms of their ability to express emotions; and in line with Jinsai's teaching, he particularly sees popular (*zoku*) genres like *haikai* poetry (as opposed to classical *waka*) and the vernacular novel (as opposed to *The Tale of Genji* or *The Tales of Ise*) as fit to do so. But most interesting in Seigyo's discourse is his category of "licentious books"—obviously books about love, including the Heian-period literary classics as well as erotic Chinese novels (the *Jinpingmei*, the *Rouputuan*, etc.) and chaste scholar and beauty works. He juxtaposes, under the generic label of *shōsetsu*, *The Tale of Genji* with vernacular Chinese novels, showcasing the beginning of a discursive trend that would last well into the late Edo period.[61] But particularly noteworthy is the ambivalence in Seigyo's treatment of these writings. Although seeing them as morally reprehensible and labeling them licentious, he still finds value in them, for their ability to express emotion "as it is" but also for their didacticism. The *Jinpingmei* punishes all its wanton protagonists, both male and female, and thus illustrates the "principle" of *kanzen chōaku*. It does so even more successfully than the chaste scholar and beauty novels, where this principle, in Seigyo's view, remains shallow.

William Hedberg has discussed the institutionally and socially ambiguous position of vernacular-Chinese studies in eighteenth-century Japan. Although connected to the venerated tradition of classical sinological (*kangaku*) scholarship with its highbrow ethical and political ambitions and thus enjoying a social prestige it did not have in China, the discipline, in comparison with classical scholarship, was marginalized as it partook of the "heterodox, plebeian, and the morally dubious."[62] *The Water Margin*, undoubtedly the vernacular novel most venerated in Japan, was indeed a morally problematic text that glorified outcasts and bandits, giving headaches to early-modern Japanese readers and critics. Bakin, most notably, attempted to correct its moral shortcomings by writing *Hakkenden*.[63] When labeled as licentious, however, the position of the vernacular novel became even more problematic. With Seigyo's remarks, the discourse on vernacular fiction in Japan rejoined broader and more traditional anxieties about literature, like *Shijing* poetry or *The Tale of Genji*, as writing that could incite desire. Whereas in the eighteenth century the notion of licentious books remained largely a matter of scholarly discourse, after the turn of the century it came to permeate the Japanese literary imagination more broadly.

A significant awareness of Chinese works like the *Jinpingmei* and scholar and beauty fiction as the material for adaptations and literary rewritings emerged only in the early nineteenth century to fundamentally shape the narrative practices of *ninjō* in the Japanese novel. This new tendency was most notable in the genre called *ninjōbon* and also in the *yomihon* by Bakin. Faithful virtue and licentious vice, chastity and sexuality, transgression and didacticism—these entangled and antagonistic concerns became major themes of the Japanese novel. I examine Bakin's work in the next chapter; the following discussion surveys the emergence of the *ninjōbon* and what I call *ninjōbon* discourse.

LICENTIOUS BOOKS: THE EMERGENCE OF *NINJŌBON* AND *NINJŌBON* DISCOURSE

Literary histories generally describe the moment around 1800 as comprising a series of interlocked paradigmatic shifts: the emergence of Edo as dominating cultural and literary capital superseding in dynamism the Kansai region, particularly the cities of Kyoto and Osaka, as the country's traditional cultural center; the transformation of *gesaku* (playful writing), formerly the leisurely pursuit of a relatively circumscribed group of scholars and literati, into a commodified mass-produced and mass-circulated popular literature; the growth in literacy and the emergence of a broad group of sufficiently educated readers of both genders in the big cities and the countryside; and the aesthetic shift, partly brought about by the censorship of the Kansei-era (1789–1801) reforms, from a literature of wit, parody, and satire (often focused on the pleasure quarter) to the darker, more violent, and more moralistic "worlds" of the new early nineteenth-century genres of the Edo-based *gōkan* and *yomihon*. Indeed, this period witnessed the transformation of the *shōsetsu*, or *yomihon*, into a distinct genre that focused primarily on martial themes and adopted the format of the long Chinese historical novels such as *The Water Margin*.

The moment around 1800 also witnessed, particularly within the *yomihon* genre, another important shift pertaining to the representation of *ninjō*. In eighteenth-century *yomihon*, the works of Tsuga Teishō (b. 1718), Ueda Akinari (1734–1809), or Morishima Chūryō (1756–1810), emotions, desire, and sexuality were important themes, often explored through the adaptation of Chinese stories of the supernatural. In these texts—stories like the

"Reed-Choked House" (Asaji ga yado) or "The Chrysanthemum Vow" (Kikka no chigiri) in Akinari's famous collection *Ugetsu monogatari* (*Tales of Moonlight and Rain*, 1768)—emotions and desire are dramatized as a strong force that can transcend life and death as well as materialize in dreams and supernatural apparitions (ghosts). These texts, replete with references to both the classical Chinese and Japanese traditions, were aestheticized literati (*bunjin*) fantasies. The didactic message, although not absent, is often complex and ambiguous.[64] Emotion and desire, in order to materialize as supernatural apparition, are necessarily excessive and can lead to death, through the embrace, for instance, of a beautifully deceptive ghost that in truth is a skeleton exuding lethal energy.[65] But desire as materialized in ghostly form can also serve ethical ends, like the fulfillment of a vow made to a friend in "The Chrysanthemum Vow"—a story that, however, also ambiguously points to the excess of male-male erotic longing. In such a fashion, the early *yomihon*, as adaptations of Chinese literary sources, translate some of the anxieties and glories attributed to the power of *qing* in late imperial Chinese discourses.[66]

This schematic summary here of an otherwise complex genre serves primarily to emphasize a difference: the shift toward the new, more dominant regime of the representation of *ninjō* in the early nineteenth century. This shift is toward what I call, in the broadest sense, the scholar and beauty paradigm—a new interest in plots dramatizing the chastity, faithfulness, and sincerity, often against adverse circumstances, of morally exemplary male and female protagonists in love (the moral focus tends to be, although not exclusively, on women). This interest necessarily includes, as its flip side, a fascination with desire, evil depravation, and licentiousness. The morality and didactic message inherent in these plots are often simpler and less ambiguous than in the early *yomihon* and fit the aesthetic format of the more popular mass-produced literature of the early nineteenth century. *Kanzen chōaku* is a key term in the didactic discourse surrounding this type of fiction. The scholar and beauty paradigm shaped the genres that became essential for the definition of the novel in a longer nineteenth-century perspective: Tamenaga Shunsui's *ninjōbon* that came to maturity in the 1830s and particularly Bakin's *yomihon*. I use the term "scholar and beauty paradigm" rather loosely here to indicate the concern with ethically exemplary chastity and faithfulness—or, on the contrary, licentious desire—that these nineteenth-century Japanese genres shared with the Chinese genre.

Although some *yomihon* by Bakin were indeed adaptations of specific Chinese scholar and beauty works, most *ninjōbon* were not because the literacy of their authors, including Shunsui, was too low. However, a broader infiltration of scholar and beauty plots—through adaptations and a more general genre consciousness produced in this process—shaped the emergence of the *ninjōbon* and, more broadly, the nineteenth-century aesthetic of representing *ninjō*.

The *ninjōbon* became firmly established as a genre with the publication of Shunsui's extremely popular *Shunshoku* (Spring colors) series from 1832 to 1841 and, in particular, the series' first canonical work, *Shunshoku umegoyomi*, published in four installments in 1832–1833.[67] This series merits attention as it was seen, from the beginning, as paradigmatic for the *ninjōbon* genre, which continued to thrive well into the early Meiji years. Shunsui indeed repeatedly labeled himself the "ancestor of the *ninjōbon* authors."[68] But his *ninjōbon* also marked the culmination of prior literary developments that underline the genre's affiliation, even if indirect, with Chinese vernacular fiction and the genealogy of the *shōsetsu* (or *yomihon*) in Japan. In a seminal essay on the *ninjōbon*'s genesis, Nakamura Yukihiko has demonstrated their generic connection to the *yomihon* and its themes.[69] He argues that the *ninjōbon* originally emerged out of a variety of the *yomihon*, the so-called *chūhon* (middle-sized book)—a publication format that was smaller than the *yomihon*'s usual *hanshibon* (folded book) format but also bigger than the *sharebon*'s (books of wit) *kohon* (small book) format. Nakamura's argument was important because it corrected the previous view that the *ninjōbon* had simply grown out of the *sharebon*, a genre that introduced the art of buying courtesans in the pleasure quarter through humorous dialogic scenes but was mostly devoid of plot. The middle-sized books, however, combined the focus on courtesans with sentimental—sometimes melodramatic—plots that stressed (female) virtues such as chastity and faithfulness and derived from various sources, including Chinese scholar and beauty fiction and the theater. While middle-sized books, Nakamura argues, were a hybrid genre accommodating a variety of topics that could not be integrated in other, more established formats, beginning in the late Kansei years (after 1800) works focusing on male-female love (involving mostly courtesans) came to dominate—works penned by authors, to name only the more famous, such as Umebori Kokuga (1750–1821), Hanasanjin (1791–1858), and Shunsui himself.[70] As a rule, these were linguistically more accessible than both *sharebon* and regular *yomihon* and targeted the expanding market of less-educated readers. But they were also intertextually aware of the more literate, regular *yomihon* in which similar *ninjō*-related themes abounded, often as direct adaptations of Chinese scholar and beauty fiction, including works by the famous Santō Kyōden (1761–1816) and Bakin.[71] Shunsui, for instance, who did not have the sinological expertise to write an adaptation himself, was certainly aware of Bakin's rewritings of Chinese scholar and beauty plots.[72]

In this context, the publication of Shunsui's *Shunshoku* series was an important event. Shunsui's *ninjōbon* are of tremendous literary-historical significance. The specific innovations of their literary format and discourse not only subsequently defined the genre but also came to be seen, by the early Meiji period, as largely synonymous with the novel as such, often in negative terms as a licentious genre. Particularly important was Shunsui's discourse on *ninjō* and its representation. More systematically than previous authors, he presented the novel as a literary medium that was to exclusively depict *ninjō*. Whereas earlier discourses had broadly defined the *shōsetsu* as representing human emotions and social customs, Shunsui filled this vague premise with a more concrete and programmatic discourse. He used the term *ninjō* primarily in the sense of male-female love, but in distinction from other terms like *koi* (love—a word traditionally used in *waka* poetry), *ninjō* carried strongly ethical connotations pointing back to earlier philosophical and literary discussions. In one of the prefaces to his *ninjōbon Shungyō Hachimangane* (The Hachiman Shrine bell at spring dawn, 1836–1838), Shunsui famously remarked,

What does human emotion mean? It does not mean simply the path of love [*koiji*]. Only someone who does not sneer at the everyday silly laments of men and women and their futile sufferings and who does not look down on ordinary people's delusions, only someone who empathizes with the feelings of various people [*sono omoiomoi no hito ni narete*] and who intimately and wholeheartedly knows to be moved by them [*aware o shiru*]—only such a person can be said to truly understand human emotion. If my writings are not read with this in mind, it will be hard to understand them.[73]

Scholars have debated whether Shunsui was aware of Motoori Norinaga's notion of empathy or "knowing *mono no aware*." Hino Tatsuo argues that

Shunsui was not educated enough to have read Norinaga's scholarly writings and points to the broader popular dissemination by the early nineteenth century, for instance through the theater, of philosophical notions of empathy and catchphrases like *mono no aware*.[74] Maruyama Shigeru, in contrast, has stressed Shunsui's unsystematic education (*zatsugaku*), which covered the Japanese classics and nativist (*kokugaku*) writings, including Norinaga's works.[75] Whether Shunsui was aware of Norinaga or not, for both the emotion most worthy of empathy—the emotion that could most strongly produce suffering and delusion—was love. Shunsui's discourse stressed that literature should depict *ninjō* and thus reiterated, whether consciously or not, the tradition of earlier discourses on *Shijing* poetry and *The Tale of Genji* on a popular level.

Shunsui's emphasis on *ninjō* was predicated on a strong awareness of ethicality and didacticism. One aspect of this awareness was his strategic move away from the pleasure quarter and the conventions of the earlier *sharebon* genre that focused on the techniques of courtesan buying and the satirical "exposing" (*ugachi*) of the mistakes of boorish customers.[76] He remarks, "Since this book is mostly about the depiction of the emotions of [the female protagonists] Yonehachi and Ochō, its goal is not to expose flaws in the pleasure quarter. I have never been familiar with courtesan houses and therefore I cannot talk much about them. This book therefore should not be judged in the same way as a *sharebon*."[77] Shunsui spatially distances his action from the Yoshiwara quarter, which dominated most previous Edo-based *sharebon* literature and those middle-sized books that introduced romantic plots in the early nineteenth century. In *Shunshoku umegoyomi*, Yonehachi, a former Yoshiwara courtesan, works as a geisha in the unlicensed Fukagawa quarter while the younger girl Ochō, her romantic competitor, has a townsman (*chōnin*) background. The most important type of "futile suffering" induced by love in Shunsui's texts and worthy of empathy is female jealousy. With her characteristic temperament of *iji* and *hari* (strong-willed combativeness), Yonehachi repeatedly bursts out in anger against the women who are also in love with her lover, Tanjirō. In a dialogue with her geisha friend Ume, she reaches the following insight after one such scene of romantic competition and angered desperation at her rival, Ochō:

Yone: "This is really embarrassing, but how was it possible that I could go astray in such a way [*naze konna ni mayottarō*]?" . . . Ume: "Truly, even if selling your body is not your profession, you might think that you have everything under your control, but when you're truly in love [*horeru*] you cannot help becoming really stupid." Yone: "Ah, in the past I used to laugh at other people, but when you feel so frustrated and helpless, it's because of that Way [love]."[78]

Anger is an emotion typical of an amateur (*shirōto*) but inappropriate for a geisha or courtesan. Shunsui labels Yonehachi's behavior inelegant (*yabo*)—the most dreaded adjective in Yoshiwara aesthetics but one that showcases the emotional authenticity of a woman in love (*horeta onna*). These authentic emotions are worthy of empathy, the ethical feeling that Shunsui seeks to address in his readers. Although his writings allude to sexual intercourse in titillating fashion, unlike in Bakin's *yomihon*, their phenomenology of love never includes desire (*jōyoku*) as sexual excess and wantonness.

Even more important than his emphasis on empathy was Shunsui's didactic outlook on the chastity and faithfulness of his heroines. In an authorial aside, he makes the following remark:

If I fill my book with [erotic] scenes, I may seem to be teaching indecent behavior to women. Some people say this is despicable but, ah, it is not true!... Since my books are written mostly for women, they are certainly clumsy. However, the women I depict are indecent only in appearance. In truth, they possess the deep feeling of chastity and faithfulness [*teisō setsugi no shinjō*]. I do not depict women who associate with more than one man, desire money, behave immorally, or are deficient in the Womanly Way. Although my books contain many amorous words, the determination of the men and women in them is pure and unstained. Although my four heroines Konoito, Chōkichi [Ochō], Oyoshi, and Yonehachi are all different, they are faithful and courageous, not unlike any male hero. At the end, you shall see how each of them protects her man with female virtue and proves peerless.[79]

Umegoyomi's ideology of female morality is not merely rhetorical camouflage but is deeply inscribed into the work's structure. One of Shunsui's important innovations was the staging of the erotic man (*irootoko*) protagonist Tanjirō, who, temporarily weak and fallen but still attractive and emotionally manipulative, must rely on the faithful support of the women who love him. Through this help in the face of adversity, Yonehachi and

Ochō prove their wifely faithfulness, even despite their jealousy. Their attitude inverses the *sharebon* topos of the coldhearted courtesan who manipulates her clients for money. Ochō even sells herself into a geisha contract to provide Tanjirō with financial assistance. Female jealousy also ultimately transforms into homosocial empathy, for instance when Yonehachi chivalrously supports her rival, Adakichi, in *Shunshoku tatsumi no sono* (Spring color southeast garden, 1833–1835), *Umegoyomi*'s sequel.[80] This inversion of gender roles, with an attractive and manipulative man and chivalrous women, is not truly subversive but on the contrary drives home a profoundly conservative message. Shunsui himself notes that his goal in depicting several women in love with the same man is to teach the control of jealousy and to promote female virtue.[81] Unlike Bakin, he would never depict women indecently involved with more than one man.[82] Shunsui also repeatedly notes that his work's goal is *kanzen chōaku*, the key formula underlying Bakin's didactic understanding of fiction.[83] *Shunshoku umegoyomi* is loudly explicit about the fact that the faithfulness of the women Ochō and Yonehachi is rewarded when both are allowed to marry Tanjirō after his social rehabilitation (it turns out that he is a high-ranking samurai), as his first and second wife, respectively, reflecting their difference in social status. The work's indirect scholar and beauty structure thus becomes apparent, culminating in a marriage with one or two faithful, chaste, and talented— although, in the case of the *ninjōbon*, not literate—wives. With Shunsui, moreover, previously philosophical assumptions about *ninjō* have clearly arrived in the popular sphere: Itō Jinsai's, Ogyū Sorai's, or Norinaga's belief that emotion can teach empathy and the neo-Confucian idea that emotion can be good, that it can produce virtuous behavior, despite its potential to be the origin of all evil as well. Shunsui's heroines are profoundly virtuous *because* they are in love.

The conservative Confucian outlook of Shunsui's *ninjōbon* notwithstanding, a discursive construction of the genre as licentious was under way from its inception. What I call *ninjōbon* discourse was tremendously powerful well into the Meiji period and, through metonymical reduction, often decried the novel per se as a mediator of dangerous desire. Shunsui, in various authorial asides, defended himself against critics who chastised him for fanning indecent desire in his (female) readers.[84] Contemporary critics who pointed out the licentiousness of Shunsui's works included Terakado Seiken (1796–1868), the author of the famous *Edo hanjōki* (Record of the prosperity of Edo, 1832–1836), Bakin, and Kimura Mokurō.[85] In his "Kokuji shōsetsu tsū," Mokurō presents a vociferous critique of the *ninjōbon*:

There is nothing as bad as the *ninjōbon* written for the entertainment of women. . . . They depict only male-female licentiousness and obscenity [*danjo inpon waisetsu no koto*] and do not have the intent to promote virtue and chastise vice. They consist of small booklets whose illustrations and character carvings are poorly executed. Their authors do not invest much labor in them, and they are easily published, thus providing an opportune income to penniless book lenders. The recent government edicts that discontinued their publication can only be lauded as a most appropriate measure.[86]

Mokurō's critique of the *ninjōbon* is noteworthy, as his view on other lowbrow subfields of the *shōsetsu*, including the heavily illustrated *kusazōshi*, is rather generous. Mokurō compares the *ninjōbon* to "extremely obscene" Chinese novels such as *The Carnal Prayer Mat*.[87] The "recent government edicts" allude to the Tenpō Reforms of 1842 to 1844 that initiated a severe censorship crackdown on the *ninjōbon* and Shunsui in particular. Subjected to a punishment of fifty days in manacles and having his works' printing blocks destroyed, Shunsui died shortly thereafter. The censorship regulations that led to Shunsui's downfall precisely singled out the obscenity of his writing.[88]

Why *ninjōbon* discourse focused on obscenity requires some closer examination. Unlike the Chinese erotic novels to which Mokurō compares the genre, Shunsui's works were only mildly erotic, containing allusions to sexual intercourse but lacking graphic details. Chastity (*misao*) in *Shunshoku umegoyomi* certainly did not imply the absence of sexual relations—an impossibility given the *sharebon* tradition and the world of geisha society that forms most of the work's backdrop. But as noted, Shunsui was careful to never let desire itself be the focus of his depiction. While titillating, the erotic allusions were the necessary extension of his ideology of faithful, even monogamous, female love. One reason for the genre's discursively stated obscenity was perhaps its perceived vulgarity that was in important ways linguistic. Large portions of Shunsui's texts consisted of dialogue that accurately reproduced the characters' Edo speech—a feature that the *ninjōbon* shared with the earlier *sharebon* as well as the *kokkeibon* of equally middle-sized printing format. The depiction of speech imparted liveliness and emotional authenticity to the text, but this vernacular direct-ness could also be a problem. Bakin, in line with previous discourse on the vernacular, notes that only vernacular language (*zokugo*) expresses emo-tions (*jōtai*) appropriately. However, contemporary vernacular speech in Japan (*rigen zokugo*) is dialectal and vulgar (*shuri hizoku*) to an extent that makes it inappropriate for literary composition (*bun*). Bakin explains that, for his *yomihon*, he therefore devised a highly mixed and eclectic (*haku-zatsu zusan*) style mediating between the elegant (*ga*) and the vulgar (*zoku*) as well as between Japanese (*wa*) and Sinitic (*kan*) elements.[89] Bakin's lin-guistic sensibility and attempt to negotiate between "vulgar" but emotion-ally authentic vernacular language and literary sophistication bespeaks the complexity of his own literary project but also sheds light on the perceived vulgarity of Shunsui's *ninjōbon*.

Yet the appeal and strength of the *ninjōbon* lay precisely in their figures' dialogic interaction, through which power relations between the genders could be negotiated and erotic tension produced. Shunsui's *ninjōbon* staged playful and sometimes titillating dialogues.[90] The skillful manipulation of eroticized linguistic interplay was the prerogative especially of the erotic man. In one *Tatsumi no sono* scene, for example, Yonehachi—half plead-ing, but also half performing her characteristic strong will—urges Tanjirō to see her rival, Adakichi, less openly, as this would hurt her pride and pique her jealousy. Tanjirō's reaction to Yonehachi's pleas is ambiguous:

As hard as Tanjirō might try, there was no way to find any defect in [Yonehachi's] forceful reasoning. Although, in his heart, he did not despise Adakichi, when hear-ing Yonehachi's arguments, he could not but praise her as a most extraordinary woman, born so clever and so beautiful with a nuance of weakness. But then he said in a deliberately light tone, "Why all this talk about 'understand me' and 'I apologize'? There is nothing to worry about, Yonehachi! I will make sure very soon that everything will be the way you like. There is really no need to talk like this and to worry. Calm down and stop arguing—I will make you feel totally relieved!"[91]

The skillful interplay between the narrator's psychological insight into Tanjirō's thoughts and male eroticizing gaze and his playfully manipula-tive response (and performance of coolness) reflects the subtle appeal of the genre. At the same time, Shunsui consciously contrasts his virtuous and chaste heroines, dedicated in their love, with a male protagonist who perhaps not criminally, but with manipulative skill and without moral restraint, indulges in erotic play with several women. Not unlike Chikamatsu's earlier *sewamono* plays, Shunsui's text dramatizes the ambivalence of *ninjō* in gendered terms as both virtuous and licentious, thus simultaneously showcasing the narrative's moral-didactic and dangerously titillating potential.

It was therefore particularly the licentious attitude of Shunsui's male protagonist, in addition to his socioeconomic reliance on women, that marked the genre as problematic and obscene. Other male figures in Shunsui's works, such as Tōbei in *Shunshoku umegoyomi* and Bairi in *Harutsugedori* (The warbler announcing spring, 1836–1837), are socioeconomically independent and display a strong moral (and financial) responsibility for the women with whom they interact. The profligate Tanjirō, however, became the prototypical *ninjōbon* hero, to the extent that his name was regularly invoked as the epitome of male licentiousness. His shockingly amoral, if not immoral, masculinity was a major reason the *ninjōbon* were devalued as socially pernicious. Bakin, in contrast, while illustrating the criminal effects of erotic desire in his evil figures, was very careful, at least on the surface, to depict his virtuous male protagonists in *Hakkenden* as truly virtuous and chaste—as "good people," to use Tsubouchi Shōyō's later term. As I show in subsequent chapters, in Tanjirō's flawed masculinity, Meiji readers and authors continued to see the emblem of the *ninjōbon*'s—and more broadly, the novel's—licentiousness, and it was precisely on the male hero as the epitome of the nation that major efforts at literary reform would concentrate.

This chapter has cast light on the interlocked layers of literary and discursive history underlying the emergence of Shunsui's *ninjōbon* in the early nineteenth century. More than other genres and despite their lowbrow popular outlook, these works, by their emphatic reference to *ninjō* as what they represent, connected to previous discourses on literature and emotion as well as to the literary works at the center of them—the *Jinpingmei*, *The Tale of Genji*, or *Shijing* poetry. The common thread linking these works across an otherwise almost unbridgeable gap in historical time, linguistic register, and social status was that they all belonged to a lineage of literature whose social and moral standing, by virtue of its focus on emotion, remained unstable. These works were situated in a field of tension between legitimizing discourses that highlighted their morality and didactic value (even, in the *Shijing*'s case, canonical sanctity as a Confucian classic) and the threat of discursive devaluation as licentious.

The specific significance of Shunsui's *ninjōbon*, reaching far beyond the historical moment of the early 1830s, was that they firmly installed this traditional discursive field of tension within the relatively new category of the *shōsetsu* in Japan. Eighteenth-century scholarly discussions had situated vernacular Chinese novels like the *Jinpingmei* and scholar and beauty fiction within the parameters of didacticism and licentiousness, but especially with the *ninjōbon* as a mass-circulated and popular genre in the Japanese vernacular did those parameters—and the idea of licentiousness—permeate the literary imagination of the Japanese novel more broadly and in a longer nineteenth-century perspective. By the early Meiji period, the *ninjōbon* defined to a large extent what the novel was: a lowbrow narrative medium focusing on *ninjō* and therefore potentially dangerous.

On a narrative level, Shunsui's texts pitched the representation of titillating licentiousness, most notably in Tanjirō's profligacy, against moral-didactic ambitions. This epitomized nineteenth-century narrative practices surrounding the novel's ambiguous status as both licentious *and* socially useful writing. A similar ambiguity, although on a more highbrow literary level, also lay at the heart of Bakin's *yomihon*. As I describe in the next chapter, Bakin's writings, more explicitly than Shunsui's *ninjōbon*, displayed an intertextual awareness of "licentious books" from China. Given the *yomihon*'s great literary sophistication, their narrative practices highlighting the licentiousness of *ninjō* and the novel's didactic ambivalence in representing it reached a complexity unprecedented in any Japanese texts. Before turning to the Meiji novel, therefore, a close examination of Bakin's writing of *ninjō* is in order.

Chapter Two

QUESTIONING THE IDEALIST NOVEL

Virtue and Desire in *Nansō Satomi hakkenden*

Whereas Tamenaga Shunsui's *ninjōbon* were seen as licentious and epitomized, well into Meiji years, the novel as a dangerous entertainment for the uneducated, the *yomihon*, especially those by Kyokutei Bakin, embodied the novel's more highbrow potential. Bakin and his former mentor, Santō Kyōden, both based in Edo, had redefined the *yomihon* in the first decades of the nineteenth century following the venerated model of the long masterworks of Chinese historical fiction. In his "Kokuji shōsetsu tsū" (1849), Kimura Mokurō states the difference in status between *ninjōbon* and *yomihon*. He not only decries the *ninjōbon* for their "licentious poison" but also posits the *yomihon* as the *shōsetsu*'s apogee, along with Chinese vernacular masterworks like *The Water Margin* and *The Romance of the Three Kingdoms*.[1] *Ninjōbon* and Bakin's *yomihon* (and Chinese historical fiction) were thus situated at opposite ends of the *shōsetsu*, with immoral licentiousness on one end and moral exemplarity and social value on the other. Various factors elevated the status of the *yomihon*: Bakin's complex stylistic experiment that avoided vulgarity while still attempting to convey the authenticity of vernacular language; the plethora of learned references and intertextual connections that authors like Kyōden and especially Bakin included to appeal to an educated readership (people like Mokurō) while still entertaining, by the sheer thrill of their plots, the less educated; and the adoption of the long and structurally complex format of the Chinese historical novel. In his own critical treatise and historical genealogy of the *yomihon*, titled *Kinsei mononohon Edo sakusha burui* (Recent storybooks: A classification of Edo authors, 1834), Bakin qualifies as novels in native script (*kokuji no haishi*) only works that, like his own, display a high degree of sophistication as adaptations of vernacular Chinese fiction.[2]

The most important factor, though, that imparted value and weight to the *yomihon* was their didactic quality—what Tsubouchi Shōyō later referred to as Bakin's writing of ideal novels (*aidiaru noberu*).[3] Bakin was particularly obsessed with the notion of *kanzen chōaku* that he highlights, in many prefaces and authorial notes, as the teaching he intends to give the reader by providing examples of virtuous behavior to follow and vicious behavior to avoid.[4] He also systematized *kanzen chōaku* as the leading structural principle of his plots. His undisputed masterwork, *Nansō Satomi hakkenden*, revolves around the martial exploits of the eight so-called dog warriors (*kenshi*) on behalf of the Satomi military house.[5] Fighting against a plethora of evil supernatural beings but also against the corrupt feudal warlords of medieval Japan (the typical historical frame of *yomihon* fiction), they help restore the fallen house of the Satomi. One important ideological message of Bakin's monumental plot is the moral goodness of these male protagonists and the Satomi lords, which is the condition for their long-term martial and political success, thus especially exemplifying the principle of "promoting virtue." A key aspect of the novel's positive ending is the writing of political utopia, the vision of a realm governed by a perfectly benevolent ruler as the ultimate reward for virtue.[6] The immense critical and structural importance that Bakin thus ascribed to *kanzen chōaku* underscores the radical and unprecedented degree to which he attempted to morally, socially, and even politically legitimize his enterprise of literary fiction.

Bakin's systematization of *kanzen chōaku* both as plot paradigm and as the novel's moral ideology—a strict dichotomy of good and evil—defined what Glynne Walley, in his recent authoritative study of *Hakkenden*, calls Bakin's "seriousness" in writing *yomihon*. Walley also sees Bakin's *yomihon* as divided between the opposing impulses of seriousness and play. As fictions belonging to so-called *gesaku* (playful writing), early nineteenth-century *yomihon* had to be entertaining to a broad group of readers, especially since Bakin was making a living from his income as a writer.[7] *Yomihon* had to please by the colorful diversity of their ever-changing plots, the thrill of their martial scenes, and the almost infinite variety of their characters, good and evil, human, animal, monstrous, and divine. Bakin was a master of the craft of literary entertainment—the very essence of *gesaku*—and his works thus certainly belong to the broader landscape of early nineteenth-century popular fiction. Yet he also, more than any other contemporary author in Japan, defined the *yomihon* as an inherently moral genre with a serious or idealist mission. As I discuss in subsequent chapters, Bakin's idealism—to repeat Shōyō's term—had a profound impact on attempts to assert the novel's value and legitimacy in the Meiji period, and the need to write morally good protagonists continued to be an important concern for Meiji writers.

This chapter, however, sheds light on an aspect that complicates the role of *yomihon* as idealist fiction and that has scarcely received attention in critical discussions: the significance of emotion and desire in shaping Bakin's fictional plots. His *yomihon*, including *Hakkenden*, were martial novels that, unlike Shunsui's *ninjōbon*, did not seem to focus primarily on love. Yet Bakin's works displayed a strong interest in *ninjō* and reflected, more conspicuously than Shunsui's writings, what I have called the scholar and beauty paradigm: a strong awareness of, even an obsession with, virtuous chastity and, as its flip side, licentious desire. Bakin also rewrote Chinese scholar and beauty novels and even produced the first and only Japanese adaptation of the *Jinpingmei*—those writings that the eighteenth-century scholar and novel aficionado Katsube Seigyo had labeled licentious books.[8]

I start with Bakin's critical reception of Chinese licentious books and contemporary Japanese *ninjōbon*, which informed the narrative practices surrounding amorous emotion and desire in his own *yomihon*. The remainder of the chapter explores the significance of *ninjō* in *Hakkenden* within and against the broader narrative framework of *kanzen chōaku* and Bakin's ideological conception of the novel's morality. Indeed, *Hakkenden*'s narration often associates sexual desire with evil and crime, whereas it predicates virtue on the chaste absence or suppression of desire, exemplifying a strict dichotomy of good and evil. However, the novel also dramatizes how erotic desire affects and humanizes virtuous figures, thus blurring their goodness. This produces a dimension of ethical ambivalence that subverts the novel's discourse and narrative of *kanzen chōaku* relying on the reward of virtue. The ambivalence comes to the fore particularly in connection with the virtue that *Hakkenden* posits as superior: the benevolence of the ruler or his compassion toward the people, which Confucian discourse saw as the foundation of good government and the ideal political order. Bakin consciously positions amorousness as the ideological antipode of benevolence but also illustrates how desire continually resurges from within the sphere of benevolence. This ambivalence destabilizes the writing of political utopia as the reward for virtue at the end of *Hakkenden*.

Walley has argued that Bakin destabilizes established notions of gender, social class, and animal-human distinctions while maintaining "the one great distinction that unifies *Hakkenden*, and that *Hakkenden* proclaims to be, alone, inviolable: that between good and evil."[9] I would contend, however, that Bakin's writing of *ninjō* precisely blurs this seemingly unshakable dichotomy. More fundamentally, it also questions the novel's ability to contribute to moral, social, and political norms. Bakin promotes *kanzen chōaku* as the essence of literary fiction, thus highlighting the novel's moral and social legitimacy. But his narrative practice also points to fiction's alternative nature as licentious illusion that incites dangerous desire in the reader and subverts the discursively stated goal of *kanzen chōaku*. In dense and sophisticated fashion, *Hakkenden* renegotiates conflicting traditional attitudes—both Confucian and Buddhist—toward literature as a medium that could have the didactic potential to lead to virtue and truth but could also derail readers.

BAKIN'S CRITICAL RECEPTION OF LICENTIOUS BOOKS

Hakkenden playfully makes reference to innumerable sources, both Chinese and Japanese, classical and vernacular, some of which are openly acknowledged and others hidden.[10] To insert intertextual pointers and decode them was one major pleasure that Bakin as author and contemporary educated readers derived from engaging with *yomihon*. Although many intertextual references in *Hakkenden* have been discussed, Bakin's critical reception of licentious amorousness in Chinese vernacular works and its significance for narrative practices of *ninjō* in his *yomihon* have not been sufficiently addressed. Note, for instance, the following passage included in Bakin's preface to the eighteenth installment of *Hakkenden*, written in 1839:

The great novelists in China are all well learned and knowledgeable about the Great Way of the Confucian Gentleman. There are, however, obscene and licentious passages [*inpon waichō no dan*] in their works. An observer without discernment would think they depict hideous lust [*shūjō*] to cater to the readers' taste. But this is not true! The licentious figures are men and women of great cruelty who act in a way a virtuous person would never behave. *The Water Margin*, for instance, depicts the infamous adulterous affairs between Pan Jinlian (Wu Dalang's wife) and Ximen Qing and between Pan Qiaoyun (Yang Xiong's wife) and Pei Ruhai. Pan Jinlian, Pan Qiaoyun, Ximen Qing, and Pei Ruhai are criminals of the worst caliber whose deeply evil sins cannot be atoned for even by death. How could a reader wish to emulate those adulterous men and licentious women who indulge in immoral and obscene desire [*fugi no in'yoku*]? It is important to discern here the author's hidden intent to promote virtue and chastise vice and to prevent such licentious atrocities from happening again. There are also those works [scholar and beauty novels] about the wondrous encounters of talented men and beautiful women that take *Pingshanlengyan* [Ping, Shan, Leng, and Yan, 1680] as their ancestor—stories like *Haoqiuzhuan* [*The Fortunate Union*] or *Liuyingzhuan*—that have been recently imported from China as small-sized prints in countless numbers.[11] All these stories are very similar and cater to the public's taste, but they depict true emotion [*shinjō*] and do not waste their brush on licentious and obscene things. Just think of the emotion [*jōtai*] of Shino and Hamaji in this tale! With respect to emotion, there is a difference between good and evil people, as the examples of [the adulterous couples] Funamushi and Komiyama Yoritsura as well as Takabayashi Tatsumi and Otoko in this tale show. I have the same intent as the author of *The Water Margin*, who created figures like Pan Jinlian and Ximen Qing to divert readers from licentiousness.[12]

This rich critical elaboration is noteworthy in several respects. For one, Bakin discusses several evil figures from *The Water Margin* and their correlates in *Hakkenden*, whose evilness lies in their "hideous lust" and other crimes (such as murder) that they commit to satisfy their lust. The criminal Pan Jinlian and her lover, Ximen Qing, for example, are not only figures in *The Water Margin* but also the central licentious protagonists in the *Jinpingmei*, which is a long sequel of sorts to the former elaborating on the couple's adultery. Pan Jinlian conspires with Ximen Qing to murder her old and unattractive husband (Wu Dalang) to satiate her erotic appetite. Both are punished when they die at the hands of the brother of Pan Jinlian's late husband, Wu Song, a tiger-slaying hero (the tiger slaying is an important motif in *Hakkenden* as well, to which I return).[13] This is why Bakin proclaims that the representation of licentiousness in *The Water Margin* still conforms to the principle of promoting virtue and chastising vice. He also states elsewhere about *Jinpingmei* that the episodes revolving around the tiger slaying and Pan Jinlian's punishment are the most noteworthy scenes in the novel, whereas the rest focusing on the erotic escapades of Ximen Qing and his household is "nothing but licentiousness" (*tada inpon no koto nomi*).[14] With these literary models in mind, Bakin consciously staged protagonists in his own works who openly indulge in their desire. An example is the notorious murderess and adulteress Funamushi, one of the most negatively charismatic figures in *Hakkenden*, whom Bakin sees as an intertextual double of Pan Jinlian. As a punishment for her crimes, he has her die a gruesome death. Bakin can thus claim that by representing her criminal lust and her punishment, he intends not to incite his readers' desire but to morally educate them. His didactic association of desire with vice was probably also a major reason his works, unlike Tamenaga Shunsui's, did not invite a reputation for licentiousness and the ire of the censors.[15] Yet Shunsui had a point when he criticized Bakin for depicting licentiousness and took pride in the fact that his *ninjōbon* heroines, while not sexually inactive, were chastely faithful to only one man. Despite their *kanzen chōaku* rhetoric, Bakin's *yomihon* indeed display a strong fascination with criminally licentious desire that is absent from Shunsui's works.

In his preface, Bakin also discusses virtuous "true emotion" that he opposes to evil "hideous lust." He sees true emotion expressed particularly in early Qing-period scholar and beauty fiction—novels like *Ping, Shan, Leng, and Yan* and *The Fortunate Union* that he explicitly mentions in the preface. These texts displayed a strong interest in virtuous chastity and even virginity and thus consciously resisted, but also implicitly reiterated, the *Jinpingmei*'s fascination with desire. In *The Fortunate Union*, the virtuous and literate protagonists resist engaging in sexual intercourse even after their marriage to prevent malicious rumors that could taint the Confucian propriety of their relationship. Bakin's unfinished novel *Kaikan kyōki kyōkakuden* (Open them and marvel at their wonders: Biographies of chivalrous heroes, 1832–1835), written while *Hakkenden* was being serialized, was an adaptation of *The Fortunate Union*.[16] Whereas in the Chinese novel male success at the imperial examinations leads to the reward of a chaste marriage, Bakin's adaptation makes the hero and heroine scions of the proimperial medieval Kusunoki and Nitta warrior houses defeated after the failure of the Kenmu Restoration (1333). Their union prefigures the revival of their families but also, implicitly, the return to power of the imperial house.[17]

As Bakin writes in his preface, even *Hakkenden*, while not an adaptation of any specific novel, depicts the dog warrior Shino and his fiancée, Hamaji, as chaste romantic heroes in line with the scholar and beauty genre. One of the most iconic and beautifully written scenes, included in almost all anthologies of late-Edo fiction and probably the best-known episode of Bakin's novel even today, is their emotional farewell. Bound to fulfill his duty to his father and lord (by delivering an heirloom sword to the latter), Shino is about to leave his native village and Hamaji, never to see her again. Hamaji, sobbing, reproaches him for deserting her as her promised future husband. Their chaste romance and tearfully melodramatic farewell, dramatizing the conflict between emotion and duty (and implicitly sexual desire), was particularly popular among historical readers. The Meiji writer, critic, and translator Uchida Roan (1868–1929) notes that the lending-library aficionados of the mid-1880s, mostly male students, loved to recite by heart this passage in particular.[18] This reception is remarkable and suggests that Bakin's *yomihon*, in their writing of chaste romance, almost served as the *ninjōbon* for educated men. (Shunsui's *ninjōbon*, on the contrary, were dismissed as reading for uneducated women, although educated men indulged in them as well.) Moreover, like most scholar and beauty plots and Shunsui's *Shunshoku umegoyomi* as well, *Hakkenden* ends with auspicious marriages that involve the "talented" dog warriors (including Shino) and the eight daughters of the Satomi lord.[19] The marriages are the warriors' reward for their tribulations but also a romantic happy ending superimposed onto the novel's utopia of benevolent rule.[20]

The affinity to Shunsui's *ninjōbon* was not coincidental. In a letter written in 1840, addressed to his friend Ozu Keisō (1804–1858), Bakin notes that his publisher, Chōjiya Hanbei, urged him to leave *Hakkenden* aside for a while and instead write a *chūhon*—a middle-sized book or *ninjōbon*—owing to the great reader demand for this genre. Bakin prepared to adapt material from the early Qing-period scholar and beauty novel *Erdumei* (The plum blossoms twice), but before he could launch this project his publisher asked him to return to *Hakkenden*. He adds the sneering remark that, because of his high royalties, his publisher in the end probably opted for "Shunsui's cheap works" (*yasumono no Shunsui no saku*).[21] Bakin also planned to adapt material from the eighteenth-century masterwork *Hongloumeng* (*The Dream of the Red Chamber*) in a middle-sized format.[22] In the aforementioned preface, moreover, he notes that scholar and beauty works, although not licentious and representing virtuous true emotion, are repetitive in their plots and ultimately do no more than cater to the public's taste. According to this assessment, the romantic elements in *Hakkenden* are a concession to the reader; they may be more sophisticated and less openly erotic than Shunsui's "cheap" *ninjōbon* but are not fundamentally different in their entertaining function. This would correspond to what literary scholar Mizuno Minoru has called Bakin's *yamu o enai ninjō*—the emotions that Bakin "could not help but depict" in order to please and entertain his readers but that were also distant from his more-elevated ethical concerns.[23] Similarly, Hattori Hitoshi argues that because Bakin's *yomihon* were primarily idealist novels (*risō shōsetsu*) aiming at writing moral and political utopia and could only schematically depict their protagonists as either good or evil, their representation of *ninjō*—despite convincing episodes like Shino and Hamaji's farewell—had to remain inherently limited in comparison with Shunsui's *ninjōbon*. Hattori even calls this "the tragedy of Bakin's *yomihon*."[24]

However, Bakin's *yomihon* displayed a strong awareness of *ninjō* that, partly at least, derived from the reception of Chinese vernacular novels.[25] Indeed, the vicious lust of the *Jinpingmei* (or *The Water Margin*) and the virtuous sentiment of scholar and beauty fiction are narratively transposed into *Hakkenden*. Yet, more subtly, the work also dramatizes at important narrative junctures how immoral desire affects and blurs virtue, thus questioning the didactic dichotomy of good and evil and—more fundamentally—the moral idealism of the novel as a genre.

DESIRE AT THE HEART OF VIRTUE AND THE PRODUCTION OF ETHICAL AMBIVALENCE

An important aspect of *Hakkenden*'s *kanzen chōaku* plot is the political utopia in which the narrative culminates. *Hakkenden* starts with the arrival of Lord Satomi Yoshizane—the scion of a defeated warrior house—in the province of Awa, the Nansō region in the book's title, a politically dysfunctional territory controlled by corrupt and belligerent warlords.[26] The novel shows how Yoshizane and later his son Yoshinari, with the help of the eight dog warriors, successively bring order to the province, and it ends with the vision of Awa as a pacified realm ruled with perfect benevolence by the Satomi house. This is possible thanks to the virtuous exploits of the dog warriors, including numerous martial adventures and especially their final victory against the corrupt shogunal Kantō governors who attempt to crush the Satomi in a last great battle. Perhaps more important, *Hakkenden*'s final utopia is also the reward for the Satomi lords' benevolence. Satomi Yoshizane and his son Yoshinari are almost consistently depicted as ideal rulers. Benevolence (*jin*), the ruler's integrity and compassion toward the people, is one of the key moral concepts in the narrative and the central Confucian virtue around which the ethical universe of *Hakkenden* revolves. Each dog warrior embodies one Confucian virtue, including loyalty and filial piety, by possessing a magical bead on which his virtue is inscribed. Shinbei, however, the owner of the bead with the character of benevolence, implicitly leads the group of peers otherwise depicted as equals, and his exploits carry a particular symbolic weight. An important narrative telos in *Hakkenden* lies in illustrating, via a plot of *kanzen chōaku*, the possibility of bringing about a benevolently governed ideal state.

The presence of amorous emotion and desire complicates this telos. It is no coincidence that *Hakkenden*'s monumental narration is brought into motion by a mistake (*ayamachi*) of Lord Satomi Yoshizane's that involves desire and, if only briefly, calls into question his benevolent virtue as a ruler. The scene of this mistake, *Hakkenden*'s *Urszene* as it were, leads to the creation of the dog warrior protagonists, the hybrid product of the union between a human princess (Yoshizane's daughter) and a dog allegorizing sexual desire. The dog's strong association with desire reflects the Buddhist concept of the animal realm as more distant from enlightened truth and more susceptible to sensuous delusion and desire than the human realm. Although the dog warriors' implicit animal nature—their animal-human hybridity—does not seem to affect their virtue, it at least casts a shadow on their moral nature and points to the powerful presence of amorousness in *Hakkenden*. Moreover, the need to overcome the consequences of Lord Yoshizane's mistake symbolically structures the remainder of the long plot. Desire resurges at important junctures, to be consistently vanquished by virtue, but also, ineluctably, to resurge again. This challenges virtue, especially benevolence, and subverts the political utopia at *Hakkenden*'s end.

When Yoshizane first arrives in Awa, the province is a politically corrupt territory of which large portions are controlled by an immoral usurper.
Yoshizane defeats the usurper and becomes the lord of Awa. He puts on trial
the usurper's mistress, the attractive but evil woman Tamazusa, whose
crimes are numerous. She not only used her "state-toppling" erotic charms
to meddle in political affairs and help demote loyal retainers but also plot-
ted to initiate the murder of Awa's former legitimate ruler, whose mistress
she had been. At her trial, Tamazusa skillfully plays down her criminal past
and pleads her innocence. It is at this point that Yoshizane's fatal mistake
occurs. For one, he feels compassion for her and grants her a pardon. When
a loyal retainer of the former lord remonstrates against this decision,
Yoshizane—even worse—changes his mind and orders Tamazusa's execu-
tion. Before her death, Tamazusa utters a resentful curse denouncing Yoshizane's fickleness and incapacity as a ruler. She curses his children and
grandchildren to follow the Way of the Beasts (*chikushōdō*) and to turn into
dogs of worldly desire (*bonnō no inu*), beings defined primarily by their
lust.[27] Through this curse with a strongly sexual subtext, the karmic chain
of events leading up to the dog warriors' birth is set in motion.[28]

One dimension of Yoshizane's mistake is his careless speech, his utter-
ing a promise and retracting it shortly after. It is indeed this fickleness,
inappropriate for a ruler, that sparks Tamazusa's anger and motivates her
vengeful curse. Yet the reason for making this inappropriate promise in the
first place is Yoshizane's momentary attraction to the criminal seductress.
Tamazusa's smiling face has the "allure of an aronia bush in rain," and her
beautiful black hair resembles "drooping spring willow leaves beckoning
one closer."[29] Only after being affected by these erotic charms does Yoshizane feel compassion for Tamazusa. In the Confucian understanding, the
ruler's virtue of benevolence consists in compassion, and the young Yoshizane already has the reputation of a benevolent lord who "makes recom-
penses heavy and punishments light."[30] His compassion for the captive
Tamazusa, however, is tainted as he seems to confound his unacknowledged
desire with compassionate benevolence, a mistake that is later mirrored by
the erotic nature of the curse. Yoshizane's desire and the careless speech it
engenders cast a problematic shadow over his otherwise exemplary virtue
as a ruler. At the same time, as the term "mistake" indicates, his improper
behavior is deplorable but not evil—it is human. Unlike evil *tout court*, emotions and desire have the power to affect virtuous figures.

Karmic retribution manifests its powerful effect when Yoshizane makes a second mistake by promising the hand of his daughter, the princess Fusehime, to the dog Yatsufusa. The dog is the reincarnation of Tamazusa's resentful spirit. After violently forcing Lord Yoshizane to keep his promise, Yatsufusa abducts his daughter to a solitary cave in the wilderness of Toyama Mountain, with the likely intention to sexually consummate his marriage. Yatsufusa's desire fulfills Tamazusa's resentful curse, literally forcing Fusehime to follow the Way of the Beasts. But Fusehime is a paragon of virtue and chastity. Instead of yielding to the dog, she succeeds in pacifying and subduing his animal desire through her incessant invocations of *The Lotus Sutra* (*Hokekyō*), whose scrolls she has brought to the mountain cave for her protection. The key phrase summarizing this process suddenly appears on the magical crystal beads, previously given to Fusehime by the mountain ascetic En no Gyōja: "In this way, the beast conceived the heart for enlightenment." This narrative turn is particularly important for *Hakkenden*'s *kanzen chōaku* plot because it auspiciously subdues the disastrous legacy of Tamazusa's curse and Yoshizane's mistake. Fusehime's chaste virtue brings about a positive karmic result or, in the logic of *kanzen chōaku*, a reward—the birth of the eight dog warriors whose virtue and future martial exploits will consolidate the glory of the Satomi house and pave the way for *Hakkenden*'s utopian ending.

Although the explicit discourse of Bakin's narrator supports this reading, also generally accepted in *Hakkenden* scholarship, the powerful presence of desire in this passage complicates Fusehime's virtue.[31] Yatsufusa's canine sexuality uncannily resurges by inscribing its mark onto the princess's body. She becomes pregnant with the dog's puppies, the future dog warriors, even without—as she repeatedly asserts—having had sexual intercourse with her animal husband. Shortly after realizing that her menstruation has stopped, Fusehime momentarily sees in the river a reflection of her head as that of a dog. She is terrified by the idea that people, including her father, could believe her to have succumbed to Yatsufusa's animalistic desire. Fusehime decides to commit suicide to prove her chastity and innocence. At the pinnacle of her confusion, she miraculously encounters a flute-playing and ox-riding reaper boy, the divine manifestation of the sage-ascetic En no Gyōja. With laughing irony, the boy explains to Fusehime that her pregnancy resulted from the mysterious principle of a "mutual attraction between kindred things" (*butsurui sōkan*).[32] Such attraction, according to the boy, can occur between inanimate objects in nature like trees or stones and lead to the production of offspring even without sexual intercourse. Some of the learned Chinese references that he cites, however, are obviously sexualized and obscene, like the story of the consort of the King of Chu, who enjoyed rubbing herself against a steel pillar only to give birth to an iron block. The boy's explanation for the "mutual attraction" between Yatsufusa and Fusehime is the following:

It is true, your body was not sullied by the dog. And now Yatsufusa also does not have any desire [*yoku*] for you anymore. But you were married to him, and this is why he brought you to these mountains; he had obtained you, and this is why in his heart he thought you to be his wife. Since he loves you [*on-mi o mezuru yue*], he enjoyed listening to your intonations of the sutra, and when you saw him embracing the Buddha's Law, you felt compassion for him as if he were your equal. Through these emotions [*jō*] you became attracted to each other, and even if your bodies did not come together, why should this not suffice to make you pregnant?[33]

On the one hand, the passage reiterates the idea that Fusehime's virtue and reliance on the power of *The Lotus Sutra* could annihilate Yatsufusa's sexual desire, leading to the dog's salvation and the creation of the eight dog warriors as the future loyal supporters of the Satomi house. On the other hand, however, the boy's discourse also points to the strong emotional bond developing between the two unequal yet "kindred" partners. Yatsufusa enjoys listening to Fusehime's sutra invocations because of the loving feelings that he harbors for her. Fusehime's compassion for the dog, developing as she witnesses his Buddhist devotion, makes her forget that he belongs to a different species. These mutual "emotions" suffice to bring about Fusehime's pregnancy. Although they are embedded in a context of Buddhist devotion, the eroticized subtext is undeniable. The "mutual attraction" between Fusehime and Yatsufusa is not unambiguously chaste. The presence of human emotion and desire produces a polysemy that subverts, or at least complicates, the discursive assertion of Fusehime's chastity.

At a slightly later point, Lord Yoshizane also provides the following explanation for his daughter's pregnancy: "When Fusehime saw that his [Yatsufusa's] licentious desire [*in'yoku*] had disappeared, she felt compassion for him. With this deep compassion in her heart, she was unconsciously responsive to his vital energy [*shirazu shite sono ki o kanji*] and became pregnant. How wondrous this is!"[34] It is worth pointing to the ambiguity in this explanation. Although Yatsufusa allegedly forsook his licentiousness, his animal being still carries vital energy (*ki*) that has procreative power. Paradoxically because of her compassion, a virtuous Buddhist emotion, Fusehime is responsive to this vital energy, which impregnates her. Recall that in contemporary neo-Confucian discourses, vital energy was seen as a dangerous material force that could jeopardize virtue—the immovable moral principle inherent in every human being—and produce the physical movement of potentially immoral emotion and desire. This movement was thought to disrupt the original human state of moral goodness and was seen as the source of evil. The fact that Fusehime is "unconsciously responsive" to the dog's vital energy casts a shadow upon her otherwise immutable virtue and provides an explanation for her pregnancy that from the mere standpoint of virtue—inborn moral principle—must remain incomprehensible. There is a powerful subtext suggesting that Fusehime, despite her virtue, is emotionally and erotically receptive to her canine husband. Like her father, Fusehime seems to briefly mistake, even if unconsciously, her compassion for an emotional bond that subsumes erotic attraction.

In "Ken'i hyōbanki" (Critique of *Hakkenden* and *Asaina shimameguri no ki*, 1818), an important critical dialogue, Bakin states that the eight dog warriors should not be understood as the progeny of a dog.[35] Instead, they should be seen as the result of the "good deeds" performed by their mother, Fusehime, and their spiritual father, Chudai.[36] Understanding this is the hidden key (*hiken*) to his authorial intent. Bakin provides this explanation in response to his interlocutor, his friend and critic Tonomura Jōsai (1779–1847), who asks why the eight dog warriors, supposedly paragons of virtue, can be the product of a dog that is the reincarnation of a criminal seductress (Tamazusa). Whereas Jōsai's question points to the subtext of the dog warriors' sexualized animal nature, Bakin again defines the interpretive direction for his text as one in which virtue and chastity come to triumph over animalistic lust. Considering the possibility, however, that "Ken'i hyōbanki" was a dialogic fiction written by Bakin alone, he was probably aware of the tension between his authorial discourse and a more subversive erotic reading of the Fusehime episode.[37]

Emotions and desire in fact constantly resurge in *Hakkenden* at symbolically important textual junctures and challenge the interpretive direction Bakin defines for his text. One such juncture is the initial scene of Lord

Yoshizane's desire. The particular significance of his mistake is that it is the ruler's. But amorous emotion and desire also affect numerous other figures, both good and evil, including Fusehime. Yatsufusa's desire, while seemingly dormant in his dog warrior sons, resurges in protagonists who bear the implicit traces of his animality. One good example is the antagonistic pair Obayuki Yoshirō and Awayuki Nashirō—human figures who, although not directly connected to each other, carry canine elements in their similar-sounding names that mark them as doppelgänger. The name Yoshirō alludes to Yatsufusa because it is identical with the name of the house dog that the dog warrior Shino kept as a boy and that was a reincarnation of Yatsufusa.[38] Yoshirō is a loyal samurai retainer who as a young man had an illicit sexual affair, and he later expiates his sin through loyal deeds. Yoshirō epitomizes the susceptibility to desire at the heart of loyal virtue. His doppelgänger Awayuki Nashirō, however, is an adulterer and murderer, embodying the evil and criminal nature of lust. *Hakkenden* abounds in such pointers or "hidden subtleties" (*inbi*)—to use Bakin's own term—that expand the powerful presence of desire as ethically ambiguous and blur the demarcation between moral principle and the licentiousness of emotion.[39]

It is no coincidence, therefore, that the major antagonists of the dog warrior Shinbei, who embodies the major virtue of benevolence, allegorize the power of desire and sensuous illusion. Shinbei must symbolically slay them for the utopia of benevolent government to be realized. Yet Shinbei's symbolic slaying of desire and sensuous illusion is never complete. This has profound implications with respect to Bakin's critical awareness of the nature and value of *Hakkenden* as a novel.

SLAYING THE TIGER, ALLEGORIZING FICTION

Shinbei is an exceptional protagonist in *Hakkenden*, destined to embody the royal virtue of benevolence. He is the last dog warrior to join the group because of a divine abduction (*kamikakushi*) that causes his absence over a long portion of the narrative, and his miraculously young age also contributes to his divine aura. The main exploit of the remaining seven dog warriors on behalf of the Satomi house is to defeat the armies of the two shogunal Kantō governors (*kanrei*), a long plot sequence filling several hundred pages toward the end of the book. As Hamada Keisuke points out, the Kantō governor wars fulfill an important function in *Hakkenden*'s plot, resolving the dog warriors' private feuds and cementing their loyalty to the Satomi house as well as laying the ground for the establishment of a utopian state.[40] A main difference between the remaining seven dog warriors' opponents and Shinbei's, however, is that the Kantō governors and their allies are human whereas Shinbei's antagonists are symbolically loaded figures with strong supernatural powers. Shinbei slays two powerful and allegorically dense opponents in the second half of *Hakkenden*. The first is an evil sorceress, in fact a shape-shifting tanuki, who appears under the human guise of a beautiful nun called Myōchin; the second is a miraculous tiger wreaking havoc in the city of Kyoto. Both of these animalistic antagonists are associated, in different ways, with desire. Myōchin continues to enact the sexualized curse of the seductress Tamazusa and extends the negative effect of Lord Yoshizane's mistake. The miraculous tiger is linked to desire in an even more fantastic way. The two opponents—and this aspect is of crucial importance—also embody the power of desire to produce illusions. The assumption that desire has this power derives from the Buddhist idea that all material phenomena are sensuous illusions grounded in desire. As I show, the symbolic significance of Myōchin and the tiger is that they explicitly link the idea of illusion to the fictional text.

Myōchin continues to embody the lingering resentment (*yoen*) of Tamazusa, who had cursed the descendants of the Satomi to follow the Way of the Beasts. Accordingly, her method is sexualized and reenacts the dog Yatsufusa's lust. She plots to wed Satomi Yoshizane's beautiful granddaughter Hamaji, the future wife of Shino and the surrogate of his dead fiancée, to the lustful and criminal usurper Hikita Motofuji. The name Hikita means "field of toads" and denotes a repellent animal nature. By marrying Motofuji, the human princess Hamaji would, like Fusehime, be made to follow the Way of the Beasts. To realize her plan, Myōchin relies on an illusionary magic (*genjutsu*) capable of conjuring up hallucinations that incite desire. She produces an alluring illusion of Hamaji before Motofuji to instill in him the desire to marry her. When Yoshizane's son Yoshinari—Hamaji's father and successor as lord over Awa—refuses to grant his daughter's hand, Motofuji with Myōchin's aid launches military rebellions against the Satomi. Relying on his magical bead of benevolence, Shinbei quells those rebellions and slays Myōchin. Although her plan thus ultimately fails, her illusionary magic was able to incite Motofuji's desire as an evil force jeopardizing Satomi rule.

Myōchin also conjures up visions of desire in members of the Satomi household. She makes Lord Yoshinari believe that his daughter Hamaji has started an affair with Shinbei. One night, Yoshinari discovers a fake love letter produced by Myōchin's magic and overhears the whisperings of the purported lovers in an adjacent room. Myōchin had previously schemed to bring about an inappropriate proximity between Hamaji and Shinbei. Not only did she create eroticized visions to haunt Hamaji at night, but she also managed to make Shinbei serve as Hamaji's bedroom guard in the castle's women's quarters to fend off the visions. This allows Myōchin to produce the illusion of an affair between the dog warrior and the princess. Her plan is to estrange Shinbei from Lord Yoshinari; upon his hallucinated discovery, Yoshinari commits the mistake of sending the youth away on a long journey. Shinbei's subsequent absence allows Myōchin more freedom in realizing her intent to abduct Hamaji and subject her to Hikita Motofuji's desire. In this episode, Yoshinari is receptive to Myōchin's hallucinations, which make him commit a "mistake" mirroring his father's earlier mistakes and questioning his virtue as a ruler.

One textual detail in this plot sequence is of particular interest: Hamaji's reading of *The Tale of Genji*.[41] Once Shinbei assumes duty as Hamaji's bedroom guard, the vision that haunted the princess disappears. The "marvelous power of Shinbei and his magical bead" seem to manifest their effect.[42] Hamaji recovers, and all her doctors and guards except for Shinbei withdraw. During the day, her ladies-in-waiting while away their tedium by playing various games, and in the evening hours they read *The Tale of Genji* to the princess. It is precisely at this point that Yoshinari, tricked by Myōchin's magic, hallucinates his daughter's affair with Shinbei. This scene contains one of the few references to *The Tale of Genji* in *Hakkenden* and is significant in several respects. It suggests that Myōchin's magical vision of Shinbei and Hamaji as lovers extends the content of the Heian-period tale. Hamaji's interest in *The Tale of Genji* reveals her susceptibility to romantic fiction. Myōchin did not incite Hamaji's ladies-in-waiting to read the tale to their mistress; on the contrary, their book selection appears to reflect the atmosphere in Hamaji's quarters and perhaps, even worse, at Yoshinari's court. Myōchin's technique extends a vision that Hamaji, by virtue of listening to *The Tale of Genji*, already hallucinates herself. Like her grandfather, father, and aunt Fusehime, Hamaji is responsive to desire despite her otherwise virtuous conduct.

Hamaji's reading of *The Tale of Genji* conspicuously contrasts with Fuse-hime's earlier recitation of *The Lotus Sutra*, through which Yatsufusa's lust was attenuated. Whereas only the recitation of a holy text like the sutra could have probably dispelled Myōchin's evil magic, the reading of the Heian-period tale must be inappropriate for this task. Although, in a critical note, Bakin explicitly acknowledges *The Tale of Genji* as a towering model for classical Japanese prose (*wabun*), he also labels the work licentious and incapable of *kanzen chōaku*.[43] Murasaki Shikibu's writing exemplifies the power of narrative fiction to incite desire in the reader. Although her work may represent an extreme case of licentious fiction, other scenes of literary reading in *Hakkenden* suggest that for Bakin the ability to produce emotions and desires inhered in the medium of fiction itself. One particularly powerful scene has Shino reading passages from the medieval *Taiheiki* (*The Chronicle of Great Peace*, ca. 1340s–1371), all concerning amorous longing. While he is reading, the ghost of his dead fiancée, Hamaji, appears to him. Shino's own longing is here superimposed onto the content of his reading, materializing in his vision.[44] An awareness of the power of literary fiction and fictional illusion underlies Bakin's text. Myōchin's hallucinations that realize the literary intertext of *The Tale of Genji* have the power to deceive Lord Yoshinari and his household. They constitute an evil force to be slain by Shinbei and his bead.

Shinbei's second antagonist, the tiger, even more fantastically embodies this enigmatic power. The tiger is an allegorically dense figure, intertextually originating in the famous episode of *The Water Margin* that Bakin complicates significantly. In the Chinese novel, the chaste martial hero Wu Song slays a murderous tiger before going on to take revenge against the adulterers Pan Jinlian and Ximen Qing, who conspired in murdering his older brother. Wu's slaying of the animal prefigures the punishment of the licentious figures and connects the tiger motif with criminal lust. As noted, the tiger episode also constitutes the narrative kernel of the *Jinpingmei*. In *Hakkenden,* Bakin appropriates the motif and complicates it with new layers of allegorical meaning, especially by connecting it to the idea of fiction and sensuous illusion. In Bakin's novel, the tiger is not a true tiger but initially an inanimate object on a scroll painting that miraculously crosses the confines of its medium and comes to life as an apparition to wreak havoc in the city of Kyoto. Unlike its model in the Chinese novels, Bakin's tiger allegorically reflects the subtle boundary between fiction and truth as well as the powerful impact of fiction on reality. But Bakin also associates the tiger with desire by weaving it into the prehistory of the tiger painting that gestures to but also complicates the intertextual reference to *The Water Margin* and *Jinpingmei*. This prehistory is embedded in a narrative digression that focuses on the adulterous lovers Tatsumi and Otoko. Recall that in the preface previously quoted, Bakin explicitly identifies these figures as modeled on the licentious Ximen Qing and Pan Jinlian.

A brief summary of this complex digression is in order. The eloped lovers Tatsumi and Otoko live a life of debauchery until Tatsumi falls ill and loses his eyesight, a divine punishment for his vice. His sickness and blindness produce a moral conversion in the couple. They not only give up their adulterous relationship but also start living exemplary lives devoted to religion and goodness. As a reward, Tatsumi miraculously regains his eyesight and resumes his initial business, painting animal votive plaques for pilgrims to a nearby Buddhist temple. Around this time an unknown youth of alluring beauty visits Tatsumi in his workshop and presents him with an old scroll painting of a tiger, allegedly executed by the early-Heian master Kose no Kanaoka. The painting is stunningly true to life, but the tiger's eyes are without pupils. The youth warns Tatsumi never to paint in the pupils, which could bring the animal to life and lead to dreadful consequences. Bakin's narration provides hints that the youth could be a manifestation of the tiger zodiac deity, the so-called tiger boy (*tora dōji*) worshipped by the local people in the nearby temple. The youth continues to visit Tatsumi and gives him painting lessons, especially for painting tiger votive plaques modeled after the scroll. He exhorts Tatsumi to paint only a limited number of these plaques and specialize in Buddha images instead. Painting a great number of tiger images would drag him down the Way of the Beasts. Tatsumi's former paramour Otoko eventually finds out about the tiger boy; suspecting Tatsumi and the youth to be lovers, she bursts into a rage of jealousy. Although Tatsumi and Otoko are able to make up, as a token of their reconciliation they resume their former sexual relationship and immoral lifestyle. Otoko also plots to kill the tiger boy, but the bullet meant for him miraculously hits her instead.[45]

In a dramatic succession of events, Tatsumi commits murder and flees to the capital, where he takes the precious scroll of the empty-eyed tiger to sell it. The scroll is soon presented to the shogun's governor, Hosokawa Masamoto (1466–1507). Masamoto agrees to purchase it on behalf of the antique-loving ex-shogun Yoshimasa (1436–1490), but he also forces Tatsumi to paint in the empty pupils. The tiger thereupon comes to life, jumps off the scroll, and bites off Tatsumi's head. It then wreaks havoc in the city of Kyoto and its surroundings, especially by killing sinful people. Masamoto's attempts to subdue the magical animal fail. Masamoto had been illegitimately detaining Shinbei, whom he wishes to make his lover. Aware of his martial prowess, Masamoto asks Shinbei to subdue the tiger; the latter agrees under condition of being granted the freedom to return to Awa. Shinbei succeeds in slaying the tiger by shooting arrows into its eyes. The animal thereupon returns to the painting and its eyes become empty again.

The tiger episode in *Hakkenden* is heavy with allegorical meaning. For one, the holy monk Ikkyū (1394–1481), whom Bakin stages in fictionalized form, provides a powerful political interpretation of the animal. In a conversation with the ex-shogun Yoshimasa, the last owner of the scroll, Ikkyū severely criticizes the retired ruler:

With your unrivaled greed for luxury you have assembled in the past numerous treasures, precious stones, rare plants, and old paintings . . . and for many years the sufferings of the people did not matter to you. This is why the resentment of the people and the gods' anger accumulated and became that beautiful youth and tiger without pupils, to warn and terrify the world. That you still do not understand . . . shows the extreme degree of your mental inebriation and delusion![46]

Ikkyū here presents the tiger as a punishment for Yoshimasa's lack of concern for the people, epitomized by his extravagant habit of collecting precious artworks. Ikkyū explains that "bad omens" like the tiger have a "deep meaning" (*fukaki kokoro*): they "promote virtue and chastise vice." The tiger is an instrument of *kanzen chōaku* insofar as it punishes only evil people and serves as a moral admonishment to the ruler. Literary scholar Tokuda Takeshi even reads Yoshimasa, in roman à clef fashion, as a veiled reference to the notorious contemporary Tokugawa shogun Ienari (1773–1841), who retired in 1837, shortly before the tiger episode was written. Ienari was famous for his aestheticist lifestyle and, above all, his sexual escapades.[47] The veiled reference to Ienari, like Tatsumi's death, indirectly makes the tiger into an agent of punishment for excessive lust.

But the tiger itself also belongs, like the dog Yatsufusa, to the Way of the Beasts. Its humanized incarnation, the exceedingly beautiful tiger boy avatar, is obviously an object of desire. The erotic allure of the boy—his exceptional beauty—even carries over into his incarnation in the scroll picture, the ex-shogun's desired plaything. Animalistic tiger references, moreover, are inscribed into the names of the protagonists Tatsumi and Otoko, who are depicted primarily as figures of adulterous crime.[48] Their implicit animal identity closely echoes their lustful nature. Bakin's text establishes a subtle affinity between the tiger and dog motifs. Although the narrative does not mention this detail, the illustration depicting Tatsumi and Otoko's reconciliation shows a dog watching the scene (figure 2.1). This is the moment when the couple is about to give up their chastity and relapse into their former licentiousness.[49] Bakin's tiger also mirrors the dog Yatsu-fusa when the holy monk Ikkyū recites a Buddhist prayer on behalf of the tiger scroll, allowing the scroll and the animal painted on it to achieve enlightenment and disappear. The tiger's salvation by Ikkyū's prayer echoes Yatsufusa's earlier salvation thanks to Fusehime's sutra recitation. This

FIGURE 2.1 The reconciliation between Tatsumi and Otoko, with dog watching the scene at the right. From chapter 141 of *Hakkenden*; illustration by Keisai Eisen (1790–1848). Courtesy of Waseda University Library, Tokyo

correspondence reiterates the idea in *Hakkenden* that licentious desire is to be overcome by virtue and Buddhist prayer.

The salvation and ultimate disappearance of the tiger scroll point to the important metaphor of eyesight and blindness—visibility and invisibility—that recurs throughout this episode in *Hakkenden*. Both Tatsumi and the tiger oscillate between stages of seeing and blindness, reflecting the oscillation of their moral attitude. Whereas the seeing Tatsumi was evil and licentious, he radically shifts to goodness and chastity once he is struck blind. After regaining his eyesight, he reverts to lust and crime. Similarly, the tiger is motionless and harmless when blindly fixed on the scroll painting, but it wreaks havoc after gaining eyesight. When the animal reaches salvation, it can leave the sphere of visibility for good. Visibility and eyesight here metaphorically refer to the activity of the senses, connected to sensuous desire and delusion—the opposite of enlightenment. The seeing tiger's violence is an emblem for the ravaging danger of delusion. Only when Tatsumi can no longer see does he understand the necessity of doing good. At the same time, there is a paradoxical moral blindness inherent in his former ability to see. The holy monk Ikkyū explains as follows:

In fact, of all those sentient beings with eyes, many are as if without pupils. They read books but do not understand the meaning of the text; this could be called literate blindness. Moreover, some people . . . although they can see, do not see; although one shows it to them, they do not understand; although they have eyes, they do not know how to use them. These people are all without pupils. How could it be only that tiger in the scroll painting?[50]

The pupilless tiger serves as a metaphor for the blindness of human delusion or the inability to see the Buddhist truth, yet it is also the very object of that delusion. Ikkyū continues to explain that the tiger is in fact visible only to deluded rulers like the ex-shogun and his governor, who neglect their duties and indulge in aesthetic or erotic escapades. Ikkyū asserts that the tiger, with or without pupils, would not appear again to the ex-shogun if he mended his ways. The tiger is an illusion; its visibility, both within and outside the painting, depends on the delusion and moral blindness of the viewer. Once this delusion is overcome and the viewer enlightens to virtue, the tiger and scroll disappear.

The ultimate complexity of Bakin's tiger allegory lies in its commentary on the problematic relationship of fiction to truth. *Hakkenden*'s tiger is illusionary insofar as it initially constitutes the subject of a painting—a fiction—whose verisimilitude is stunning. This has to do with the scroll's alleged origins. According to the explanation provided by the tiger boy, the artist, Kose no Kanaoka, obsessively attempted to "sketch the truth" (*shashin*) of a living tiger, a tribute from the country of Wu to Japan.[51] His painting so successfully sucked in the spirit (*seishin*) of the living animal model that it died. The painted tiger thus appears alive, and only the emptiness of its eyes identifies it as a fiction. Adding the pupils makes its verisimilitude absolute and annihilates the boundary between painting and reality, fiction and truth. As Ikkyū reminds us, though, the fictional tiger appears real only to those who are morally blind. Ultimately there is no boundary between fiction and reality; the tiger that seems alive is as fictional as the one without pupils in the painting. Buddhist truth and moral goodness lie only in the enlightened invisibility to which the scroll, thanks to Ikkyū's prayer, eventually reverts. At the same time, the tiger allegorizes the power of fiction, here a painterly fiction, to come to life and have a devastating impact on the nonfictional world.

QUESTIONING UTOPIA

Bakin's narrator claims that Shinbei's tiger slaying serves merely as an expedient means (*hōben*) to free him from his detention by the Kyoto governor and let him quickly return to the Satomi in Awa. But this reading only superficially conceals the animal's allegorically complex nature. On the one hand, it is an agent of *kanzen chōaku*. Unlike the many evil human figures and animalistic monsters in the novel, the tiger does not kill at random or in order to fulfill its base desires. It kills evil and lustful figures only as a rightful punishment for their crimes. On the other hand, however, the tiger also follows the Way of the Beasts and facilitates Tatsumi and Otoko's relapse into lust and crime. It is an illusion visible only to those who are morally blind owing to their desire. Finally, it is a fiction that can have a murderous impact on the real world.

The tiger allegory, in its ambiguity, aligns with Bakin's understanding of narrative fiction. In one of the prefaces to *Hakkenden*, Bakin notes that the novel would merely "teach licentiousness and incite [readers] to desire" if it were devoid of the impulse to "promote virtue and chastise vice."[52] However, if motivated by *kanzen chōaku*, fiction can help "blind people quell the dogs of their worldly desire and steer away from the road of delusion."[53] It is intriguing that Bakin here posits his potential readers as blind—deluded by desire—and possessed by an inner dog (an inner Yatsufusa, as it were) that would drag them down the Way of the Beasts. Fiction, by providing entertaining illusions, can cater to readers' desire or, even worse, teach licentiousness.

Kanzen chōaku is thus a strategy to sanitize the potential for licentiousness deeply inherent in the fictional medium. Bakin argues that, by realizing the narrative principle of *kanzen chōaku*, potentially dangerous fiction can be made morally meaningful and readers can be rescued from their inner dog. He even elevates the fictional novel over factual history, which had traditionally enjoyed a high moral status, arguing that only fiction can realize *kanzen chōaku*, whereas the historical sources he consulted are devoid of it. He explains,

What I am writing is not the story of the historical dog warriors. However, although it is not the story of the historical dog warriors, the protagonists are the dog warriors of the [historical] Satomi clan. Why is this? The goal of unofficial history is to borrow the names [of historical figures] and make their story new. In this way, virtue can be rewarded and vice chastised. The Confucian gentlemen [*kunshi*] will find the hidden subtlety between the lines [*bungai no inbi*] and understand the deep meaning of the moral teaching; for women and children, however, it will be no more than another replacement for a daylong theater performance, helping them through the tedium of long spring days or autumn nights.[54]

Bakin here clearly shows his awareness of the two-sided nature of his readership.[55] While the "women and children"—the set phrase for the less-educated reader—will see only the entertainment value of his works, the educated gentlemen will understand the "deep meaning" of *kanzen chōaku*. Like Bakin's other novels, *Hakkenden* fictionalizes historical sources and constitutes unofficial history (*haishi*), a fictional rewriting of history that diverges from nonfictional official historiography (*seishi*). By arguing that *kanzen chōaku* adds a deep meaning to the fictionalization of its historical sources, Bakin makes a radical claim for fiction as a medium encoding a moral and political message for morally conscious, educated readers.

Elsewhere, he even cites as the models for his fictional project canonical Confucian texts such as the *Zuozhuan* commentary to the *Chunqiu* (*Spring and Autumn Annals*) and the *Shijing*, both purportedly edited by Confucius.[56] Confucius's editorial projects were famous for relying on a technique of reading that decodes a hidden moral and political meaning in otherwise not explicitly moral texts, like *Shijing* love poetry. Bakin here followed the lead of late-Ming and Qing-period fiction critics, figures like Jin Shengtan (1608–1661) and Mao Zonggang (1632–1709), who connected the lowbrow genre of the novel to venerated models in the Confucian tradition.[57]

Terms like "deep meaning" and "hidden subtlety" (*inbi*) recur in Bakin's critical discourse. Scholars have provided various interpretations for *inbi*, reflecting the breadth of Bakin's use of the word. For the current context, I particularly agree with Kamei Hideo's understanding of *inbi* as encapsulating Bakin's desire to fictionally enact in his novels moral possibilities that could not be realized in factual history and—I would add—that correct history's moral deficiencies.[58] In *Hakkenden*, the fictional refashioning of history through *kanzen chōaku* culminates in the writing of political utopia, the vision of an alternative historical realm where absolute peace and harmony prevail under the benevolent rule of the Satomi lords. Whereas *Hakkenden* started with the arrival of the future ruler Satomi Yoshizane in Awa province as a politically corrupt territory, the text ends with the vision of Awa as an ideally governed state. This writing of utopia relies on the fictional principle of *kanzen chōaku* insofar as the ending is the result of, or the reward for, the Satomi lords' consistent benevolence as well as the dog warriors' and other figures' virtuous exploits. An important aspect of the moral and political "teaching" encoded in the novel's plot, and to be decoded by its gentlemen readers, is this fulfillment.

In this plot, Shinbei's slaying of the tiger and the sorceress Myōchin, preceding the advent of benevolent utopia, is of utmost symbolic importance. As critics have remarked, it constitutes an important turning point in the text, where the regime of fantastic fictionality—the nightly world of animals, monsters, and supernatural creatures—is deposed and makes room for the brightly rational and afictional realm of political utopia.[59] But it also allegorizes the demise of fiction's moral instability and affinity to desire—in other words, the demise of fiction as illusion and the triumph of fiction, not history, as the narrative fulfillment of *kanzen chōaku*.

Are desire and illusion completely slain, however? One of the most remarkable and enigmatic moments in Bakin's long work is the short epilogue in the last narrative chapter—the grand finale (*daidan'en*)—which offers an overview of the ten generations of Satomi rule in Awa beyond Yoshinari's utopian reign. This epilogue presents a dystopic history of decline and a disquieting swan song of the Satomi house. Yoshinari's second son, who becomes regent after his older brother's premature death, is already "full of desire" (*tayoku*) and an evil schemer.[60] The virtue and benevolence that had characterized Yoshizane and Yoshinari's reigns are lost. Bakin asserts that this final future outlook merely reproduces the content of the historical sources he had consulted.[61] Yet this brief return to history after the end of fiction also marks the demise of *kanzen chōaku* as a plot-generating logic. Why does Bakin deconstruct his political utopia in such a fashion? Is the grand finale an ironic comment on the ethical contingency of history as opposed to the fictional moral order of *kanzen chōaku*? Or could this ending be interpreted, on the contrary, as an ineluctable resurgence of Tamazusa's curse? In this scenario, contrary to the narrator's assertions, the curse would not have been completely quelled but continue to lure the Satomi "children and grandchildren" onto the Way of the Beasts. One of the few scholars to discuss *Hakkenden*'s ending, Glynne Walley intriguingly reads the novel's conclusion as Bakin's attempt to bring back the utopian world of the text to the dystopic reality of most readers and to thus instruct them morally. In other words, by deconstructing his textual utopia, Bakin would urge his readers to build their own utopia in the real world.[62] My reading, however, sees the resurgence of desire in *Hakkenden*'s dystopic ending as a final necessary destabilization and subversion of the novel's *kanzen chōaku* teleology.

The narrative movement of *Hakkenden*, with regard to emotions and desire, is a double one. Desire in particular is seen as potentially evil and constantly subjected to the narrative impulse to subdue it. Yatsufusa's salvation through Fusehime's sutra recitation, Shinbei's slaying of Myōchin and the tiger, and the tiger scroll's salvation through Ikkyū's prayer are all important episodes, culminating in the vision of a benevolently ruled realm devoid of desire. Desire, as the origin for political evil of all sorts, constitutes the ethical antipode particularly to the royal virtue of benevolence. However, emotions and desires constantly resurge, often affecting even virtuous figures. It is not so much Tamazusa's licentious evilness in itself but

Lord Satomi Yoshizane's mistake as a ruler, his brief receptivity to her deceptive allure, that lies at the origin of *Hakkenden*'s plot machine. Princess Fusehime's receptiveness to Yatsufusa's animalistic vital energy, the susceptibility of Satomi Yoshinari (Yoshizane's son) to Myōchin's deceptive illusions, Princess Hamaji's reading of *The Tale of Genji*, and finally the resurgence of desire in *Hakkenden*'s grand finale—all suggest the implicit presence of dangerous desire at the very heart of the Satomi house.

Emotions and desires thus constantly challenge Satomi benevolence not so much as an evil other but, more problematically, from within. If a major aim for Bakin in writing *Hakkenden* was to illustrate the fulfillment of *kanzen chōaku* and to thus produce a social and political teaching suitable for gentlemen readers, why does he let desire complicate and challenge the integrity of benevolence and the utopian trajectory of his text? One possible answer is that Bakin in his critical discourse repeatedly points out that one of the novel's primary aims is to depict emotion, which includes erotic desire.[63] He explores how emotion and desire humanize otherwise perfectly moral protagonists (including his ruler figures) and introduce a dimension of ethical instability that exceeds and subverts the *kanzen chōaku* framework of the text.

Another reason for the resurgence of desire at the end of the novel lies in Bakin's awareness of literary fiction as an illusion radically opposed to the telos of *kanzen chōaku*. In this respect, the complex tiger allegory has a revealing metacritical significance. Bakin's tiger—partly instrument of *kanzen chōaku* and partly animalistic illusion associated with desire—in fact can serve as a metaphor for the contradictory nature of literary fiction itself, for its simultaneously moral and illusionary quality. Although symbolically slain by Shinbei, fiction's illusionary nature is never entirely suppressed (or suppressible) and constantly resurges throughout the text. In the same way as many of *Hakkenden*'s figures participate in virtue and transgression, thus producing ethical ambivalence, Bakin highlights the contradictory and unstable nature of his novel as literary fiction with strong moral-didactic ambitions but also grounded in licentious illusion.

Bakin's tiger recalls the even more drastically explicit mirror allegory in chapter 12 of Cao Xueqin's (ca. 1715–1763) eighteenth-century masterwork *Hongloumeng*. Given to the lecherous Jia Rui as a cure for his sexual longing by a Taoist priest, the mirror on one side displays a frightfully grinning skeleton, looking at which, according to the priest, would be the immediate cure for his desire. But the other side of the mirror shows the alluring image of the woman Jia Rui desires beckoning him to come closer. Opting to enter the image of his desire and engaging in imaginary intercourse, he finally dies in a pool of his own ejaculated semen, reverting to the skeleton that was initially shown to him by the mirror. In Cao Xueqin's novel, the mirror is a recurring motif that points, like Bakin's tiger, to the Buddhist antinomy of illusion (desire) and truth, key themes in the novel's complex symbolic architecture.[64] In the Jia Rui episode, however, the mirror serves above all as a metacritical allegory for the contradictory power of narrative fiction and *Hongloumeng* itself: the novel's moral and didactic power, but also its ability to entice the reader to dangerously alluring imaginary worlds. If the novel's didactic message is not seen, masturbation and death are the ultimate nature and consequence of the act of reading—what traditional discourse identified as fiction's capacity to "teach licentiousness and incite to desire."

Bakin was aware of *Hongloumeng* and even considered using its material for a literary adaptation in the *ninjōbon*'s middle-sized book format in the late 1830s, at around the time when (or shortly after) he wrote the tiger episode. As mentioned, Bakin's publisher, Chōjiya Hanbei, had urged him to publish in this format. His adaptation, however, was never realized, and he also had to give up reading *Hongloumeng* owing to his worsening eye ailment.[65] It is not certain, therefore, whether Bakin was sufficiently knowledgeable about the Chinese novel to be aware of the Jia Rui episode and the mirror allegory.[66] An enormous gap also separates *Hakkenden*, a martial novel greatly indebted to *The Water Margin*, from *Hongloumeng* and its purely domestic literary space foregrounding its characters' emotions and interiority in great depth. Nonetheless, a similar understanding of the contradictory power of literary fiction, both didactic and illusionary, unites both works. As I have shown in my analysis, moreover, Bakin's reception of Chinese scholar and beauty fiction and "licentious books"—*Hongloumeng* certainly among them—allowed for an increasingly complex understanding of amorous emotion and desire in his own novel writing. Part of this complexity is that Bakin did not reduce emotion and desire to the stabilizing moral poles of either virtue or vice; they belonged to both poles or to the gray zone between them, as did the medium of narrative fiction itself.

In the Meiji period, Tsubouchi Shōyō famously criticized *Hakkenden* for what he saw as the novel's failure to represent *ninjō* and for staging protagonists—the eight dog warriors—who were no more, in his eyes, than idealized "specters of the eight Confucian virtues like benevolence and righteousness" (*jingi hakkō no bakemono*).[67] These protagonists stood for what he referred to as Bakin's idealism. There is a significant blindness in Shōyō's critical discourse on Bakin's writing of *ninjō*—a blindness grounded in Shōyō's own literary project and understanding of the term. However, his own novel writing continued to be torn, like Bakin's, between the problematic representation of what he called vulgar passion and a strongly didactic impulse that reflected his continuous admiration for Bakin's idealism despite his earlier criticism. He saw the novel as a dangerous "morphine," able to incite the reader to licentious desire and unreasonable actions, but also as a civilizing agent that could elevate the reader's spirit. In this ambiguity lay the potential and difficulty of literary reform. Within the new parameters of Meiji enlightenment and civilizational reform discourse, Shōyō's literary project continued to showcase the contradictory power of the novel as narrative fiction, thus bridging the Edo-Meiji transition while laying the foundation for the subsequent Japanese novel. It is to the new permutations of the older ambiguities of the novel in the Meiji period that the following chapters turn.

PART II

The Age of Literary Reform

TRANSLATING LOVE IN THE EARLY-MEIJI NOVEL

Ninjōbon and *Yomihon* in the Age of Enlightenment

In 1885, almost twenty years into the Meiji period, the progressive Christian educator and literary critic Iwamoto Yoshiharu (1863–1942) serialized
an essay titled "Fujin no chii" (The position of women) in *Jogaku zasshi* (The
journal of women's education), founded in the same year. In this essay, he
differentiates among three historical stages of civilizational development
in the relationship between men and women: the barbarian age of lust (*iro*),
the half-civilized age of foolish passion (*chi* or *chijō*), and the civilized age
of love (*ai*). In the age of lust, Iwamoto states, male-female relationships were
reduced to the mere satisfaction of carnal desire (*nikuyoku*), and women
were subjected to the arbitrary violence of men. The half-civilized age in
Japan extends from the Heian period to the Edo period.[1] Although he does
not explicitly state this, what Iwamoto calls foolish passion corresponds to
the type of extramarital romance, both sexual and emotional, between male
aristocrats and noblewomen at the Heian imperial court as depicted in *The
Tale of Genji*, or between courtesans and their male lovers as depicted in
genres like *ninjōbon*. The age of love, finally, corresponds to the civilized
Meiji present as envisioned by Iwamoto and other progressive Meiji intellectuals. Civilized love is the relationship of the married couple grounded
not in lust or passionate foolishness but in mutual respect. It implies the
husband's protection of the wife and the wife's support at home—what

Iwamoto calls happy home (*happī hōmu*)—for the husband's public endeavors in service to the nation.[2] His essay's point is to emphasize the high position enjoyed by women in the civilized age and the need to enhance the social status of women and thus promote civilization.

Iwamoto's text, modeled on the new genre of civilizational history in vogue in Japan since the 1870s, highlights the epistemological changes in the discourse on love and sexuality from Edo to Meiji.[3] Whereas earlier discourse was articulated primarily from a Confucian moral perspective, pitting virtuous chastity against immoral licentiousness, Iwamoto argues from the standpoint of civilizational progress. "Civilization and enlightenment" (*bunmei kaika*) was an all-encompassing catchphrase in the 1870s and 1880s and offered a framework for conceptualizing the status of Japan in the new international order, confronted with the threat of Western imperialism.[4] Civilization was a way of describing the perceived superiority of the social and cultural customs of Western countries, allegedly the key to their military and economic strength, as well as the need for Japan to reform in order to face the challenge of imperialism. As Iwamoto's essay suggests, the position of women and, by extension, the nature of gender relations and sexuality were seen as a major indicator of the civilizational level of the nation and as an important domain for efforts at social reform.[5]

Iwamoto's notions of lust, passion, and love derived from contemporary Western—particularly Victorian—discourse that differentiated between carnal lust and spiritual chaste love, with strong Christian connotations.[6] Whereas the concept of a spiritual love was new, passion and lust overlapped with the traditional notions of emotion (*jō*) and desire (*yoku*).[7] Iwamoto's negative view of uncivilized lust and half-civilized passion also resonated with the critique of the *ninjōbon*'s licentiousness in the early Meiji period. As noted, the *ninjōbon* had been discursively denigrated as licentious from their inception, culminating in the harsh censorship measures of the Tenpō Reforms in the 1840s. In early-Meiji discourse, the critique of the *ninjōbon* overlapped with a broader critique of the novel from a utilitarian and civilizational perspective. In 1876, for example, an article published in the *Tōkyō nichinichi shinbun* (Tokyo daily newspaper) saw the reading of novels (*haishi shōsetsu*) as a waste of time when "civilization [*bunka*] advances every day" and everyone's efforts should be directed to strengthening and enriching the country. The author notes that *ninjōbon* are particularly dangerous to women, the future mothers of the nation, because they do nothing but teach licentious behavior.[8] Another commentator criticized Shunsui's *Shun-shoku umegoyomi* for inciting foolish passion in readers.[9]

Concurrently, the introduction of the Western notion of civilized spiritual love allowed for the possibility of a new, reformed novel that would focus on civilized gender relationships and emotions instead of the *ninjōbon*'s lust and passion. In *Shōsetsu shinzui*, Tsubouchi Shōyō famously defined the novel's main focus as *ninjō*, but in the sense of civilized male-female love (*airen*).[10] Alternatively, the novel should represent the (male) protagonist's struggle, using civilized reason, with his sexual passion.[11] The civilizational concerns of Meiji-period critics, including Iwamoto and Shōyō, explain the great importance accorded to *ninjō* in discourses of the novel's reform in the late 1870s and 1880s. By providing examples of civilized gender relations and thus instructing the reader, the novel could be made an agent of enlightenment that could help build a strong nation.

The didactic interest in the representation of *ninjō* also explains the continuous importance of the early nineteenth-century genres *ninjōbon* and *yomihon* in Meiji-period attempts to reform the novel. The *ninjōbon*, although disqualified as uncivilized, was the only genre well into Meiji that focused primarily on the representation of love and gender relations. These works provided an important reference, even if as a negative foil, but also epitomized the continuous anxiety about the novel's licentiousness that underlay Meiji critical discourse and narrative practice. At the same time, there was a continuity in highlighting the novel's didactic purpose, connecting back to Bakin's *yomihon*. The previous chapter explored Bakin's interest in emotion and desire, but Meiji discourses and narratives were especially aware of what Shōyō called Bakin's idealism, the assertion of the novel's moral and social mission. The continuous ideological concern, especially for elite male authors and readers, with the representation of exemplary male subjects—virtuous, civilized, and socially useful—connected the reformed Meiji novel to the moral didacticism of Bakin's *yomihon* as well.

An important ambiguity, however, complicated Meiji-period attempts to reform the novel. Shōyō states, as noted, that the reformed novel—what he calls the true novel—should depict the male protagonist's struggle, led by reason, against his vulgar passion (*retsujō*), another term for Iwamoto's foolish passion. Only a protagonist whose reason prevails is a "good person," not unlike Bakin's dog warriors. Although Shōyō here clearly articulates the novel's moral and civilizational mission, the plot he envisions implicitly integrates the representation of sexual passion—what Iwamoto saw as the epitome of a half-civilized age and what contemporary commentators associated with the *ninjōbon*. This ambiguity contributed to a continuous anxiety about the novel's licentiousness that destabilized Shōyō's project of literary reform.

The ambiguity at the heart of Shōyō's project, while extending the ambiguities examined in previous chapters, was also related to Western translations, which produced the new literary field that allowed for the novel's reform. This chapter examines in detail the acclaimed novel *Ōshū kiji: Karyū shunwa* (A strange story from Europe: Spring tale of flowers and willows, 1878–1879), the abridged translation, by Niwa Jun'ichirō (1851–1919), of Edward Bulwer-Lytton's novel *Ernest Maltravers* and its sequel *Alice*.[12] The exact circumstances of *Karyū shunwa*'s translation are unclear. The translator, Niwa, apparently enjoyed reading the novel while traveling by ship from England back to Japan and therefore decided to translate it.[13] Once published, however, his translation was a major event that fundamentally challenged the Japanese novel. It triggered a boom not only in new translations of Western novels, most notably by Bulwer-Lytton, but also in adaptations and rewritings.[14] In 1885, moreover, Shōyō described most Japanese fiction produced up to that point as the "dregs of Bakin" and "copies of Tanehiko and Shunsui"—those canonical early nineteenth-century authors who defined the canon of popular fiction well into the mid-Meiji period. Only translations like *Karyū shunwa*, according to Shōyō, introduced a literary format of "great novelty" and made visible the "essence of the Western novel" that could serve as the model for the reform of Japanese fiction.[15]

But *Karyū shunwa* also incorporated elements of previous Japanese genres, particularly *ninjōbon* and *yomihon*, defining a continuity rather than a radical rupture with the earlier literary field. It also connected these elements with the discursive and literary concerns of 1870s Japan, which explains the work's contemporary success. This dynamic exemplifies Lydia Liu's seminal notion of translingual practice. Following Liu, I here understand translation not primarily as a medium through which new meaning and knowledge become unilaterally transplanted from the "guest" language or text (Bulwer-Lytton's English novel) onto the "host" language or text (*Karyū shunwa*). Rather, the meaning-making process of translation relies on the dynamic translingual interplay between the guest and host languages, in such a way that the translated text is shaped as much by its host environment (linguistic, discursive, literary, cultural) as by the guest environment.[16]

That the translation *Karyū shunwa* could translingually integrate elements of *ninjōbon* and *yomihon* was a result of the contradictory literary format of Bulwer-Lytton's source text, the novel *Ernest Maltravers*. As a typical proponent of the nineteenth-century European bildungsroman, it relied on the representation of essentially conflicting ideological worldviews. On the one hand, this novel presented a story of youthful sexual passion, the emplotment of the egalitarian European enlightenment ideal of the free choice of the heart that could transcend class barriers and social conventions. This passion, a key term in Bulwer-Lytton's text, was also an implicit political figure of democracy embracing the ideals of individual freedom and equality. On the other hand, *Ernest Maltravers* emphasized the need to move from youthful freedom to maturity and to control erotic passion through virtue, reason, and a monogamous love marriage. This narrative was the attempt to subject especially the male protagonist to the norms of the family, society, and nation—precisely those norms that his passion had challenged.

The novel *Karyū shunwa* appropriated this narrative format in a peculiar way. Although validating the European enlightenment ideal of free and egalitarian "passion"—translated in Japanese as *jō*—it also associated this passion with the uncivilized sexual love of the *ninjōbon* that transgressed social and moral norms. Importantly, it was then in the novel's plot surrounding the control of passion that Meiji-period civilizational, utilitarian, and enlightenment concerns would converge. This plot included the potential integration of passion into a monogamous marriage that could inhibit uncivilized licentiousness, and it also allowed for the representation of a socially useful and exemplary male subject. This correlated with the narrative integration of important new themes in contemporary Japanese discourse, such as the idea of advancement through hard study and work (*risshin shusse*) and democratic political activity—an integration that transposed the prowess of the *yomihon* hero into the discursive framework of the Meiji present.

Karyū shunwa's plot that could simultaneously present uncivilized passion and its control and social integration provided a new narrative format for the representation of *ninjō* that was instrumental in defining the literary space for the reform of fiction in the decade of the 1880s. This format was ambivalent, though, as it allowed for the representation of titillating romance as in a *ninjōbon* but could also respond to readers' expectations connected to the *yomihon* by highlighting the novel's didactic value as a civilizing and moral agent. Scholar Saeki Junko and others have argued that Christian enlighteners like Iwamoto Yoshiharu introduced, in the decade of the 1880s, the new concept of a chaste, spiritual, and civilized love— designated by the later term *ren'ai*—that fundamentally challenged the representation of gender relations in the Japanese novel. According to Saeki, the new concept of spiritual love led to the discursive devaluation and demise of premodern cultural forms of erotic love associated with the *ninjōbon*.[17] However, even before Iwamoto launched his challenges, *Karyū shunwa* had already provided a sophisticated literary narrative not only for civilized married love but also for the new notion of erotic passion, which, while carrying new enlightenment connotations, was reminiscent of the *ninjōbon*. The translation of multiple competing models of love considerably complicated the early-Meiji literary field and subsequent attempts to reform the Japanese novel through its representation of *ninjō*.

The following discussion first surveys the new discursive space of the 1870s as pertaining to gender, sexuality, and readership. I then analyze *Karyū shunwa*, a narrative fraught with ambiguity where licentious passion is never completely controllable despite its civilizational and didactic ambitions. I close with a reading of Kikutei Kōsui's novel *Sanpū hiu: Seiro nikki* (Winds of adversity and rains of sadness: Diary of getting on in the world, 1884). This important intertextual rewriting of *Karyū shunwa* into a Japanese novel significantly reduced its model's ambiguity. Kikutei's narrative more strongly highlighted the enlightenment implications of youthful passion, its potential to lead to individual freedom. It also presented a plot where the successful control—but not the elision—of passion could facilitate a monogamous marriage and the representation of a virtuous and useful masculinity fulfilling the tropes of social advancement and political activity.

GENDER AND SEXUALITY IN THE AGE OF ENLIGHTENMENT: *KARYŪ SHUNWA'S* READERS

The decade of the 1870s in Japan is generally identified as the age of civilization and enlightenment. After Japan's confrontation with the Western powers in the 1840s and 1850s, the country's forced opening to Western military and economic interests, and the regime change of the Meiji Restoration (1868), Japan was swept by wide-ranging reforms that aimed at strengthening the nation against foreign imperialist aggression. "Civilization" was a key term invoked as synonymous with the West's perceived strength. Civilizational histories divided the world into civilized and uncivilized regions and relied on a teleological model of stages of world-historical development. The term was also widely debated in the public sphere, in connection to the reform of national customs. In the 1870s, these debates were dominated by the Meirokusha (Meiji Six Society) and disseminated by its print organ, *Meiroku zasshi* (Meiji Six journal). Members of the group included the towering private intellectual Fukuzawa Yukichi (1834–1901) and government officials like Mori Arinori (1847–1889) and Nishi Amane (1829–1897), who had gathered extensive knowledge of the West through travel. An avowed goal of their publications was to promote civilization, including areas as diverse as script reform, the introduction of new fields of knowledge like philosophy and religion, and—one of *Meiroku zasshi*'s most urgent topics— parliamentarian politics.

The ideology of civilization and enlightenment also produced a reconfiguration of discourses on emotion, sexuality, and gender relations. Issues debated by the Meirokusha intellectuals, but also by 1870s and 1880s journalists and the newspaper-reading public, included monogamous versus polygamous marriage, concubinage, prostitution, the question of the equality between the sexes, and women's education.[18] Mori Arinori's "Saishōron" ("On Wives and Concubines") was probably the earliest and most influential treatise on the reform of gender relations and the management of male-female sexuality.[19] Serialized in *Meiroku zasshi* in 1875–1876, this essay promoted monogamous marriage and the necessity to end the "barbarous custom" (*banzoku*) of concubinage. Mori defined marriage as an exclusive emotional union in which both partners "mutually love and protect each other" without directing their emotions (*jō*) to any third party. Legally sanctioned and widely practiced among the Japanese elite, concubinage—or a husband's affairs with servant women and prostitutes—in Mori's eyes served only to satisfy male sexual desire (*jōyoku*), a term he associated with the "barbarous" Japanese tradition. Mori's views resonated with the writings of contemporaries like Fukuzawa Yukichi, who, in his popular treatise *Gakumon no susume* (*An Encouragement of Learning*, 1872), denounced concubinage as an uncivilized practice of "birds and beasts."[20] These arguments also promoted the idea that men and women in marriage were fundamentally equals—husbands should behave as chastely as they expected their wives to behave—although they were not yet to have, in legal terms, the same rights.[21]

An important reason for Mori to promote monogamous marriage and the equality between husbands and wives was a newly perceived importance of women as mothers and educators of their children—the future of the nation. Women should no longer be considered the sexual playthings of men, Mori argued, but as bearing the difficult responsibility of educating their offspring. The education of women began to be seen as a task of urgent national importance. Nakamura Masanao's famous essay "Zenryō naru haha o tsukuru setsu" ("Creating Good Mothers," 1875), published in the wake of Mori's article in *Meiroku zasshi*, explicitly states the connection between female education and the nation's future. Nakamura's essay is also interesting for anticipating the vision of marital family life held together by female love (*ai*):

Those who are concerned about the potential harm of equal rights for men and women only fear that an uneducated woman could make her husband henpecked. If women, however, [thanks to their education] are in awe of Heaven and God, relish the arts and knowledge, support their husband, and love and respect him, then such a concern will be groundless. Set aside the question of equal rights, men and women must have an equal education. A woman who has feelings of deep love [*shin'ai no jō aru fujin*] will give bliss and comfort to her husband and assist him in accomplishing great deeds for the country.[22]

Nakamura's essay was probably the first formulation of the notorious ideology of the "good wife and wise mother" (*ryōsai kenbo*), but it also provided a new formula of conjugal love as mutual respect, predicated on the educated wife's ability to support her husband in serving the nation. Her support, in turn, relies on the husband's willingness to restrain his sexuality within a monogamous marriage. This gender interrelationship foreshadowed the ideological linkage, in Meiji novels, of female education and conjugal love as the nurturing ground for male achievement and national progress. It also anticipated the 1880s discourse on spiritual love promoted by enlighteners like Iwamoto associated with *Jogaku zasshi*.

The position of sexuality and desire in enlightenment discussions was complex, though. In a *Meiroku zasshi* essay, Tsuda Mamichi (1829–1903) argues that desire (*jōyoku*) is not only necessary for the continuation of mankind but also a legitimate source of pleasure.[23] Similarly, Fukuzawa Yukichi, in *Gakumon no susume*, affirms that desire is the motivational force of human activity and its fulfillment the condition for happiness. Yet he also emphasizes the need to control desire through reason (*dōri*) to prevent it from becoming excessive and harmful to society.[24] As noted, the opposition between emotion (*jō*)/desire (*yoku*) and moral principle (*ri*) had been one of the fundamental dichotomies in neo-Confucian discourse, and Fukuzawa translates the earlier dichotomy into a Meiji enlightenment framework. Although his use of the term *dōri* retained a moral connotation, his notion of the control of desire through reason (informed by morality) was new. This resonated with contemporary discourse on gender relations and marriage, and it became a trope in literary discussions, including *Shōsetsu shinzui*, that saw the novel's protagonist as susceptible to erotic passion but also as able to control it.

The sexually restrictive aspect of enlightenment discourse, paralleled by the contemporary critique of the *ninjōbon* and novel as licentious, should not obscure the fact that the decade of the 1870s witnessed a great interest in and proliferation of sexual themes. This had important implications for the readership of novels like *Karyū shunwa*. The year 1875, for instance, saw the publication of the first sexological treatise in Japan, titled *Zōkakiron* (Discourse on procreation). This translation, written like the Meirokusha publications in a rather difficult Sinified style without phonetic glosses, was followed by a linguistically more accessible popular (*tsūzoku*) version only one year later. These publications were the beginning of a long series of *zōkakiron* texts, published well into the 1880s, that enjoyed popularity among a diverse readership, including students.[25] The texts introduced anatomical reproductions and explanations of the genital organs as well as sexological knowledge pertaining to intercourse, contraception, abortion, and childbirth. This information was intended primarily for the married couple. Jim Reichert rightly points out that the ideological framework of early-Meiji sexology "effectively limited sexual activity to genital-genital procreative intercourse" and excluded other forms of sexuality like male-male desire.[26] Despite these limitations, however, *zōkakiron* publications focused closely on the minutiae of love (*aijō*) and desire (*jōyoku*), including the pleasures of intercourse. Marriage, while seen as grounded in the couple's love, was described as highly sexualized.[27]

The breadth of the contemporary reception of the *zōkakiron* genre can be gauged from a newspaper article of 1880, lamenting that these well-illustrated publications, although not "obscene," provide for "solitary pleasure in student lodgings."[28] The author points to the boom of *zōkakiron* in recent years in conjunction with republications of romantic writings in literary Sinitic, including the 1878 Japanese abridged version of Feng Menglong's (1574–1645) *Qingshi leilüe* (History of emotion in encyclopedic categories), scholar and beauty novels, and Hattori Bushō's (1841–1908) satirical journal *Tōkyō shinshi* (New Tokyo chronicles). This last featured stories about courtesans but also investigative journalism exposing the sexual escapades of powerful bureaucrats.[29] These or similar writings, in addition to Shunsui's *ninjōbon* and the *Jinpingmei*, make up the readings that excite the male protagonists in Mori Ōgai's (1862–1922) semiautobiographical novels *Gan* (*The Wild Goose*, 1911) and *Vita sexualis* (*Vita Sexualis*, 1909), both resurrecting student life in the 1870s, the decade of Ōgai's youth.[30] The eclectic reading tastes of students of the late 1870s and 1880s mixed sexological translations, Chinese scholar and beauty works, and the late Edo-period *gesaku* canon, especially *ninjōbon* and Bakin's *yomihon*—the literary horizon of expectation within which *Karyū shunwa* was received. Students who flooded the bigger cities in pursuit of education and advancement were an important new group of readers beginning in the mid-1870s. They also made up probably the most important subgroup of *Karyū shunwa*'s readers.[31]

Karyū shunwa addressed the diversity of the discourse and reader interest surrounding gender and sexuality in the 1870s by presenting a plot that highlighted desire and passion while also responding to enlightenment concerns regarding the control of passion through reason, civilized gender relations, female education, and monogamous marriage. Stylistically, it also stood in a middle ground. Advertised in the widely popular *Yomiuri shinbun* (Yomiuri newspaper) and providing ample phonetic glosses (*furigana*), the translation was accessible to a broader group of readers. At the same time, the novel's Sinified translation style, sustained even through dialogue and romantic scenes, emphasized its affinity to highbrow writings, including *Meiroku zasshi* essays, Western translations, and *yomihon*.[32]

An idea of the novel's ambiguous generic position in the eyes of contemporary readers can be gained from its paratexts. One important paratext is

Karyū shunwa's foreword, written by the famous scholar and journalist Narushima Ryūhoku (1837–1884):

Do grasses and trees have emotions? I respond: No. If that is the case, on what basis is the quarter of softness and warmth [the pleasure quarter], full of incomparable emotion, called the world of flowers and willows? I respond: There is an explanation. Flowers do not have emotion, but when their fragrant lips graciously open in the rain as though smiling, who would think them devoid of emotion? Willows do not have emotion, but when their alluring hips elegantly move in the wind as though dancing, who would think them devoid of emotion?. . . The sages are full of emotion, fools of course are full of emotion, the entire world is a world of emotion. Narrow-minded scholars claim that the people in Western countries care only about gain and profit and do not value elegance and the foolishness of emotion [*fūryū jōchi*]. This is absolute nonsense. I myself traveled to the West for a year and could see that the emotions here and there are equivalent. There is not even a tiny bit of difference. . . . Those narrow-minded scholars will certainly say that love stories [*jōshi*] do not have any benefit in the world and only incite to licentiousness and teach depravity. Ah! People with emotion like me were born into a world of emotion and read love stories. This also is a gift of the Creator—how could we humans be the same as trees and grasses?[33]

Literary histories often refer to Ryūhoku's foreword for its bold attack on utilitarian views of literature under the banner of emotion (*jō*)—a term humorously repeated twenty-one times in a very condensed textual space.[34] The preface was indeed epoch-making as the first major voice defending emotion and the novel's representation of it against the criticism of licentiousness. As Matthew Fraleigh notes, Ryūhoku was never against Meiji enlightenment per se but advocated a "more balanced, less exclusively utilitarian, form of 'civilization and enlightenment'" that—as the foreword suggests—could even include stories about sexual love.[35] Ryūhoku's argument relied on the unprecedented observation that the West, like Japan, was a "world of emotion" and that there was no contradiction between Western civilization and emotion. His concept of emotion, however, derived from a traditional understanding grounded in the ideal of the erotic sophistication (*fūryū*) of pleasure-quarter culture—the world of "flowers and willows." *Karyū shunwa* did not feature courtesans, but Ryūhoku significantly read the novel as a *jōshi*, which was the traditional term for love stories in vernacular Chinese or literary Sinitic, including scholar and beauty fiction, but also used synonymously with *ninjōbon*.[36] His thought-provoking point was that this genre did not have to be banned from the civilized Meiji present.

Whereas Ryūhoku still understood *Karyū shunwa* along the line of *ninjōbon* and Chinese erotic literature, Niwa Jun'ichirō's translator's afterword opens up a new interpretive view: "The twenty-two [*sic*] books of Lord Lytton's novel examine in detail the human emotions of old and new times and record the different customs in distant and near places. They let the reader clearly see the joy and sorrow as well as the right and wrong in the human world. However, they also differ from those books in our land like Tamenaga Shunsui's *Plum Blossom Calendar* [*sic*] that vainly excite their readers' foolish passion."[37] Niwa here argues that the human emotions (*ninjō*) in *Karyū shunwa* are different from the foolish passion (*chijō*) to be found in *Shunshoku umegoyomi*, Shunsui's famous *ninjōbon*. The important implication here is that *Karyū shunwa* does not "incite to licentiousness and teach depravity"—to use the words of Ryūhoku's narrow-minded scholar-critics. Although Niwa does not elaborate, he implies that the novel's representation of love and gender relations conforms to new enlightenment standards. Although brief, his statement is groundbreaking, as it integrates the traditional term *ninjō*, hitherto associated primarily with *ninjōbon* licentiousness, into a more respectable enlightenment framework and conceives of a novel that centers on *ninjō* without being a traditional *ninjōbon*. Niwa's understanding of *Karyū shunwa* breaks the generic model defined by *Shunshoku umegoyomi* and anticipates Shōyō's discourse in *Shōsetsu shinzui*.

Ryūhoku's and Niwa's readings, while reflecting the diversity of contemporary reader interests, also attest to the complexity of *Karyū shunwa*, which allowed for both erotic (licentious) and enlightened (civilized) readings. There was a third available reading, though, that connected reader expectations to commercial publishing strategies. *Karyū shunwa*'s advertisement in the *Yomiuri shinbun*, published shortly before the novel's first installment, labeled it a *jōshi*, glossed *ninjōbon*. It promised readers that the novel would "not only show customs and emotions [*fūzoku ninjō*] different from those to be found in our popular *Plum Blossom Calendar* but also blow your mind by new wonderful ways of storytelling."[38] Although the advertisement emphasized *Karyū shunwa*'s difference from Shunsui's *ninjōbon*, it did so only to highlight the translation's exciting novelty as a commercial publication. The ad here presents *Karyū shunwa* as a praise-worthy addition to the *ninjōbon* genre—a new addition from the West. This demonstrates, contrary to Niwa's dismissal of Shunsui's *ninjōbon*, that the term still had a strong pull on readers and could be positively exploited for commercial ends.

BULWER-LYTTON'S *ERNEST MALTRAVERS* AS BILDUNGSROMAN

The contradictory way *Karyū shunwa*'s paratexts and the advertisement appropriated the novel was a direct result of the bildungsroman structure of Bulwer-Lytton's source narrative. The nineteenth-century European bil-dungsroman, as Franco Moretti has argued, was a contradictory literary form that mirrored the conflicting sets of aspirations inherent in capitalist modernity: mobility versus stability, change versus identity, freedom versus happiness. The bildungsroman symbolically represents the conflict between these aspirations by staging the opposite poles of youth and maturity— unbounded freedom and mobility on the one hand and social integration on the other—between which the often male protagonist must negotiate.[39]

Bulwer-Lytton's *Ernest Maltravers* is about the eponymous hero's passage from youth to maturity and the thorny path of his social integration. The beginning depicts Maltravers, a scion of the landowning English gentry, as an eccentric and talented young man with a strong poetic inclination, the opposite of the "sober Englishman" type. On his way home from Ger-many, where he was a university student and an idealist political activist, he is almost robbed and murdered, but the robber's beautiful daughter, Alice, rescues him. Maltravers and Alice start living together in an isolated, idyl-lic country cottage, which he rents to provide the destitute girl with a tem-porary home. As Alice is illiterate and lacks knowledge of the world, Mal-travers educates her. The intimacy of their teacher-pupil interaction soon evolves into a sexual love relationship, a youthful and passionate "German romance." Through adverse circumstances, however, the couple's country-side idyll soon ends and they are separated. To compensate for the loss of Alice, Maltravers travels again and during a stay in Italy falls in love with the beautiful, witty, and educated Valerie de Ventadour, the wife of a French aris-tocrat. Ventadour, however, despite her own feeling of "passion" for Mal-travers, resists the adulterous temptation and holds on to her "virtue." The amorous rejection triggers a moral conversion in Maltravers. He awakens not only to the moral worth of "all womanhood" but also to the possibility of his realizing deeds that would merit "praise and honor." This experience and the encouragement of two fatherly friends spur his "ambition," and he soon launches a career as a much-acclaimed public writer, the first step toward his social integration.

At the same time, his eccentric distaste for the superficiality of upper-class life keeps him from more actively contributing to society, in particular as a politician. This aversion changes when Maltravers encounters the beautiful and intelligent Florence, a wealthy English heiress. Through anonymous letters, Florence encourages Maltravers to give up writing and instead realize his ambition by embracing an active political life that would suit his talent. Although skeptical at first about Florence's high-class urbanity, Maltravers awakens to her moral superiority, and after swearing mutual friendship, the two enter a love relationship that culminates in their decision to marry. Maltravers, now a successful politician, is offered a ministerial post. Yet the promise of social integration, epitomized by a bourgeois marriage and political success, remains unfulfilled as the slanderous machinations of a political rival dissolve his marriage and career. This tragic undoing marks the end of *Ernest Maltravers*. The sequel, *Alice*, largely omitted from the Japanese translation, shows the protagonist leading a restless life. Only in the end does he miraculously reencounter Alice and marry her. The novel's last page also hints at the possibility of social redemption, as Maltravers resumes his career "with an energy more practical and steadfast than the fitful enthusiasm of former years."[40]

A plot surrounding love often lies at the heart of the bildungsroman's contradictory symbolic form. On the one hand, Maltravers's passion for the illiterate and low-class Alice epitomizes the enlightenment ideal of individual freedom that defies social and moral norms, including traditional arranged marriage. The class difference between the lovers is an implicit figure of democracy, the political guarantor of universal freedom and equality.[41] It is no coincidence that one of Bulwer-Lytton's important intertexts is Rousseau's *Julie, ou la nouvelle Héloïse* (*Julie, or the New Heloise*, 1761), which in staging a socially unequal teacher-student relationship, the model for the romance between Maltravers and Alice, dramatizes these enlightenment ideals.[42]

However, the novel also revolves around a plot of maturation that rein-states the norms previously challenged by Maltravers's youthful artistic per-sonality and passion. This narrative includes relationships with educated and upper-class women that validate the normativity of virtue and reason. It also prefigures the protagonist's integration into the stabilizing institu-tions of the family and the nation, through a love marriage—what Anthony Giddens calls "romantic love" as opposed to "passionate love"—and socially useful male activity, including public writing and work as a politician.[43] The other major intertext for Bulwer-Lytton's novel is, significantly, Goethe's *Wilhelm Meisters Lehrjahre* (*Wilhelm Meister's Apprenticeship*, 1797), often seen as the archetype of the bildungsroman.[44] Goethe's novel emphasizes the possibility of reaching male maturity through marriage and the aban-donment of a youthful artistic vocation. Bulwer-Lytton's plot, however, never completely resolves the ideological contradictions of the bildungsroman form. Passion always destabilizes relationships even with the educated and upper-class women, and the novel's ideological ambivalence is confirmed by Maltravers's ultimate marriage with his first lover, Alice, the seeming redemption of his former passion.

TRANSLATING PASSION IN *KARYŪ SHUNWA*

Karyū shunwa is quite an accurate translation of *Ernest Maltravers*. Although it adds and omits words and sentences and sometimes provides additional authorial reflections and explanations, in general it follows the original's wording and plot and retains the English names in Japanese tran-scription for all protagonists.[45] At the same time, the translation of the contradictory bildungsroman format into a Japanese text produced a com-plex array of new valences and meanings. The translation of romantic pas-sion is an important case in point.

To a limited extent, the translation of passion in *Karyū shunwa* intro-duced the notion of free and egalitarian love as an intrinsically valuable feeling. An important scene in this respect is at the beginning of the trans-lation. Unaware of his host's criminal intent, Marutsurabāsu (as "Maltrav-ers" is transliterated in Japanese) playfully asks Arisu ("Alice") for permission to kiss her. The short scene, here translated back into English, is noteworthy for the subtle shift in genre expectations:

The master of the house [Arisu's father] stood up and left the room. When the guest [Marutsurabāsu] looked around and saw that Arisu was sitting alone in one corner, he thought that this was his opportunity to talk to her. He therefore said, "If I were to be so fortunate to have a taste of your crimson lips, I would certainly sleep peacefully tonight!" Arisu, covering her face with her sleeve, seemed intent to answer but did not reply. The guest: "Please do not be angry with me." Arisu: "I am not. How could I be?" The guest then came closer to take her hand, but Arisu inquired, "Do you carry a lot of money with you?" The guest was appalled at the greed of the destitute girl and asked, "If your crimson lips were not of too high a price, would you not sell them to me?" With a frown, Arisu replied in a low voice, "If you carry money with you, please do not tell my father."[46]

As one scholar has pointed out, Niwa's translation of the English word "kiss" is awkward, only circumscribing the act ("to have a taste of your crimson lips") without directly naming it.[47] Although the concept of kiss was probably exotic and foreign to the codes of representation in previous Japanese genres, there is an unmistakably erotic dimension in Marutsurabāsu's behavior, reminiscent of *ninjōbon*. However, his desire to kiss Arisu also points to a different, new type of erotic romance, dramatized by the small misunderstanding in the scene's dialogue and underlined by Niwa's highbrow translation style, starkly different from the *ninjōbon*'s colloquial diction. The hero expects his kiss to be for free and is appalled when Arisu reacts like a courtesan or prostitute. The exotic symbolism of the kiss here subtly implies a different type of romantic behavior that is egalitarian and free, in the economic but also in the political sense, insofar as it transcends the boundaries of social class. In the Japanese context, this behavior mirrored the Meiji-enlightenment repudiation of prostitution as an uncivilized practice.

Besides the kiss, *Karyū shunwa* stages another exotic signifier of passion: Marutsurabāsu's later declaration of love to Arisu, to my knowledge the first instance of such a speech act in Japanese literature. In an important climactic scene that marks the beginning of the couple's sexual relationship, he declares, *Yo jitsu ni kei ni renchaku su* 余實ニ卿ニ戀着ス (I truly love you).[48] The neologism of *renchaku* and the declarative sentence structure clearly replicating the English syntax, with the explicitly stated "I" (*yo*) as subject and "you" (*kei*) as object, here produce the sense of romantic passion, the absolutely individualistic feeling of love of the other as other that could potentially transcend all social and moral norms.[49]

It remains questionable, though, to what extent this translation could convey the meaning of such an absolute and exclusive passion. Two extrinsic factors also add value to the passion here, especially in the context of contemporary Japanese civilizational ideology. One is Marutsurabāsu's attempt to educate the illiterate Arisu before declaring his love to her. As she flees from her criminal father and depends on him for her subsistence, he decides to stay with her, not as her lover but as her teacher. In the English novel, Maltravers's decision to teach the girl only reconfirms his youthful romantic personality susceptible to "strange and eccentric" ideas, and he even fantasizes about acting "the Saint Preux to this Julie of Nature."[50] Saint Preux and Julie were the famous lovers in Rousseau's *Nouvelle Héloïse*, a teacher and his student. Julie, however, was not illiterate, and Maltravers's fantasy of Alice as a "Julie of Nature" gestures to both Rousseau's novel and eighteenth-century French enlightenment ideas about the state of nature and its potential for education.[51] *Karyū shunwa*'s translator left these references out, and the atmosphere of French enlightenment utopia was probably lost on him. But Marutsurabāsu's decision to teach Arisu also leads to an enlightenment experiment in the Japanese context—a gender experiment. By conceiving of an educational and nonerotic relationship between a young man and woman not married to each other, the text provided a fantasy of civilized gender relations that even exceeded the proposals of the Meirokusha and anticipated ideas of the free and platonic "association of men and women" (*danjo kōsai*) in 1880s discourse.[52] Although Marutsurabāsu is aware of the danger of erotic infatuation in living with Arisu, he believes that their relationship will not offend the Moral Way (*kōdō*).[53] He even declares that it is his duty (*gi*) to give the woman an education so that she can professionally sustain herself as a female teacher in the future, without—and this is the enlightenment implication of the idea—having to work as a prostitute.

Not only the association with female education but also his moral discourse adds value to Marutsurabāsu's love in the Japanese translation. He is a morally exemplary protagonist. Especially in the first half of the novel, this quality paradoxically derives from his awareness of the immorality of his erotic attraction and his attempt to overcome it. He is subject to passion, and the initial trigger for it is Arisu's outstanding beauty. "Spring feelings" (*shun'i*) surge up in him while teaching her, but he also feels shame (*haji*) when awareness of her innocence dawns on him. His moral awareness lets him struggle to resist his passion. His attempt to end the teacher-student relationship significantly precedes his declaration of love. Arisu's beauty has increased the more she has advanced in her learning, and he is aware of his resurging desire and recognizes the futility of his educational project. In a climactic scene, he explains to Arisu that if they were to "commit a mistake" and give up their restraint (*kinshin*)—the word in the English novel is "prudence"—this would lead to inescapable sin (*tsumi*). Chastity (*teisō*) is the most important virtue for a woman. Arisu should independently continue with her studies and aim to make a living as a teacher. He even bemoans her beauty, thus revealing his inner struggle. The outcome of the scene, however, is unexpected. In an outburst of emotion, Arisu swoons and Marutsurabāsu, while attempting to rescue her, suddenly kisses her. The English novel is explicit in mentioning the kiss, but Niwa again avoids a translation and has the hero spill cold water onto the woman's "crimson lips." The illustration nevertheless shows both partners in an awkward kissing pose. The scene ends with the declaration of love and the beginning of sexual romance.

In this episode, Marutsurabāsu's love is indirectly given value as a feeling that affects a male subject purposely engaging in enlightened female education and morally aware of his dangerous passion. This love fundamentally differs from *Shunshoku umegoyomi*, where Tanjirō engages in erotic acts without distancing them through a moral discourse or any useful social activity. However, Marutsurabāsu's educational project and his moral discourse also remain extrinsic, even opposed, to his passion. His love powerfully erupts only at the moment when both fail, and to Japanese readers it was probably as titillating as any earlier *ninjōbon* plot. Marutsurabāsu's kiss and love declaration could serve as the signifiers for a free, egalitarian, and therefore enlightened passion but also as the emblems for an erotic love that, although exotic, had a strong affinity to *ninjōbon*. This was precisely why the *Yomiuri shinbun* advertisement claimed *Karyū shunwa* to be a *ninjōbon* full of novelty—that is, new Western elements like kisses and love declarations. There is a subtle shift in the translation of passion in *Karyū shunwa* from a morally problematic but still valuable enlightened feeling in the English novel into the exciting type of *ninjōbon* love that was

FIGURE 3.1 Ānesuto Marutsurabāsu kissing Arisu. From chapter 6 of *Karyū shunwa*; illustrator unspecified. Courtesy of Waseda University Library, Tokyo

cherished by readers but denigrated by contemporary discourse.[54] "Love" (*renchaku*) and "passion" (*jō*) were indeed new Western terms introduced by *Karyū shunwa*, but as Iwamoto's essay "Fujin no chii" suggests, Japanese discourse came to see especially passion as synonymous with half-civilized *ninjōbon* love.

Indeed, various references in *Karyū shunwa* implicitly gesture to the *ninjōbon*. Arisu, for example, although not a courtesan or prostitute, remains strongly associated with prostitution. At the beginning, her father implicitly states to her his evil intention to sell her as a mistress or prostitute. She does not understand and instead insists on working in a nearby factory to sustain the family. Although she is predestined to prostitution or a life in the pleasure quarter given her beauty and low-class background, her inborn virtue resists this fate by pointing, in enlightenment manner, to the possibility of female work. Yet her titillating potential as a *ninjōbon* heroine also comes to the fore, especially after the failure of her education and the beginning of sexual romance. Marutsurabāsu similarly possesses qualities of a *ninjōbon* hero. He is the second son born into a wealthy land-owning family and can indulge in a life of luxury without having to assume the responsibilities of a household heir.[55] While a student in Germany, moreover, he frequents "elegant circles"—*fūryū shakai*—and has the reputation of a "talented and attractive man" (*saishi binan*).[56] Whereas the English novel underlines Maltravers's romantic, Byronic temperament by specifying that he "had been already the darling of the sentimental German ladies," the references to male attractiveness and *fūryū* (erotic elegance) in the Japanese translation—also highlighted by Narushima Ryūhoku—again gesture to the elegant but (to Meiji enlighteners) uncivilized *ninjōbon* world.[57]

CONTROLLING PASSION

Bulwer-Lytton's novel is a bildungsroman insofar as it gradually replaces the narrative of passion with a narrative of maturation that highlights the hero's compromise with social norms. In the Japanese translation, this produces a new narrative arc away from the *ninjōbon* aesthetic. *Karyū shunwa*'s later plot stages the transformation of the protagonist from a passionate and licentious to a socially useful and moral masculinity, thus aligning with the interest of contemporary Japanese young men in social advancement and political activity—new themes that resonated with the *yomihon* and their representation of male exemplarity. In unprecedented fashion, moreover, this narrative featured a new type of civilized love that could facilitate male social integration.

The idyll of Marutsurabāsu and Arisu's romance dissolves when the hero must return to his family to look after his dying father—the symbol of the value system of the family and social morality—and Arisu is abducted by her own criminal father. Marutsurabāsu subsequently falls in love with the married Bentadoa—*Karyū shunwa*'s transliteration for "Ventadour."[58] His attraction is triggered not only by her beauty but also by her talent and intelligence, in strong contrast to Arisu's illiterate innocence. Bentadoa, in turn, is impressed by Marutsurabāsu's uprightness, and she views him as an "exceptional talent" (*kisaishi*) and the antipode to the superficial "upper-class society" (*jōtō shakai*) around her. Their conversation topics also reflect their intellectual equality: Roman democracy, people's rights, the function of newspapers—also important topics in Meiji enlightenment discourse—as well as, a bit surprisingly perhaps, the importance of love (*aijō*) in modern society.[59] All this cultivated, enlightened, and civilized talk, however, is overshadowed by the sudden eruption of amorous tension. One balmy spring night, overwhelmed by the lady's attractiveness and the beauty of the surrounding Neapolitan landscape, Marutsurabāsu catches her hand and again declares, "You might despise me, but I truly love you [*shin ni renbo su*]." He also boldly states, "I am committing a mistake, but I hardly feel ashamed of it." His visual focus is on her physical beauty mediated by the translation's exoticizing Sinified style: "Her flowery face, illuminated by the starlight, was glittering on the jeweled balustrade; her cloudy hair, moved by the soft breeze, fell on her pearl-like cheeks—her delicate figure was unspeakably enticing."[60]

The peculiar mixture in this passage of enlightened conversation, stylistic elegance, and erotic tension was quite different from the *ninjōbon* aesthetic.[61] Bentadoa's education, which strongly differentiates her from Arisu and previous *ninjōbon* heroines, also leads to a radically surprising outcome: the rejection of Marutsurabāsu's love. Unlike Arisu, Bentadoa is able to "control" (*sei-su*) her feelings and prevent adultery (*fugi*) from happening. Her rejection is all the more heroic because her feelings are strong. Her words to her suitor are unambiguous: "In my heart, my love for you [*ken-ren no jō*] is truly as strong as yours. How could I ever hide it? Last night, after separating from you, a thousand thoughts and sorrows let me see my unhappiness, and my entire heart was with you and no one else. I can yield my heart to you, but I cannot yield my body. I wish you to understand."[62] In the English novel, Ventadour concludes her reflection by making the important distinction between reason and passion: "I reasoned calmly, for my passions did not blind my reason."[63] *Karyū shunwa*'s translations for the conceptual antonyms are *jō* and *ri*. Bentadoa decides to "curb her passion and abide by reason" (*jō o kujiki ri o mattō suru*).[64] She also refers to her conscience (*ryōshin*) as opposed to her passion. Her virtuous rejection of Marutsurabāsu's advances triggers a moral conversion in him. He exclaims, "Now standing before such a virtuous woman, even an unworthy fellow like me must arouse his ambition [*kokorozashi o tatan to su*]!"[65] "Ambition" (*kokorozashi*) is a key word in both the English novel and the translation, and it motivates the hero's subsequent decision to give up his socially useless life of passion and instead serve society and the nation as a public writer. His writings soon gain resounding fame for their integrity and adherence to truth.

Bentadoa's inner conflict between passion and reason (or virtue and conscience) again brings to the fore the bildungsroman's tension between contradictory aspirations. However, whereas Marutsurabāsu's earlier similar conflict in the face of Arisu's beauty gave precedence to immoral passion, Bentadoa's education and intelligence allow her to opt for virtuous reason. It is certainly relevant that the subject able to enact reason and virtue is an educated woman, not the equally educated male hero. Yet the more important point was that educating women could facilitate the conversion of men from uncivilized passion to reason and thus turn them into useful members of society and the nation. This resonated with the Meirokusha writings about the role of female education and love in facilitating male achievement within the new framework of the nation.

Marutsurabāsu's conversion to reason and subsequent career, moreover, allowed for integrating contemporary male readers' concern with *risshin shusse*. The early Meiji period witnessed a new social mobility of young men, often of former samurai background, who flooded the big cities to study and in search of social opportunity. Contemporary journals like *Eisai shinshi* (New talent chronicle) featured reader submissions that expressed the desire for success, fame, and to a lesser extent wealth through "hard study" (*benkyō*), either by climbing the ladder of the new Meiji governmental bureaucracy or, beginning in the early 1880s, by launching a political career.[66] The publication and circulation of *Eisai shinshi* significantly peaked in the year 1878, when *Karyū shunwa* was published. The novel indirectly refers to the journal's discourse by incorporating major key words like "hard study," "rising in the world" (*mi o tatsuru*), and "high-flying ambition" (*seiun no kokorozashi*) into its translation idiom. *Risshin shusse* was also an important theme in the later Meiji novel, and *Karyū shunwa* was probably the first work to bring it to the fore.[67]

At the same time, *Karyū shunwa* combined the focus on male advancement and success with a concern for morality that was absent from *Eisai shinshi*'s essays and connected back to the narrative format of the *yomihon*. Reader submissions to that journal often straightforwardly emphasized fame and wealth as desirable goals, whereas *Karyū shunwa* didactically devalues those goals for Maltravers. His intentions are "pure" and not contaminated by the vulgar desire for profit (*ri*) and fame (*na*) that two scheming villains instead embody. Yet the novel still skillfully presents him as a role model for success. In this fashion, *Karyū shunwa* integrated the contemporary discourse into a didactic narrative framework of male exemplarity that could fulfill the more highbrow reader expectations connected to *yomihon*.

Social integration through marriage was another important element in *Karyū shunwa*'s new narrative of the control of passion and a civilized love. This narrative revolves primarily around the woman Furorensu ("Florence"), an English bourgeois heiress. Like the French aristocrat Bentadoa, Furorensu is beautiful and educated, but unlike the almost adulterous romance with the former, Marutsurabāsu's relationship with her more intrinsically conforms to new civilizational norms. As Maeno Michiko has noted, Bulwer-Lytton's novel purposely associates adulterous love with the French aristocracy, whereas a bourgeois marriage is possible only with Florence.[68] The translation *Karyū shunwa* and contemporary Japanese discourse were aware of these specificities of nation and class. Bentadoa indeed notes that French aristocratic marriage, like hers, is not free, as it is forced upon the children by their parents.[69] The protagonists in Shōyō's slightly later novel *Imotose kagami*, moreover, make a similar point about French customs, adding that their practice of forced marriage (*kyōhaku kekkon*) is the breeding ground for licentious adultery—uncivilized behavior not different from Japanese feudal customs. Only in Britain are marriage customs free (*jiyū*) from parental intervention, thus allowing for truly civilized relationships between the sexes.[70] The important implication, in *Karyū shunwa*, of the hero's relationship and marriage plans with Furorensu is this British— bourgeois or middle-class—model of civilized gender relations. Indeed, her love derives from her intellectual and spiritual attraction to Marutsurabāsu's writings. Convinced of his "talent in governing the realm" (*keizai no sai*), she sends him anonymous letters, urging him to embrace a career in politics. As she states in one of her letters, "I have never met you and I also do not desire to meet you. This is because I do not love you as a person, but I long for your ideas" (*sono hito o shitawazu shite sono i o shitau*).[71]

With this encouragement, Marutsurabāsu enters national politics (*kokusei*) and becomes a member of parliament. His virtuous aim is to benefit the nation (*tenka no yō o nasu*). The years of *Karyū shunwa*'s publication witnessed the first peak of the People's Rights Movement, a nationwide campaign, promoted especially by young men of former samurai status, for political participation through a parliamentarian system. Marutsurabāsu's career as a politician resonated with the desire of Japanese young men not only for advancement but also for political engagement, an important topic discussed by contemporary enlightenment media like *Meiroku zasshi*. *Karyū shunwa* can thus be seen as the first Japanese political novel with a politician protagonist, a new genre that greatly flourished throughout the 1880s.

As in subsequent political fiction, Marutsurabāsu's career as a politician— the pinnacle of his social utility and virtue, reminiscent of *yomihon*—relies on a new enlightened love based not on erotic attraction but on respect. This educated and spiritual dimension in Furorensu's feelings qualifies her as his ideal marriage partner and anticipates Iwamoto's views on married love in a civilized age. When Marutsurabāsu finds out that she was the author of the anonymous letters, they become aware of their mutual love and decide to marry. One of the novel's illustrations labels the couple a "talented man and beautiful woman" (*saishi kajin*), indirectly referring to the scholar and beauty genre, where marriage was the recompense for the protagonists' chastity and virtue.[72] But *Karyū shunwa*'s marriage plot also reflects the new valences of Japanese enlightenment discourse, especially the idea of chaste monogamy as the nurturing ground for a useful masculinity serving the nation.[73]

One of the complexities of *Karyū shunwa*, however, is that it does not end with such an exemplary marriage. Despite its enlightened quality, Marutsurabāsu's relationship with Furorensu soon transforms into a passionate love (*renjō*) that defies social integration. Their passion most violently erupts when their marriage plans dissolve owing to the machinations of his evil rivals. Consumed by "foolish passion," Furorensu dies; Marutsurabāsu, similarly subject to "mental fatigue" (*shinshin no hirō*), abandons his political and public career.[74] Despite *Karyū shunwa*'s seemingly teleological trajectory moving from youthful passion to maturity, mirroring the ideology of progress and civilization in Meiji discourse, passion resurges and jeopardizes the hero's career. The bildungsroman's contradictory format reemerges as unresolved. The ambiguity is particularly conspicuous in the ending, where Marutsurabāsu reencounters and marries his first lover, Arisu—a revalidation of sorts of his former infatuation. As indicated, this ambiguity allowed for a contradictory range of readings. Presenting a new type of enlightened love, *Karyū shunwa* could integrate the *yomihon*'s focus on exemplary masculinity as well as contemporary concerns for male social utility, advancement, and political participation. At the same time, the novel continuously staged titillating foolish passion, reminiscent of what Meiji discourses decried as the *ninjōbon*'s licentiousness unfit for the civilized present.

NARRATING THE SUCCESSFUL COMPROMISE: THE NOVEL *SEIRO NIKKI*

Karyū shunwa's contemporary success can be gauged from the number of novels that were published in the late 1870s and early 1880s with very similar titles. Shōyō's first published work, a translated fragment of Walter Scott's *The Bride of Lammermoor* (1819) titled *Shunpū jōwa* (Spring breeze love tale, 1880), is one of them. The most important rewriting of *Karyū shunwa*, though, its retranslation of sorts into a Japanese novel, was *Seiro nikki*, written by the journalist and later author of political fiction Kikutei Kōsui.[75] *Seiro nikki*'s publication history is complex. The two first volumes were originally serialized under the title *Geppyō kigū: Ensai shunwa* (Strange encounter in the moonlight: Spring tale of love and talent) in a regional Oita newspaper, the *Inaka shinbun* (Country newspaper), in 1880. A one-volume edition with the same title and content appeared in Tokyo in 1882.[76] *Seiro nikki* was the new title for the complete three-volume edition published by Tōkyō Haishi Shuppansha (Tokyo novel publishing house) in 1884. The novel's intertextual indebtedness to *Karyū shunwa* is dense. It adopts the bildungsroman's contradictory format, pitching the value of unbridled passion against a more mature form of love compatible with a respectable marriage. However, *Seiro nikki* reduces the ambiguity through a narrative that highlights the successful compromise between passion and freedom on the one hand and maturity and control on the other. This allowed for a more thorough integration of passion into a plot of social advancement and political activity that epitomized a virtuous and useful masculinity serving the new Japanese nation.

Seiro nikki differs from *Karyū shunwa* in more explicitly highlighting the enlightenment potential of passion. The novel's protagonists are a young male teacher, Hisamatsu Kikuo, and his even younger female student, Matsue Take, whose romance unfolds in their rural elementary school (*shōgakkō*). The recent implementation of compulsory elementary education reflects the efforts of the early-Meiji state to integrate rural peripheries into the national community and instill civilization and enlightenment on the local level. Although the exact time of the story is not specified, it is obviously the Meiji present—"that enlightened reign" (*kaimei no yo*), as Kikutei writes, when elementary schools "were established everywhere all over the realm well into the remotest corners."[77] *Seiro nikki* reenacts Marutsurabāsu's teacher-pupil relationship with Arisu, but it integrates this reference into the symbolically loaded spatiotemporal context of Meiji civilization and enlightenment. The love between the protagonists in *Seiro nikki*, besides their being teacher and student, is enlightened in several respects. When Kikuo declares his "love" (*kenren no jō*) to Take—in an early-morning schoolroom scene that significantly contrasts with the more titillating late-night settings of Marutsurabāsu's love declarations—he emphasizes her extraordinary talent and knowledge. Take's physical attractiveness recedes to the background while Kikuo's respect is foregrounded. An illustration accordingly shows the couple surrounded by implements of teaching, including a world map, glasses, and animal and plant sketches.

The most important enlightenment implication of Kikuo's love for Take, however, is that it can lead to a marriage grounded in the partners' free consent and not in their parents' will. Japanese discourse in the 1880s, especially as disseminated by *Jogaku zasshi*, promoted free marriage (*jiyū kekkon*) as opposed to the traditional practice of forced marriage, which it decried as cruel and barbarian.[78] The idea was directly connected to the notion of an enlightened "association of men and women" (*danjo kōsai*). In *Seiro*

FIGURE 3.2 Hisamatsu Kikuo declaring his love to Matsue Take. From chapter 3 of *Seiro nikki*; illustration by Teisai Nensan (dates unknown). Courtesy of the National Diet Library, Tokyo

nikki, free marriage also validates passion as the enlightened choice of the heart that could realize individual freedom against traditionalist propriety and social class. Whereas *Karyū shunwa* downplayed the enlightened quality of this love, equaling it with foolish passion, *Seiro nikki* more strongly foregrounds this quality.

However, like *Karyū shunwa*, *Seiro nikki* also sees the freedom of passion as in need of regulation and control. The 1882 edition, still titled *Ensai shunwa*, starts with a preface, written in literary Sinitic, that defines the necessity to restrict *jō* (emotion or passion) and *yoku* (desire) as the novel's main theme. The preface begins with the following enlightenment apology reminiscent of Tsuda Mamichi's evolutionist argument about desire previously published in *Meiroku zasshi*: "The creator bestowed both passion and desire on humankind. These two are of the utmost importance in human life; even if only one of them were lacking, how could human life ever be reproduced?" Yet Kikutei continues,

However, if there is no method of limiting and controlling [passion and desire], the harm produced by them will surely bring a youthful life to a premature end. How important it is to exercise restraint! Confucius once said, "There are three things the gentleman should guard against: in youth when the blood and *qi* [life force] are still unsettled he should guard against the attraction of feminine beauty."[79] This refers to the need to limit and control passion and desire. Yet when the control is too severe, it can bring harm and lead to sickness. When, on the other hand, there are no limits, this will lead to life-threatening debauchery. The method of limiting and controlling is difficult indeed![80]

Kikutei's preface highlights the erotic quality of passion and desire, which, although human and necessary, must be contained to avoid the danger of life-threatening debauchery (*hōtō*). It thus points to the licentious underside of passion that contemporary discourse associated with the *ninjōbon*. *Seiro nikki* in fact abounds in titillating scenes. In several instances, Kikuo and Take are about to lose control and give free rein to their desire. In a dream, for example, after arguing to Take about the need to give up the "mere pleasure of one moment," Kikuo soon reverses his stance because "life is so short."[81] Only the end of the dream frustrates the promise of sexual fulfillment.

As in *Karyū shunwa*, the plot of *Seiro nikki* revolves around the control of passion, necessary to produce a virtuous and useful masculinity. Shortly after declaring their love to each other, Kikuo and Take are separated by adverse circumstances. Owing to slander, Kikuo is forced to move to another school, and Take's seemingly evil stepmother forces her to marry a brutish relative embodying the backwardness of traditional customs. Yet Kikuo approves of this separation. He argues that, although he "loves" Take (*ken-ren su*), their union would be an "illicit affair" without their parents' consent; "sinking body and soul into a sea of passion [*jōkai*]" would mean giving up his "long-cherished ambition" (*shukushi*) that goes far beyond the "lowly profession" of elementary-school teaching.[82] With the intent to build his "own independent base" in life, he soon leaves his school and embarks on a six-year period of "painful study" (*kugaku*) in Osaka to polish his talent and realize his high-flying ambition. The control of passion is here again linked to the major key words of *risshin shusse* discourse.

It turns out, however, that Take's forced marriage was an expedient means devised by her stepmother to only temporarily distance her from Kikuo. The stepmother explains that, although she approved of the couple's love, she did not think they could have a happy future if they married too early. Her plan was to wait for Kikuo's "success in his enterprise and return home" (*seigyō kikoku*) before allowing her stepdaughter to marry.[83] Kikuo's control of his passion and painful study qualify him to marry Take and gain access to the wealthy landowning rural elite to which she belongs. This mature and socially acceptable marriage—a compromise between the couple's freedom and their parents' consent—is the true fulfillment of his ambition, and it also provides the financial basis for his future political activity. The final scene of the novel tellingly takes place in the spring of 1881, when an imperial edict announced the opening of the National Diet for the year 1890. Kikuo is seized by the general political fever that erupts in the wake of the edict's proclamation, embracing both reformist and liberal doctrines (*kaishin jiyū no setsu*) and embarking on a new political life in Tokyo.[84]

Unlike *Karyū shunwa*, *Seiro nikki* presents a successful compromise between youthful passion and maturity, freedom and control. It thus almost brings to perfection a new narrative of male-female love that, unlike earlier *ninjōbon*, could include the representation of male virtue and usefulness, directly connected to the representational sphere of the *yomihon*. Like Marutsurabāsu, Kikuo is a virtuous protagonist. As an elementary-school teacher, he abides by righteousness (*seigi*) and is the victim of the intrigues of inefficient school officials. By his talent and sense of mission, he contributes to the thriving of his local school and the state's enlightenment project. As a student in Osaka, he selflessly nurses his friend until the latter's death. Kikuo's uprightness in the face of adversities is an important quality shared by *Hakkenden*'s dog warriors as well.

Seiro nikki's connection to Bakin's *yomihon* also pertained to publishing and readership. The 1884 version of Kikutei's novel was published by Tōkyō Haishi Shuppansha, which up to that point had almost exclusively republished *yomihon* by Bakin, including a full movable-type reprint edition of *Hakkenden* in 1882–1885. This important, albeit short-lived, publishing venture also increasingly focused on publications of contemporary texts, including *Seiro nikki*, the shorthand transcription of San'yūtei Enchō's (1839–1900) *Kaidan botan dōrō* (*Peony Lantern Ghost Story*, 1884), and—at least in planning—Shōyō's treatise *Shōsetsu shinzui* and novel *Tōsei shosei katagi*. Shōyō's epoch-making texts ultimately appeared elsewhere, but the specific sense of mission and understanding of the novel reflected by the scope of Tōkyō Haishi Shuppansha's publications deserve attention. As Isobe Atsushi has shown, this publisher understood the novel as a highbrow genre promoting literature (*bungaku*).[85] A publisher's memorandum defined Bakin's novels as masterworks depicting the intricacies of "human emotion and social customs" as well as the exploits of "chivalrous heroes, beautiful women, and talented men" (*eiyū gōketsu kajin saishi*).[86] This description fit the plot of *Seiro nikki* as well.[87] Linguistically, the novel, with its rather difficult Sinified style far removed from the *ninjōbon*'s everyday language, was also reminiscent of Bakin's *yomihon* and other highbrow contemporary publications, including translations. The genealogy that linked, through Tōkyō Haishi Shuppansha, Bakin's *yomihon*, *Seiro nikki*, and finally Shōyō's writings highlights the emergence of the novel as a respectable genre for educated readers focusing on male exemplarity and civilized love. This genealogy anticipated the possibility for the novel's reform in the 1880s.

With the publication of *Karyū shunwa* and *Seiro nikki*, *ninjō*, rather than being denigrated as licentious, for the first time became the explicit focus

of the novel as a respectable genre. This was a result of the new enlightenment discourses in Japan that saw gender relations and male-female love
as important indicators of civilizational progress. The novel was particularly suited to depict human emotion and social customs, one of the core
domains in contemporary efforts to implement civilization. By didactically
presenting civilized gender relations and love, it could actively promote
enlightenment and progress. Both *Karyū shunwa* and *Seiro nikki*, moreover,
represent civilized love as the attribute of a virtuous and educated hero, who
could serve the new nation. This met the literary expectations especially of
male elite readers, often students, who were enthusiastic readers of Bakin's
yomihon. An important continuity thus links Bakin's didactic-moralistic
understanding of the novel and representation of male exemplarity (in the
eight dog warriors, for instance) to the new Meiji novel focusing on social
customs and *ninjō*.

However, the peculiar bildungsroman structure inherent in *Karyū
shunwa* and its intertext *Seiro nikki* also allowed for the inclusion of a narrative focus on foolish passion. Although both novels ideologically relegate
passion to immature youth and subject it to a didactic narrative of control,
especially successful in *Seiro nikki*, passion and the erotic scenes it engenders remain constitutive elements of the text. This allowed for a reception
according to the genre expectations of *ninjōbon*, focusing on titillating
elements—what critics condemned as the novel's licentiousness and the
remnants of a half-civilized age. These elements obviously catered to different literary obsessions of often the same student readers.

In previous chapters, I argued that the early nineteenth-century Japanese novel, especially Shunsui's *ninjōbon* and Bakin's *yomihon*, negotiated
in differing ways the tension between legitimating discourses that highlighted the novel's moral-didactic value and the representation of licentious emotion and desire. In doing so, Shunsui's and Bakin's narratives were
more complex than contemporary and later discourses that reductively
associated *ninjōbon* with licentiousness and *yomihon* with didactic idealism. Novels like *Karyū shunwa* and *Seiro nikki* transposed the tension inherent in *yomihon* and *ninjōbon* and their narrative practices of *ninjō* to the
age of enlightenment. This tension refueled anxieties about literary licentiousness that considerably complicated subsequent attempts to reform the
novel in Meiji Japan.

Chapter Four

HISTORICIZING LITERARY REFORM

Shōsetsu shinzui, Translation, and the
Civilizational Politics of *Ninjō*

In *Shōsetsu shinzui*, Tsubouchi Shōyō famously defines the main focus of the reformed novel to be human emotion (*ninjō*) and, next in importance, social customs (*setai*). He specifies that the novel should focus on the realist depiction (*mosha*) of emotions and customs "as they are" (*ari no mama*) and that the novelist should be an observer and psychologist digging out the interior emotions of his characters and making them visible to the reader. He also postulates that the novel is "art" (*bijutsu*) giving aesthetic pleasure to the human mind. These core ideas in Shōyō's treatise were greatly influential in a longer literary-historical perspective. In the late 1880s and 1890s, it became common to define the realist depiction of *ninjō* as the novel's main purpose, and by the turn of the century discourses promoted an increasingly naturalized understanding of literature as an imaginative art focusing on emotion and passion. This is why twentieth-century scholarship until recently saw in *Shōsetsu shinzui* the origin of Japanese literary modernity. Shōyō's critical terms that could be read as the manifesto of a mimetic and psychological realism seemed to suggest that the Japanese *shōsetsu* had finally caught up with the dominant literary paradigm of the nineteenth-century European novel.[1]

While *Shōsetsu shinzui*'s importance in shaping later discourses of Japanese literary modernity is undeniable, this chapter seeks to historicize Shōyō's fictional project in its immediate literary and discursive context. On the one hand, I stress the importance of contemporary civilizational and enlightenment concerns in his reform of fiction. Although highlighting the novel's role as art, Shōyō attempts to make it a didactic and civilizing agent, especially in its representation of gender relations and *ninjō*. He responds to contemporary discourses that viewed gender relations and love as important indicators of a nation's level of civilization. Moreover, I highlight the significance of prior Japanese genres, especially *ninjōbon* and *yomihon*, as a major literary reference for Shōyō's reform. The canon of early nineteenth-century popular fiction, or the *gesaku* classics, formed the basis for the understanding of the novel in Japan well into the 1880s. It is no coincidence that, in *Shōsetsu shinzui*, Bakin's *Hakkenden* and Shunsui's *Shunshoku umegoyomi* are by far the most cited works, not only in quantity but also in quality.[2] Shōyō's reception of Western novels and critical ideas, including key notions like "realist depiction," did not lead to an effacement of the contemporary literary field. Instead, Shōyō's reform of Japanese fiction according to civilizational and enlightenment imperatives incorporated an awareness of important elements of previous genres, particularly the *ninjōbon*'s focus on *ninjō* and the *yomihon*'s didacticism. In this respect, *Shōsetsu shinzui* and Shōyō's reform were a product of the literary field opened up by the translation *Karyū shunwa*, whose new narrative format recombined elements of the *ninjōbon* and *yomihon* while responding to Meiji enlightenment concerns.

My discussion starts with an important topic often overlooked in critical studies: Shōyō's reception and translation in the early 1880s, immediately after *Karyū shunwa*'s publication, of a limited group of English novels, in particular historical fiction by Bulwer-Lytton and Walter Scott. Shōyō's translations of these works had a strong affinity to *Karyū shunwa* and specific aspects of prior Japanese fiction. They were historical novels with martial and virtuous protagonists, and Shōyō was well aware of their affinity to Bakin's works he had admired as a youth. More than Bakin's *yomihon*, however, Shōyō's translations foregrounded plots of romance that, like *Karyū shunwa*, staged the conflict between passion and reason or a civilized love. These works could be read as reformed *yomihon* or *ninjōbon* with a focus on gender relations and emotion that illustrated new civilizational norms.

I then move to *Shōsetsu shinzui*, which must be seen as a theoretical elaboration of Shōyō's experiments with translation. He famously criticizes both *ninjōbon* and *yomihon*. Although lauding Shunsui's writings for their ability to depict *ninjō*, he also condemns them, in line with broader Meiji discourse, for their focus on uncivilized, licentious passion. He attacks Bakin's *Hakkenden* for focusing primarily on didactic moralism and for staging protagonists, the eight dog warriors, whom he sees as dehumanized "specters of the eight Confucian virtues" lacking *ninjō*. Instead, the novel should show how protagonists are subject to "vulgar passion" but can overcome it by reason. Despite this critique, Shōyō's model reintegrates important elements of both genres: the *ninjōbon*'s focus on passion but also Bakin's didacticism. *Shōsetsu shinzui*'s conception of the realist depiction of *ninjō*, far from being simply a model of mimetic representation, was in fact inherently didactic. The representation of *ninjō* should show the protagonist's struggle against passion and thus help readers reflect on and vanquish their own passion. Elsewhere, Shōyō even states that, while the first emphasis of the "true novel" is the depiction of *ninjō*, its second emphasis is *kanzen chōaku*. This realism must be historicized within a critical framework that responded to both traditional moral and Meiji civilizational concerns.

I finally contextualize Shōyō's literary project in contemporary political discourse and fiction. Literary histories have often claimed that Shōyō's new emphasis on *ninjō* and his criticism of Bakin implied a critique of contemporary political fiction and its didactic agenda. Political novels (*seiji shōsetsu*) flourished in the 1880s, promoting the ideas of the People's Rights Movement, a nationwide campaign for democratic political participation opposing the Meiji government. Shōyō's reform of the novel was indeed directed against a specific type of political fiction, associated with the Japanese Liberal Party (Jiyūtō), that sought to promote violent and revolutionary political change. Because of their focus on martial action and moralistic dichotomies, these novels have been discussed as an extension of Bakin's *yomihon*, and Shōyō himself dismissed them as inferior imitations of Bakin. However, his didacticism that relied on the realist depiction of emotions and customs resonated with a different type of 1880s political fiction, associated with the Constitutional Reform Party (Rikken Kaishintō). This type of fiction emphasized, instead of violent action, gradual political, social, and civilizational reforms and nation-state building. Reform Party–inflected novels were greatly invested in the didactic representation of civilized customs and emotions, including love, with the goal of civilizing the nation and bringing it to political maturity. Shōyō's literary project thus did not promote a demise of politics. On the contrary, it shared a strong interest with Reform Party–inflected political discourse and fiction in nation-state building and social reform.

ENGLISH LITERATURE, TRANSLATION, AND THE MAKING OF SHŌYŌ'S LITERARY REFORM

Shōyō's reform of fiction was in important ways the product of his reception and translation of specific English novels. This reception was highly contextualized, though, and a closer examination of the institutional and literary-historical context for his reading and translation of Western works elucidates his literary and critical project. The origins of this project go back to Shōyō's student years at the University of Tokyo in the late 1870s and early 1880s. A graduate of the prestigious Aichi Gaikokugo Gakkō (Aichi foreign language school) in Nagoya in 1876, Shōyō was one of the few outstanding students selected to take the entrance examination for Tōkyō Kaisei Gakkō (Tokyo Kaisei school), which became the University of Tokyo (Tōkyō Daigaku) in 1877, the only university in Japan at the time. Shōyō passed the exam, moved to Tokyo, and started to study in 1876, first in the preparatory course (*futsūka*) and, from 1878 until his graduation in 1883, in the main course (*honka*), at the university's newly founded Literary Faculty (Bungakubu). His major was political science, but students would enroll in specialized courses of their major only in the last year and, before doing so, studied a broad curriculum including history, English literature, and psychology as well as the Japanese and Chinese classics.[3] Although not a major in itself—the majors available in the Literary Faculty were history, philosophy, political science, and the Japanese and Chinese classics—English literature (*Eibungaku*) was an important new subject. Shōyō's teacher was the American scholar William Houghton (1852–1917), who, resident in Japan between 1877 and 1882, played a fundamental role in instituting English literature as an academic discipline at the university. The textbook used in Houghton's classes, Homer Sprague's (1829–1918) *Masterpieces in English Literature* (1877), contained well-annotated excerpts from canonical authors up to the seventeenth century, including Chaucer, Spenser, Shakespeare,

Milton, and Bunyan. Shōyō and his cohort belonged to the first generation of Japanese students to be systematically exposed to Western literature, at least as defined by this limited canon.

However, the motivation for Shōyō's reform of fiction did not derive primarily from these academic studies. It was the result of the circulation and reading of a set of nineteenth-century English novels, excluded from the university curriculum, among the small group of his cohorts and friends in the Literary Faculty. Shōyō's biographer Yanagida Izumi has termed this sudden surge of interest in English fiction a "Western literature fever" (*Seiyō bungaku netsu*).[4] Students affected included such future eminent men as Takata Sanae (1860–1938), the later president of Waseda University and Shōyō's lifelong friend, and the writer and critic Okakura Kakuzō (1862–1913). Their "fever" broke out approximately in the fall of 1878, Shōyō's first year of study in the university's main course. Yanagida convincingly assumes that it was sparked by the publication of *Karyū shunwa* at around the same time.[5] As noted, this translation was a resounding success among contemporary students and a broader readership, as it presented a new model for the novel. But Shōyō and his group of friends, unlike the majority of general readers, were able to consume a greater amount of fiction in the original English. Thus, despite the timely outbreak of their literature fever, the circulation and consumption of English-language novels within this small student group remained local yet nonetheless had a lasting legacy. In his memoirs, Takata Sanae confirms this impression:

As far as I know, Tan-kun [Tan Otsuba] was among the very first who ever read Western novels in Japan.[6] Tan started to read a novel (I do not remember which one it was), talked to me about it, and strongly urged me to read it. He said it was very interesting. I also got into the mood and started to read two or three Western novels. Then, one day when I was taking a walk in the neighborhood, I discovered this splendid volume with a golden edge in a used-book store titled *Waverley Novels*. . . . The first novel I read was *Rob Roy*, which was about a group of bandits in Scotland. . . . As I said before, because my head had been trained by *Hakkenden* and [*Chinsetsu*] *Yumiharizuki* [Strange tales of the crescent moon, 1807–1811], I somehow managed to follow the plot to its end [despite the linguistic difficulties owing to the use of Scottish dialect]. This got my interest aroused and I was full of excitement when reading *Ivanhoe*, *Kenilworth*, and *The Talisman*. Tan-kun urged me to read the novels he had read before, and by reading, following Tan-kun's recommendation, Edgar Allan Poe's novels—which at the time were still largely unknown but now [in 1927] are treasured by the public—and Bulwer-Lytton's works, I became quite an aficionado of Western novels [Seiyō shōsetsu tsū].[7]

Takata subsequently introduced his appreciation of Western-novel reading to his close friend Tsubouchi Shōyō, who, as Takata notes a bit later, became an "aficionado" as well.[8] In his own memoir, titled "Kaioku mandan" (Reminiscences in idleness), published in 1925–1926, Shōyō provides the following account:

At the time, around the years 1880 and 1881, only surprisingly few students at the University of Tokyo had a critical interest in Western literature [Seiyō no junbungaku]. As far as I know, among those who broadly read Western novels, there were only Hanpō-kun's [Takata Sanae's] now deceased friend Tan Otsuba, Hanpō-kun himself, the now deceased Okakura Kakuzō, and Tanaka Shōhei.[9] . . . During the coldest months of the year, the stove in the janitor's room was the warmest place in the student dorm, and students would regularly congregate there. So it often happened that Takata and Okakura would have animated discussions about novels there. Their discussions about the strengths and weaknesses of Dumas and Bakin, Scott and Lytton, still faintly reverberate in my ears. At the time, I was merely their passive listener.[10]

This passage complements Takata's account and provides a lively glimpse of the reception of Western novels among Shōyō and his friends. In this context of social intercourse and critical discussion, important seeds for Shōyō's literary project were sown.

Waverley Novels, the title that Takata cites, refers to a series of historical novels by Walter Scott, published between 1814 and 1831, that were extremely popular throughout the nineteenth century in Europe. The book titles all belong to Scott's series. The reference to Edgar Allan Poe is exceptional as, to my knowledge, there is no mention of it in Shōsetsu shinzui or other critical discussions in the early 1880s. As Takata notes, Poe's broader reception in Japan belonged to a later moment.[11] However, Scott and Bulwer-Lytton were instrumental in shaping Shōyō's early understanding of the novel and his ideas of literary reform that led up to the writing of Shōsetsu shinzui.

My aim is not to present an argument about the impact of Western literature in general on the reform of traditional Japanese fiction or Shōyō's literary project. There was no such general impact, and we must get away from wide-sweeping assumptions about the influence of Western literature in Meiji Japan. What needs to be emphasized instead is the significance of the appropriation of often very limited bodies of texts and authors in highly specific contexts of reception. The reading of Scott's and Bulwer-Lytton's novels by Shōyō and his cohort at the university around the year 1880 is a case in point. Many of the major names of the eighteenth- and nineteenth-century Western canon, Russian, French, and German, are absent from Shōyō's reading list; and although the names of today more canonical nineteenth-century English novelists like Dickens, Thackeray, and George Eliot are mentioned in *Shōsetsu shinzui* and other critical texts by Shōyō, their significance to him seems marginal. An important reason for the "feverish" but also highly selective interest that Shōyō and his friends showed in Bulwer-Lytton and Scott's novels in the late 1870s and early 1880s was the affinity of these works to Bakin's *yomihon*.

As sophisticated, plot-driven works of historical fiction, replete with learned references and often staging martial protagonists in a universe of moral dichotomies, Scott's novels in particular had strong parallels to Bakin's fiction. As Takata notes, his ability to appreciate and even to follow the plot of *Rob Roy* (1817), despite its linguistic difficulty, was predicated on the fact that his "head had been trained by *Hakkenden* and *Yumiharizuki*." Similarly, Shōyō was a noted lover of Bakin's fiction. As a youth in Nagoya, he had avidly frequented the Daisō lending library, an important local business that covered a broad range of popular fiction, from the early nineteenth century (and partly before) well into Meiji times.[12] Shōyō had acquired extraordinary knowledge of *gesaku* fiction, but he also thought Bakin to be superior over all other Japanese fiction writers.[13] In this assessment, he agreed with many of his contemporaries. As Takata's reading experience and Shōyō's report about students discussing the weaknesses and strengths of Scott, Bulwer-Lytton, Dumas, and Bakin testify, the novels of these authors were comparable, even translatable into one another in the eyes of contemporary elite readers.[14]

However, the Western novels in question also bore the potential to inspire literary reform, by offering a vision of what Shōyō later called the "essence of Western fiction" (*Nishi no shōsetsu no shugan*) that differed from what Japanese authors, including Bakin, had previously produced.[15] This is probably why Shōyō started to translate novels by Scott and Bulwer-Lytton. He produced unfinished translations of two historical novels, Scott's *The Bride of Lammermoor* (1819) and Bulwer-Lytton's *Rienzi* (1835), published in 1880 and 1885, respectively.[16] The significance of these translation experiments comes to light in their prefaces, which make reference to the critical paratexts surrounding *Karyū shunwa* while anticipating some of the core ideas in *Shōsetsu shinzui*. In a nutshell, Shōyō's reform of the novel through translation consisted in rewriting the *yomihon* as novels foregrounding plots of *ninjō* more explicitly than Bakin's works did. At the same time, the translations provided a vision of *ninjō* that was more civilized than in prior *ninjōbon*, thus extending the new literary format of *Karyū shunwa*.

Shunpū jōwa (Spring breeze love tale), Shōyō's translation of chapters 2 to 5 of Scott's *The Bride of Lammermoor*, was published in April 1880 by the publishing house Banseidō. Shōyō probably labored on this project in the winter of 1879–1880, and it is his earliest extant literary text. The translation appeared in the immediate aftermath of *Karyū shunwa* and even imitated its title. Shōyō later reminisced that, because of the earlier work's success, publishers insisted that Western translations include words like "spring," "flowers," or "love tale" in their title to appeal to the public.[17] *Shunpū jōwa*'s affinity to *Karyū shunwa*, however, was not limited to the title. Shōyō's preface strongly echoed Narushima Ryūhoku's famous foreword in its emphasis on the importance of *ninjō* in the novel:

This book was composed by the English writer Sir Walter Scott, and it is about Edgar Ravenswood and the woman Lucy. The tale is based on the principle of cause and effect [*inga ōhō no kotowari*], and it skillfully depicts and presents in a highly moving manner [*aware ni okashiku*] the intricate details of human emotion and the various aspects of social customs in the world. In this way, it is an extremely interesting book. Since it very much resembles the historical novels [*denki shōsetsu*] that our countrymen value, readers will understand that, even in countries separated from us by the eightfold oceans and whose customs are different from ours in myriad ways, the depth of emotion [*mono no aware*] is the same, and the novels that depict it have naturally a similar character.[18]

This preface is written in a dense *wabun* style, and the use of terms like *mono no aware* recalls Norinaga's discussion of *The Tale of Genji*, contrasting with Ryūhoku's Sinified diction. But Shōyō's point about his translation's role in demonstrating the identity of emotions in the West and the East is the same as in Ryūhoku's foreword—as is the emphasis on *ninjō* as the primary focus of the novel. Shōyō's interest in *ninjō* therefore dated from the early moment of his work on *Shunpū jōwa* and was embedded in the literary space established by *Karyū shunwa*. Unlike Ryūhoku, however, Shōyō also points to the affinity of his translation with the "historical novels that our countrymen value," an unmistakable reference to Bakin's *yomihon*.[19] That the historical novel's complicated plot should illustrate the "principle of cause and effect" was also a core idea in Bakin's literary thought. More explicitly than *Karyū shunwa*'s paratexts, Shōyō's preface thus links the format of Bakin's *yomihon* to a new emphasis on *ninjō*.

Scott's *The Bride of Lammermoor* revolves around the tragic love of Edgar Ravenswood, the heir to a fallen Scottish aristocratic house, for Lucy, the daughter of the man responsible for the downfall of his family. Shōyō's translation, like Scott's novel, starts off with the moral dichotomies typical of *yomihon* fiction. Especially the beginning sections translated by Shōyō oppose Edogaru ("Edgar"), with his venerable warrior (*bushi* or *gōzoku*) pedigree, to the wealthy social climber Uiriyamu Ashuton ("William Ashton"). Ashuton is the father of Rushī ("Lucy") and the man who bought up the estates of Edogaru's father, bringing shame and financial ruin to him. The latter dies with deep resentment (*urami*), or "hatred" in the English novel. Edogaru is a martial and chivalrous hero, consistently referred to as *masurao* (brave man), and a filial son (*kōshi*) who swears to exact revenge on his father's enemy. Ashuton, on the contrary, is a small-minded person (*shōjin*), concerned merely with the increase of his status and wealth but cowardly and lacking Edogaru's martial skills. While this narrative setting can be read as an allegory of the triumph of bourgeois capitalism over the doomed warrior class and its ethical values (a theme that certainly resonated with Japanese readers of former samurai status), the text also recalls the moral universe of *yomihon* fiction. Bakin's dog-warrior heroes are all filial sons, and some of them prove it by exacting revenge on their fathers' foes, often "small-minded" and corrupt. However, Edogaru's revenge fails. He even saves his enemy's life because of his "passion"—a key word in the English novel—for Rushī, his enemy's daughter.[20] The translation stops after Edogaru's rescue of Ashuton and the lovers' subsequent encounter, and it does not depict the tragic ending of their story. In the English novel, the lovers are consumed by their passion as they are unable to consummate their love through marriage because of the resistance of Lucy's mother. The narrative ends with Lucy's madness and the death of both protagonists.

Like *Karyū shunwa*, Shōyō's translation introduces passion as an ambivalent emotion.[21] It is "foolish," to use Iwamoto Yoshiharu's epithet that linked the new notion to the eroticism of an uncivilized age.[22] Although the relationship of Edogaru and Rushī remains chaste, it is destructive and radically opposes social norms. But passion also again, in enlightenment fashion, validates the lovers' freedom. Moreover, like *Karyū shunwa*'s protagonist, Edogaru is susceptible to morality and reason, able to struggle against his passion. Owing to various factors, his social integration, as in a bildungsroman, fails, tragically escalating his passion's destructiveness. But he is still depicted as an exemplary hero. This male exemplarity, while speaking to Meiji enlightenment concerns, also provided the link to Bakin's *yomihon* that Shōyō's translation highlighted more explicitly than *Karyū shunwa*. *Shunpū jōwa* showcases Edogaru's identity as a historical, martial hero not only by its *yomihon* style, closely echoing Bakin's, but also by the illustrations that show the Scottish protagonist as a Japanese samurai, indeed emphasizing an affinity to those "historical novels that our countrymen value."

Shōyō's other important translation in the early 1880s, also unfinished, was of Bulwer-Lytton's historical novel *Rienzi*, published under the title *Kaikan hifun: Gaisei shiden* (A tale of indignation: Chronicle of a patriot's life) in February 1885. Shōyō labored on this translation while writing *Shōsetsu shinzui*, whose serialization started about half a year later. *Rienzi* is about the eponymous medieval popular hero Cola di Rienzi (ca. 1313–1354), who became tribune of the Roman people and organized their uprising against the city's corrupt aristocratic elite. The novel thus responded to the political sensibilities of the People's Rights Movement, which reached an important peak at the time Shōyō was working on the translation (1883–1884). At the same time, it was the novel's representation of *ninjō* that was particularly relevant for the reform of fiction in his eyes. In the preface to his translation, he writes,

Passages like the one in chapter 7 that focus on the encounter between the hero and the heroine [*masurao to memasurao*] illustrate most clearly the difference between the novelists' intent in the West and the East. It may seem strange to see

FIGURE 4.1 Edgar Ravenswood depicted as a Japanese samurai. Frontispiece of *Shunpū jōwa*; illustration by Teisai Nensan. Reproduction from the National Diet Library Digital Collections, Tokyo

a dauntless hero [gōmai naru shunketsu] embrace a womanish heart [memeshige naru kokoro], but this is precisely the nature of human emotion [hito no jō], and it will produce unspeakable charm to those who pay attention. If readers bear this in mind, they will, despite my translation's clumsiness, realize the essence of the true novel [shin no shōsetsu haishi no shushi].[23]

Shōyō here argues again from the generic perspective of Bakin's yomihon, where "dauntless heroes" were not primarily depicted as protagonists of love plots. In Gaisei shiden, however, as in Shunpū jōwa, a "dauntless" man is receptive to "womanish" love in a way that greatly exceeds the potential for ninjō—as male-female romance—in Bakin's protagonists.

Chapter 7 of Shōyō's translation, the one referred to in the preface, illustrates the relationship between Rienjī ("Rienzi") and his female lover, Naina ("Nina").[24] Unlike the destructive passion depicted in Shunpū jōwa, Naina's love supports and strengthens Rienjī's political ambitions. In Bulwer-Lytton's original, Nina sees it as her role to "share [her lover's] schemes—to cheer [him] in doubt—to whisper hope to [him] in danger." This makes Rienzi exclaim, "Perhaps, in those long and solitary hours of coolness and exhaustion . . . perhaps I should have failed and flagged, and renounced even my dreams of Rome, had they not been linked also with my dreams for thee!. . . Sacred, strong, enduring must be, indeed, the love which lives in the same pure and elevated air as that which sustains my dreams of patriotism, of liberty, of fame!"[25] Nina's love helps Rienzi realize his "dreams of patriotism." In turn, he awakens her to his "elevated and generous ambition."[26] Shōyō translates Rienzi's last sentence quoted here in slightly altered fashion: "Since your sincerity values liberty, fame, and hope for the future, our love [renjō] is not ordinary love [koi], but it will always be pure and elevated [kōshō]!"[27]

Elsewhere, Shōyō defines the relationship between the two lovers as "high-class love" (kami no koi), grounded in mutual support and respect for a partner's "elevated spirit," thus indicating the highest degree of civilization.[28] This definition closely echoed Iwamoto's notion of the civilized age of love, where a married woman supports her husband's public endeavors by her service in the family. Although Naina and Rienjī are not married, Shōyō presents their relationship as high-class and civilized, benefiting the nation. The love in Gaisei shiden thus markedly differs from the destructive passion in Shunpū jōwa. Taken together, however, both foolish passion and civilized love were important elements of the new bildungsroman format introduced by *Karyū shunwa*.

In his preface, Shōyō also refers to *Rienzi* as a "true novel," whose qualities his translation sought to convey as "material for instruction" to the as yet unenlightened Japanese novelists. He places his translation *Gaisei shiden* alongside two recent publications, the novels *Karyū shunwa* and *Seitō yodan: Shun'ōten* (A political digression: Orioles warbling in spring, 1884). The latter was the translation, by Seki Naohiko (1856–1934), of Benjamin Disraeli's (1804–1881) political novel *Coningsby* (1844). Shōyō admiringly notes that both translations "very much exhibit the characteristics of the [true] novel" with the potential to reform contemporary Japanese fiction.[29] He opposes them to all recent Japanese novels, which he calls the "dregs of Bakin" or "copies of Tanehiko and Shunsui"—inferior imitations of those early nineteenth-century classical *gesaku* authors.[30] The preface to Shōyō's more famous *Shōsetsu shinzui* contains a similar diatribe against the contemporary literary field, but it elides the reference to contemporary Western translations, including *Gaisei shiden*, as models for the novel's reform. This was probably the result of Shōyō's emphasis, in *Shōsetsu shinzui*, on the reform of original fiction—not translation—and his ideological rhetoric of "surpassing the European novel." The lack of reference to those early translations in *Shōsetsu shinzui*, however, has largely precluded a critical awareness of their importance in shaping Shōyō's understanding of the novel's reform. Translations like *Shunpū jōwa*, *Gaisei shiden*, and *Karyū shunwa* presented a reformed vision of *gesaku* genres. They exposed the exemplary masculinity of Bakin's *yomihon* protagonists—"dauntless heroes"—to *ninjō* in a way that was more enlightened than the passion or lust that Meiji critics saw in *ninjōbon*. It was to a great extent this reform, mediated by translation, of elements of traditional genres under a civilizational agenda that Shōyō defined as true novel.

HISTORICIZING REALISM: PASSION AND DIDACTICISM IN *SHŌSETSU SHINZUI*

Shōsetsu shinzui is highly canonized today and sometimes invoked as instrumental in bringing about an epistemological shift that led to the demise of *gesaku* fiction.[31] Although, in this section, I demonstrate the significance of the continuity in Shōyō's critical engagement with the earlier literary field, *Shōsetsu shinzui* indeed introduced a critical idiom that challenged previous discussions of the novel in Japan. One of the new notions that Shōyō presented was his definition of the novel as "art" (*bijutsu*) seemingly divorced from didactic or utilitarian value. He relied on the new Western concept of "art" as introduced by Ernest Fenollosa (1853–1908) in his lecture "Bijutsu shinsetsu" (An explanation of the truth of art, 1882) and by Ōuchi Seiran (1845–1918) in the editorial to the first issue of *Dai Nippon bijutsu shinpō* (Great Japanese art journal), published in 1883. Shōyō quotes from both sources in *Shōsetsu shinzui*. The American Fenollosa had been Shōyō's teacher at the university, and the Japanese transcript of his 1882 lecture, originally given in English, soon became highly influential in various contemporary contexts.[32] In the quote that Shōyō provides, Fenollosa defines the aim of art—in the sense of fine arts, including painting and sculpture—as "giving pleasure to the heart and elevating [people's] deportment" (*kikaku o kōshō ni su*). Ōuchi Seiran, as quoted by Shōyō, provides the same definition and also summarizes the aim of art as its ability to "nurture civilization" (*jinbun hatsuiku*).[33] Shōyō, then, in a seemingly radical and provocative gesture, rejects these still too utilitarian definitions and claims that these purported aims are mere "incidental effects" but not art's "original aim," which is to "transport to an enraptured realm [*yūshu kakyō*] where the soul can fly and the spirit wander."[34] He thus presents art as an inherently aesthetic medium, whose goal is to "please the human heart."[35]

For the first time, moreover, he classifies the novel as art, alongside other genres like music and painting. Accordingly, he defines the true novel as the "artistic novel" (*āchisuchikku noberu*), which he differentiates from the "didactic novel" (*jidakuchikku noberu*) or *kanchō shōsetsu*—a type of novel that, like Bakin's *yomihon*, pursues primarily didactic goals.[36] The primary goal of the artistic novel is realist depiction (*mosha*). The artistic novel is therefore synonymous with what Shōyō calls the realist novel (*mosha shōsetsu*), or simply "novel" (*noberu*), concerned with the depiction of human emotions and social customs. It is in this sense that Shōyō famously states, "The novel's main focus is on human emotion. Social customs come next in importance." The artistic novel's goal is to realistically depict emotions and customs as they are. Shōyō also argues that the novelist should be a bystander (*bōkansha*) or psychologist (*shinrigakusha*), making visible the emotions that are hidden in individual figures but nonetheless "true" or "real" (*shin*).[37]

Shōyō's critical vocabulary in *Shōsetsu shinzui*, especially the key notion of *mosha*, was new and derived from the English-language sources he had consulted. One of these was Robert Chambers's (1802–1871) article "Rhetoric and Belles Lettres," which was part of the encyclopedia *Chambers's Information for the People* (edition of 1867) and had been translated into Japanese by Kikuchi Dairoku (1855–1917) in 1879.[38] In *Shōsetsu shinzui*, Shōyō cites two longer excerpts from Kikuchi's translation. One of the passages contains the following sentence, here directly quoted from the original English: "The greatest and most important peculiarity in the recent course of such productions [novels], is the endeavour to make what is exciting in plot and character coincide more and more with what is *real* in life. . . . All such works [novels] deal in representations of the transactions or doings of men and women, and put the air of *reality* upon these as much as possible."[39] Kikuchi, as quoted by Shōyō, translates Chambers's expressions "real in life" and "reality" as *jinsei no jitsuji* (truth in life) and *shin* (truth), respectively— terms (especially *shin*) that Shōyō uses in *Shōsetsu shinzui*. Shōyō therefore had an at least rudimentary understanding of realism, as the novel's depiction or imitation of truth or reality. Elsewhere, he also used the English word "realist" (in the meaning of "realist novelist"), glossed in Japanese as *shujitsu haishika* (novelist focusing on truth).[40]

Shōyō's emphasis on the realist depiction of truth or reality has led critics until recently to see in *Shōsetsu shinzui* the first important theory of modern realism in Japan. Literary scholar Yamada Shunji, for example, views in Shōyō's discourse a new orientation toward the visual representation of "things as such," liberated from the rhetorical, stylistic, and representational conventions of traditional genres.[41] Maeda Ai also stresses the visuality of *Shōsetsu shinzui*'s realism and its contemporaneity to new technologies like photography.[42] As noted, critical discussions since the early twentieth century saw in Shōyō's discourse the manifesto for a mimetic and psychological realism characteristic of the nineteenth-century Western novel and a new Westernized literary modernity. Shōyō's treatise became discursively produced as the origin of modern literature (*kindai bungaku*) in Japan—a notion that emerged concurrently with Shōyō's canonization as its founding theorist.[43]

My goal is not to question *Shōsetsu shinzui*'s canonical status in modern Japanese literary history but to sever Shōyō's notion of the realist depiction of emotions and customs from its later appropriations in discourses of literary modernity and resituate it in the initial context of his literary reform. As mentioned, Shōyō possessed an at least rudimentary understanding of the novel's imitation of reality or truth. But his notion of *mosha* had important connotations that were not reducible to a theory of mimetic realism. To understand these, it is necessary to reconsider how Shōyō critically engaged with the earlier narrative genres that he sought to reform, especially Bakin's *yomihon* and the *ninjōbon*.

Shōyō's scathing critique of Bakin's *Hakkenden* in *Shōsetsu shinzui* is well known. He claims that Bakin's protagonists, the eight dog warriors, are not depictions of true human beings but morally ideal figures, "specters of the eight Confucian virtues," meant solely to support the didactic goal of *kanzen chōaku*:

If seen from the standpoint of promoting virtue and chastising vice, *Hakkenden* is unsurpassed in both the East and the West, but when judging it from the [novel's] main focus on human emotion, the work cannot be called peerless. Why is this? Look at the behavior of those eight protagonists! Or even leaving their behavior aside, all they think entirely matches the Confucian Way, and never does vulgar passion arise in them. . . . They are Kyokutei Bakin's ideal figures [*risōjō no jinbutsu*] and not true depictions [*shashin*] of human beings in this world.[44]

Shōyō here criticizes *Hakkenden* from his understanding of the novel's realist depiction of *ninjō* "as it is." *Hakkenden*'s figures are "ideal" creations, and therefore their representation is not truthful. His signifier for the truth of *ninjō* is "vulgar passion."

The major genre in Japan that had realistically depicted vulgar passion was the *ninjōbon*. Shōyō indeed repeatedly lauds Shunsui's works for their ability to depict "human emotion as it is" (*ari no mama no ninjō*), and he states that the undifferentiated rejection of *ninjōbon* by contemporary critics is "untenable nonsense."[45] His overall view of the genre, however, remained much in line with the prior discourse on *ninjōbon* and licentious books:

When critics in China condemned the novel for teaching licentiousness and inciting to desire [*kaiin dōyoku*], they must have meant novels like the *Jinpingmei* and *Rouputuan*; or when people in our country rejected tales [*monogatari*] as books disturbing our customs, they probably referred to those love stories [*jōshi*] depicting the intricacies of the foolish passion [*chijō*] between men and women and indulging in licentiousness and depravity. Books like the *Jinpingmei* and *Rouputuan* and these obscene love stories are pseudonovels. They are not true novels.[46]

Although realistically depicting "foolish" or "vulgar" passion—sexual love and desire—*ninjōbon* and their Chinese antecedents, in Shōyō's eyes, remain essentially immoral and uncivilized, far distant from what he envisions as the true novel.

The contradiction in this argument is worth noting.[47] On the one hand, Shōyō criticizes Bakin's *yomihon* for their moralistic idealism and their inability to realistically depict *ninjō* as it is, especially vulgar passion. On the other hand, his civilized true novel, unlike Shunsui's *ninjōbon*, cannot focus on vulgar passion alone, even if this focus is realist. What does Shōyō understand, then, by the realist depiction of *ninjō* in the true novel? In one passage, he states that the novel must focus on spiritual love (*airen*) and psychology (*shinri*) instead of the "unspeakable details" brought to the fore by the "authors of the Tamenaga school."[48] However, although such a focus would conform to Shōyō's civilizational ambitions for the reformed novel, it would exclude vulgar passion, which he previously defined as the signifier for the truth of *ninjō*. Shōyō's core argument about the novel's realist depiction of *ninjō* is in fact more complex:

Since human beings are animals of desire [*jōyoku no dōbutsu*], it rarely happens that even wise men or virtuous people are exempt from desire. Because wise men and fools, without distinction, are subject to desire, what then distinguishes a wise man [*kenja*] from a small-minded person [*shōjin*] and what makes a good man [*zennin*] different from an evil person [*akunin*] is their ability to suppress their desire by the strength of their reason [*dōri*, also "morality"] or the force of their conscience and to thus chase away the dogs of their desire [*jōyoku no inu*].[49]

This passage encapsulates Shōyō's understanding of the depiction of *ninjō* in the reformed novel. Its protagonists are foolish "animals of desire" but also able to control their desire by the civilizing force of their reason and conscience. This model replicates the narrative structure of contemporary translations like *Karyū shunwa* that allowed for the representation of titillating passion but also subjected it to the control of virtue and reason.

In this model of realism, despite his previous criticism of *ninjōbon* and *yomihon*, Shōyō, significantly, lets important elements of both genres in through the back door. One is the *ninjōbon*'s focus on vulgar passion. While defining *ninjō* as the novel's main focus, the various synonyms that he provides for the term are mostly negative: "vulgar," "foolish," or even "animalistic passion" (*jūjō*) and the "one hundred eight lusts" (*hyaku hachi bonnō*)—terms that contemporary discourse associated with the *ninjōbon*'s licentiousness as the epitome of an uncivilized age.[50] Shōyō thus viewed even the civilized protagonists of the reformed novel as subject to licentious passions.[51]

At the same time, Shōyō's model reintegrates Bakin's dichotomy of "good" and "evil." Only a protagonist able to control his vulgar passion or animal nature, Shōyō argues, is a "good person." Moral and civilizational ideology essentially intersect when he superimposes Bakin's ethical categories onto the enlightenment idea of the ability (or inability) to control licentious passion through reason. Thus, while integrating a focus on vulgar passion that brought back an affinity to the *ninjōbon*, Shōyō's notion of *mosha* also includes an idealist element reminiscent of Bakin: the "good" protagonist's inner struggle with and, ideally, control of passion. This dimension made Shōyō's realism inherently didactic.

Indeed, Shōyō identifies two didactic "indirect benefits" that derive from the novel's realism and that are of particular importance.[52] One is the novel's ability to "elevate [people's] deportment" (*kikaku o kōshō ni nasu*)—that is, to bring readers to an elevated level of civilization by showing them civilized behavior and thus diverting them from their own foolish passions. The novel here assumes a function similar to reason, but unlike reason, Shōyō argues, it is able to influence readers in a gentle and entertaining way that is more efficient, especially if they are still immature.[53] The other indirect didactic benefit is the novel's ability to "encourage and admonish" (*kanshō chōkai*), a rephrasing of *kanzen chōaku*, by bringing readers to self-reflection (*hansei*). This idea was related to Shōyō's notion of the novel as a "criticism of life" (*jinsei no hihan*) that derived from an essay by the Victorian literary critic John Morley (1838–1923). What Shōyō means becomes clear from his rather free summary of the essay:

John Morley has said that one of the greatest pleasures in life is the criticism of the world of men. The novel is therefore a critique [*hyōbanki*] of life; it offers to the critical view of the reader the reasons A failed and B was successful, or how someone gained power and lost his morality [*dōgishin*], or how someone was led astray by passion [*jō*] and his reason was destroyed. If sharp-eyed people read about this, they will be moved more deeply than if they were reading the Confucian classics [*keisho*] or books of official history [*seishi*].⁵⁴

Shōyō argues that the artistic novel's realism—focusing, for example, on the conflict between reason and passion—has the power to bring readers to moral self-reflection. In other words, by witnessing the protagonist's inner struggles and their outcomes, readers can be brought to a reflection about their own lives. This is why the artistic novel presents a didactic criticism of life.

Shōyō's important claim is that the "realist novel [*mosha shui no shōsetsu*], without intending to do so, contains the principle of admonishment and encouragement and implicitly has the power to educate [*kyōka suru*] the reader."⁵⁵ In a civilized age, the realist novel is even more efficient didactically than the didactic novel itself (that is, works like *Hakkenden*), not to speak of the Confucian classics.⁵⁶ Key for Shōyō is the expression "without intending to do so" (*motomezu shite*). The realist novel does not intend to be didactic, although it necessarily will end up that way. Elsewhere, he also argues that Western novels, while putting their first emphasis on the realist depiction of *ninjō*, have as their second emphasis *kanzen chōaku*.⁵⁷ The artistic novel thus does not stage idealized protagonists like Bakin's eight dog warriors but will nonetheless continue to morally instruct and civilize by virtue of its realist depiction of emotions and customs. This reversal of priority between *kanzen chōaku* and *ninjō* was an important, yet only gradual, departure from Bakin.⁵⁸

Shōyō's theory of *mosha* opens up a new and potentially mimetic literary mode emphasizing the representation of the "real" and "true." Yet a historicization of Shōyō's realism must also take into account its reintegration of contradictory *ninjōbon* and *yomihon* elements. That the realist depiction of *ninjō* could focus on vulgar passion brought to the fore an affinity to the *ninjōbon*. Yet despite the fact that Shōyō stressed the "vulgar" quality of *ninjō* as passion, he did not explore its destabilizing implications in *Shōsetsu shinzui*. As I show in the next chapter, his fictional works written in the wake of *Shōsetsu shinzui* indeed explored the problematic power of erotic passion at the heart of the novel, not only for its protagonists but also for its readers, who could be led to dangerous passion instead of self-reflection by reading fiction. This brought back an anxiety about the novel's licentiousness that jeopardized Shōyō's fictional project.

The primary emphasis in *Shōsetsu shinzui*, then, was clearly on the didactic potential of *mosha*—the focus on the protagonists' struggle with passion. Highlighting the novel's moral, social, and civilizational value, this didacticism was an updated version of Bakin's *kanzen chōaku*. Shōyō labeled the novel's didactic "benefits" as merely "indirect" and not as its main artistic purpose, but they were in fact the fundamental precondition for the novel to qualify as art and deploy its "direct benefit" of providing aesthetic pleasure. This is particularly obvious when, in discussing the novel's indirect benefits, he makes reference to a friend (probably Takata Sanae), who, although having the highest moral standards and being well versed in Japanese, Chinese, and Western learning, still felt ashamed of his own moral inadequacy upon reading about the exemplary behavior of *Hakkenden*'s dog warriors.[59] Bakin's novel, in other words, induced this educated friend to self-reflection. Similarly, the reformed true novel, while able to elevate the minds of the less educated, will provide material for self-reflection to cultured "men of worth" (*taijin*) and "learned men" (*gakusha*), whom Shōyō sees as the most appropriate readers.[60] They will read the novel as art, whose realist depiction of emotions and customs will transport them to an aesthetic "enraptured realm." However, this realm is aesthetically appealing to them only *because* it is civilized and moral. The artistic novel certainly provides material for self-reflection in a more indirect way than the—in Shōyō's eyes—purely didactic novel *Hakkenden*, but it can also be artistic only as long as it is didactic. Not surprisingly, the "learned" readers of *Hakkenden*, like Shōyō and Takata, were the implied readers of the artistic novel as well.[61]

THE CIVILIZATIONAL POLITICS OF *NINJŌ*

Shōyō's theory of the novel was implicated in the social and political environment of its time. The mid-1880s witnessed a profound sociopolitical transformation related to the breakdown of the radical wing of the People's Rights Movement because of government pressure and the ensuing reorientation of political energy toward nation-state building through cultural, social, and civilizational reform. Shōyō's literary project must be reconsidered for its awareness of and affinity to contemporary political discourse and fiction, the dominant mode of the Japanese novel in that decade.

The People's Rights Movement had emerged in the mid-1870s as a nationwide protest movement, especially among members of the disenfranchised former samurai class as well as among rural and urban elites, who embraced Western enlightenment ideas of freedom and democratic political participation to voice their opposition to the oligarchic and authoritarian Meiji government. The movement had gained considerable momentum in the late 1870s and early 1880s, and one important success was the government's consent in 1881, proclaimed through an imperial edict, to grant a constitution and open a National Diet in the year 1890. This prompted the foundation of political parties, especially the Liberal Party and the Constitutional Reform Party, which both epitomized, in different ways, the fate of the political movement throughout the 1880s.

The Liberal Party is associated with the political radicalization of the People's Rights Movement in the first half of the decade, when members of the party became involved in so-called violent incidents (*gekika jiken*), including the Fukushima Incident (1882), the Kabasan Incident (1884), and the Chichibu Incident (1884).[62] Although not necessarily connected to one another, these incidents were all expressions of violent resistance against the Meiji government, with the goal to implement instantaneous democratic reforms in a revolutionary manner. The intellectual atmosphere in the early 1880s was extremely politicized and heated, and this was the moment when most educated male youth, including eminent future intellectuals and writers, envisioned activism and a future political career.[63] The violence associated with the Liberal Party, however, met severe government repression, and by the middle of the decade the radical wing of the People's Rights Movement had been almost entirely suppressed.

The political movement of the early 1880s provided the context for an important revalidation of literature as a didactic medium able to promote political ideas. Activists used poetry and songs to mobilize support, and the theater and especially the novel were seen as didactically efficient genres.[64] For example, in a newspaper editorial titled "One Means to Propagate the Seeds of Freedom in Our Country Is to Reform the Novel and Theater," an anonymous author called the novel a "splendid teacher of knowledge for women, children, and the lower social classes."[65] After the 1870s enlightenment critique of the novel as useless and licentious, the early

1880s political movement restated the social-use value of fiction and facilitated the emergence of the political novel as a new genre, referring back to the traditional idea of literature and fiction as a didactic medium. Important works of political fiction produced in this context include translations by Liberal Party intellectuals—authors like Sakurada Momoe (1859–1883) and Miyazaki Muryū (1855–1889)—of French novels by Alexandre Dumas (1802–1870) that thematized the French Revolution and encouraged violent resistance against an oppressive government.[66] Socialism and Russian anarchism were also major references in early 1880s radical political fiction.[67]

As Atsuko Ueda has shown in her readings of Sakurada's and Miyazaki's French translations, these works were closely connected to the Fukushima uprising in 1882 and might even have influenced its leaders' revolutionary antigovernment stance.[68] She also demonstrates that these texts relied on an ideological and rhetorical framework of good versus evil—that is, good revolutionary resistance against evil government oppression—that was indebted to Bakin's moral-didactic principle of *kanzen chōaku*. Indeed, the early 1880s witnessed a strong revival of Bakin's *yomihon* and *Hakkenden* in particular among People's Rights activists, who could identify with the dog warriors' virtuous fight against corrupt government officials.[69] As Ueda persuasively argues, *Shōsetsu shinzui* rejected this type of political fiction associated with the revolutionary activism of the Liberal Party. To Shōyō, these works neglected the realist depiction of emotions and customs and, like Bakin's *yomihon*, put their main emphasis on *kanzen chōaku*— the didactic support of a political ideology through protagonists who, like the eight dog warriors, embodied political and moral ideals. Shōyō still admired *Hakkenden* as the unsurpassed masterwork of didactic fiction, but the Liberal Party–inflected political novels were certainly no better, in his eyes, than what he derogatively called the dregs of Bakin.

I agree with Ueda's analysis of Shōyō's rejection of radical political fiction, whose disappearance by the middle of the 1880s owing to government repression coincided with the publication of *Shōsetsu shinzui*. However, I disagree with her argument that Shōyō's new emphasis on the depiction (*mosha*) of emotions and customs instead of *kanzen chōaku* was implicated in an epistemological shift that led to an effacement (or "concealment") of politics in Japan. This shift, she contends, also concealed Bakin's moralistic "style of language" inherent in radical fiction and instead produced modern "literature" as a morally and politically "neutral" domain.[70] As

I previously demonstrated, Shōyō's discourse does not conceal Bakin's moral-didactic categories of "good" and "evil" but instead reintegrates them into the model of the realist depiction of emotions and customs to assert the novel's didactic civilizational—and implicitly moral—role in teaching readers good civilized customs and bringing them to self-reflection. Shōyō's reform of fiction, moreover, had a strong affinity to the political discourse and fiction associated with the other important political party in 1880s Japan, the Reform Party.

Unlike the political radicalism of some members of the Liberal Party, the Reform Party, especially in the aftermath of the unsuccessful violent incidents in the middle of the decade, emphasized gradual and nonviolent political, social, cultural, and civilizational reforms. A major goal was to make democratic popular participation, based on civilized customs and behavior, in the soon-to-open National Diet possible and effective. Whereas the opposition associated with the Liberal Party tended to be revolutionary and bottom-up, the Reform Party stance was elitist and top-down, emphasizing the need to mobilize the relatively wealthy and educated middle-class segments of society for civilized political participation— precisely the social group that Shōyō envisions as the most appropriate readership for the artistic novel.[71] Although not a member himself, Shōyō was closely affiliated with the Reform Party through his friends at the University of Tokyo—Takata Sanae and Ichijima Kenkichi (1860–1944), among others—who were involved in founding the party in 1882, immediately after their graduation. This group belonged to the social elite with strong ambitions for political participation.

The reform of fiction was an important component in the broader Reform Party call for social and civilizational reform. The 1885 writings of the former Liberal Party politician and novelist Sakazaki Shiran (1853–1913), for instance, reflect interest in the reform of social customs (including gender relations, writing, hairstyles, etc.), which he saw as intrinsically connected to political reform. Shiran is a good example of the general tendency of the oppositional movement in the mid-1880s, including former Liberal Party affiliates, to adopt a reformist and gradualist Reform Party stance in the wake of the government repression of violent activism.[72] Shiran also published an essay in the political newspaper *Jiyū no tomoshibi* (Torch of freedom) in which he envisioned a new type of novel as a reformed *ninjōbon*. This novel should have a socially more useful male protagonist than

Shunsui's Tanjirō—one who could be a bureaucrat, medical doctor, student, public speaker, or newspaper journalist.[73] The similarity between Shiran's essay and *Shōsetsu shinzui*—the emphasis on civilized *ninjō* in the new novel, seen as a reformed type of *ninjōbon*—is obvious. Shōyō in fact separately published *Shōsetsu shinzui*'s core chapter, "Shōsetsu no shugan" (The main focus of the novel), in *Jiyū no tomoshibi* in August 1885. This demonstrates the extent to which *Shōsetsu shinzui* must be contextualized in a political discourse and media network where politics was understood as intertwined with social reform and civilizational progress.

Civilized gender relations and emotions were indeed a core component in the Reform Party political novel, whose foundational text—although published before the foundation of the party and not explicitly connected to its ideology—was *Karyū shunwa*. In this translation, as noted, a civilized male-female love served as the guarantor for the hero's political career. *Karyū shunwa* had a great impact on a type of political fiction in Japan that differed from the revolutionary works associated with the Liberal Party. Important examples include *Seiro nikki* and the famous novel *Kajin no kigū* (Encounter with beautiful women, 1885–1897), where the political intrigue and discourse are embedded in the civilized, platonic relationship between the male Japanese protagonist and two highly educated Western women.[74] *Karyū shunwa* also strongly influenced the emergence of the parliamentarian novel in Japan, which reflected the political stance of the Reform Party. The first important work in this vein, also written before the party's foundation, was titled *Minken engi: Jōkai haran* (A tale of people's rights: Stormy waves in a sea of passion, 1880) and published shortly before the imperial edict granting a National Diet.[75] This short allegorical novel predicates the male protagonist's participation in the future Diet on his ability to leave behind uncivilized sexual promiscuity in the pleasure quarter. Instead, he must enter a civilized monogamous relationship with a woman who allegorically embodies his people's rights (*minken*). His chaste marriage with her prefigures his future political engagement in the Diet. The novel's allegory thus interlocks the civilizing reform of emotions, sexuality, and social customs with the prospect of political reform and democratic participation in the future Diet.

The most important parliamentarian novel promoting Reform Party ideology was written after the publication of *Shōsetsu shinzui* and was probably influenced by it. At least partly, it also met with Shōyō's enthusiastic approval. Published in 1886, it was titled *Seiji shōsetsu: Setchūbai* (A political novel: Plum blossoms in the snow) and written by the well-known journalist and politician Suehiro Tetchō (1849–1896). Tetchō explicitly lays out his Reform Party ideas through the mouth of his male hero, Kunino Motoi (literally, "Foundation of the Nation"), who is a poor young intellectual and political activist.[76] In Kunino's (and Tetchō's) view, the violence associated with Liberal Party radicalism must be renounced and all democratic groups, especially the intellectual and wealthy segments of society, united. Kunino rejects the political participation of the uneducated masses through universal suffrage. Instead, only the educated, wealthy, and entrepreneurial— that is, the intellectual and business-owning—elements of society should stand united for and in the future Diet, thus ensuring the long-term prosperity of Japan as a nation. At the core of the novel is a male-female romance, which allegorically mirrors Tetchō's elitist political ideology, revolving around the marriage between the student Kunino Motoi, the intellectual "foundation of the nation," and Tominaga Oharu (literally, "Spring of Eternal Wealth"), the daughter of a rich landowner. The particularly civilized dimension of this union is exemplified by the fact that Kunino and Oharu are engaged rather than married at the end of the novel and therefore must defer consummation of their desire. One of the novel's last sentences reads, "The excitement in their hearts [anticipating marriage] was not less than our people's in the years 1885 and 1886 awaiting the year [of the Diet opening in] 1890."[77] As Christopher Hill has noted, "the element of self-restraint extends from Kunino and Haru to the nation as a whole."[78] Through this allegory, civilized gendered customs and emotions were again interlocked with the promise of social reform, political participation, and national revitalization.

Shōyō's reaction to Tetchō's novel was enthusiastic. In a two-part review of *Setchūbai* that appeared in the fall of 1886, he notes,

After finishing reading *Setchūbai* I could not help but exclaim, "Has our nation now finally produced its Disraeli?" The interest of its plot and the vividness and clarity of its style are unseen in any of the other recent novels. Nobody besides master Tetchō, who is full of patriotic thought and political feelings, could have ever reached such a height. This master, who already has a name as a writer and politician, does not need to feel shame. Harunoya Oboro [Shōyō], however, who aspires to be a novelist, cannot but feel shame in many respects upon reading this novel. Its greatness in truth and its depth in interest make it a truly captivating book![79]

Shōyō's points of critique about *Setchūbai* lay primarily in the novel's "allegory" (*gūi*), the fact that the protagonists embody abstract principles in a way reminiscent of Bakin. Shōyō also criticizes the improbable and unrealistic elements in *Setchūbai*'s plot and laments that the figures' emotions are not sufficiently well developed. However, he seems to approve of the novel's political message and its romance plot, as they show a great affinity to Benjamin Disraeli's political fiction, which he obviously admires and which probably served as the model for *Setchūbai*. Disraeli's novel *Coningsby* had been translated into Japanese under the title *Shun'ōten* in 1884. As noted, Shōyō approvingly singled out *Shun'ōten* alongside *Karyū shunwa* as recent noteworthy translations and models for the true novel in the preface to his *Rienzi* translation. Like Tetchō's *Setchūbai*, *Coningsby* promoted political and social reform instead of revolutionary violence, and its romance

FIGURE 4.2 Harry Coningsby's wedding. From volume 4 of Seki Naohiko's translation *Shun'ōten*; illustrator unspecified. Reproduction from the National Diet Library Digital Collections, Tokyo

plot allegorized the union between the old English aristocratic and new industrialist classes, but at the exclusion of the uneducated masses.[80] This type of novel appealed to the political and literary sensibilities of the Reform Party, and a mere look at the illustrations of the Japanese translation indicates the extent to which it promoted romance as high-class and civilized.

In another essay published in August 1885 in *Jiyū no tomoshibi*, Shōyō lauds Disraeli's political novels for not bringing the viewpoints of the author's party to the forefront but instead "depicting primarily the emotions [*jōtai*] in the political world."[81] Shōyō here reiterates his point that Western novels put their didactic and allegorical intent (*gūi*) second while making the depiction of emotions and customs their "main focus." Interestingly, he cites Harriet Beecher Stowe's (1811–1896) *Uncle Tom's Cabin* (1852) as an exemplary novel that, while promoting a political message, depicts the emotions of both slaves and slaveholders in impartially realist fashion. Japanese political novels, however, are only concerned, like Bakin's *yomihon*, with the promotion of their allegory (*aregorī*) in the *kanzen chōaku* mode and cannot be called true novels. Shōyō took the novel's political mission very seriously, though:

[That Japanese political novels are mere allegories and not true novels] has, I believe, to do with the severity of the government's censorship ordinances, which make the depiction of true emotions very difficult. If, in the future, it becomes possible to make use of all kinds of things in utilitarian fashion [*riyōshugi nite*], I intend to make use of art to promote reforms for our nation [*kokka no kairyō*]. But since I cannot bear killing the purport of art just to exploit its benefit, I must be patient until the freedom of writing [*hikken no jiyū*] is granted. To all those who strongly care about the use value of things, I beg you not to view artists as indifferent to our nation.[82]

Hampered by censorship ordinances or not, the didactic and political mission of the artistic novel lies in the key phrase "reforms for our nation." Although Shōyō's formulation seems a bit vague, what he means by "reforms" becomes clear through his intimations, later in the essay, about the didactic intent of his own novel *Tōsei shosei katagi* (Characters of present-day students). This novel, he states, intends to show the "transformation of the students' emotions" (*shosei no jōtai no hensen*) and the "change in their customs" (*fūgi no henka*)—that is, their renunciation of revolutionary violence and licentious debauchery and, as a result, their metamorphosis into civilized gentlemen (*shinshi*), able to build Japan's future democratic public sphere.[83] Shōyō explicitly reflected *Tōsei shosei katagi* as a novel that is *not* primarily political fiction; and *Shōsetsu shinzui* is careful to avoid references to the artistic novel as political.[84] This conforms to his assertion that the novel's main focus should not be didactic. At the same time, the artistic novel's indirect didactic benefits or its second emphasis on *kanzen chōaku* still allowed for a strong affinity to contemporary political discourse and fiction. As discussed in the following chapter, Shōyō continued to write explicitly political, even allegorical, works shortly after publishing *Shōsetsu shinzui*. This was because his reform of fiction remained intimately tied to the broader contemporary project of national reform that predicated the prospect of political participation upon civilized behavior, including in gender relations and love.

Shōyō's literary project must be situated within the broader historical and discursive space in the mid-1880s that emerged with the government's suppression of the violent uprisings of the People's Rights Movement and the ensuing concerted effort, in both the government and the oppositional public sphere, to build a strong national community in anticipation of the 1890 National Diet opening.[85] The Reform Party–inflected interest of political intellectuals like Sakazaki Shiran in social and civilizational reforms was an important example, as was Iwamoto Yoshiharu's promotion of female education through the journal *Jogaku zasshi*. At the same moment, the major public intellectual and journalist Tokutomi Sohō (1863–1957) also formulated the new ideal of the "country gentleman" (*inaka shinshi*) and "youth" (*seinen*) as civilized male elite figures who had left revolutionary violence behind and were capable of building the national democratic public sphere.[86] Sohō famously criticized political novels like Tetchō's *Setchūbai* for their romance plots and saw the new type of love promoted by Iwamoto as inappropriate for the new youth, but his nationalistic and civilizational agenda was ultimately similar to Tetchō's, Iwamoto's, and Shōyō's.[87] In this context, literature and especially the novel were seen as important media that could contribute to social reform and national consolidation. Major journals founded in the mid to late 1880s, in particular Iwamoto's *Jogaku zasshi* and Sohō's *Kokumin no tomo* (The nation's friend), were greatly invested in offering a forum for literary discussion and the publication of novels in the wake of Shōyō's reform.

Shōyō's emphasis on the realist depiction of emotions and customs in *Shōsetsu shinzui* provided the critical formula for the new novel as an agent able to promote social reform and civilization. By realistically focusing on civilized protagonists as well as their emotions and customs—in Sakazaki Shiran's words, letting a medical doctor or journalist be the hero instead of Tanjirō—the novel could teach the same emotions and customs to the reader. Or, in *Shōsetsu shinzui*'s terms, it could be an aesthetically pleasing art by virtue of its ability to elevate readers' deportment and bring them to self-reflection. Such an understanding of the novel's social, moral, and political significance remained didactic and connected to Bakin's *kanzen chōaku*. Although Shōyō criticized Bakin for writing exclusively didactic fiction, he still envisioned a novel that could be indirectly didactic through its civilized realism. Shōyō thus subtly shifted from Bakin's Confucian didacticism to one more strongly concerned with social reform, but Bakin's idealism remained an important component of his literary theory. Indeed, novels that inspired or echoed Shōyō's reform—his own early translations, *Karyū shunwa*, Disraeli's *Coningsby*, and Tetchō's *Setchūbai*—were all similar to Bakin in staging exemplary male heroes who were moral and civilized and, by virtue of these qualities, could benefit the nation.

In *Shōsetsu shinzui*, Shōyō states that the novel's depiction of emotions and customs focuses on how a good protagonist fights and overcomes his vulgar passion using his reason and conscience. The exemplary nature of this fight and especially its success could certainly serve as edifying material for self-reflection. However, the presence of vulgar passion at the very heart of the novel's realism also had the potential to subvert the didactic teaching, as *ninjōbon* allegedly did, by inciting readers to passion rather than self-reflection. *Shōsetsu shinzui* defines *ninjō* in largely negative terms as vulgar and even animalistic but otherwise does not explore its destabilizing power. That passion remains *Shōsetsu shinzui*'s blind spot becomes obvious when considering Shōyō's own novels written in the late 1880s that dramatize foolish passion and its irreconcilability with social reform. It is to the destabilization and, ultimately, breakdown of Shōyō's literary project that I turn in the next chapter.

Chapter Five

THE NOVEL'S FAILURE

Shōyō and the Aporia of Realism and Idealism

Tsubouchi Shōyō's novel *Shinmigaki: Imotose kagami* (Newly polished: Mirror of marriage, 1885–1886), written shortly after *Shōsetsu shinzui*, contains an important scene of misreading. The novel's hero, Misawa Tatsuzō, a recent university graduate and government bureaucrat, reads Bulwer-Lytton's *Ernest Maltravers*, probably in the original English. He misreads the novel to the extent that he commits the "greatest mistake in his life": marrying an uneducated low-class woman inappropriate for someone with his career prospects. Engrossed in reading about Maltravers's love for Alice, Misawa only delves deeper into his "foolish passion" for a woman he should shun from the perspective of reason:

Spring had passed by like a dream and the gloomy season of the fifth-month rains had arrived. . . . Misawa Tatsuzō was hunched over his writing desk at the open southern window and intently reading a Western book. The book was the novel *Maltravers* [*sic*], written by the English master Lord Lytton—there is a partial translation by a certain Oda [Jun'ichirō] titled *Karyū shunwa*. The book's plot is the following: A student named Maltravers, on his way back from Germany, fortuitously encounters a girl called Alice. Thanks to her sincerity, he manages to escape from a dangerous situation, and taking her with him on his journey, he lives with her for some time as husband and wife. Saddened by her lack of education and learning, Maltravers conscientiously teaches her every day, thus gradually giving her an understanding of the world. This and other details are delicately described. Misawa Tatsuzō had for a long time pursued the study of Western learning and was knowledgeable in the practical sciences, but he had never studied literature or poetry [*bungaku shiika*] and until this day had rarely read any novels [*haishi shōsetsu*]. This novel fit his fantasies very well and left a deep impression on him. He read through it with much emotion and could hardly put down the volume. What could be done about the fact that his delusions [*bōsō*] were increasingly excited, but—ah!—was it the sin of the reader or the author? When Lytton wrote his novel, his intent was to provide a strict admonishment. Maltravers's story to a certain extent resembles the love stories [*jōshi*] by the authors of the Tamenaga school, but in its deep meaning there is an unbridgeable difference. Tamenaga sees the essence of human emotion in the pleasure of the body, which he has described at length. But Lytton, while narrating emotions and social customs, depicts the most ardent of all emotions, love [*aijō*]. It would be a great mistake to believe that he depicts obscene animalistic passion as a means to describe love! From reading Lytton's novels, readers with sharp eyes can gain an understanding of the depths of human emotion and the mysteries of social customs, and their benefits will be numerous! That the delusion of Misawa Tatsuzō only increased from reading the book resulted from the dullness of his eyes. When a critic of the *Jinpingmei* once said that the sin was in the reader's heart and did not have anything to do with the book, was he not coming to the author's defense?[1] The *Jinpingmei* is a depraved work, and even if differentiating between ethics and art, it is hard to agree with such a critique. Yet this critic claimed that even the *Jinpingmei* was without sin. Readers of novels in this world must see them with utmost precaution! Novels are like morphine: one must love them, but also fear them.[2]

This passage reflects *Shōsetsu shinzui*'s theory in a nutshell, but it also subverts it. The Western novel *Ernest Maltravers* is what Shōyō calls a true novel because it does not depict animalistic passion like Shunsui's *ninjōbon*, but civilized love. Or, to be more precise, it shows the hero's inner struggle between passion and reason. Despite his initial infatuation with Alice, Ernest Maltravers vanquishes his passion and almost enters a love marriage that facilitates his career as a politician and service to the nation. Such a depiction of emotions and customs should provide sharp-eyed readers with a "strict admonishment" and lead them to self-reflection. Had Misawa Tatsuzō been sharp-eyed, his self-reflection induced by the act of reading would have diverted him from passion. But his dullness causes him to misread Bulwer-Lytton's novel as an invitation to marry an unworthy woman for no other reason than the "pleasure of the body." Misawa, in other words, misreads the true novel *Ernest Maltravers* as a *ninjōbon*. Why does Shōyō here let collapse the relationship of didactic instruction between novel and reader that *Shōsetsu shinzui* postulated?

To use the narrator's critical terms, there is a sin of the book and a sin of the reader. The sin of Bulwer-Lytton's novel is that it indeed "resembles the love stories by the authors of the Tamenaga school" by representing "animalistic passion," most notably in the romance between Maltravers and Alice. Readers who fail to see his battle between passion and reason, the moral qualms that precede his sexual gratification, will probably misread the novel as an invitation to the *ninjōbon*'s lust. Although *Shōsetsu shinzui* defined the novel's protagonist as subject to vulgar passion, it did not explore this passion's destabilizing potential for the reader. Misawa's misreading, however, foregrounds the passion depicted in *Ernest Maltravers* as powerful enough to disrupt the novel's didactic and artistic mission. The misunderstanding refers back to the traditional anxiety about the novel—every novel—as a dangerous, desire-inducing morphine.[3] It uncovers the problematic continuum between the artistic novel and works traditionally seen as licentious, including *ninjōbon*, the *Jinpingmei*, and even *The Tale of Genji*, to which the cited passage also subtly alludes.[4]

At the same time, the sin of the book can be made visible—or *Shōsetsu shinzui*'s blind spot be exposed—only through the sin of the reader. The dullness of Misawa Tatsuzō's eyes needs to be understood in the context of contemporary civilizational discourse. Despite his elite university education, the Japanese man Misawa is not yet mature enough to correctly read the realist depiction of emotions and customs in the British artistic novel.[5] His misreading reflects the not yet civilized reality of Japanese customs in comparison with the West. In *Shōsetsu shinzui*, Shōyō proclaimed the artistic novel, in social Darwinian fashion, as the product of the highest stage of civilizational progress. He also posited the novel's readers as "men of worth," able to appreciate its aesthetic pleasures and didactic admonishments. However, Misawa's lack of civilization despite his education and gender, both as a reader and protagonist, jeopardizes the project of the artistic novel. His misreading demonstrates that it cannot yet be appropriately understood in Japan. Even worse, the realist depiction of Misawa as a Japanese hero must describe his failure to live up to the ideal of the British gentleman. At the heart of *Shōsetsu shinzui* lay the assumption that the artistic novel's realism is civilized. Shōyō's own novels, however, subvert this assumption. With an unprecedented radicalness, his *mosha* zooms in on Japanese customs and emotions "as they are": vulgar and animalistic passions, uncontrolled and uncontrollable by reason. This realism brought back an anxiety about the novel's licentiousness that *Shōsetsu shinzui*'s discourse had concealed. Realistically focusing on nothing but vulgar passion would essentially reduce the reformed novel to a *ninjōbon*, devoid of a social, political, and artistic mission.

This is why Shōyō's narratives continued to stage idealist elements, illustrating how Japanese customs and emotions *should* be. An ideal (*aidiaru*), however, as Shōyō self-reflexively puts it, is a "propensity of wanting to realize things that cannot be realized in the world."[6] It contradicts realism. In his novels, then, the result is an aporia or fundamental contradiction between irreconcilable realist and idealist elements. Shōyō's works are driven by the contradictory impulses to depict emotions and customs *as they are* and *as they should be*, without providing a strong narrative link from one to the other. This aporia also breaks up the bildungsroman form that relied on the integration of (or compromise between) contradictory aspirations: most notably, passion and reason. The disintegration of the bildungsroman, moreover, generates a new narrative culminating in failure. *Imotose kagami* ends tragically with the wife's suicide and the hero's unemployment, the exact opposite of previous narratives culminating in the representation of an exemplary masculinity supported by a civilized marriage. Shōyō's narratives of failure encapsulate his difficulty of integrating the novel's realism with its idealist mission. Within the new context of Meiji civilizational discourse, they extended and even radicalized the earlier ambiguity in nineteenth-century narratives—Bakin's, for instance—that pitched the novel's writing of licentious *ninjō* against the genre's moral-didactic ambition and legitimacy.

This chapter surveys Shōyō's literary production following *Shōsetsu shinzui* up to his abandonment of novel writing in the early 1890s. I start with a discussion of his most famous novel, *Ichidoku santan: Tōsei shosei katagi* (Reading it once and sighing thrice: Characters of present-day students), and its sequel of sorts, *Imotose kagami*. Both works showcase the difficulty of reconciling realist and idealist elements and break up the bildungsroman form. I then move to Shōyō's literary experiments later in the decade that, more radically, pursue the representation of idealist and realist extremes: the Reform Party–inflected political utopia in *Naichi zakkyo: Mirai no yume* (Mixed residence with foreigners: A dream of the future, 1886) with its didactic focus on future reformed customs, and especially *Saikun* (The wife, 1889), whose pessimistic realism highlights the failure and impossibility of civilizational reform in the present. I close with a brief examination of Shōyō's idiosyncratic attempt, in the early 1890s, to synthesize realism and idealism in what he calls the theory of "submerged ideals" (*botsurisō*), a synthesis he finds tellingly realized not in the novel but in Shakespeare's plays.

WAITING FOR THE TRANSFORMATION OF STUDENTS: *TŌSEI SHOSEI KATAGI* AND THE APORIA OF LITERARY FORM

A peculiarity of Shōyō's first novel, *Tōsei shosei katagi*, is its literary form that eclectically reenacts various late Edo-period genres of *gesaku*.[7] A major portion of the novel consists of humorous slapstick scenes reminiscent of the *kokkeibon* (books of humor).[8] These dialogue-heavy and not primarily plot-centered scenes focus on the customs of contemporary students in a private academy, modeled after the University of Tokyo, and particularly their sexual escapades with prostitutes. The bawdy behavior and slang of various student characters in their interaction with one another and the young women are a major component of the humor. Another important strand of the novel's plot revolves around the romance between the student Komachida Sanji and the geisha Tanoji. In flashback accounts, we learn that Tanoji, whose birth origin is unknown, was taken as a child into Komachida's family, where she grew up as his sister. Owing to the financial difficulties of his father (a former samurai), however, she had to leave and become a geisha. The novel starts when Komachida and Tanoji meet again after many years of separation. The plot follows their ensuing infatuation until Komachida decides to break up the relationship. His reason is the imminent threat of being expelled from school for his amorous transgression, which would end his study and career prospects. The dialogue-focused narrative mode in which Shōyō presents this romance, in addition to its general setting in the pleasure quarter, where Tanoji sees Komachida as her customer, recalls the generic conventions of the *ninjōbon*.[9] Another section of the novel is in a narrative format reminiscent of the *yomihon* and particularly Bakin's style. This narrative presents a long historical flashback and uncovers the social origins of Tanoji, who, contrary to what her lowly geisha profession suggests, is the sister of Komachida's friend and fellow student Moriyama Tomoyoshi, the scion of an affluent *shizoku* family.[10]

Critical discussions of *Tōsei shosei katagi* have often seen in these seemingly unrelated *gesaku* modes a symptom of the novel's failure, its transitional and hybrid status on the path toward modernity and its inability to fully live up to the standard of the modern novel and its realism as defined by *Shōsetsu shinzui*.[11] However, particularly the literary formats reminiscent of the *kokkeibon* and *ninjōbon* were well suited for what Shōyō intended to be the realist depiction of contemporary Japanese emotions and customs as they are (I return subsequently to the *yomihon*). The students' debauchery with low-level prostitutes and the romance between Komachida and Tanoji realistically reflect what Shōyō calls vulgar or animalistic passion— still unenlightened gender relations, involving prostitution and pleasure-quarter romance. In an important digression in his narrative, he indirectly qualifies the types of *ninjō* depicted in his novel as low-class love (*shimo no koi*) and middle-class love (*chū no koi*), respectively, echoing Iwamoto Yoshiharu's model of the civilizational stages of love.[12] The lowest class (*kaikyū*) of love, according to Shōyō, is the carnal pleasure (*nikuyoku*) sought in prostitution, equaling the "desire of birds and beasts" and characteristic of Iwamoto's barbarian age of lust. Middle-class love is losing oneself (*mayou*) in foolish passion, like the geisha Tanoji and her customer Komachida, but this class is also "a relic of uncivilized times," belonging to the manner of beasts (*kedamono ryūgi*). Iwamoto qualified the age of foolish passion as half-civilized. These are, in Shōyō's view, the emotions and customs realistically depicted in his novel. That they involved university students, the future male elite of the country, only adds to the weight of his civilizational commentary.

Civilized love and gender relations, however, are not entirely absent from *Tōsei shosei katagi*. They constitute what Shōyō calls high-class love (*kami no koi*), not coincidentally in reference to a Western novel: Bulwer-Lytton's *Rienzi*. High-class love describes the relationship between Rienzi and Nina, and its source is the respect (*keibo*) for the partner's "elevated spirit" and "exceptional character." This definition was in line with Iwamoto's age of love, where a monogamous marriage assured the husband's protection of the wife and the wife's support, at home, of the husband's public endeavors.

But in *Tōsei shosei katagi*, these civilized emotions and customs remain the idealist fiction of a Western text divorced from the realism available to the Japanese novel. Inspired by the intertextual model of *Rienzi*, the novel's protagonists—and through them Shōyō—engage in a metacritical reflection about the difference between reality and ideal. Idealism (*aidiarizumu*) is an important term that the figures discuss in several instances and that is often glossed *kakūheki* (propensity to fiction).[13] Significantly, this "propensity" opposes the novel's impulse to engage in *mosha*.

Komachida clearly reflects the difference between ideal and reality because he is aware that his relationship with Tanoji does not conform to the "high-class" standard set by Bulwer-Lytton's novel. In one scene, his student friend Kurase parrots enlightenment gender wisdom, claiming that the strength of a beautiful woman (*kajin no chikara*) can help a "great man" accomplish eminent deeds. Even a hero like Rienzi, he states, can fulfill his high-flying ambition only if he has a woman like Nina by his side.[14] Kurase's intent in likening Rienzi's love to Komachida's is to cheer his friend, who deeply suffers from his decision to cut his ties with Tanoji to pursue his study and ambition. Komachida's reply, however, pessimistically points to the futility of such a comparison:

What I resent is that I am so idealistic [*aidiaru*] that I sometimes have weird illusions [*myō na mōsō*] and attempt to *fallaciously* [original English]—in foolish fashion—apply Western thought to Japanese society. And then I fail. But this problem is not only mine, it is the problem of Japan as a whole. Kurase, it is even yours. You just brought up the example of *Rienzi*, but how can this ever be a model for getting on in the world? If one has high-flying ambitions yet needs the help of a beauty to arouse one's courage and accomplish something, is this not extremely weak [*wīku*]? When he wrote with his talented brush, Bulwer-Lytton merely laid bare the intricacies of human emotion, but this does not mean that [arousing one's courage with the help of a beauty] is laudable.[15]

Komachida here presents Rienzi's heroism depending on the support of a beautiful woman as "weak" and argues that love is an impediment to male ambition. His deeper problem, however, is that Western thought (*Seiyō shisō*) cannot be directly applied to Japan. Western enlightened customs and emotions, as epitomized by the relationship between Rienzi and Nina, must remain a "weird illusion" given the current state of Japanese society. Any attempt at similar gender relations in Japan would be idealist fallaciousness. Komachida also notes "how stupid I was to act as if I could model my behavior after the wondrous encounters of beautiful women with talented men"—his definition of what he calls ideal love (*aidiaru no renjō*), in opposition to traditional Japanese ordinary love (*tsune no koi*).[16] He even goes on to label Tanoji an "unfortunate victim" (in English) of his idealism, and the narrator ironically notes that all these thoughts are the product of his reading of novels from Western countries (*Nishi no kuni no haishi*).

The key difference between Komachida's situation and Rienzi's is that Tanoji, unlike the aristocrat Nina, is a geisha—the very epitome of uncivilized Japanese customs that enlightenment gender discourse sought to eradicate. The relationship therefore cannot evolve into a high-class marriage predicated on the mutual respect of the partners. For one thing, Tanoji is bound by her geisha contract, and Komachida does not have the financial means to ransom and marry her. Although the novel makes clear that, after graduating and finding government employment, Komachida would have those means, simply ransoming Tanoji would still not erase the social stigma of marrying a former geisha.[17] Marrying Tanoji in the future would impede his career, despite her exceptional intellectual and moral qualities, constantly highlighted, that raise her above the geisha profession and indeed qualify her for ideal love.

The realist depiction of Japanese customs cannot write Komachida's marriage as an ideal union involving two equal partners who support each other. This predicament leads to Shōyō's failure to write *Tōsei shosei katagi* as an artistic novel representing an enlightened marriage. Recall that marriage was an important concept not only in contemporary gender discourse but also in the Japanese bildungsroman in the wake of *Karyū shunwa*, a major implicit reference for *Shōsetsu shinzui*. In these novels, civilized gender relations culminating in marriage facilitated the hero's advancement through hard study and (political) career. In *Seiro nikki*, the protagonists were a schoolteacher and his student, which gave their relationship a sufficiently enlightened context—the nation-state's educational policies—to turn it into a socially appropriate marriage, despite the initial budding of erotic passion. In *Tōsei shosei katagi*, however, Shōyō places the romance squarely in the pleasure quarter, the "real" locus of contemporary gender relations. An enlightened student-teacher relationship would probably have been too idealistic.[18] It is true that Komachida could qualify as the type of civilized protagonist envisioned by *Shōsetsu shinzui* because he struggles against his passion and breaks up with his lover, motivated by his ambition and intellectual self-awareness. But unlike in previous novels, his struggle leads nowhere. He neither advances in his career nor fulfills his ambition. Instead, he remains despondent, suffering in his brain and nerves.[19] His despondency results from lovesickness, but also from his awareness of the unbridgeable gap between his ideal love and the half-civilized reality of his passion for a geisha. The path from reality to ideal—his *Bildung*, in other words—is obstructed. The novel ends with this inconclusive lack of "elevation," to use a key concept from *Shōsetsu shinzui*, and the disintegration of the bildungsroman.[20]

In one of the two prefaces to *Tōsei shosei katagi*, Shōyō acknowledges that the speech depicted in his novel is vulgar and the emotions (*jōtai*) are lowly. But as long as the author's intent is elevated, concentrating on the realist depiction of emotions and customs, his writing will differ from Shunsui's *ninjōbon* that depict the same vulgar customs, but with the mere intent to "flatter licentious tastes."[21] In the other preface, he states that his "critique of errors in the student world"—that is, licentious customs—is art (*bijutsu*) with the potential to bring readers to self-reflection about good and bad behavior and to elevate their deportment.[22] The line of demarcation he draws between artistic novel and *ninjōbon* is subtle, though, and related primarily to the author's intent, not to literary representation. How problematically subtle this line was is obvious from the reaction of contemporary readers. Iwamoto Yoshiharu, for instance, notes that *Tōsei shosei katagi*, in describing the students' debauchery with women, is not much different from Shunsui's *ninjōbon*, which he sees as greatly distant from the elevated and pure customs of the West. But he also states that the novel is not to be held responsible for representing depravity, because it "mimetically depicts the sins of society" (*shakai no zaiaku o chokusha shitaru*).[23] Despite Shōyō's assertion to the contrary, the lack of elevation in his realism and its affinity to the *ninjōbon* were problematic in the eyes of contemporary critics and probably for Shōyō as well, since these qualities had the potential to undercut the novel's didactic and artistic mission—especially if readers like Misawa Tatsuzō were not sufficiently sharp-sighted to understand its "teaching."

This probably explains the strong impulse in *Tōsei shosei katagi* to write an ideal content, even if exceeding the sphere of realism. As discussed,

Shōyō defines idealism as "propensity to fiction," the opposite of *mosha*. His emphasis on fictionality is of critical importance. Unable to integrate the representation of idealist elements into the realist depiction of Japanese emotions and customs, *Tōsei shosei katagi* indeed exhibits a strong propensity to bring them back onstage as "fiction." Nonrealist fiction lies at the heart of the novel's *yomihon* subplot that uncovers Tanoji's true class origins. Revolving around complicated details, countless minor characters, and unlikely coincidences, this subplot consciously defies the principle of realist representation. Although not staging ideal characters as did Bakin, the narrative sequence nonetheless leads to a highly idealistic outcome: the seemingly lowborn geisha Tanoji is the sister of Komachida's university friend Moriyama Tomoyoshi, who is of *shizoku* descent. Significantly, these newly discovered class origins make the enlightened marriage between Komachida and Tanoji realistically possible and facilitate the transformation of their foolish passion into an ideal love. The *yomihon* subplot paradoxically enables the transformation of *Tōsei shosei katagi* into a bildungsroman, culminating in an exemplary marriage.

Shōyō's novel contains metacritical reflections about the idealism of this subplot. One such reflection occurs in a dialogue between Komachida and his friend Moriyama, later identified as Tanoji's brother.[24] Moriyama attempts to dissuade Komachida from his infatuation with Tanoji by telling him about his own prior involvement with a Yoshiwara courtesan and his decision, after some painful struggle, to stop seeing her after only one visit. Moriyama states that his decision came from the awareness of the danger of "the heart's delusion" or "idealism." Idealism would perhaps be the romantic infatuation with that woman, but more important, it would be the enticing idea that she could be his long-lost sister, as some details about her seem to suggest. Idealism, according to Moriyama, is clinging to something "romantic" (*romanchikku*)—the katakana gloss for *kōtō kii na koto* (something absurd and fantastical)—that only happens in novels (*shōsetsu haishi*). Significantly, in *Shōsetsu shinzui*, the epithets *kōtō* and *kii* qualify what Shōyō terms "romance" (*rōmansu*), the kind of not yet civilized narrative that abounds in fantastical incidents like Bakin's *yomihon* and precedes the advent of the realist true novel.[25] Moriyama Tomoyoshi is aware that, if the Yoshiwara courtesan was indeed his lost sister, this would be like a fantastical coincidence in a *yomihon*, unrealistic and impossible from the standpoint of reason. He is right that the courtesan is not his sister. However, it is revealed over the course of the novel's convoluted *yomihon* subnarrative that Tanoji is his sister.

It seems ironic that *Tōsei shosei katagi* metacritically qualifies its own plot as "absurd and fantastical" while privileging *yomihon*-type romance over the realism of the true novel. Literary critic Ochi Haruo has argued that in order to overcome the static scene-centered aesthetic of the earliest *kokkeibon* drafts and shape them into a novel centered on plot and narrative, Shōyō could not but have recourse to a traditional *yomihon* format.[26] His recourse to such a format, however, also allowed for a reintegration of idealism, at least as fiction, since the writing of ideal love was not possible in a realist way. The not yet civilized idealism of the *yomihon* plot paradoxically makes it possible to write a civilized love: the marriage between Komachida and Tanoji, not as geisha but as *shizoku* daughter—Bulwer-Lytton's Nina in Japanese clothes, as it were. The affinity between Rienzi's ideal love and the *yomihon* is indeed noteworthy. In *Tōsei shosei katagi's* universe, both Rienzi and Bakin's dog warriors must be what Shōyō, in *Shōsetsu shinzui*, calls ideal figures, not conforming to the reality of Japanese emotions and customs. Although Shōyō and his protagonists denounce idealism as a negative "propensity" (*kuse*) to be deluded by unrealistic fictions, there is an undeniably strong propensity in the novel to precisely stage those ideal figures. This predicament results from the problematically vulgar reality of Japanese customs. In a civilized society, such a predicament would not arise as Rienzi would not be the ideal but reality and the unproblematic hero of the true novel.

However, at the point of possibly staging Komachida's marriage in the last chapter, the novel significantly hesitates, leaving open whether it will happen or not. Writing it would certainly give *Tōsei shosei katagi* the veneer of an artistic novel and bildungsroman, but it would also be a deception, since it would rely not on *mosha* but on the fantastical artifice of a *yomihon* plot. The novel's avoidance of marriage makes sense, but it also lays bare the aporia between realist and idealist elements and impulses. Previous novels like *Karyū shunwa* and especially *Seiro nikki* were able to integrate foolish passion and a love marriage within a coherent plot. In *Tōsei shosei katagi*, however, this synthesis dissolves into irreconcilable *gesaku* components: the students' debauchery presented in the *kokkeibon* mode, Komachida's foolish passion for a geisha reminiscent of the *ninjōbon*, and the prospect of writing ideal love and marriage brought about by a *yomihon* plot. The integration of *ninjōbon* passion and *yomihon* idealism into one coherent format of realist representation would have produced an artistic novel and bildungsroman, but here the *gesaku* elements remain incongruous fragments. That Shōyō thus failed to write an artistic novel was a result not so much of his lack of ability or training—his being mired in *gesaku* conventions, unable to be truly modern—but of a fundamental difficulty integrating these fragments and their underlying impulses given what he perceives as the vulgar reality of Japan.

Shōyō initially intended to write *Tōsei shosei katagi* as a bildungsroman, though. This is clear from his remarks about his failure to write the "transformation of students" (*shosei no hensen*). The beginning of the following quote refers to the fact that the novel depicts events occurring in the years 1881–1882, predating the time of publication in 1885–1886.

When the author initially undertook the writing of this novel, he wanted to extend the plot to the years Meiji 18–19 [1885–1886], and while sufficiently laying bare the emotions [of students], he also planned to show their transformations . . . the transformations of their customs and their behavior. For example, an initially imprudent person can become serious over the years. Or somebody who was a licentious prodigal while a student becomes an experienced entrepreneur. Or somebody, upon graduation, is good for nothing. Or somebody's learning is superficial, but he can still be employed. The transformations take myriad shapes and I cannot list them all, but depicting them sure provides limitless fascination! For example, Komachida in this novel is nothing better than a poor-looking, nervous, pitiable young man, but who knows how he could evolve after gaining some experience over five or six years? There are child prodigies in the world, and sometimes there are people born with great intelligence, but these are exceptional, and a realist novelist [*shujitsu haishika*, glossed "realist" in English] does not like them. In any case, the author greatly regrets that he was not able to depict this principle [of transformation]. If he is lucky enough to find time, he wants to take up his pen again and compose a volume titled *The Characters of Present-Day Students Continued*. This continuation will provide the later account of Komachida, Moriyama . . . and it will introduce new figures. The new figures will be the main ones and will be students. The old figures will come second and will be gentlemen [*shinshi*]. For this reason, the continuation should be seen as a character study of students and gentlemen.[27]

Shōyō initially intended to write the transformation of, for example, Komachida from a "poor-looking, nervous, pitiable" student into a "gentleman." While this transformation constitutes the maturation process of individual figures—their passage from youthful debauchery and passion to adult maturity—it also allegorically anticipates the progress of Japanese society as a whole from a half-civilized past (the years 1881–1882 and before) to a civilized present and future. Elsewhere, Shōyō also notes that his novel's didactic intent (gūi) is to "correct effete customs [bunjaku no fū] and violent behaviors."[28] "Effete customs" include the students' debauchery and Komachida's foolish passion, whereas "violent behaviors" is a reference to the political radicals of the People's Rights Movement.[29] This didactic intent, as mentioned, closely echoed the political agenda of the Constitutional Reform Party and its attempt to mobilize the intellectual and wealthy segments of society for nonviolent democratic participation in the National Diet. Especially the gentleman (shinshi), promoted as a new cultural and political ideal, served as the emblem of civilization and the new democratic public sphere.

In Tōsei shosei katagi, however, Shōyō largely avoids writing the transformation of students. The novel ends before Komachida can turn into a gentleman, but some characters indeed undergo change. Moriyama Tomoyoshi in particular, probably modeled on Takata Sanae, is described as a truly gentlemanly figure from early in the novel. He is the only one to successfully struggle against fictional delusion, and he indirectly criticizes the novel's plot for being unrealistic romance. It is not surprising, then, that upon graduation—Moriyama graduates within the novel, whereas Komachida does not—he becomes a lawyer and enters the Reform Party. Moriyama, however, is not the main protagonist. Komachida is, stuck in half-civilized passion, and the novel hesitates to unite him with Tanoji in an enlightened marriage. In his authorial discussion, Shōyō states that the realist novelist does not like child prodigies (shindō). But is the civilized gentleman not also like a child prodigy, an impossible ideal, given the reality of Japan? This explains the novel's strong realist hesitation about Komachida's transformation, despite the equally strong idealist longing for precisely such a transformation to occur.

In his "Critique of Tōsei shosei katagi" (Tōsei shosei katagi no hihyō, 1886), Takata Sanae lauded Shōyō's work for being a social novel (sōsharu noberu) and not an ideal novel (aidiaru noberu). According to Takata, whereas the ideal novel or romance (*rōmansu*), like the works of Bakin and Scott, seeks to promote "feudal morality" by staging ideal heroes, the goal of the social novel is the "criticism of social customs," which are described "as they are," as in the works of Dickens and the eighteenth-century British humorists.[30] Contemporary critics like Takata and Iwamoto thus viewed *Tōsei shosei katagi* primarily as a realist social novel, but the relationship between social and ideal in the novel is more complex. Torn between a realist impulse (the writing of emotions as they are, even if vulgar) and an idealist impulse (the writing of the civilized transformation of students), it ends with an unresolved aporia between the representation of the ideal and the social. This aporia comes to the fore even more sharply in Shōyō's next novel, *Imotose kagami* (Mirror of marriage).

MIRROR OF MARRIAGE: RADICALIZING THE APORIA

Scholars have rarely discussed *Tōsei shosei katagi* in connection with *Imotose kagami*, although the latter can be seen as a sequel to the former.[31] *Imotose kagami* writes a transformation of students of sorts featuring a young male protagonist, Misawa Tatsuzō, who, unlike Komachida, has recently graduated from the university and found a well-paid job in the government bureaucracy. Of greater significance is the fact that the novel focuses, as its title indicates, on marriage, the theme that *Tōsei shosei katagi* avoided. Shōyō's preface explicitly reflects on this evolution:

The focus of the novel is on human emotion, and the strongest human emotion is love [*ai*]. . . . No kind of love [*aijō*] is stronger than the affection [*renjō*] between men and women. This is why a love story [*jōwa*] between a man and a woman must be the backbone of the novel's plot. However, since the main focus of this novel is on the relationship between husband and wife [*imo to se no kōjō*] and not unmarried lovers [*jōfu jōrō*], it greatly differs from the love stories of the Tamenaga school.[32]

By focusing on the emotions of husband and wife, *Imotose kagami* takes the wind out of the sails of critics who, like Iwamoto, bemoaned the affinity of Shōyō's first novel to the *ninjōbon*. Given that marriage, in contemporary discourse, had become the ideological locus for the formulation of enlightened gender ideals, the new focus of *Imotose kagami* was part of a maturation process. It could be seen as the fulfillment of the idealist impulse to finally depict civilized love. *Imotose kagami* also no longer juxtaposes incongruous *gesaku* formats but is written in a more unified literary style that, while stylistically reminiscent of Bakin's *yomihon*, is closer to a Western novel.[33] However, the representation of a high-class love again fails, and this radicalizes the aporia between the representation of idealist and realist elements.

At the horizon of *Imotose kagami* lies the possibility of an enlightened love marriage, between the hero, Misawa, and Oyuki, the educated, beautiful, and exemplary daughter of a high-ranking Meiji bureaucrat. This union is perceived by everybody, including Oyuki's parents, as ideal, but it fails because Misawa happens to eavesdrop on a conversation in which the potential bride pretends to despise him, although, in truth, she wants to conceal her affection for him. As a consequence, Misawa chooses to marry an attractive, but uneducated and low-class woman, Otsuji, the daughter of a fishmonger, and Oyuki, against her feelings and under pressure from her parents, marries an unworthy social climber and opportunist. Both marriages end unhappily. The primary didactic aim of the novel, repeatedly articulated by the narrator, is to illustrate the pitfalls inherent in these two types of union: "free marriage" (*jiyū kekkon*) and "forced marriage" (*kanshō kekkon*), respectively. This intent was not lost on contemporary readers. In his review of the novel, fittingly published in *Jogaku zasshi*, the young critic Ishibashi Ningetsu (1865–1926) saw the "didactic revelation" of the "two evils" of freedom and parental interference as the true benefit for the journal's female upper-class readers (*jōryū ni kurai suru on-katagata*).[34]

The two evils identified by Ningetsu epitomize the not yet fully civilized status of Japan. Oyuki's forced marriage is a result of the barbaric tyranny of parents. In his "Kon'inron" (On marriage, 1891), published in *Jogaku zasshi*, Iwamoto Yoshiharu labels this type of marriage old-fashioned, and he defines *Jogaku zasshi* as an educational tool for daughters to resist it.[35] Shōyō's *Imotose kagami* similarly sees in Oyuki's parents the "tyrannical attitude of old *bakufu* times" (*kyūbaku no sensei-hada*).[36] The main focus of the novel, however, is on the failure of Misawa's free marriage with the lower-class woman Otsuji. At least since the publication of the essays by Fukuzawa Yukichi and Iwamoto, both titled "Danjo kōsairon" (On the association of men and women), in 1886 and 1888, respectively, "freedom" in the relations between the sexes became a major concept in the enlightenment discourse on gender. Iwamoto argues that this freedom of association will engender the "habit of mutual respect" (*ai-kei suru no shūkan*) and "equality" (*dōtō*) between the sexes, ultimately strengthening women's rights. The absence of freedom in gender relations in the past favored prostitution, as courtesans were the only women whom Japanese men could freely access.[37] Freedom was thus perceived as a necessary precondition for a new kind of enlightened marriage and love.

The failure of Misawa's free marriage results from his misunderstanding of freedom. In an inner monologue, he states,

According to customs that have been in place since ancient times, parents always interfered with the marriages [of their children], and if you chose your partner yourself, people often stared at you, thinking this inappropriate. . . . If she loves me and I love her [*kare ware o ai-shi ware kare o omoi*] and if [only then] we receive our parents' permission, then this is true freedom [*shinsei no jiyū*] and even resembles the national customs of England [*Ei no kokufū*]![38]

The "national customs of England" are of course civilized. Misawa's misunderstanding is to believe that his love for the low-class woman Otsuji is high-class love. He does not know that what he feels is in fact foolish passion. To a certain extent this is understandable, though, given the ambiguity of passion. As noted earlier, "passion" was a new concept in Meiji Japan with an enlightenment potential. In Bulwer-Lytton's *Ernest Maltravers*, the hero's love for an uneducated, low-class woman (Alice) could epitomize the freedom of the heart's choice against social norms, including the practice of arranged (or forced) marriage. At one point, Misawa even exclaims, in English, "Tsuji, Tsuji, I love thee," parroting Maltravers's earlier love declaration and, at least rhetorically, highlighting the individualistic and exclusive (and therefore enlightened) quality of his passionate feeling.[39] Shōyō's narrator, however, disqualifies Misawa's passion as "vulgar," "foolish," and "animalistic," opposing it to the "true freedom" inherent in English customs:

His belief that a marriage that is based just on mutual affection is a free marriage was a truly deplorable mistake! People who have no respect but only foolish longing for each other [*itazura ni ai-omou mono*] have sunk into so-called animalistic lust [*jūjō*]. This is not what is called true love [*shin no ai*]! The difference between common animalistic lust and true love is whether or not there is respect! Did Misawa Tatsuzō have any respect for Otsuji? Was there anything in her qualities, besides her looks and her attitude, that he loved with respect? Did he respect her extraordinary talent or the firmness of her chastity? No! Misawa loved Otsuji for her looks only.[40]

Misawa's "foolish longing," reducible to physical attraction, is not much different from what Meiji discourses decried as the licentiousness depicted in *ninjōbon*. Not unlike previously with the translation *Karyū shunwa*, Shōyō's narratorial discourse devalues the enlightened quality of passion by likening it to uncivilized lust.

This judgment of passion was not unrelated to Shōyō's Reform Party ideology. He makes this connection explicit in a short political parable written concurrently with *Imotose kagami*, titled *Fūkai: Kyō waranbe* (A satire: Capital braggart, 1886).[41] In this work, the male student protagonist, Nakatsu Kunihiko (literally, "Hero of the Middle Land"), is an allegory of the Japanese people. He fails to marry the educated princess who embodies his people's rights (*minken*). Instead, led astray by animalistic passion, he ends up frequenting prostitutes and neglects his studies, thus giving away the princess to a despicable competitor, who stands for the oligarchic Meiji government. Unable to legitimately make the princess his wife by virtue of his achievements, he even attempts to abduct her, incited by his lust, foolishly mistaking his violence for "freedom." This behavior, we learn, represents the antigovernment revolutionary activism of the Liberal Party in the mid-1880s that Reform Party ideologues repudiated. The overall interpretive key that Shōyō provides for his parable is that the Japanese people are not yet ready and civilized enough for democratic political participation in the National Diet.[42] That Misawa, in *Imotose kagami*, fails to marry the educated woman predestined to him and presumes his attraction for a low-class woman to be free enlightened love is his mistake from the elitist top-down perspective of Reform Party ideology. Enlightened customs or true freedom, both political and romantic, were the prerogative of the wealthy and educated, whereas the lower classes were to be excluded from the national politics of the Diet and from civilized love. Attempting to include them, like Misawa, could not but indicate political immaturity—or foolish passion.

Shōyō's short parable, *Kyō waranbe*, presents an inversion of the Reform Party political novel. Works like *Jōkai haran* (Stormy waves in a sea of passion) and Suehiro Tetchō's novel *Setchūbai* (Plum blossoms in the snow) allegorically linked the success of civilized gender relations and love to the prospect of a democratic public sphere. Shōyō inverts the paradigm by focusing on the failure of enlightened gender relations and, allegorically, civilized national customs and democratic politics in the Diet—a failure resulting from the civilizational backwardness of the Japanese people. The didacticism of the allegory, but also of the realism in *Tōsei shosei katagi* and *Imotose kagami*, seems clear: to bring especially educated readers to self-reflection about their behavior and thus promote the transformation of customs.

However, the inversion of the realist focus from civilized to uncivilized *ninjō* threatens to subvert the didactic economy of the novel. By focusing on uncivilized customs reminiscent of *ninjōbon*, the novel risks being misread. As Shōyō's narrator notes in discussing Misawa's misreading of *Ernest Maltravers*, the novel can be "morphine" to readers, inciting them to inappropriate desire. Significantly, the failure of civilized national customs—the depiction of licentiousness—at the heart of Shōyō's realism also implies the failure of the artistic novel, whose success in educating readers relied precisely on the success of those customs, at least as represented by the novel. It is to avoid such a total failure of the artistic novel that Shōyō, in the second half of *Imotose kagami*, presents his failed hero, Misawa, despite the paradoxical incongruity with the first half, as what in *Shōsetsu shinzui* he calls a good person. The novel's plot is thus divided into two incongruous parts. Whereas the first part focused chiefly on Misawa's foolish passion leading up to his inappropriate marriage, the second part sees him transform into a surprisingly active, socioeconomically responsible, ethical, gentlemanly, and therefore civilized hero, despite the initial mistake of his marriage.

The second half of *Imotose kagami* revolves around a seemingly strange yet, given Shōyō's interest in civilizational reform, still meaningful plot: Misawa's attempt to ransom a courtesan from the pleasure quarter not to satisfy his lust but from a profoundly ethical and civilized motive. This plot sequence develops from the novel's prehistory, recounted in several flashbacks, that centers on Misawa's deceased father, a high-ranking government official but also a sexual profligate who enjoyed himself, in unenlightened fashion, with prostitutes and a mistress while neglecting Misawa and his mother.[43] One of the father's greatest misdeeds was to financially ruin a high-ranking courtesan in Osaka, Kouno, who had selflessly vouched for his considerable pleasure-quarter spending. Since Misawa's father never paid her back, Kouno died in desperation, harassed by her debtors. Her financial ruin and death also weighed heavily on her family and forced her sister to sell herself to the Nezu quarter in Tokyo. When Misawa Tatsuzō incidentally learns about these circumstances involving his father's profligacy, he chivalrously swears to ransom Kouno's sister to clear his father's name and atone for his wrongdoings.

Spurred by his mission, he develops an ethical discourse that condemns his father's misdeeds and the civilizational evil of prostitution: "Why did Oshimo [Kouno's sister] fall into this dreadful world of suffering and shamefully become a prostitute, why was she innocently buried in the world of mud for seven years, why did she become a slave in the world of lust, fodder for animalistic passion, why did she become a cow or a horse, whose fault was this?. . . How could I not feel ashamed if I pretended that this wasn't my business!"[44] Misawa, earlier a "slave" of animalistic passion himself, now has transformed into its most fervent detractor. He feels bound by "the shackles of morality" (*tokugi no kōsoku*) and a strong sense of "duty" (*giri*) toward the women wronged by his father. His actions, moreover, are led by an awareness of shame (*haji*), and in another passage he refers to his "conscience" (*ryōshin*) that he wishes to appease. In this discourse, major elements of the bildungsroman plot promoted by *Shōsetsu shinzui* are in place. Through his reason or conscience, the good person overcomes vulgar passion.

Yet by paradoxically frequenting the pleasure quarter for an ethical and civilized reason, Misawa becomes subject to misunderstandings. Even the courtesan Oshimo doubts his motivation, and his wife, Otsuji, believes that he intends to replace her with a new mistress. Compounded by instances of eavesdropping and the spread of false rumors, the misunderstandings about Misawa's mission lead to his dismissal from government employment. Angered at the uneducated Otsuji for her lack of understanding and himself misled by false assumptions drawn from eavesdropping (and now disillusioned by the great "mistake" of his marriage), Misawa declares that he will divorce his wife. The novel ends tragically with Otsuji's suicide.

Misunderstandings, including those produced by eavesdropping, here stand for the difficult negotiation between civilizational ideals and a half-civilized reality of unenlightened social practices that include pleasure-quarter prostitution.[45] The misunderstandings also directly pertain to Misawa as a person. This is how he attempts to explain his actions to his wife: "I only wanted to fulfill my duty!. . . Ah, even Wakazato [Oshimo] had doubts about me and said all kinds of things, so I can understand that you doubted me. But how could I ever be like the vulgar men from the *Plum Calendar* [sic] or *kusazōshi* booklets! Honor and reputation are what count, and even if in my heart I thought stupid things, my reason [*dōri*] would never acknowledge these!"[46] Despite his own former vulgar passion, Misawa remarkably dissociates himself from the "vulgar man" of Shunsui's *Shunshoku umegoyomi*—that is, Tanjirō—while highlighting his enlightened reason and duty. And yet an uncivilized environment constantly questions and impedes his reasonable acts. At the same time, Misawa not only is the object of misunderstandings but also produces them himself. Although he seems to have undergone a transformation and left behind his initial "stupid" infatuation with Otsuji, he continues to stupidly eavesdrop on others and misunderstand them, thus precipitating the novel's tragic ending. Misawa thereby remains part of the uncivilized reality around him.

Imotose kagami radicalizes what I previously called the aporia in representation in *Tōsei shosei katagi* by staging a male hero who realistically enacts the failure of civilized customs in Japan while displaying the idealist qualities of a good person led by reason and moral duty. While oscillating between these two spheres, Misawa, as his own remark suggests, also negotiates the two genres that intertextually lurk behind *Imotose kagami* and, more broadly, the 1880s Japanese novel: *ninjōbon* and *yomihon*. On one level, Misawa is perceived as, and truly is like, a licentious Tanjirō, but he also, to borrow Shōyō's earlier definition, has the *yomihon* hero's idealist "propensity of wanting to realize things that cannot be realized in the world": ransoming a courtesan not for the sake of pleasure but out of duty. Spurred by an anxiety about the realist representation of licentious customs and the breakdown of the artistic novel's political mission, Shōyō continued to stage a type of idealism—a "goodness"—worthy of Bakin's heroes. The incongruity, however, generates a narrative of failure: the failure of marriage, the failure of the hero's ambition and career, and Otsuji's tragic suicide. Whereas the bildungsroman à la *Karyū shunwa* could (more or less) happily reconcile the contradictory spheres of reason and passion (or idealism and realism) through the writing of a civilized marriage, the uncivilized marriage in *Mirror of Marriage* crudely lets these spheres break apart. The incongruity has become unbridgeable.

EXTREME IDEALISM, EXTREME REALISM

Imotose kagami's narrative culminating in failure was certainly not satisfactory for Shōyō. This is obvious from his next novelistic project, titled *Mirai no yume* (A dream of the future) and serialized in 1886, simultaneously with the latter part of *Imotose kagami*.[47] *Mirai no yume* differed radically from *Imotose kagami* in that it was conceived as an idealist utopia in the near future. Shōyō left the project unfinished, and the extant version offers only the beginning of the plot, but the work's general concept can be gauged from the following advertisement that appeared in the two-volume edition of *Tōsei shosei katagi* published in April 1886:

In this newly conceived work, Harunoya Sensei [Shōyō] depicts, with the brush of his imagination, the [future] state of mixed residence [with foreigners] as if one could see it with one's own eyes. At the center of the work is the story of Atsumi Kyōsuke, an eminent man who for a long time has harbored the great vision of making the country rich and who, against many hardships and struggles, attempts to strengthen Japan's commerce and bring prosperity to its manufacturing, thus elevating the country's dignity against the competition of the round-eyed [Westerners]. The novel features a politician, a novelist, an investor, a magician . . . The workings of the Diet, the transformation of customs, and the renewed state of public debates can be naturally seen in its pages. . . . This is an extremely useful new novel that contains the didactic intent of admonishment [*fūshi shōkai no gūi*] amid its playful words. You gentlemen, read it with pleasure![48]

The issue of cohabitation with foreigners (*naichi zakkyo*) was hotly debated in 1886 and 1887 in connection with the government's unsuccessful attempts to renegotiate the unequal treaties with the Western powers. The years 1887–1888 also saw the peak of production of political fiction in Japan, triggered by the intense public debates and the revival of the People's Rights Movement linked to the critique of the government failure in asserting national sovereignty vis-à-vis the West.[49] Shōyō's novel needs to be read in this context. It envisions a future after treaty revision when mixed residence with foreigners, a result of the demise of imperialist extraterritoriality, has become a reality. *Mirai no yume*, as its advertisement indicates, has a Reform Party utopian plot that depicts the results of political, social, and entrepreneurial reforms: democratic politics in the National Diet, the transformation of social customs, and successful business enterprises, all making Japan strong and prosperous against the competition of the Western powers.

Mirai no yume situates literature and the novel within a broader social utopia that comprises politics, business, and commerce. The three main protagonists are a novelist, a politician, and the successful businessman and manufacturer Atsumi Kyōsuke, who is the true hero of the novel. Atsumi is thoroughly idealistic and strives to realize his "fictitious plans" (*kakū no hōsaku*) of entrepreneurial enterprise meant to enrich and strengthen Japan. Atsumi also states the need to overcome passionate desire (*aiyoku*) in order to achieve his "great enterprise" of business and his "ideals" (*risō*).[50] *Mirai no yume* was an ambitious attempt to finally depict civilized customs and emotions, enacting the elitist Reform Party fantasy of universal reform in all major sectors of social life and national culture: art as epitomized by the novel, politics in the Diet, and business. In a sense, this was the culmination of Shōyō's literary project as conceived by *Shōsetsu shinzui*, the attempt to fulfill in the mode of the future what his previous novels could not capture in the mode of the present: the realist depiction of transformed customs.

Shōyō, however, could not but leave this novel unfinished. In an essay titled "Miraiki ni ruisuru shōsetsu" (On novels written as future records) and published in the *Yomiuri shinbun* in 1887, about one year after *Mirai no yume*'s serialization, he indirectly provides the reason for abandoning the project. He contends that recent Japanese novels about the future have successfully illustrated "the transformation of human emotion" (*ninjō no hensen*) in Japan or the "evolution of human emotion" (*ninjō no shinka*) toward a more civilized level. Although not explicitly mentioned, novels like Tetchō's recently published *Setchūbai* were probably among the titles Shōyō had in mind, besides his own work.[51] His fundamental critique of these novels is that the future transformation of a society cannot be known: "We cannot know how the Japanese people will transform in the future. We imagine that they will become more enlightened [*kaika subeshi*], but to what extent they will become enlightened is hard to say. Even a philosopher, I believe, would not be able to gauge the degree of their future enlightenment."[52] In other words, a novel like *Mirai no yume* is an idealist fantasy that fundamentally lacks realism, the depiction of Japanese society "as it is." *Mirai no yume*, the most idealist of all Shōyō's novels, could be produced only as a "future record," the intrinsic literary mode of the Reform Party political novel, but ultimately it does not withstand Shōyō's skepticism and realist impulse. The old aporia resurfaces in his abandonment of the project.

In 1888, however, the year when his reflections on the novel as future record were published, he wrote another essay, titled "On the Ideal Novel" (Aidiaru noberu no koto ni tsukite), that explicitly lauds Bakin as the model for this type of fiction in Japan.[53] Shōyō defines an ideal (*gokubi*, glossed *aidiaru*) as "what is highest in goodness and beauty" and, for a human being, as "somebody whose flawlessness cannot be conceived of as higher by the human imagination."[54] The ideal novel stages good people (*yoki hito*) as protagonists. The essay hails Samuel Richardson, Walter Scott, and Edward Bulwer-Lytton as the major authors in the West, whereas Bakin is the only noteworthy master in Japan. Moreover, Shōyō disqualifies novels that merely present humorous, realist satire (*fūshi*) as too lowly in their choice of material and unable to reach the didacticism of the ideal novel. He links this point to a scathing critique of contemporary fiction in Japan:

The current political novels or scholar and beauty novels, with the exception of two or three works, all have a didactic intent. They stage young ladies in Western dress and praise their talent, laud their virtue, and thus seem to instruct the younger generation; or they depict dauntless men of high purpose and hail their acts, foreground their achievements, and thus seem to encourage our young men. Are these not didactic novels [*shōkai shōsetsu*]? Are these not ideal novels? But beware and examine these novels closely! Those whom their authors hail as good people are talented men only on the surface, in fact they are all half-learned, dumb, and small-minded; and the women are, without exception, pseudoladies—impudent, half-educated, precocious, rash, talkative, and of little talent. . . . Figures like this can be in a satirical novel [*fūshi shōsetsu*], but [that authors] embrace the ideal novel and still display such shortcomings is truly difficult to understand![55]

The political novels or scholar and beauty novels referred to here were probably works by Reform Party–inspired authors like Sudō Nansui (1857–1920), who were themselves influenced by Shōyō's literary reform and who were prolific in the latter half of the 1880s.[56] But Shōyō's remarks probably also constitute an oblique critique of the realism in Futabatei Shimei's (1864–1909) famous novel *Ukigumo* (Floating clouds, 1887–1889), whose first two volumes had just been published. Since early in 1886, Shōyō and Futabatei had been engaged in an intense literary friendship, and Futabatei's literary experiments, particularly *Ukigumo*, were influenced by Shōyō's works. An important dimension of *Ukigumo*'s realism was indeed to satirically and didactically illustrate the shortcomings of civilized society, by staging a "pseudolady" like Osei and "talented men only on the surface"—figures like the social climber Noboru and even the male protagonist, Bunzō. At the same time, Shōyō's criticism should be seen as targeting his own earlier novels, including especially *Tōsei shosei katagi* and *Imotose kagami*.

His remarks render palpable a dislike for works that depict contemporary Japanese customs and emotions with their blatant defects and a preference for the flawless, good heroes of the ideal novel. However, it was precisely with the type of realism he despised that Shōyō continued to experiment in the late 1880s, probably influenced by Futabatei's work. His most noteworthy experiment in this vein was his last novel, *Saikun* (The wife), published in the new journal *Kokumin no tomo* in 1889.[57] This short narrative has often been hailed as a masterpiece of realism and, for this reason, as the culmination of Shōyō's development as a realist novelist.[58] This praise probably reflects the fact that there is no longer any obviously idealist element in the novel. By focusing with great realist detail and psychological insight on the sufferings of an educated upper-class woman in her unhappy marriage with a profligate husband—a gentleman and former student—who enjoys himself with a Western mistress, *Saikun* highlights the breakdown of idealism as the belief in civilizational progress. Although marriage, alluded to by the title, still serves as a signifier for enlightened gender ideals, unlike in *Imotose kagami* there is no impulse toward transformation. The novel merely depicts the failure of enlightened customs in a realist mode. This is precisely the reading that Iwamoto Yoshiharu provides in his critique published in *Jogaku zasshi*. Iwamoto writes that the novel mirrors the *real* hardships of educated women, who are aware, through their reading, of "enlightened learning," "enlightened freedom," and "enlightened male-female relationships," but then have to face the unenlightened reality of married life.[59] As a masterpiece of realism that contained an indirect social critique, *Saikun* had an important influence on the development of the Japanese social novel of the 1890s. Higuchi Ichiyō's (1872–1896) "Jūsan'ya" ("The Thirteenth Night," 1895), to name one famous example, could be seen as a rewrite of Shōyō's text. In this respect, *Saikun* was certainly a success. As Shōyō's diary entries demonstrate, however, the composition process was a source of great suffering and self-doubt, and upon completing it he officially declared the end of his writing of novels.[60] Given the mastery of *Saikun* as a realist work, critics have tended to view his decision as a contradiction. But considering his earlier promotion of the good person as protagonist and his return to Bakin as the unrivaled model for the ideal novel, the extent of his suffering in writing *Saikun* can be gauged. Like the extreme idealism of *Mirai no yume*, the extreme realism of *Saikun* must have felt a failure.

After abandoning the novel, Shōyō famously turned to the reform of drama and a lifelong engagement with the study and translation of Shakespeare's plays. While bringing an end to his frustration with novel writing, this engagement also offered a solution to the aporia in representation of realist and idealist elements that had complicated his novelistic and critical project. In a series of remarkable essays published in 1890–1892, produced in the context of his literary "debate over submerged ideals" (*botsurisō ronsō*) with Mori Ōgai, he came to conceive of a synthesis of realism and idealism through Shakespeare's work. For one, he devised a new notion of realism that considerably broadened his earlier notion of *mosha*. Shakespeare's realism, to Shōyō, did not merely depict the limited details or "particularities" (*tokushusō*) of a historical locale, as previous Japanese novels had done, but could replicate nature in its "universality" (*fuhensō*).[61] What Shōyō meant includes the following: "Although taking their names from old England or ancient Rome, Shakespeare's plays depict their Elizabethan present. But since Shakespeare is a born poet and fortunately not the slave of small ideals, his descriptions follow the Creator's universe, thus even moving our intellect and emotions today and, between the lines, foretelling our future."[62] Encompassing past, present, and future and the universe's entire nature, Shakespeare's realism is truly universal.

This realism is also not devoid of ideals, although it is not idealist. Shōyō brings this important distinction to the point in the following way: "When I say that Shakespeare greatly resembles nature, I do not mean that the events and figures he describes are the same as in reality [*jissai no ni onaji*]. That his works can be interpreted in myriad ways by his readers greatly resembles the universe's Creator."[63] The argument is that Shakespeare's plays resemble the natural world (reality) insofar as an infinity of interpretations (*kaishaku*) can be projected onto them, in the same way as myriad human ideals have attempted to explain the natural world. Shakespeare's universal realism does not uphold any single ideal—as an individual author with individual ideals he disappears in his works—but it can contain and "submerge" all the various ideals or interpretations that his readers have projected onto him. In a parable titled "A Famous Place in the World of Letters: The Bottomless Lake" (Bunkai meisho: Soko shirazu no mizuumi, 1891), Shōyō compares nature to a vast ocean and Shakespeare to a big lake into which all conceivable human ideals—Christianity, Buddhism, modern science, and unlearned superstitions—are successively submerged without ever exhausting the watery space.[64] This is precisely the meaning of his new concept of "submerged ideals." He writes, "When I say that Shakespeare submerges ideals, I of course do not mean that he is without ideals, but I also do not mean that he has superhuman or great ideals. I mean that the many ideals his critics think to be his are not his own and that his own ideals cannot be easily seen.[65]

The universal realism that Shōyō finds in Shakespeare is, by the same token, a universal idealism that does not herald any ideal in particular but contains and sublates them all. By a remarkable dialectical movement, Shōyō finds in Shakespeare's work a synthesis that will allow him to transcend the old realism-idealism aporia, one that contains both realist and idealist impulses without being caught by their inherent limitations. This is the deeper significance of Shōyō's thought experiment that Ōgai and later critics have tended to ignore.[66] Moreover, he came to believe that drama, more than the novel, could realistically represent protagonists in their universal fullness without the mediation of the author's ideals and thus submerge them. He argues that *King Lear*, written as a novel, would not fundamentally differ from *Hakkenden*. *Hakkenden*'s heroes, although some seem realistic, are always predicated on the ideal of *kanzen chōaku* of Bakin the author. Only a dramatic format could free them from *kanzen chōaku* while leaving this ideal submerged as a potential standard of interpretation alongside others.[67] Although perhaps not entirely persuasive, this argument shows that Shōyō came to see the novel as a limited form bound by the realist depiction of historical particularities and the author's individual "small ideals" (*shō-risō*). Shakespeare, on the contrary, encompasses the entirety of the universe's creation—past, present, and future—and thus sublates all particularistic realist details and small ideals, thus achieving a universality that the novel as a form will never fulfill. The promise of this synthesis drove Shōyō into his new obsession with Shakespeare and theater reform that would occupy him more or less for the rest of his life.

That Shōyō should have enjoyed the relief of a synthesis is a comforting idea, but what most concerns me here is that the aporia complicating his literary project in the 1880s and underlying his efforts at synthesis again brought to the fore the tensions surrounding the imagination of the novel's social danger and value in a broader nineteenth-century perspective. Shōyō's "particularistic" realism focusing on foolish passion—not yet civilized *ninjō* and *setai*—revived the anxiety about the novel's potential to instill licentious desire in readers, like a *ninjōbon*, and to annihilate the genre's artistic and didactic mission. At the same time, his idealist attempt to stage good people as protagonists, also as a response to this anxiety, extended the notion of the novel's sociopolitical legitimacy, most notably defined by Bakin, into the ideological parameters of Meiji civilization and enlightenment. Shōyō's inability to reconcile the contradiction between these realist and idealist spheres, like the previous bildungsroman à la *Seiro nikki*, only radicalized earlier tensions in the Japanese novel, for instance those in Bakin's work. As shown in the next chapter, Shōyō's literary project and its contradictions continued to influence the literary and critical field in the 1890s and beyond. While *ninjō* became a major concept underlying the novel and literature more broadly in the wake of Shōyō's reform, it also continued to be seen as problematic content, engendering narrative practices that aimed at containing its potential danger.

PART III
Late-Meiji Questionings

Chapter Six

NINJŌ AND THE LATE-MEIJI NOVEL

Recontextualizing Sōseki's Literary Project

Natsume Sōseki is widely thought of today as one of the greatest novelists of modern Japan, but it is less well known that throughout his writing career he was highly ambivalent, if not suspicious, of the novel and may not have even thought of himself as a novelist. An early masterpiece by Sōseki is the acclaimed *Wagahai wa neko de aru* (*I Am a Cat*, 1905–1906), which he labeled *shaseibun* (sketch prose).[1] In his short essay "Shaseibun" (1907), a key reflection on his literary writing, Sōseki defined the difference between *shaseibun* and the novel in primarily emotional or affective terms. He argues that the novelist is strongly affected by, or drawn into, his or her characters and their emotions. The stance of the *shaseibun* author, on the contrary, is one of gentle and humorous detachment, like that of a parent toward a child. Even if the child cries, Sōseki remarks, a good parent does not cry with the child. Similarly, the *shaseibun* author observes and describes (or "sketches") his or her figures and their emotions—their love, their tears, their greed— not coldly but with amused interest, unlike the novelist, who passionately sheds tears together with his or her characters.[2] In short, Sōseki envisions the *shaseibun* genre in emotional terms as a type of prose writing that allows for more affective distance from the narrated world and its emotions than the novel.

Sōseki defines the novel in reference to *ninjō*, through its propensity not only to represent emotions ("tears") but also to incite them in readers and even authors. This generic understanding must be contextualized in the literary and discursive space of the late Meiji postdating Tsubouchi Shōyō's reform of fiction. The realist depiction (*mosha*) of emotions and customs (*ninjō setai*), key to Shōyō's critical discourse, had become the major concept defining the novel as a genre. Concurrently, discussions beginning in the 1890s promoted a new understanding of literature (*bungaku*) as imaginative writing focused on the representation and expression of emotion, particularly love and desire. In his 1907 essay, Sōseki complicates this understanding by conceiving of *shaseibun* as a genre that belongs to literature as a type of writing representing and mediating emotion, but in a more detached fashion than the novel. In other words, he defines *shaseibun* as a genre less exposed to *ninjō* and its dangers. Sōseki's interest in *shaseibun* in the first decade of the twentieth century idiosyncratically reconfigures the earlier awareness of *ninjō* as the problematic, if not licentious, core of the novel and literature more broadly.

This chapter has two goals. First, it surveys the discourses through which a focus on *ninjō* became constitutive of the Meiji novel and the concept of literature in the wake of Shōyō's reform. I outline the increasingly sentimental aesthetic of the novel to which Sōseki refers by highlighting the genre's tearful quality. I also trace the contemporaneous transformation of the literature concept. Critical discourses in the 1890s continued to denounce the novel for depicting frivolous love and failing to promote moral and social ideals, thus extending Shōyō's suspicion about the novel's realism. At the same time, an increasingly naturalized, new understanding of literature based on the categories of emotion and love (*ren'ai*) made the traditional anxieties about *ninjō* recede into the background. It was in reaction to these developments that the notions of *shasei* (sketching) and *shaseibun*, first promoted by Sōseki's friend and poetic mentor Masaoka Shiki (1867–1902), emerged around the turn of the century. *Shaseibun* presented an alternative type of prose that, instead of on love and desire often focused on the natural landscape as well as human beings and their emotions embedded in that landscape. This allowed for an affectively more detached narratorial stance that questioned the naturalized primacy of emotion in contemporary literary discourse.

The chapter then moves to the literary and critical writings by Sōseki that elaborated on *shaseibun* and its critique of the novel and literature. Sōseki's interest in *shaseibun* was part of a broader theoretical and literary project that sought to redefine, with a strong awareness of the contemporary novel and in distinction from it, various genres of literature in terms of their capacity to represent, express, or relate to emotion. While previous scholarship has pointed to Sōseki's resistance to the novel, his appropriation of the discourse on emotion in an attempt to experiment with alternative genres or literary modes in distinction from the novel and the newly naturalized regime of literature has been largely overlooked.[3]

My discussion focuses on Sōseki's experimental work *Kusamakura* (The grass pillow, 1906) and on his critical writings, demonstrating that throughout these works he engaged in a persistent investigation of the ways in which literary writing in general and specific genres in particular mediate and produce emotion. *Kusamakura* is a text that critically highlights, in exemplary fashion, various genres—*shaseibun*, haiku, *kanshi* (Sinitic poetry), and even English verse—as literary media representing and conveying emotion. The work's narration performs and investigates the emotionally loaded quality of these genres, probing and dramatizing their relative proximity to, but also their distance from, the novel and new literature concept. I also examine how a similar investigation lies at the heart of Sōseki's critical writings, in particular his seminal treatise *Bungakuron* (Theory of literature, 1907) and essay "Sōsakuka no taido" (The attitude of the literary writer, 1908). These texts theorize literature in general as well as specific literary modes in terms of their capacity to represent and convey emotion, and they thus complement the *Kusamakura* project in important ways. In particular, I pay attention to the literary mode that Sōseki, in highly idiosyncratic fashion, defines as "idealist" or "romantic." In *Bungakuron*, he subsumes under this label those writings that, unlike the novel, do not exclusively focus on the human element but instead juxtapose, as did haiku and Sinitic poetry or *shaseibun* prose, the human element with the landscape. This juxtaposition allows for a more indirect representation of emotions than that found in what he defines as the "realist method" (*shajitsuhō*) of the novel, with its exclusive focus on human content. At the same time, he argues that the emotional impact on the reader produced by idealist or romantic texts is stronger than that engendered by realist writings.

While *Bungakuron* meticulously defines the criteria that enhance or reduce the emotional impact of literary texts, *Kusamakura* consciously highlights, reflects, and objectifies the amount of emotion inherent in the various genres that it performs. *Kusamakura* itself constitutes a literary

performance of Sōseki's theoretical writings. At the same time, his analytical deconstruction of various literary modes and genres, including the
novel, highlights their commonality as literature that represents emotion.
Sōseki's project was to define literature as a universal category that could
potentially subsume all genres. It sought to deconstruct, but also to reinte-
grate, the new Meiji discourses on the novel and literature, thus attempting
to come to terms with *ninjō* as literature's increasingly naturalized core.

TOWARD THE TEARFUL NOVEL

As noted, Shōyō's notion of the realist depiction of emotion and customs
became a major concept in critical discussions surrounding the novel
throughout the 1890s and beyond. The mainstream of the Japanese novel
in the wake of Shōyō's reform emerged as what literary historian Hiraoka
Toshio has labeled "novels of human emotion and social customs" (*ninjō
setai shōsetsu*), revolving around plots of love, often with the satirical depiction of manners.[4] The most important and one of the earliest examples
was Futabatei Shimei's novel *Ukigumo*. Owing to its experimentation with
genbun itchi (literally, unification of the spoken and written languages), the
modern Japanese vernacular style, and its exploration of the hero's delu-
sional interiority, this novel has traditionally been hailed as the first Japanese masterwork of psychological realism.[5] But influenced by Shōyō,
Futabatei's novel also critically highlighted the shortcomings of modern
civilization in a plot of failed romance. As in Shōyō's works, the realist
depiction of *ninjō* and *setai* was here largely synonymous with what contemporary criticism qualified as "satire" (*fūshi*), the partly humorous depiction of not yet civilized, licentious gender relations and customs. Another
early work in a satirical vein was written by Miyake Kaho (1868–1944), a
young female writer, and titled *Yabu no uguisu* (*Warbler in the Grove*, 1887).
This was the stated rewriting of Shōyō's *Tōsei shosei katagi* with upper-class
female students as protagonists, a literary experiment that critically engaged
with the new enlightenment ideals surrounding marriage and love. Like
Ukigumo, it also shed a satirical light on the depravity of superficially
enlightened customs.[6]

The major upsurge in the production of novels of human emotion and
social customs began in the late 1880s. The years 1889 and 1890 were particularly important, witnessing, among other works, the publication of

Mori Ōgai's *Maihime* (*The Dancing Girl*, 1890), which restaged, fully aware of Shōyō's critical ideas, the bildungsroman's contradictions.[7] The work is about a young elite Japanese bureaucrat who, while studying in Berlin, starts a relationship with a local uneducated dancing girl, neglecting his studies and almost giving up his career in service of the nation. Although he ultimately leaves the pregnant woman behind and embraces a career in Japan, his decision produces resentment (*urami*) in him that keeps validating his passion. The resentment also motivates him to write a first-person memoir—the text of *Maihime*—that reflects on the unsolvable inner conflict between love and ambition. This conflict subsequently became a major indicator for *Maihime*'s modernity, cementing the text's literary-historical fame, as it epitomized the emergence of the modern individual as the subject of passion resisting subjection to social utility and the nation. Love here did not refer so much anymore to licentious customs but instead signified the individual's enlightened freedom challenging social and moral norms.[8]

Maihime's lasting fame notwithstanding, the most immediately influential appropriation of Shōyō's ideas was by Ozaki Kōyō (1867–1903) and the group of young authors around him known as the Ken'yūsha (Friends of the Inkstone Society).[9] The most widely read novelist throughout the 1890s until his death in 1903, Kōyō cemented his fame with *Ninin bikuni: Iro zange* (Two nuns: A love confession, 1889). He started this short piece of historical fiction, centering on two beautiful young nuns who tearfully reminisce about their love for the same man, with a prefatory remark that boldly redirected Shōyō's terms: "The main focus of this novel is on tears" (*Kono shōsetsu wa namida o shugan to su*).[10] Kōyō's reappropriation of Shōyō's famous dictum ("the main focus of the novel is on human emotion") epitomized the increasingly sentimental quality of the new realist novel in the 1890s. This type of fiction formed the new mainstream of novels of human emotions and social customs, from the largely Ken'yūsha-based Shincho hyakushu series (1889–1891) well beyond the turn of the century—what Ken Ito has aptly called "an age of melodrama."[11]

The novel in the late nineteenth century thus underwent a subtle qualitative shift. Throughout the 1890s and later, the earlier enlightenment and civilizational anxieties about *ninjō* receded to the background. This was linked to the broader sociocultural climate marked by the consolidation of the Meiji nation-state, perceived by many as a major civilizational achievement.

With the promulgation of the Meiji Constitution and the opening of the National Diet in 1890, Japan's successive victories in the Sino-Japanese and Russo-Japanese Wars, and the revision of the unequal treaties, completely realized in the early twentieth century, the need to civilize and enlighten, to become on a par with the Western powers, was less acutely felt. Instead, other issues surfaced, especially "social problems" (*shakai mondai*) that Carol Gluck has identified as the central concern of ideological discourse in the late Meiji period—problems of the family, social class, or the capitalist divide of poverty and wealth that also increasingly dominated novels.[12] The mode of representation for these problems in 1890s novels, often in conjunction with the representation of gender relations and love, tended to be sentimental or melodramatic, as in works by authors as famous as Izumi Kyōka (1873–1939), Higuchi Ichiyō, and Kunikida Doppo (1871–1908). The depiction of sentiment was often predicated on a social critique that in Doppo's case was even close to socialist concerns.[13] At the same time, *ninjō* became discussed in terms of a literature that incites both readers and novelists to tears.

Another aspect of the novel's new focus on sentiment was its increasing commercialization, in response to the development of a mass readership associated with widely distributed new magazines and an ever-expanding newspaper industry. Kōyō's cooperation with the *Yomiuri shinbun* was emblematic of this development. Two particularly successful examples of turn-of-the-century melodramatic novels published in newspapers were Tokutomi Roka's *Hototogisu* (Cuckoo, 1898–1899) and Kōyō's *Konjiki yasha* (Gold demon, 1897–1903).[14] *Hototogisu* culminated in the tearful death of the heroine, forced by an unfeeling mother-in-law to divorce her loving husband because of her tuberculosis. *Konjiki yasha* sensationally weighed the lure of capital against the power of passion. In *Kusamakura*, Sōseki pointed to these two contemporary works as typical examples of the novel as a genre.[15] It was melodramatic works of this kind, in addition to Western novels with which he was familiar as an English-literature scholar, that Sōseki had in mind when, in his 1907 essay on *shaseibun*, he characterized the novelist as passionately crying with his or her characters. His suspicion was thus directed against a novel of human emotion and social customs, whose tearful and sensational sentimentality, focused on love and social problems, had become the genre's increasingly naturalized core.

TOWARD A LITERATURE OF EMOTION

Concurrently, the concept of *bungaku* underwent a transformation by which it came to refer to a mode of textuality expressing and representing emotion. Traditionally, *bungaku* had designated mainly the study of the Confucian classics and the highbrow literacy of Sinitic poetry and prose, genres ascribed social, moral, and political value.[16] It was still from the perspective of such an understanding that contemporary discussions criticized the new novel in the 1890s. Various critics, even those who were rather open to Shōyō's reform and the novel's focus on *ninjō*, attacked the "smallness" of recent fiction and its frivolous love and tears, claiming the need for a "great" literature with moral and civilizational standards that would benefit the nation.[17]

For example, in an essay titled "Bungaku sekai no kinkyō" (The current state of the world of literature, 1890), an anonymous author bemoaned the fact that novelists depict the tears of beautiful women and "small love" (*shōai*) instead of the "great love for the nation and the people" and the tears of men of high purpose (*shishi*).[18] In the same year, the important critic Kitamura Tōkoku (1868–1894) wrote the following:

The novels by Aeba Kōson [1855–1922] seem to satirically criticize customs in the world, but ultimately they are not better than the product of an inebriated brush.[19] Kōyō skillfully depicts human emotion in an old-fashioned way, but his skillfulness ends there, and no other particular light is to be seen in his writings. How talented are the authors in the literary world! Their wondrous ability to understand the principle of love [*aijō no tetsuri*] and to write long novels [about it] truly deserves our admiration. It is true that there is nothing greater than love [*airen*] in the great universe, and its exploration is the novelist's duty. But I also do not believe that the novelist's duty simply ends there. There is no difference between the hero of literature and the hero of arms. If he does not have the courage to drink up the four oceans, the strength to have great ideas containing the whole universe, it will be hard for him to become a hero of letters [*moji no eiyū*]. Does fearfully scrutinizing the small details of the world and piling up beautifully embroidered words fulfill the duty of a man of letters?[20]

Tōkoku's ambivalence is worth noting, as his essay subsumes the novel and its representation of love under the conceptual banner of *bungaku* while emphasizing the need to embrace "great ideas" worthy of a "hero of arms," transcending love and the novel. Tōkoku agreed with Shōyō's reform and recognized the importance of *Tōsei shosei katagi* as a new model for the novel depicting emotions and customs, but without the expression of great ideas, in his view largely absent in Shōyō's texts, such literature would remain superficial and problematic. Iwamoto Yoshiharu, too, while not rejecting novels depicting emotion emphasized the need for ideals (*risō*), which he understood in the vein of the ideas propagated by earlier political fiction.[21] Tōkoku's and Iwamoto's views were symptomatic of the literary criticism in the wake of Shōyō that acknowledged the realist depiction of *ninjō* in the novel while asserting the moral-didactic necessity of a literature of great ideas. These debates clearly replicated Shōyō's own concern with the novel's idealism that could not be fulfilled by the mere depiction of vulgar customs and licentious love. In 1898, critic Uchida Roan still urged novelists to turn their attention away from the world of love (*ren'ai sekai*) and instead write political fiction. Roan valued realism (*shajitsu*), but instead of love the type of novel he promoted should realistically and satirically depict the politics of the new Diet.[22]

Out of their awareness of the idealist limitations of the novel, critics like Iwamoto, Tokutomi Sohō, and Tōkoku devised the new concept of the "poet" (*shijin*) as a transcendent savior figure that could embrace the political and social ideals that contemporary fiction lacked. Sohō, whose rhetoric was informed by his Christian faith, defined the poet as a "purifier, preacher, teacher, comforter, and transformer of human society."[23] Tōkoku's thought experiment of the poet was even more radical and derived from a new type of transcendent inner experience predicated on religion (Christianity) and love.[24] Ironically, one of the major concepts that became associated with the poet and literature through Tōkoku was love (*ren'ai*). In his essay "Ensei shika to josei" (The disillusioned poet and women, 1892), published in *Jogaku zasshi*, Tōkoku famously exclaimed, "Love is the secret key to life. Only after there is love is there a human world; without love, human life would be flavorless."[25] In this essay with a deep impact on contemporary and later readers, Tōkoku postulates love as the totalizing, spiritual experience of the poet, opposed to the licentiousness depicted by "pseudo-novelists." Love is also the "citadel giving refuge to the defeated general of the world of ideas."[26] This points to the important continuum of Tōkoku's social and political ideals, especially those of the People's Rights Movement, in which he had been involved as a youth.[27] However, Tōkoku also asserts the irreconcilability between love and society as epitomized by marriage, which "vulgarizes" love, producing the poet's "disillusionment." Unlike earlier enlightenment discussions linking civilized love to marriage, as well as the family and the nation, Tōkoku reverts to a notion of absolute passion irreducible to social norms. This spiritual transcendence of the poet as the subject of love radically widened Shōyō's earlier notion of the realist depiction of *ninjō* in the novel. However, both together became greatly influential in redefining *bungaku*, now including chiefly poetry and the novel, as concerned with the representation of emotion and love.

Even before the publication of Tōkoku's essay, however, and under the impact of Shōyō's reform, a new discourse had started to emphasize the emotional and imaginative quality of literary writing. In the first literary history of Japan, published in 1890, the university graduates Mikami Sanji (1865–1939) and Takatsu Kuwasaburō (1864–1921) defined "pure literature" (*junbungaku*) as what "skillfully expresses thought, emotion, and imagination."[28] Their broader notion of *bungaku* comprised the humanities in general, including disciplines like history, philosophy, and political science.[29] But they also specified that especially emotion (*kanjō*) and imagination (*sōzō*), rather than thought, befit literature in the narrower sense of pure literature—a term they use in reference mainly to poetry (*shiika*) and the novel (*shōsetsu*).[30] Writing in 1890, Mikami and Takatsu were clearly aware of the recent boom in novels of emotion and customs following Shōyō's reform.[31] Unlike other contemporary discourses, they referred to emotion and imagination as positive qualities. But like Shōyō and other critics, they also highlighted the need for a didactic "great purpose" and "practical benefit" of literature in "elevating the spirit of the nation."

However, it was only with Tōkoku's discourse and its wider dissemination through the writings of the young authors associated with the romantic movement in the 1890s that the narrower concept of "pure literature," defined primarily by emotion and love, became naturalized as literature *tout court*.[32] This process was more or less completed by the time Fujioka Sakutarō (1870–1910) published his comprehensive history of Heian literature in 1905, shortly after Japan's victory in the Russo-Japanese War. This study presents an already established notion of literature predicated on emotion (*jōshu*) as love. Historically, Fujioka finds this notion exemplified in its purest form in works like *The Tale of Genji*. He privileges the Heian period as an "age of emotion" that valued love over moral righteousness and beauty over goodness, and he notes that Heian courtiers were able to live an "aesthetic life" (*biteki seikatsu*) grounded in emotion, nature, and the "satisfaction of instincts" (*honnō no manzoku*).[33] The term "aesthetic life" had been coined by the young critic Takayama Chogyū (1871–1902), who appropriated Tōkoku's notions of love and the poet in a more specifically turn-of-the-century context. Chogyū had been influenced by his eclectic readings of Nietzsche and fin de siècle European authors like Zola, Sudermann, and Ibsen, and he wrote essays that provocatively questioned contemporary civilization and its values, including morality and truth.[34] He promoted instead the new formula of an aesthetic life based on the pursuit of beauty, nature, individuality, love, and the satisfaction of instincts, including sexual desire. He particularly highlighted love as "one of the most beautiful" aspects of the aesthetic life, and he saw the poet and artist (*bijutsuka*) as privileged subjects to realize it.[35]

Chogyū's essays and their reception by literary historian Fujioka Sakutarō were part of the discursive production of the new literature concept in the wake of Shōyō and Tōkoku. Like Tōkoku and other romantic critics, Chogyū continued to emphasize the high-cultural significance of literature, the "sublime and grand calling" of the literary writer (*bungakusha*) and poet as critics of contemporary civilization and culture (he uses the German term *Kulturkritiker*). He also dismissed contemporary Japanese novelists for their inability to pursue high "ideals."[36] However, unlike earlier critics, Chogyū attacked the Japanese novel not for its depiction of small love but for its inability to engage in the critique of civilization and to embrace the aesthetic life grounded in love and the satisfaction of instincts. By the early twentieth century, emotion and love as the content of literature had become naturalized and were no longer perceived as licentious.

The most radical formulation of this new understanding was provided by the critical discourse and literary writings of so-called naturalism (*shizenshugi*) in the first decade of the twentieth century. Influenced, like Chogyū, by contemporary European authors like Zola and Nietzsche, naturalist critics equally promoted terms like nature (*shizen*) and instincts, but instead of emphasizing beauty and the aesthetic life, they highlighted the need to depict desire, even if ugly, dark, and animalistic.[37] For example, in the afterword to his 1902 novel *Jigoku no hana* (The flowers of hell), the young Nagai Kafū (1879–1959), under the spell of Zolaism, expressed his determination to "vividly depict without hesitation the multiple dark facets of desire [jōyoku], aggression, and sexual violence resulting from the [figures'] milieu and ancestral heredity."[38] Other critics and writers hailed the power of nature and sexual instincts while relativizing socioethical norms. In his acclaimed 1902 novel *Jūemon no saigo* (*The End of Jūemon*), which cemented his fame as a naturalist author, Tayama Katai (1871–1930) celebrated the abnormal sexuality and the criminal, antisocial violence of his protagonist as manifestations of the "greatness of nature," thus realizing in a slightly altered sense Chogyū's earlier call for literature as a critique of civilization. In distinction from the earlier 1890s and turn-of-the-century sentimental novels of human emotion and social customs, naturalist novels and criticism brought back an explicit focus on sexual passion reminiscent of Shōyō's discourse. But, whereas for Shōyō and other critics such a focus recalled the *ninjōbon*'s problematic licentiousness, naturalist criticism came to literally naturalize it as an artistic program.

The naturalization of emotion—tearful sentiment, spiritual love, or dark sexualized passion—as the novel's and literature's new core was the context for the emergence of *shasei* and *shaseibun*. *Shaseibun* has often been discussed in terms of its promotion of realism and the *genbun itchi* style, but it also presented a literary mode of mediating emotion in a way that radically differed from the novel and what contemporary discourses postulated about literature.[39] In his essay "Jojibun" (On narrative description, 1900), for instance, Masaoka Shiki defined the object of *shasei* as either natural landscape (*keshiki*) or human affairs (*jinji*).[40] He argued that the lively narrative description or realist depiction (*mosha* or *shajitsu*)—that is, the "sketching"—of natural objects and human beings, when freed from the conventions of traditional poetic diction, would have great power to move the reader. This type of narrative prose did not revolve around plots of *ninjō* but instead highlighted the visuality of narrative description, which treated human beings more distantly like a landscape or, as Shiki emphasized, part of a "painting" (*kaiga*) of a landscape.[41] Similarly, in Kunikida Doppo's "Wasureenu hitobito" ("Those Unforgettable People," 1898), the narrator predicates his sketches (*suketchi*) of nature on a stance that distances the human beings encountered in the landscape. His "unforgettable people" are ironically those who lack individualized features and do not affect him emotionally.

While appropriating loaded terms like "nature" and "realist depiction," *shaseibun* discourse gave them a radically different significance. Instead of using *shajitsu* and *mosha* in reference to *ninjō* and *setai*, Shiki applied these terms to the depiction of natural objects or human beings as embedded in the landscape. His notion of "nature" (*tennen*) also did not refer to instincts or sexual desire. He instead realigned it with traditional poetic discourse, where the categories of landscape (*kei*) and emotion (*jō*) had been interlocked.[42] This reflected the aesthetics of premodern poetic genres—Sinitic poetry, *waka*, and haiku—that, rather than directly expressing emotions, often represented them through the mediation of natural imagery. This aesthetics allowed for a more indirect and subdued representation of emotions than in the novel. In classical *waka*, for instance, love (*koi*) was, together with the four seasons, a major topic of poetic composition, expressed mostly in conjunction with natural tropes.[43] Haiku, while less focused on love, as a rule juxtaposed human topics with seasonal tropes, often in a humorous manner.[44] Sinitic landscape poetry differed from both *waka* and haiku by more strongly relying on an allegorical reading mode that saw in natural metaphors the expression of the poet's moral and political feelings.

Both Shiki and Sōseki were highly proficient in haiku and Sinitic poetry (Shiki also in *waka*), and these genres' poetic sensibility lay at the heart of their notion of *shasei*. Shiki, however, did not explicitly reflect on the distinction between *shaseibun* and the novel or the newly naturalized concept of literature. It was Sōseki who, in his essay "Shaseibun," first theorized the sketcher's stance toward the sketched human beings as emotionally more detached than the stance of the novelist, thus reappropriating the discourse on emotion that had hitherto been connected to the novel and literature. Sōseki had been experimenting with *shaseibun* prose from the turn of the century, and he cemented his fame as a literary author with the novel-length serialization of *Wagahai wa neko de aru* starting in 1905.[45] His *shaseibun* texts indeed focused on what Shiki called human affairs, although less on landscape, in an affectively more detached mode mediated by humor, carefully distancing, even marginalizing, the theme of love that had been central to the novel.[46] This experimentation was part of a broader critical investigation of literature through the lens of emotion. *Kusamakura* participated in this investigation while bringing back to the foreground, unlike Sōseki's other early works, Shiki's discourse on *shaseibun* that privileged landscape and nature, as well as painting and poetry. But *Kusamakura* ironically performed and parodied this discourse, thus investigating its critical parameters.

THE PERFORMANCE OF LITERATURE IN *KUSAMAKURA*

Kusamakura constitutes a performance of *shaseibun* prose that highlights constitutive elements of the genre.[47] The narrator is an unnamed young male painter in the Western style and a poet.[48] Traveling through the natural landscape of Kyushu, his stated goal is to not be strongly affected by the people and human affairs (*jinji*) that he encounters during his journey, thus seeking to realize the emotionally detached state that Sōseki envisioned for the *shaseibun* author.

An artist traveling through nature in the pursuit of beauty, an "aesthetic life" of sorts, Sōseki's narrator parodically reenacts postromantic discourse. Ironically, however, what he seeks is not love and the satisfaction of instincts but detachment. He aims to experience human affairs or human emotion without becoming directly involved with them and by only sketching them in his landscape paintings, in his poetry, and in his *shaseibun* prose; he even goes so far as to specify that he will observe a distance of three feet between himself and the figures in his painting. His assumption is that this distant way of approaching the world will enable him to overcome the "suffering" (*kurushimi*) inherent in deep involvement with human affairs and that his encounter with the world will thus be rendered "charming" (*omoshiroi*). He states, "When I walk through the mountains and approach the objects of the natural landscape [*shizen no keibutsu*], all that I see and hear is charming. It is merely charming, and no pain whatsoever arises. . . . But why is it that there is no pain involved? This is because I am viewing the landscape just as I would see the scroll of a painting or read a volume of poetry."[49] A bit later, he also claims, "I intend to treat the human beings that I will encounter—farmers, village people, the clerks at the village office, old men, and old women—without exception as accessory figures in the big landscape of nature. . . . It is my design to observe the people whom I will now encounter at my leisure from a high vantage point so that there will be no electric current of human emotion [*ninjō no denki*] between us."[50]

Sōseki's presentation in *Kusamakura* of the narrator's discourse and the *shaseibun* genre is both performative and ironic, constantly testing the limits of his postulated narratorial distance toward human affairs and the possibility of its being breached. At the beginning, for instance, the narrator stumbles over a stone on his path, which serves as a physical reminder that the landscape his discourse sought to reduce to the status of aesthetic artifact is capable of impacting him in painful ways.[51] The stone, however, is only a metaphorical anticipation of the alluring and mysterious woman Nami, who jeopardizes the young man's emotional detachment after he encounters her at the hot spring resort Nakoi. Nami, in other words, threatens to drag him into the suffering of love and desire. Her presence in *Kusamakura* serves a highly self-reflexive and critical purpose. Through his narrator's increasing attraction to Nami, Sōseki investigates the subtle line of demarcation between *shaseibun* prose and the novel. Were the narrator's affective distance to break down—were he to enter a love relationship with Nami and suffer—*Kusamakura*'s *shaseibun* prose would instantaneously transform into the plot of a novel, staging tearful sentiments or sexual passion. Although constantly playing with the possibility of such a turn, Sōseki consciously avoids it and instead continues to probe the ambiguous line between detachment and affective involvement, or *shaseibun* and the novel.

In a similar fashion, the narrator also investigates other genres as literary forms that might convey his attraction to Nami in a more detached fashion than is possible via the plot of a novel. He explores genres such as haiku, English verse, and Sinitic poetry as media of expression for precisely the type of emotion that had been most strongly associated with the novel and literature: male-female love. His exploration of haiku is particularly interesting, as it introduces the notion of objectivity, a central idea in *Kusamakura* with regard to the performance of various literary genres as emotionally detached modes of expression. The narrator asserts that any strong feeling, for instance one's reaction to an event initially experienced as frightening, can be turned into poetry or painting and thus placed at an emotional distance if it is viewed "objectively" (*kyakkanteki*). If thus severed from the poet's immediate experience, strong feelings such as heartbreak (*shitsuren*) can be transformed into an appropriate topic for painting and poetry because the initial suffering inherent in the feeling has been excised, with only its "gentle" aspect and less-violent emotions such as compassion and sorrow remaining.[52]

For example, on the night of his arrival at the Nakoi hot spring resort, *Kusamakura*'s narrator confronts the following scene: Nami, to tease him, hides in a dark corner of the garden and uncannily intonates a *waka* allegedly composed by a madwoman who once inhabited the place.[53] Under the influence of Nami's "frightening" performance, the narrator composes the following haiku poems:

春の夜の雲に濡らすや洗ひ髪

Haru no yo no / kumo ni nurasu ya / araigami

(The spring night's clouds dampen the [woman's] freshly washed [and untied] hair!)

春や今宵歌つかまつる御姿

Haru ya koyoi / uta tsukamatsuru / onsugata

(This spring night [I see] an elegant form humbly offering a poem [to me].)[54]

In these poems, the narrator's feelings triggered by Nami—his attraction and his fright—are encapsulated in expressions like "freshly washed hair" and "an elegant form." Such images point to the aspect of human affairs, or the danger of emotional entanglement, in the poems. At the same time, these faintly eroticized expressions are set alongside natural imagery such as the "clouds," which, through elegant poetic superimposition, seem to fuse with and dampen the woman's hair. The objectification of feeling through poetry, as theorized by *Kusamakura*'s narrator, consists of this merger of human affairs (and emotions) with specific objects in the landscape, which also reduces the intensity inherent in emotion and renders it gentle and even elegant. However, although poetry thus produces detachment, the narrator's discourse on objectivity and his poetic compositions simultaneously highlight haiku composition as a medium that carries erotic attraction.

Sōseki's narrator even amplifies the dynamic of self-reflexive emotional objectification by quoting English poetic intertexts. A good example is George Meredith's (1828–1909) poem "Sadder than is the moon's lost light," which first appeared in Meredith's novel *The Shaving of Shagpat: An Arabian Entertainment* (1856). In *Kusamakura*, the first two stanzas of the poem are cited in the English original after a scene in which the narrator has unexpectedly encountered Nami's seductive gaze. After a brief moment of intense silent communication and Nami's sudden withdrawal from the scene, the narrator reflects in the following manner:

Suddenly what came to my mind was the following poem:
> Sadder than is the moon's lost light,
>> Lost ere the kindling of dawn,
>> To travellers journeying on,
> The shutting of thy fair face from my sight.

If I were in love [*kesō shite*] with the woman [Nami] wearing the gingko-leaf hairstyle [*ichōgaeshi*] and wished to meet her at all costs and if, shortly before being able to meet her, I had to part from her with this one glance that, so overwhelmingly unexpected, would fill me with joy and regret, I think I would compose exactly such a poem. And I would probably also add these two lines [from the same poem]:
> Might I look on thee in death,
> With bliss I would yield my breath.

Luckily, I have already left behind me the realm of what is called longing or love [*koi to ka ai to ka iu kyōgai*], and even if I wished to feel this kind of suffering I could not. But the poetic flavor [*shishu*] of the incident that just occurred now for a brief moment is very well captured in these five or six lines. Even without such a painful longing between me and the woman with the gingko-leaf hairstyle, it would still be charming to match our current relationship to the content of this poem. Or it would also be pleasing to interpret the meaning of this poem with our case as an illustration.[55]

In this scene, a dynamic of objectification unfolds, similar to the one that was possible with the haiku poetry previously. Strong feelings that could potentially develop between the narrator and Nami are transposed into and contained within the poem so that the real relationship remains playful and "charming." Whereas the haiku objectified their composer's feelings by reducing their intensity and rendering them gentle, Meredith's poem introduces a strongly subjective first-person voice, absent in the haiku, that intensifies the feeling of longing not only by dramatically staging a determination to die but also by producing an intense dialogue between the male speaker and his imagined female interlocutor.

The narrator's reflections in this scene resonate with Sōseki's "theory of literary distance" (*kankakuron*) as developed in *Bungakuron*, his treatise on literature that I take up in detail in the next section. There, he asserts that in "lyrical poetry" (*jojōshi*) the main function is to "sing feelings" (*jō o utau*), and the speaker should be the "I" of the poet. Sōseki states,

If one wishes to sing one's feelings in poignant fashion, then the one who sings must be oneself. This is because there is [no speaker] who would possess feelings [*jōsho*] as poignant as one's own. For this reason, lyrical poetry starts with "I" [*yo*] and ends with "I." "I" should be the composer of the poem, and if this cannot be, it should be the poem's protagonist, with whom the composer has become one. This is why, with a lyrical poem, we are always able to enjoy the flavor of poetry with the least amount of distance possible.[56]

A first-person voice, as in Meredith's poem, is the most authentic medium for conveying a subjective stance and for reducing the distance between the reader and the text.

Moreover, in *Bungakuron*, Sōseki posits literary "illusion" (*genwaku*) as the power that enables a text to impact the reader, or, in other words, the means by which the reader becomes subjectively and emotionally involved with the text. Because of the strongly subjective first-person voice in Meredith's poem, the literary illusion it produces is also strong and lets poetry come to the fore as a privileged medium for producing emotional immediacy. However, Sōseki's narrator in the scene ironically highlights the emotionally loaded nature of the medium of poetic expression only to again objectify and neutralize it through his critical reflections. This ambiguous oscillation between subjective expression and affective noninvolvement is even more complex with regard to the Sinitic poems quoted in *Kusamakura*. Before examining these, however, a discussion of Sōseki's literary theory is in order.

ROMANTICISM VERSUS REALISM: MEASURING FEELING AS THEORY OF LITERATURE

The attempt of *Kusamakura*'s narrator to objectify—to self-consciously highlight and measure—the "electric current of human emotion" in the poems he cites is an inherently theoretical endeavor. A different, albeit comparable, endeavor of emotional objectification occurs in Sōseki's critical writings, which investigate the amount of emotion produced by literature and various literary genres. In *Bungakuron*, Sōseki broadly defines literature as the product of the association between specific content-related "ideas," which he labels with a capital F (probably for "focus"), and "emotions" (*jōsho*), which he labels with a lowercase f (probably for "feeling").[57] The stronger the volume of feeling (*jōsho no bunryō*), or f, that is associated with an idea (or multiple ideas) in a literary text or genre, Sōseki argues, the more powerful the literary "illusion"—the emotional impact of a text or genre on the reader—becomes. More important, the stronger the volume of feeling in a text, the more literary (*bungakuteki*) the text becomes. In short, Sōseki defines literariness by the volume of emotion that a text is able to produce and to convey, as literary illusion, to its readers. As scholars have pointed out, Sōseki's understanding of the quantification of emotion in *Bungakuron* was indebted to his reception of contemporary scientific and psychological models, especially as found in the work of American psychologist William James (1842–1910).[58] At the same time, his theoretical project must be seen as an idiosyncratic reinvestigation of the newly naturalized concept of literature as an emotionalized textual practice.

An important objective of *Bungakuron* is to determine the "means" (*shudan*) by which literary illusion is produced. Sōseki offers a detailed discussion of these means in the fourth section of his treatise, "Bungakuteki naiyō no sōgo kankei" (The interrelations between literary contents). His fundamental argument is that in most cases literary illusion and the emotional impact (f) of a text increase if two types of content (F)—most often a human and natural content—are combined in the text. The various possible combinatory modes, or "interrelations," between types of literary content are the means by which illusion is produced. In contrast, both emotions (f) and literary illusion are reduced if only one content type—for instance, human affairs—is the text's focus. This is the case in what Sōseki defines as the "realist method" (*shajitsuhō*), which is the only means he posits that does not rely on a combination of two types of literary content but focuses only on one.[59] Although *Bungakuron* does not explicitly state this, it is clear that genres combining human and natural content include *shaseibun* and traditional poetry (haiku, *waka*, and Sinitic poems), whereas the only genre that exclusively focuses on human affairs is the novel.

Nature (*shizen*) and human affairs constitute independent categories of literary content (*bungakuteki naiyō*) in *Bungakuron*. Sōseki differentiates among four different categories of literary content: "sensory *F*" (*kankaku F*), "human *F*" (*jinji F*), "supernatural *F*" (*chōshizen F*), and "intellectual *F*" (*chishiki F*). However, he downplays the ability of the latter two categories to produce a strong sense of illusion in the reader; only the first two types of content are, in general, able to produce illusion. Sōseki specifies, moreover, that the material of sensory *F* consists of the "natural world" (*shizenkai*), while the material of human *F* consists of the "human drama mirroring good and evil, joy, anger, sadness, and delight."[60]

The theoretical framework of *Bungakuron* thus resonates with the issues that lie at the core of Sōseki's essay "Shaseibun" and the literary project of *Kusamakura*. While the novelist is deeply drawn into human *F*, or the drama of *ninjō*, the *shaseibun* narrator seeks to approach this drama more distantly, often through the mediation of the natural world. In *Bungakuron*, Sōseki argues that a literary means that combines two types of literary content, human and natural, increases literary illusion and makes the emotional impact of a text on the reader stronger. What he intends to convey, however, is not the emotional involvement of tears—the kind postulated for the novelist in the essay "Shaseibun." In *Bungakuron*, Sōseki defines what he understands by illusion as "taste" (*shumi*), "poetic flavor" (*shishu*), or "poetic mood" (*shikyō*). Genres that, like traditional poetry, combine both natural and human content produce stronger poetic flavor and, to Sōseki, have a stronger emotional impact on the reader and therefore are more literary. At the same time, these genres allow for more detachment from the "drama" of *ninjō* than those, particularly the novel, that focus exclusively on the human element.[61]

A particularly interesting literary means that Sōseki discusses is the "harmonizing method" (*chōwahō*), where two different types of content are juxtaposed and therefore "harmonized" in a single text. The example that he cites to illustrate this technique is the following couplet excerpted from Bai Juyi's (772–846) "Song of Everlasting Sorrow" (Changhenge), composed in 806:

玉容寂寞淚闌干　Her [Yang Guifei's] beautiful face looked desolate, and her tears were streaming down,

梨花一枝春帶雨　the bough of a pear tree in flower bearing the rain in spring.[62]

Sōseki argues that the power of this couplet lies in the visual juxtaposition of the human image of the beautiful palace lady in tears with the natural imagery of a blooming tree under the spring rain. The aesthetic effect is heightened because the two "materials," the human and the natural, are mutually amplified by their copresence in the text.[63]

Sōseki also argues that the harmonizing technique is particularly representative of the Japanese (or Eastern) poetic tradition, while it is rare in English literature:

When human material [jinjiteki zairyō] is matched with sensory material [kankakuteki zairyō] or when sensory material is juxtaposed to human material, they naturally fuse in the text, prevent monotony, and make the text livelier. This fusion also produces an emotion that is much superior to the one that these materials would have produced separately. . . . A scholar of Chinese letters [kangakusha], in an evaluation of a poem, once remarked that "both emotion and landscape are exquisitely executed," meaning that he was praising the fact that the harmonization of human materials with sensory ones in the poem was particularly successful. Japanese people have always had an innate love for nature, and since ancient times poetry and literary prose [shiika bibun] could not be composed without this harmonization. As the background for human affairs, there always had to be nature, and the foreground for nature necessarily consisted of human affairs. People in the West do not take a particularly strong delight in the natural landscape, and the fact that they do not consider this harmonization to be a necessary ingredient for their literary compositions is indeed noteworthy for somebody from the East.[64]

The emotional effect that Sōseki associates with the Japanese and East Asian literary tradition is, as indicated, crystallized in expressions like "poetic flavor" and "poetic mood." For this reason, he criticizes Samuel Richardson's (1689–1761) novels for treating only a single kind of material—the human one—and for thus being less poetic. He characterizes the emotional impact on readers produced by "Eastern" poetry as stronger than that produced by Richardson's novels.

At the end of his discussion of the different means by which literary illusion is produced, Sōseki subsumes all combinatory methods—the ones bringing together different types of literary content in a text—as belonging to what he calls the idealist school (*risō-ha*) or romantic school (*roman-ha*). He opposes these schools to the realist school (*shajitsu-ha*), or realist method, which uses only one type of literary material (F) with only one type of literary emotion (f) attached to it. In a numeric chart, Sōseki shows that, owing to the amplificatory effect brought about by the combination of different types of content and their emotions, the volume of feeling produced by romantic (or idealist) texts is necessarily higher than that produced by realist texts.[65] As noted, although Sōseki does not explicitly relate the romantic or idealist school to a specific genre, it is clear from the majority of the cited examples that romanticism is associated with poetry, both English and Japanese. The realist school, in contrast, is the representational regime most suited to the aesthetic world of the novel. Sōseki by no means disqualifies realism, and he expresses a strong appreciation for the novel and individual novelists, including Jane Austen and Charlotte Brontë. Moreover, he meticulously lists the respective strengths and weaknesses inherent in both literary schools.[66] In *Bungakuron*, however, literariness— the ability of a text to produce illusion—is more strongly associated with romanticism (or idealism) and the language of poetry. Although the text cites mostly English literary sources, the section "Interrelation between Literary Contents," which discusses the means that produce illusion, points back to the traditional aesthetic format of haiku, Sinitic poetry, and *waka*, which harmonizes human "foregrounds" with natural "backgrounds" in the same poetic text. Moreover, Sōseki's terminology here recalls earlier Meiji discourse, where the realist depiction of licentious emotions in the novel—that is, human affairs—was criticized for its lack of idealism. But he also deftly blurs this discourse and its categories by reducing them to a purely formalist opposition of literary methods producing illusion in the reader.

Approaching romanticism from a slightly different angle is "Sōsakuka no taido," a lengthy theoretical essay that is particularly relevant for understanding the way Sinitic poetry is explored as a medium of emotional expression in *Kusamakura*.[67] In "Sōsakuka no taido," Sōseki differentiates between two fundamental attitudes of the literary writer that subtly mirror those of the novelist and *shaseibun* author described in the essay "Shaseibun." One is what he calls the attitude of the merchant or scientist, but it is clear that this is an indirect reference to the novelist. This stance entails a desire to perceive and describe the world directly as it is, using sensuous perception or (linguistic) concepts. It does not aim to "savor" or "enjoy" (*tanoshimu*) the world but merely to seek knowledge or material gain. The second is what Sōseki calls the attitude of the artist, a clear reference to both the poet and the *shaseibun* author.[68] This stance always strives for enjoyment. Moreover, it never seeks to perceive or describe things in the world directly but always through the mediation of something else, using, for example, similes, metaphors, and symbols—literary figures that juxtapose and substitute one type of "idea" or "content" (to use *Bungakuron*'s terminology) with another. Sōseki considers this attitude of the artist characteristic of romanticism (*romanshugi*). Insofar as it combines different types of literary contents (for instance, human and natural) through the use of similes, metaphors, and symbols, this attitude resonates with Sōseki's definition of the romantic or idealist school in *Bungakuron*.[69]

Especially noteworthy in connection with the romantic attitude is the problem of subjective expression or, more precisely, the question of how a subject's emotions can be conveyed and expressed by representing them with different content. In his discussion of substitution through symbols (*shōchō*), for Sōseki the most complex form of romantic expression, he introduces the concept of "mood" (*kibun*). He defines mood as a subjective content (*shukan no naiyō*) originally linked to and produced by specific objects or situations in the exterior "world dissociated from the self" (*higa no sekai*). These original objects or situations, however, are often irretrievably lost, and as the mood becomes more complex the "I" has more difficulty relating it to corresponding objects in the exterior world. This then leads to a fundamental separation between the mood and the possibility of its objective representation, a gap that triggers what Sōseki defines, in English, as an "infinite longing"—or, in Japanese, *mugen no shōkei*—for this lost state of representation. Out of this situation, the need for symbolic expression arises.

Sōseki provides the following reflection on the complex interrelation between the subjectivity of the mood and its objective representation through symbols:

It happens that you suffer and would like to give expression to your suffering, but this is just not possible. If you leave it this way, then that of course is it, but if you wanted to give at least one-tenth of it expression, be it only incompletely, then you would have to have recourse to symbols. You do not express all ten parts of it—"do not express" would be the wrong wording: you cannot express them—and so inevitably you leave it at one-tenth. Of course, if you only wanted to express your mood as mood, then you could merely say, "I am very sad" or "I am a bit happy," and there would not be any need to discuss the possibility or impossibility of expressing it fully. However, if you attempted to find an object for this somehow deep, broad, and complicated mood in the objective world dissociated from the self, then you would have to substitute the ten parts of your mood with a form [*keisō*] corresponding to one-tenth of it; the remaining nine parts are alluded to by this symbol. But since this is difficult to do even for the person who has the mood, it is even more difficult for somebody else to understand. It sometimes happens that you hear only one part and then know all ten parts of it, but this works only if you are someone who can see one part and then feel the ten parts together. And even if you can see one-tenth and then feel ten-tenths, this does not necessarily mean that you feel exactly the same as the one who produced the expression. What you use as symbols may belong to the world dissociated from the self, but what these hint at is the mood of the self. It is *my* mood, and to say it very precisely, it is not the mood of anybody else and of course not the mood of an outside object.[70]

The "forms" of the "world dissociated from the self" through which the mood of the first-person subject (*"my* mood") is, even if only incompletely, expressed are, most often, natural objects of the landscape. Nature is the privileged medium through which feelings can gain material form in poetic language.

The specific emotional quality of the mood, however, remains unspecified and thus a potentially overdetermined receptacle for different emotional types. In "Sōsakuka no taido," Sōseki differentiates among types of emotion that an artist may seek to express—for instance, the sentiments (*jōsō*) associated with the beautiful (*bi*), the good (*zen*), and the sublime (*sō*). The good, or the feeling related to moral judgments, also often subsumes the sentiments of love (*ai*) and hope (*kibō*).[71] At the same time, the fact that this romantic mood is nearly incommensurable with communication and representation—that its content remains largely indistinct—points to the extreme degree of emotional and subjective detachment that is inherent in symbolic expression. It is precisely this type of detachment that comes to the fore in *Kusamakura*'s Sinitic poems.

202

KUSAMAKURA'S SINITIC POETRY

In *Kusamakura*, Sōseki's first-person narrator similarly analyzes his subjective "mood" (*kokoromochi* or *mūdo*) prior to composing a Sinitic poem. He describes his mood as "hard to grasp" and difficult to represent through either painting or poetry. He states that this subjective "feeling" (*waga kanji*) has not come to him from the exterior world and is also not reducible to a specific object in the landscape. Yet he is aware that, in order to express and represent this mood, he must symbolically substitute it with a symbol in the form of natural imagery. He defines this challenge in the following way: "The only problem is what kind of landscape and emotion [*keijō*] to bring into my poem to copy [*utsusu*] this broad and somehow indistinct inner state."[72] And although this state is highly subjective and individual—the narrator repeatedly points out that he is seeking the representation of only his "own mood" (*jiko no kokoromochi*)—it remains "abstract" (*chūshōteki*) and detached. Out of this mood, the following poem emerges:

青春二三月	In the second and third month of spring
愁随芳草長	my melancholy grows along with the fragrant grasses.
閑花落空庭	The quietly blooming flowers have fallen in the empty courtyard,
素琴横虚堂	an undecorated zither is lying in the deserted hall.
蟠蛸掛不動	A spider is hanging motionless
篆煙繞竹梁	and incense smoke curling around the bamboo beams.
独坐無隻語	I sit alone, not saying a single word—
方寸認微光	in my heart, I perceive a small ray of light.
人間徒多事	The world of men is full of useless matters,
此境孰可忘	but who could ever forget this state [I am in right now]?
会得一日静	Having by chance earned this one day of peace,
正知百年忙	I now know exactly what a hundred years of restlessness mean.
遐懐寄何処	Where is it that I could direct my deep feelings?
緬邈白雲郷	I will send them far away to the realm of the white clouds.[73]

This poem is romantic or idealist, following Sōseki's definition in *Bungakuron*, in that it couples human affairs with natural phenomena so that the emotions relate to, or speak through, the landscape. It takes a subjective, first-person stance that expresses an affectively unspecific and detached mood through the symbolic forms of natural imagery. This happens in the first and last couplets, where the vastness of the speaker's "melancholy" and "deep feelings" is underlined and materially extended by movement through the natural landscape—the vast sweep of spring grasses in the first couplet and the limitless expanse of the sky in the last. The speaker's mood and his feelings seem emotionally loaded, and a certain ambiguity permeates the tone of the poem. The setting suggests, on the one hand, a psychological state of peacefulness and equilibrium, which is underscored by the natural imagery: the stillness of the spider's web and the quiet movements of the smoldering incense smoke in the hall are replicated by the poet's tranquil, seated posture. On the other hand, this very tranquility also makes him intensely aware of the underlying tensions and restlessness of his life in the social world beyond the ephemeral idyll of his respite inside the hall, thus producing an atmosphere of unease and resentment.

The poet's melancholia can be read as an indication of discontent resonating with certain strands in the East Asian poetic tradition, such as eremitic verse. In his early essay "Eikoku shijin no tenchi sansen ni taisuru kannen" (The conceptual attitude of English poets toward heaven and earth, mountains and rivers), written in 1893, five years before the preceding poem was composed, Sōseki defined romanticism (*rōmanchishizumu*) as the eighteenth-century English literary movement that sought to leave behind the poetic conventions and court-centered life of classicism. In his formulation, poets would leave the cities, go to the mountains and woods, and seek a mode of expression, often in nature-themed poetry, that reflected their true "Heaven-endowed nature" (*tenpu no honsei*).[74] What fundamentally motivated each poet was a discontent (*fuhei*) whose origins might have varied from one to the next. While Oliver Goldsmith (1728–1774) resented society for economic reasons, William Cowper (1731–1800) felt a religiously motivated discontent with the vanity of the people, and Robert Burns (1759–1796) was driven by the egalitarian desire for social justice.[75] Sōseki's essay is interesting in that it appropriates, and deftly merges with English literature, a major motif in the East Asian poetic tradition: discontent with the social world and the conventionality of court-centered literary culture and the renunciation of a political career in favor of an eremitic life amid the "mountains and rivers."[76]

Another Sinitic poem, composed by Sōseki in March 1898—around the same time as the two poems in *Kusamakura*, but not included there—brings to the fore in a more drastic manner the interconnection between romantic subjectivity, landscape, and social or political discontent. The untitled poem reads as follows:

吾心若有苦	My heart seems to harbor pain,
求之遂難求	but although I examine it [my pain], it cannot be easily examined.
俯仰天地際	When I survey the expanse between heaven and earth,
胡為発哀声	why do I let out this plaintive cry?
春花幾開落	The flowers of spring: how often have they bloomed and scattered?
世事幾迭更	The affairs of the world: how often have they undergone change?
烏兎促鬢髮	As sun and moon make their rounds, they urge my hair to turn white,
意気軽功名	but my ambition looks down upon fame in the world.
昨夜生月暈	Yesterday night a halo surrounded the moon,
飆風朝満城	and a whirlwind was blowing through the town in the morning.
夢醒枕上聴	I woke up in my dream and from my pillow I could hear
孤剣匣底鳴	my solitary sword emitting a scream from the bottom of its chest.
慨然振衣起	With stern determination I shook my robe and stood up,
登楼望前程	and I climbed up the tower to watch the way ahead of me.
前程望不見	But the way ahead of me I could not see—
漠漠愁雲横	obstructing my view, only clouds of grief were floating.[77]

A strong emotionality, presumably linked to discontent and thwarted ambition, permeates this poem. It appears as if the speaker whose "ambition looks down upon fame in the world" once harbored a wish to participate in politics and in the government, as would have been appropriate for a man of worth in the Confucian tradition.

This is particularly obvious when examining the original version of the poem's fourth couplet, which was subsequently rewritten by Nagao Uzan

(1864–1942), Sōseki's mentor in Sinitic poetry composition in Kumamoto. The original couplet read,

| 菲才非国器 | Someone as untalented as me could not become a vessel of the state. |
| 所願豈功名 | How could I aspire to fame in the world?[78] |

It is not clear whether the discontent in these lines is directed at the speaker's lack of talent or at a degenerate, hostile world that will not let men of worth assume positions of responsibility. However, the poem creates a heroic discourse that symbolically relates to natural and cosmic imagery.

A martial stance somehow reminiscent of poetry written by *bakumatsu* samurai activists (*shishi*) comes to the fore in the personification of the sword, screaming in discontent and exhorting the poet to participate in politics.[79] Moreover, the poem's cosmic imagery is filled with foreboding, symbolized by the halo around the moon at night and the whirlwind in the morning, underlining the speaker's martial desires. The only seasonal imagery—the blooming flowers in spring—serves as an allegory for the passing of time that gradually reduces the possibility of political participation.

A related theme that permeates this poem, indirectly at least, is youth as the period in life when political activism is possible, if not mandatory. The other Sinitic poem that Sōseki quotes in *Kusamakura* in fact explicitly mentions this theme. The second part reads,

孤愁高雲際	My solitary grief extends to the fringes of the high clouds
大空断鴻帰	and on the vast sky a lonely goose, separated from its flock, is flying home.
寸心何窈窕	My heart, how deep and calm it feels—
縹渺忘是非	in its limitlessness it has forgotten about true and false.
三十我欲老	I am thirty years old and about to turn old,
韶光猶依依	but the spring colors are still young and fresh.
逍遥随物化	I freely wander around and follow the transformation of things;
悠然対芬菲	with a calm mind I face the fragrant spring grasses.[80]

This poem displays a more detached and reconciliatory tone than the previous one, but the original passion of the speaker's ambition is still recognizable in the grandiose dimensionality of the first couplet. The poem also makes clear that the feeling of intense grief, as well as its appeasement through Zhuangzian "free and easy wandering" and an acceptance of constant transformation, is connected to the speaker's youth—his age of thirty years, the approximate age at which Sōseki composed the poem and precisely the age of *Kusamakura*'s narrator.[81]

Youth is a particularly relevant motif in that it relates not only to the theme of discontent but also to love—the theme par excellence of the novel and the newly naturalized literature. In both instances where Sinitic poetry is composed in *Kusamakura*, the erotic presence of the woman Nami is indeed particularly important. In the first instance, Nami's alluring dance in a long-sleeved kimono (*furisode*) playfully interrupts the narrator's process of poetic composition. A potential emotional subtext for the narrator's mood could, therefore, also be love.

In the poems taken up here, however, the potential emotional subtexts—political discontent or love—are extremely subdued. As Sōseki writes with regard to symbolic substitution in his essay "Sōsakuka no taido," only one-tenth of the poet's emotion seems to find expression through the poem's imagery, while his general mood remains abstract and undecipherable—or calm and peaceful. This aesthetic format creates an effect of detachment that liberates the speaker from the vicissitudes of suffering inherent in the world. In orientalizing fashion, Sōseki performs Sinitic poetry as what he calls Eastern poetry (*Tōyō no shiika*), echoing a famous eremitic poem by Tao Yuanming (365–427) that he cites from earlier in his text as an example of strong detachment.[82] However, *Kusamakura* also self-consciously reflects Sinitic poetry as a literary genre that, similarly to English verse and haiku composition, still transmits the "electric current of human emotion"—be it only one-tenth as strong and transparent as the current flowing through other genres, such as English verse and the novel.

Kusamakura critically highlights *shaseibun*, haiku, English verse, and Sinitic poems as "literary" writing in accordance with the definition in *Bungakuron*—writing particularly suited to move the reader and produce illusion. Meredith's passionate love poem, by staging a first-person lyrical voice that "sings its feelings," produces an affective immediacy that reduces the distance between reader and text and enhances illusion. *Kusamakura's shaseibun* prose as well as the haiku and Sinitic poems cited by the narrator, while obviously either less lyrical or nonlyrical, also produce illusion by juxtaposing (or harmonizing) natural and human contents and thus conforming to Sōseki's definition in *Bungakuron* of romantic or idealist writing. The various genres performed in *Kusamakura*, all their differences notwithstanding, converge in their quality as romantic writing that distances them from the novel. The novel, because of its exclusive focus on human affairs—the "human drama mirroring good and evil, joy, anger, sadness, and delight"—belongs to the literary mode that Sōseki defines as realist. As has been noted, he sees the volume of feeling produced by realist texts as weaker than that produced by romantic or idealist writings; the capacity of realism to move the reader, to inspire poetic flavor, and to be literary is less strong than that in romanticism.

The performance of genre in *Kusamakura* as well as Sōseki's critical discussions leave little room for doubt about his general preference for romantic (or idealist) over realist writing. As mentioned, romantic writing offers a more detached stance toward the drama of *ninjō* in the way postulated by Sōseki with regard to *shaseibun* in his 1907 essay. That he was ambivalent, if not suspicious, of the novel and its affectively involved plots of *ninjō* reflects a literary sensibility grounded in the aesthetic world of traditional letters or writing styles (*bun*) as epitomized by Sinitic poetry and haiku.[83] Moreover, through the exploration of these genres, Sōseki could envision an alternative type of literature that, while producing more poetic flavor and illusion, could allow for more affective detachment than the novel and the newly naturalized literature.

However, Sōseki by no means aimed for a nostalgic and naive return to traditional letters under modern conditions, nor did he simply reject the novel. The performance of various nonnovelistic and traditional genres in *Kusamakura* as media that convey emotion was possible only because of his strong awareness of the contemporary novel and new literary discourse. Through this performance, he objectified, distanced, and alienated the aesthetic world of traditional letters to distinguish it from, and weigh it against, the world of the novel. *Kusamakura's* narrator no longer inhabits the world of traditional letters but instead ironically performs it to measure how much "electric current of human emotion" it can transmit.

Similarly, Sōseki's critical investigation of traditional literary modes under the banner of romanticism or idealism takes place in an inherently modern framework that relies on distinctions made between those modes and the novel and on a critical lexicon (including such terms as "romanticisim") that was alien to traditional letters. Although the volume of feeling produced by romantic or traditional texts makes them more literary than realist writings, according to *Bungakuron*, both romanticism and realism still belong to a common literature that Sōseki defines by its inherent capacity to convey emotion.

While critically deconstructing the emotional quality of literature and thus questioning the process of naturalization through which its new concept had come into place, Sōseki's literary and critical project simultaneously reasserted literature's universally emotional nature. This paradoxical double movement was the idiosyncratic attempt to integrate, appropriate, and come to terms with not only literature but also *ninjō* as its newly naturalized core. This project remained a highly intellectual endeavor, however, fraught with self-reflection and irony. It is significant in this respect that, beginning in 1907, Sōseki started producing works that were more strongly akin to the novel, and he largely abandoned the writing of *shaseibun*, although not the composition of Sinitic poetry and haiku. However, whether in the interrogation of "natural love" in *Sorekara* (*And Then*, 1909), the breakdown of narrative plot and affectivity in *Mon* (*The Gate*, 1910), or the obsessive production of Sinitic poems while writing *Meian* (*Light and Darkness*, 1916), Sōseki continued to question the novel and the emotions it depicts. His interrogation of literature and its emotional distinctions never seemed to come to rest.

EPILOGUE

My study has outlined the nineteenth-century modernity of the Japanese novel as a coherent literary-historical space held together by a critical and narrative concern with *ninjō*. This concern was grounded in the notion that the novel is a problematic, if not licentious, genre because of its representation of *ninjō*, but also often in the attempt to assert its social, moral, and political value, often in contradiction with the depiction of licentious love and desire. A suspicion about the disruptive potential of *ninjō* had been inherent in traditional literary discourse, but only with the new centrality of the novel and its genealogy in the nineteenth century did this suspicion generate, to an unprecedented degree of intensity, narrative practices and critical scrutiny surrounding the social value and danger of literary writing. The genealogy of the licentious novel comprised early-modern Chinese vernacular works, early nineteenth-century *ninjōbon* and *yomihon*, as well as, influenced by these, Meiji critical and narrative experiments including Shōyō's and Sōseki's. To outline this genealogy, across the epistemological permutations of the early modern–modern divide, has been a major ambition of this study.

By the early twentieth century, however, the continuous literary-historical space of the nineteenth-century *shōsetsu* was waning. A broader configuration of interlocked discursive and literary transformations marked the demise of this space. As discussed, by the time the literary discourse of naturalism emerged, the novel's depiction of erotic love and desire, even if dark, ugly, and "animalistic," had become largely unproblematic and literally naturalized. The early twentieth century also witnessed, in close correlation with the establishment of naturalism as the main literary current, the emergence of a new discourse that posited Shōyō's *Shōsetsu shinzui* and its notion of the realist depiction of *ninjō* as the origin of modern Japanese literature.[1] This discourse redefined Shōyō's terms *mosha* and *ninjō* as belonging to a new mimetic psychological realism, focusing on the emotional interiority of the novel's protagonists in the vein of nineteenth-century European works, and it saw *Shōsetsu shinzui* as the necessary theoretical precursor for the contemporary naturalist novel and its rhetoric of unadorned depiction even of ugly desire.[2] This discourse already ignored the complex narrative and critical engagement with the licentiousness of *ninjō* and its realist depiction in Shōyō's own works.

The canonization of Shōyō's critical discourse as the origin of Japanese literary modernity also correlated with the decanonization of the novel's earlier genre memory that was defined by Chinese vernacular fiction and the *gesaku* classics. In 1907, for instance, literary critic Ikuta Chōkō (1882–1936) noted the following:

Shōsetsu shinzui is truly a revolutionary in the world of the novel. This revolutionary's outcry—the great outcry that urged the literary world of our nation to adopt a new and fresh intellectual trend—even awoke the slumber of our old-fashioned novelists. The silly didacticism [*kanchōshugi*] was finally vanquished in the eyes of the public and realist depiction valued; psychological description with human emotion as the main focus became the general trend. For the first time did the world of our novel have the chance to get in touch with nineteenth-century world literature, and the light of literary art [*bungei*] suddenly shone brightly. Seen at least from one angle, *Shōsetsu shinzui*'s realism was truly a manifesto of literary independence, and this manifesto's message undoubtedly made the dividing wall between Meiji literature and the literature before Meiji even thicker.[3]

Ikuta not only presents *Shōsetsu shinzui* as the "revolutionary" origin of a modern literary order but also posits "silly didacticism," an obvious reference to Bakin's *kanzen chōaku*, as opposed to this order. Although Shōyō criticized Bakin's writings for their exclusive focus on moral didacticism,

Shōsetsu shinzui by no means declared *kanzen chōaku* as obsolete, but on the contrary highlighted its importance as one of the novel's "indirect benefits." A moral-didactic, "idealist" outlook still fundamentally defined Shōyō's understanding of literary fiction. It was only with discourses like Ikuta's in the early twentieth century that Bakin's *yomihon* in particular were produced as the other of the literary modernity allegedly epitomized by *Shōsetsu shinzui*—as a premodernity defined by moralism that contradicted the novel's modern focus on psychological interiority. On the other hand, with the naturalization of "dark" desire as the novel's core in Japanese naturalist discourse, the notion of licentiousness in earlier *ninjōbon* discourse became obsolete. If a work like Tayama Katai's *Futon* (*The Quilt*, 1907), often hailed as one of the masterworks of Japanese naturalist fiction, still upheld the earlier enlightenment dichotomy of chaste spiritual love and licentious desire, it did so mainly to ironically highlight the hypocrisy of chaste spirituality in the light of desire's truth.[4]

This broader shift in the first decade of the twentieth century was interlocked with the demise of Sinitic literacy and learning, both classical and vernacular, as an active cultural field and, concurrently, the massive promotion of the vernacular *genbun itchi* style as a national language in the wake of Japan's victory in the Sino-Japanese War in 1895. Influenced by the writings of linguistic ideologues, the government had begun to actively implement the establishment of a standardized, national language, especially through new elementary-school curricula that increasingly privileged the *genbun itchi* style over traditional forms of literacy. By the 1920s, *genbun itchi* had become the dominant written language, not only in education but also in public discourse, including newspapers, general magazines, and literary writings, thus also defining the standard of vernacular Japanese as a national spoken language.[5] As shown in chapter 1, traditional East Asian notions of literary writing had provided the ideological and intellectual basis for asserting the moral-didactic, social, and political value even of the *shōsetsu*—and for asserting the licentiousness of *ninjō*. This does not mean that assertions of the moral-didactic function of literature were absent from twentieth-century literary discourse. The proletarian literary movement of the 1920s and early 1930s invested great interest in the political mission of the novel, but this interest was defined by Marxist ideological concerns that were already divorced from the moral-didactic and civilizational parameters that had defined earlier discourse.

While the broader epistemological transformations in early twentieth-century Japan certainly warrant further scrutiny, my cursory overview of them here should suffice to highlight the historicity of the nineteenth-century Japanese novel and its literary space. The genealogy of the novel outlined in this study intrinsically belonged to the nineteenth century and its modernity (its variegated epistemological and discursive contexts), but it also relied on the continuity, from premodern discussions well into the early twentieth century, of the critical concern with licentious *ninjō* and the social-didactic function of literary writing. The nineteenth-century *shōsetsu* enacted the intensification, the complexification, even the culmination of this concern but, notably, also its ending. It is in this sense that its literary space, historiographically, was transitory and hybrid. It looked back to the past by intensifying and reconfiguring it, but it also, in terms of an ending, gave way to an incommensurable future. Its key category was emotion, not as the signifier for the psychological interiority of mimetic realism but as *ninjō*, the traditional concept that came to shape nineteenth-century narrative and critical discourse in new and complex ways.

NOTES

INTRODUCTION

1. Tsubouchi Shōyō, *Shōsetsu shinzui*, in *Tsubouchi Shōyō shū*, ed. Nakamura Kan and Umezawa Nobuo, NKiBT 3 (Tokyo: Kadokawa shoten, 1974), 68. Unless otherwise indicated, all translations are mine.
2. Tsubouchi, *Shōsetsu shinzui*, 69; for the term "true novel," see 60.
3. Natsume Sōseki, "Shaseibun" [On sketch prose], in *Sōseki zenshū*, vol. 16, ed. Komori Yōichi (Tokyo: Iwanami shoten, 1995), 48–56.
4. I am aware of Michael Emmerich's important caveat, from the viewpoint of book history, against the use of the overarching term "novel" for Edo-period works of narrative fiction because "there is a reason the names used for early modern genres of fiction in Japan often refer to their material form." See Michael Emmerich, *The Tale of Genji: Translation, Canonization, and World Literature* (New York: Columbia University Press, 2013), 410n39. At the same time, it was primarily in reference to the term *shōsetsu* that assertions of the moral-didactic and the licentious nature of narrative fiction were continuously made across the Edo-Meiji transition.
5. This is the understanding of *xiaoshuo* famously presented by Ban Gu (32–92) in his *History of the Former Han* (*Hanshu*). See Judith T. Zeitlin, "Xiaoshuo," in *The Novel*, ed. Franco Moretti (Princeton, N.J.: Princeton University Press, 2006), 1:249.
6. Zeitlin, "Xiaoshuo," 256–57.
7. For helpful discussions of the *shōsetsu* concept in Japan or the equivalence of *shōsetsu* and "novel," see Tomi Suzuki, *Narrating the Self: Fictions of Japanese Modernity* (Stanford, Calif.: Stanford University Press, 1996), chapter 1; Atsuko Ueda, *Concealment of Politics, Politics of Concealment: The Production of "Literature" in Meiji Japan* (Stanford, Calif.: Stanford University Press, 2007), chapter 2; Glynne Walley, *Good Dogs: Edification, Entertainment, and Kyokutei Bakin's* Nansō Satomi hakkenden (Ithaca, N.Y.: Cornell University East Asia Program, 2017), 61–74; Jonathan E.

214

Zwicker, *Practices of the Sentimental Imagination: Melodrama, the Novel, and the Social Imaginary in Nineteenth-Century Japan* (Cambridge, Mass.: Harvard University Asia Center, 2006), chapter 1.

8. Walley, *Good Dogs*, chapter 1, cogently elaborates on what he calls Bakin's "seriousness," in opposition to the "playful" entertainment character of his works as popular fiction.

9. Tsubouchi Shōyō, "Shinkyū katoki no kaisō" [Recollections of the transition between the new and old age, 1925], in *Shōyō senshū*, ed. Shōyō Kyōkai (Tokyo: Daiichi shobō, 1977), 12:325.

10. Tsubouchi Shōyō, "Aidiaru noberu no koto ni tsukite" [On the idealist novel, 1888], in *Tsubouchi Shōyō kenkyū: Fu, bungakuron shoshutsu shiryō*, ed. Ishida Tadahiko (Fukuoka: Kyūshū daigaku shuppankai, 1988), 426–28; Tsubouchi, "Shinkyū katoki no kaisō," 320.

11. Shunsui repeatedly labeled himself the "founder" of the *ninjōbon* genre.

12. By "courtesans," I refer to pleasure-quarter prostitutes of various ranks, often called *yūjo*; geisha were professional entertainers, but the line between prostitution and entertainment was often blurry. For the difficult terminology with regard to early-modern prostitution, see Amy Stanley, *Selling Women: Prostitution, Markets, and the Household in Early Modern Japan* (Berkeley: University of California Press, 2012), 14–15; on geisha, see 66–71.

13. For an instance where Shunsui includes himself under the category of "novelist" (*shōsetsuka*), see Tamenaga Shunsui, *Shunshoku umegoyomi*, ed. Nakamura Yukihiko, NKBT 64 (Tokyo: Iwanami shoten, 1971), 135.

14. Kimura Mokurō, "Kokuji shōsetsu tsū," in *Zoku enseki jisshu*, ed. Iwamoto Kattōshi (Tokyo: Chūōkōronsha, 1980), 1:293–306. On Mokurō and his treatise, see Andrew L. Markus, "Kimura Mokurō (1774–1856) and His *Kokuji shōsetsu tsū* (1849)," *Journal of Japanese Studies* 26, no. 2 (2000): 341–70. Note that *gesaku* authors also discussed their works as *shōsetsu*, often in connection with the assertion of their didactic value. See, for example, the authorial comments in Shikitei Sanba (1776–1822), *Ukiyoburo* [Bathhouse of the floating world, 1809–1813], ed. Nakamura Michio, NKBT 63 (Tokyo: Iwanami shoten, 1957), 111; I owe knowledge of this reference to Suzuki, *Narrating the Self*, 17.

15. In his historical overview of the *shōsetsu* in *Shōsetsu shinzui* (in the section titled "The Transformation of the Novel"), Shōyō subsumes a broad variety of both Japanese and Western texts under the "novel" concept, including even ancient Japanese and Greek myths. However, the works that Shōyō had in mind when defining what he called the true novel—novels by the English authors Walter Scott or Edward Bulwer-Lytton—had a strong affinity to genres of *gesaku* fiction, especially *ninjōbon* and *yomihon*. See my detailed discussion in chapter 4.

16. Fukuchi Ōchi, "Bunron" [On literature], in *Fukuchi Ōchi shū*, ed. Yanagida Izumi, MBZ 11 (Tokyo: Chikuma shobō, 1966), 345. Originally published in the *Tōkyō nichinichi shinbun* in August 1875. While Ōchi, in "Bunron," does not make explicit reference to these works' genres, he mentions them in his contemporaneous essay "Nihon bungaku no fushin o tanzu" [Lamenting the stagnation of literature in Japan, 1875], in *Fukuchi Ōchi shū*, 343. For a similar list, see also Taguchi Ukichi (1855–1905), *Nihon kaika shōshi* [A short civilization history of Japan, 1877–1882],

in *Taguchi Teiken shū*, ed. Ōkubo Toshiaki, MBZ 14 (Tokyo: Chikuma shobō, 1977), 60.

17. For exemplary studies of the canonization of various premodern Japanese "classics," see Haruo Shirane and Tomi Suzuki, eds., *Inventing the Classics: Modernity, National Identity, and Japanese Literature* (Stanford, Calif.: Stanford University Press, 2000).

18. Barbara H. Rosenwein, *Emotional Communities in the Early Middle Ages* (Ithaca, N.Y.: Cornell University Press, 2006), and *Generations of Feeling: A History of Emotions, 600–1700* (Cambridge: Cambridge University Press, 2016).

19. James Legge, trans., *Li Chi, Book of Rites: An Encyclopedia of Ancient Ceremonial Usages, Religious Creeds, and Social Institutions*, ed. Ch'u Chai and Winberg Chai, 2 vols. (New York: University Books, 1967), 1:379 (translation modified).

20. Peter Brooks, *The Melodramatic Imagination: Balzac, Henry James, Melodrama, and the Mode of Excess* (New Haven, Conn.: Yale University Press, 1995), 12, 41. For recent studies on melodrama in nineteenth- and early twentieth-century Japan that engage with Brooks, see Zwicker, *Practices of the Sentimental Imagination*, and Ken K. Ito, *An Age of Melodrama: Family, Gender, and Social Hierarchy in the Turn-of-the-Century Japanese Novel* (Stanford, Calif.: Stanford University Press, 2008). Sentimentalism, which David Denby has defined as the narrative impulse to generate sympathy and solidarity in the reader, is also different from the narrative practices surrounding *ninjō*; see David J. Denby, *Sentimental Narrative and the Social Order in France, 1760–1820* (Cambridge: Cambridge University Press, 1994), 88.

21. For an incisive critique of Elias, see Barbara H. Rosenwein, "Worrying about Emotions in History," *American Historical Review* 107, no. 3 (2002): 821–45.

22. For a comparable approach, see also Takemitsu Morikawa, *Liebessemantik und Sozialstruktur: Transformationen in Japan von 1600 bis 1920* (Bielefeld: transcript Verlag, 2015). Morikawa argues that Genroku-period (1688–1704) writings like Chikamatsu Monzaemon's (1653–1724) famous *sewamono* (contemporary life) plays and *ninjōbon* stage an *amour passion* that Meiji-period moral and rational discourse later eclipses.

23. Saeki Junko, *"Iro" to "ai" no hikaku bunkashi* (Tokyo: Iwanami shoten, 1998), chapter 1; for a translation, by Indra Levy, of this chapter, see Indra A. Levy, ed., *Translation in Modern Japan* (New York: Routledge, 2011), 73–101. See also Saeki Junko, *"Ai" to "sei" no bunkashi* (Tokyo: Kadokawa gakugei shuppan, 2008), 7–117.

24. Gregory M. Pflugfelder, *Cartographies of Desire: Male-Male Sexuality in Japanese Discourse, 1600–1950* (Berkeley: University of California Press, 1999), chapter 1. For an incisive presentation of Edo-period *nanshoku*, see also Paul Schalow's introduction to Ihara Saikaku, *The Great Mirror of Male Love*, trans. Paul Gordon Schalow (Stanford, Calif.: Stanford University Press, 1990).

25. See Kuki Shūzō's foundational study *Iki no kōzō* (The structure of *iki*, 1930). On Kuki and his work, see Leslie Pincus, *Authenticating Culture in Imperial Japan: Kuki Shūzō and the Rise of National Aesthetics* (Berkeley: University of California Press, 1996).

26. See in particular Jim Reichert, *In the Company of Men: Representations of Male-Male Sexuality in Meiji Literature* (Stanford, Calif.: Stanford University Press, 2006); J. Keith Vincent, *Two-Timing Modernity: Homosocial Narrative in Modern Japanese Fiction* (Cambridge, Mass.: Harvard University Asia Center, 2012).

27. For a nuanced discussion of *nanshoku* in Bakin's *yomihon*, see Walley, *Good Dogs*, chapter 5. Walley's conclusion is that, while references to *nanshoku* are not absent from *Hakkenden*, the novel's predominant focus is on male-female sexuality.

28. Pflugfelder, *Cartographies of Desire*, 95, also notes the decrease of *nanshoku*-related texts in the early nineteenth century, thus complicating historical narratives that situate the demise of *nanshoku* only in connection with the advent of Meiji modernity.

29. What Habermas has in mind is the new eighteenth-century genre of sentimental fiction, works like Samuel Richardson's *Pamela* (1740) and Goethe's *The Sorrows of Young Werther* (1774). Published and mass circulated, this literature of the inner subject was inherently public from the outset. What Habermas calls the literary public sphere (*literarische Öffentlichkeit*) even "mediates" the emergence of the public sphere per se, where private subjects—already united by their universally shared emotionalized subjectivity and humanistic values through public literary discourse—congregate to articulate their political and economic interests. See Jürgen Habermas, *Strukturwandel der Öffentlichkeit: Untersuchungen zu einer Kategorie der bürgerlichen Gesellschaft* (Frankfurt/Main: Suhrkamp Verlag, 1990), 116–21. For a fascinating case study that critically engages with Habermas by exploring the capacity of emotions—as opposed to rational discourse—in shaping public opinion, see Eugenia Lean, *Public Passions: The Trial of Shi Jianqiao and the Rise of Popular Sympathy in Republican China* (Berkeley: University of California Press, 2007). An exploration of Habermas's concept of the "literary public sphere" for the context of modern China is Haiyan Lee, "All the Feelings That Are Fit to Print: The Community of Sentiment and the Literary Public Sphere in China, 1900–1918," *Modern China* 27, no. 3 (2001): 291–327.

30. Maruyama Masao, *Nihon seiji shisōshi kenkyū* (Tokyo: Tōkyō daigaku shuppankai, 2014), 106–17. For more context on these discourses, see chapter 1. For a complete translation, see Masao Maruyama, *Studies in the Intellectual History of Tokugawa Japan*, trans. Mikiso Hane (Princeton, N.J.: Princeton University Press, 1974).

31. Peter Flueckiger, *Imagining Harmony: Poetry, Empathy, and Community in Mid-Tokugawa Confucianism and Nativism* (Stanford, Calif.: Stanford University Press, 2011), 32.

32. On this aspect, see the excellent discussion in Ueda, *Concealment of Politics*, chapter 6. For a thorough historicization of the notion of the "self," see Suzuki, *Narrating the Self*, chapter 2.

33. Senuma Shigeki, "Shinri bungaku no hatten to sono kisū" [The development of psychological literature and its result, 1930], in *Bungei hyōron shū*, ed. Honma Hisao, Gendai Nihon bungaku taikei 96 (Tokyo: Chikuma shobō, 1973), 145. See also the helpful discussion of this essay in Suzuki Sadami, *Nihon no "bungaku" gainen* (Tokyo: Sakuhinsha, 1998), 272–73. Senuma's agenda was to demonstrate that the "bourgeois" psychological realism initiated by Shōyō's literary reform had to be replaced by the new movement of proletarian fiction.

34. Lee also identifies a "revolutionary structure of feeling" arising in the 1930s. While emphasizing the epistemic breaks separating these different structures of feeling, she also pays attention to transitional literary works and genres; see Haiyan Lee, *Revolution of the Heart: A Genealogy of Love in China, 1900–1950* (Stanford, Calif.: Stanford University Press, 2007), 81–91, 315n7. For the original concept of structure

of feeling, see Raymond Williams, *Marxism and Literature* (Oxford: Oxford University Press, 1977), 128–35.

35. Lee, *Revolution of the Heart*, 8.

36. For a recent critique of this narrative from the perspective of the "spatiality of emotion" in early-modern Chinese fiction and drama, see Ling Hon Lam, *The Spatiality of Emotion in Early Modern China: From Dreamscapes to Theatricality* (New York: Columbia University Press, 2018).

37. Satoko Shimazaki, *Edo Kabuki in Transition: From the Worlds of the Samurai to the Vengeful Female Ghost* (New York: Columbia University Press, 2016), masterfully describes the eruption of strong female affects on the *bakumatsu* stage, greatly contrasting with the martial, public, and male-centered "worlds" of eighteenth-century classical kabuki. Shimazaki thus describes, from an angle different from mine, the early nineteenth century as a historical moment marked by an intensified awareness of emotion. For a recent discussion of discourses surrounding the morally dubious quality of male-female love and desire in nineteenth-century Japanese poetry, see also Robert Tuck, *Idly Scribbling Rhymers: Poetry, Print, and Community in Nineteenth-Century Japan* (New York: Columbia University Press, 2018), chapters 2 and 5.

38. For a discussion of specific socioeconomic factors underlying the eighteenth-century interest in emotion, see Flueckiger, *Imagining Harmony*, 3. See also David Atherton, "Valences of Vengeance: The Moral Imagination of Early Modern Japanese Vendetta Fiction" (PhD diss., Columbia University, 2013), chapter 4, for anxieties over an increasingly capitalist economy that shaped the melodramatic aesthetic in early nineteenth-century *gōkan* vendetta narratives.

39. "Novel of human emotion and social customs" is Hiraoka Toshio's term in *Nihon kindai bungaku no shuppatsu* (Tokyo: Hanawa shobō, 1992). See chapter 3 for a discussion of the genealogy of the "novel of human emotion and social customs."

1. FROM *NINJŌ* TO THE *NINJŌBON*

1. Ki no Tsurayuki (ca. 868–945) had already made a similar point about *waka* (classical Japanese poetry) in his famous preface to the *Kokinshū* (*Collection of Ancient and Modern Poems*, ca. 905). Murasaki Shikibu probably borrowed the idea in her discourse on narrative fiction.

2. The idea of expedient means was central to the famous *Lotus Sutra* (Jp. *Hokekyō*). In its most famous parable, the Buddha likens his teachings to the toy carts that a father uses to lure his children out of a burning house, the world of sensuous delusions. See Burton Watson, trans., *The Lotus Sutra* (New York: Columbia University Press, 1993), 56–62.

3. Murasaki Shikibu, *Genji monogatari*, ed. Yanai Shigeshi et al., vol. 2, SNKBT 20 (Tokyo: Iwanami shoten, 1994), 440.

4. David L. Rolston, *Traditional Chinese Fiction and Fiction Commentary: Reading and Writing Between the Lines* (Stanford, Calif.: Stanford University Press, 1997), chapters 5 and 6.

5. For Buddhist and Confucian readings of *The Tale of Genji* in a historical perspective, see Thomas Harper and Haruo Shirane, eds., *Reading* The Tale of Genji: *Sources*

from the First Millennium (New York: Columbia University Press, 2015). For a concise overview of the ambivalent pre-Meiji reception of *The Tale of Genji* as either "woman's romance," often decried as licentious, or a "men's classic" with cultural and didactic value, see Gillian Gaye Rowley, *Yosano Akiko and* The Tale of Genji (Ann Arbor: Center for Japanese Studies, University of Michigan, 2000), chapter 1.

6. Tsubouchi Shōyō, *Imotose kagami*, in *Tsubouchi Shōyō shū*, ed. Inagaki Tatsurō, MBZ 16 (Tokyo: Chikuma shobō, 1969), 195.

7. On the Mao tradition of poetic commentary, see Steven Van Zoeren, *Poetry and Personality: Reading, Exegesis, and Hermeneutics in Traditional China* (Stanford, Calif.: Stanford University Press, 1991); Peter Flueckiger, *Imagining Harmony: Poetry, Empathy, and Community in Mid-Tokugawa Confucianism and Nativism* (Stanford, Calif.: Stanford University Press, 2011), chapter 1.

8. The translation (slightly modified) is from Stephen Owen, *Readings in Chinese Literary Thought* (Cambridge, Mass.: Harvard University Council on East Asian Studies, 1992), 41.

9. Ling Hon Lam, *The Spatiality of Emotion in Early Modern China: From Dreamscapes to Theatricality* (New York: Columbia University Press, 2018), 20–25, presents a revisionist reading of the "Great Preface" that questions the model of emotion as inner response to outside stimuli. Instead, he highlights the affinity of emotion to the concept of "winds" (Ch. *feng*, Jp. *fū*) in the treatise—also the name of the most important genre of *Shijing* poetry—as an all-penetrating and "embedding" cosmic force that does not rely on the inside-outside dichotomy.

10. Translation from Stephen Owen, *An Anthology of Chinese Literature: Beginnings to 1911* (New York: Norton, 1996), 30–31.

11. Mao commentary as cited in Owen, *Anthology of Chinese Literature*, 31. Note that the *Shijing* was traditionally believed to be the compilation of Confucius, and the first poem thus carried a particular interpretive weight for the anthology as a whole.

12. The "Great Preface" refers to not only emotion as the psychological origin of poetic composition but also human intent or will (Ch. *zhi*, Jp. *shi*), which is more unambiguously ethical. Note the famous dictum, "The poem is that to which the intent goes. In the mind it is intent; coming out in language, it is a poem" (Owen, *Readings*, 40, with minor modifications).

13. The "Record of Music" is a chapter of the *Record of Rites* (*Liji*), which had been compiled by the first century CE. For a translation of the relevant passages, see Owen, *Readings*, 50–56.

14. The most systematic early reflection on desire and the need to regulate it through ritual is found in the *Xunzi* (third century BCE); see in particular the chapter on "Ritual." For a comprehensive discussion of the early philosophical discourses, including the *Xunzi*, see Anthony C. Yu, *Rereading the Stone: Desire and the Making of Fiction in* Dream of the Red Chamber (Princeton, N.J.: Princeton University Press, 1997), chapter 2.

15. A. C. Graham, *Studies in Chinese Philosophy and Philosophical Literature* (Albany: State University of New York Press, 1990), 59–66, argues that *qing* in pre-Han literature never meant "emotion" or "passions" but "the facts" or a quality that could be translated as "essence." For a critique of this view, see Chad Hansen, "Qing (Emotions) 情 in Pre-Buddhist Chinese Thought," in *Emotions in Asian Thought: A*

Dialogue in Comparative Philosophy, ed. Joel Marks and Roger T. Ames (Albany: State University of New York Press, 1995), 181–211.

16. Useful discussions I consulted are Thomas A. Metzger, *Escape from Predicament: Neo-Confucianism and China's Evolving Political Culture* (New York: Columbia University Press, 1977); Martin W. Huang, *Desire and Fictional Narrative in Late Imperial China* (Cambridge, Mass.: Harvard University Asia Center, 2001), chapter 2; Flueckiger, *Imagining Harmony*, chapter 1.

17. The reference is to *Analects*, 7:30. For a translation, see Confucius, *The Analects (Lun yü)*, trans. D. C. Lau (London: Penguin Books, 1979), 90.

18. Translation from Wing-tsit Chan, *A Source Book in Chinese Philosophy* (Princeton, N.J.: Princeton University Press, 1963), 631.

19. Huang, *Desire and Fictional Narrative*, 28.

20. For a discussion of Zhu Xi's *Shijing* commentary, titled "Shijizhuan" (Collected transmissions of the *Shijing*), and its appropriation of the "Record of Music," see Flueckiger, *Imagining Harmony*, 43–45.

21. Nakamura Yukihiko, *Kinsei bungei shichōkō* (Tokyo: Iwanami shoten, 1975), chapter 1.

22. For one example among many of the use of the *kaiin dōyoku* formula, see Kyokutei Bakin, *Nansō Satomi hakkenden*, ed. Hamada Keisuke, vol. 10, Shinchō Nihon koten shūsei bekkan 10 (Tokyo: Shinchōsha: 2004), 261.

23. Note that *qing*, since Lu Ji's (261–303) canonical dictum that "poetry follows from emotions" (*shi yuan qing*), had been a positive term in the discourse of Chinese poetry criticism, independently of *Shijing* exegesis. The dictum is from Lu Ji's (261–303) "Wenfu" ("The Poetic Exposition on Literature") and reformulated the famous phrase from the "Great Preface" that "poetry expresses the moral intent" (*shi yan zhi*). For a discussion and translation of the "Wenfu," see Owen, *Readings*, chapter 4. A still indispensable study of *qing* in Chinese poetry criticism is Siu-kit Wong, "Ch'ing in Chinese Literary Criticism" (PhD diss., Oxford University, 1969).

24. See James McMullen's discussion and abridged translation of Banzan's treatise in Harper and Shirane, *Reading* The Tale of Genji, 385–92. A comprehensive study is James McMullen, *Idealism, Protest, and* The Tale of Genji: *The Confucianism of Kumazawa Banzan (1619–91)* (Oxford: Oxford University Press, 1999). Also note that Banzan's position here anticipates Ogyū Sorai's slightly later stance on *Shijing* poetry; on Sorai, see Flueckiger, *Imagining Harmony*, chapters 2 and 3.

25. Andō Tameakira, *Shika shichiron* [*Seven Essays on Murasaki Shikibu*], in *Hihyō shūsei Genji monogatari*, ed. Akiyama Ken et al. (Tokyo: Yumani shobō, 1999), 1:218. Translation, with minor modifications, by Satoko Naito, in Harper and Shirane, *Reading* The Tale of Genji, 402.

26. Andō, *Shika shichiron*, 220.

27. Motoori Norinaga, *Genji monogatari tama no ogushi* [The Tale of Genji: *A Little Bejeweled Comb*], in *Motoori Norinaga zenshū*, ed. Ōno Susumu and Ōkubo Tadashi (Tokyo: Chikuma shobō, 1969), 4:199. For a detailed study and translation, see Thomas J. Harper, "Motoori Norinaga's Criticism of the *Genji monogatari*: A Study of the Background and Critical Content of His *Genji monogatari tama no ogushi*" (PhD diss., University of Michigan, 1971).

28. See the excellent discussion in Flueckiger, *Imagining Harmony*, chapter 6; on Nori-naga's didacticism, see also Thomas Harper's discussion in Harper and Shirane, *Reading* The Tale of Genji, 416.

29. Throughout my study, I use "Sinitic poetry" to refer to *kanshi* poetry and "literary Sinitic" to *kanbun* prose. Both terms are potentially inclusive of writings produced by authors in China, Japan, or other regions in the Sinosphere. I follow here Matthew Fraleigh, *Plucking Chrysanthemums: Narushima Ryūhoku and Sinitic Literary Traditions in Modern Japan* (Cambridge, Mass.: Harvard University Asia Center, 2016), 20–28.

30. Flueckiger, *Imagining Harmony*, 52.

31. See Flueckiger, *Imagining Harmony*, 54 and 241n39, for Jinsai's interpretation of "considerateness" (Ch. *shu*, Jp. *jo*), a term that Confucius uses in the *Analects*.

32. Itō Jinsai, *Kogaku sensei bunshū*, in *Itō Jinsai Itō Tōgai*, ed. Yoshikawa Kōjirō and Shimizu Shigeru, Nihon shisō taikei 33 (Tokyo: Iwanami shoten, 1971), 279. The translation, with minor modifications, is from Lawrence E. Marceau, "*Ninjō* and the Affective Value of Literature at the Kogidō Academy," *Sino-Japanese Studies* 9, no. 1 (1996): 49. For a discussion of the passage, see also Nakamura, *Kinsei bungei*, 64.

33. Itō Jinsai, *Dōjimon*, in *Kinsei shisōka bunshū*, ed. Ienaga Saburō et al., NKBT 97 (Tokyo: Iwanami shoten, 1966), 157. For a translation and insightful discussion of this passage, see Emanuel Pastreich, *The Observable Mundane: Vernacular Chinese and the Emergence of a Literary Discourse on Popular Narrative in Edo Japan* (Seoul: Seoul National University Press, 2011), 166–67. The terms *yashi* and *haisetsu* are synonymous with *haishi* and *shōsetsu*.

34. Nakamura, *Kinsei bungei*, 56. The reference is to Baiu's *Kenbun dansō* [Collection of things seen and heard, probably written in 1738], ed. Kamei Nobuaki (Tokyo: Iwanami shoten, 1940), 243.

35. Hozumi Ikan, "Chikamatsu no gensetsu: *Naniwa miyage* hottanshō," in *Chikamatsu jōruri shū*, vol. 2, ed. Shuzui Kenji and Ōkubo Tadakuni, NKBT 50 (Tokyo: Iwanami shoten, 1959), 356–57. See also Michael C. Brownstein's translation in *Early Modern Japanese Literature: An Anthology, 1600–1900*, ed. Haruo Shirane (New York: Columbia University Press, 2002), 347–51.

36. For a helpful discussion of *Naniwa miyage* paying attention to the treatise's references to sinological knowledge, see Pastreich, *The Observable Mundane*, 180–82; for Ikan's indebtedness to traditional Chinese poetry criticism, see also Nakamura, *Kinsei bungei*, chapter 5.

37. Minamoto Ryōen, *Giri to ninjō: Nihonteki shinjō no ichikōsatsu* (Tokyo: Chūōkōronsha, 2013), 121–81, offers a similar interpretation of Chikamatsu's plays.

38. Harper and Shirane, *Reading* The Tale of Genji, 389.

39. Motoori, *Genji monogatari tama no ogushi*, 214–15. Norinaga dismisses a reading of "good" and "bad" in Confucian terms, instead relating these terms to human sensibility or the ability to "understand *mono no aware*."

40. The scholarship I consulted includes Martin W. Huang, "Sentiments of Desire: Thoughts on the Cult of Qing in Ming-Qing Literature," *Chinese Literature* 20 (1998): 153–84, and *Desire and Fictional Narrative*; Dorothy Ko, *Teachers of the Inner Chambers: Women and Culture in Seventeenth-Century China* (Stanford, Calif.: Stanford University Press, 1994), and "Thinking About Copulating: An Early-Qing Confucian Thinker's Problem with Emotion and Words," in *Remapping China: Fissures*

in Historical Terrain, ed. Gail Hershatter et al. (Stanford, Calif.: Stanford University Press, 1996), 59–76; Lam, *Spatiality of Emotion*; Haiyan Lee, *Revolution of the Heart: A Genealogy of Love in China, 1900–1950* (Stanford, Calif.: Stanford University Press, 2007); Wai-yee Li, *Enchantment and Disenchantment: Love and Illusion in Chinese Literature* (Princeton, N.J.: Princeton University Press, 1993); Yu, *Rereading the Stone.*

41. The mainstream of Chinese discourse on love appears to have been concerned with male-female relationships. For homoeroticism in late imperial Chinese culture and literature, see Cuncun Wu, *Homoerotic Sensibilities in Late Imperial China* (London: RoutledgeCurzon, 2004); Giovanni Vitiello, *The Libertine's Friend: Homosexuality and Masculinity in Late Imperial China* (Chicago: University of Chicago Press, 2011).

42. See Paolo Santangelo, "The Cult of Love in Some Texts of Ming and Qing Literature," *East and West* 50, no. 1/4 (2000): 439–99.

43. The five cardinal relationships are between lord and minister, father and son, older brother and younger brother, husband and wife, friend and friend.

44. Hua-yuan Li Mowry, trans., *Chinese Love Stories from* Ch'ing-shih (Hamden, Conn.: Archon Books, 1983), 6. See also Feng Menglong's (1574–1645) similar remarks in his *Qingshi leilüe* (History of emotion in encyclopedic categories), an anthology of stories about *qing*. Mowry's book is a partial translation of Feng's anthology.

45. Lee, *Revolution of the Heart*, 38.

46. For contemporary female readings of the play, see Ko, *Teachers of the Inner Chambers*, 84–89; Judith T. Zeitlin, "Shared Dreams: The Story of the Three Wives' Commentary on *The Peony Pavilion*," *Harvard Journal of Asiatic Studies* 54, no. 1 (1994): 127–79. For a recent rereading, see Lam, *Spatiality of Emotion*, chapter 1.

47. William D. Fleming, "Strange Tales from Edo: *Liaozhai zhiyi* in Early Modern Japan," *Sino-Japanese Studies* 20 (2013): 75–115.

48. On the four masterworks, see Andrew H. Plaks, *The Four Masterworks of the Ming Novel: Ssu ta ch'i-shu* (Princeton, N.J.: Princeton University Press, 1987). My discussion here follows Huang, *Desire and Fictional Narrative*, chapter 3.

49. Huang's own project is to retrace the various permutations of this intertextual awareness in vernacular Chinese works up to the *Hongloumeng.*

50. Huang, *Desire and Fictional Narrative*, 67.

51. See Richard C. Hessney, "Beautiful, Talented, and Brave: Seventeenth-Century Chinese Scholar-Beauty Romances" (PhD diss., Columbia University, 1979); Huang, *Desire and Fictional Narrative*, chapter 8; Keith McMahon, *Misers, Shrews, and Polygamists: Sexuality and Male-Female Relations in Eighteenth-Century Chinese Fiction* (Durham, N.C.: Duke University Press, 1995), chapters 5 and 6.

52. For a translation, see John Francis Davis, trans., *The Fortunate Union: A Romance*, 2 vols. (London: Oriental Translation Fund, 1829). The major seventeenth-century scholar and beauty narratives were the first Chinese novels to be fully—and, I should add, quite accurately—translated into European languages, including German and French.

53. Motoori, *Genji monogatari tama no ogushi*, 174, 215.

54. Jonathan E. Zwicker, *Practices of the Sentimental Imagination: Melodrama, the Novel, and the Social Imaginary in Nineteenth-Century Japan* (Cambridge, Mass.: Harvard University Asia Center, 2006), 134–35; Ōba Osamu, *Edo jidai ni okeru tōsen*

mochiwatarisho no kenkyū (Suita: Kansai daigaku tōzai gakujutsu kenkyūjo, 1967), and *Edo jidai ni okeru Chūgoku bunka juyō no kenkyū* (Kyoto: Dōhōsha shuppan, 1984). I am aware of William Fleming's caveat that the simple number of imported Chinese books is not necessarily a meaningful indicator of a work's dissemination and reception in Japan; see Fleming, "Strange Tales from Edo," 77. Bakin's observation, however, that scholar and beauty novels were "recently" imported in great numbers seems to indicate that the genre was quite widely received, at least by the time Bakin wrote his preface (1839); see Kyokutei, *Hakkenden*, 10:261, and my discussion of this important preface in chapter 2.

55. The vernacular Chinese language, unlike literary Sinitic, was a particular challenge for Japanese readers. On *Jinpingmei*'s difficulty, see Kanda Masayuki, *Bakin to shomotsu: Denki sekai no teiryū* (Tokyo: Yagi shoten, 2011), 525.

56. Kawashima Yūko, "Edo jidai ni okeru *Kinpeibai* no juyō (1): Jisho, zuihitsu, sharebon o chūshin toshite," *Ryūkoku kiyō* 32, no. 1 (2010): 1–20.

57. *Hachimonjiya* books broadly referred to the genre of *ukiyozōshi* (books of the floating world), a genre of narrative fiction that flourished in the first half of the eighteenth century.

58. A Japanese translation of this erotic novel was published in 1760 under the title *Tsūzoku Zui Yōdai gaishi* (A Japanese version of the history of Emperor Yang of the Sui); see Pastreich, *The Observable Mundane*, 29. The original title of the Chinese work is *Sui Yangdi yanshi* (Salacious history of Emperor Yang of the Sui dynasty [581–618]).

59. The titles of these two famous scholar and beauty novels consist of the names of their protagonists.

60. Quoted from Nakamura, *Kinsei bungei*, 253–54. For the original manuscript, see Katsube Seigyo, *Sentō zuihitsu*, 3rd fasc., n.d., National Diet Library, Tokyo, or online at http://dl.ndl.go.jp/info:ndljp/pid/2566455?tocOpened=1, frame numbers 12–13. I am grateful to one of my anonymous reviewers for pointing out two mistakes in Nakamura's transcription. In my translation, these mistakes have been revised.

61. See especially Hagiwara Hiromichi's (1815–1863) later commentarial project on *The Tale of Genji*. This project relied on the incorporation of the vocabulary of vernacular Chinese fiction criticism. For a detailed study, see Patrick W. Caddeau, *Appraising* Genji: *Literary Criticism and Cultural Anxiety in the Age of the Last Samurai* (Albany: State University of New York Press, 2006).

62. William C. Hedberg, "Separating the Word and the Way: Suyama Nantō's *Chūgi Suikodenkai* and Edo-Period Vernacular Philology," *Journal of Japanese Studies* 41, no. 2 (2015): 351. However, Pastreich, *The Observable Mundane*, 19, argues that, unlike in China, where vernacular fiction did not enjoy a particularly reputable status until the twentieth century, in eighteenth-century Japan "Chinese vernacular narrative remained within the larger, privileged, discourse of Chinese culture."

63. See Glynne Walley, *Good Dogs: Edification, Entertainment, and Kyokutei Bakin's* Nansō Satomi hakkenden (Ithaca, N.Y.: Cornell University East Asia Program, 2017), chapter 4. For an earlier Japanese critic's engagement with *The Water Margin* and its dubious morality, see William C. Hedberg, "Reclaiming the Margins: Seita Tansō's *Suikoden hihyōkai* and the Poetics of Cross-Cultural Influence," *International Journal of Asian Studies* 12, no. 2 (2015): 193–215.

64. See the discussion of Tsuga Teishō's literary adaptations in Nan Ma Hartmann, "From Translation to Adaptation: Chinese Language Texts and Early Modern Japanese Literature" (PhD diss., Columbia University, 2014). On Morishima Chūryō, see William D. Fleming, "The World Beyond the Walls: Morishima Chūryō (1756–1810) and the Development of Late Edo Fiction" (PhD diss., Harvard University, 2011).

65. As in Asai Ryōi's (ca. 1612–1691) famous story "Peony Lantern" (Botan no tōrō), in the collection *Otogi bōko* (Hand puppets, 1666), which foreshadows the *yomihon* written by eighteenth-century Japanese literati.

66. For these discourses, see Huang, *Desire and Fictional Narrative*, chapter 1.

67. *Shunshoku umegoyomi* was first published by Bun'eidō in Edo. Its illustrator was Yanagawa Shigenobu (1787–1832).

68. Tamenaga Shunsui, *Shunshoku umegoyomi*, in *Shunshoku umegoyomi*, ed. Nakamura Yukihiko, NKBT 64 (Tokyo: Iwanami shoten, 1971), 189, and *Harutsugedori* [The warbler announcing spring, 1836–1837], in *Sharebon, kokkeibon, ninjōbon*, ed. Nakano Mitsutoshi, Jinbō Kazuya, and Maeda Ai, SNKBZ 80 (Tokyo: Shōgakukan, 2000), 466.

69. Nakamura Yukihiko, "Ninjōbon to chūhongata yomihon," in *Kinsei shōsetsu yōshiki shikō* (Tokyo: Chūōkōronsha, 1982), 459–78.

70. On Hanasanjin, see Sara Langer, "Sentimental Fictions: A Study of Gender Politics in Selected Writings of Hanasanjin (1790–1858)" (PhD diss., Indiana University, 2002).

71. For the increase in *ninjō*-related themes in regular *yomihon* of the Kansei (1789–1801) and Kyōwa (1801–1804) periods, see Kigoshi Shunsuke, *Edo Ōsaka no shuppan ryūtsū to yomihon, ninjōbon* (Osaka: Seibundō, 2013), 143–67. See also the relevant chapters in Tokuda Takeshi, *Nihon kinsei shōsetsu to Chūgoku shōsetsu* (Musashi Murayama: Seishōdō shoten, 1987), and Yan Xiaomei, "Nihon ni okeru saishi kajin shōsetsu no juyō ni tsuite: Torai saishi kajin shōsetsu mokuroku," in *Yomihon kenkyū shinshū*, ed. Yomihon Kenkyū no Kai (Tokyo: Kanrin shobō, 2003), 4:124–44.

72. Yan, "Nihon ni okeru saishi kajin shōsetsu," 130, refers to a section probably authored by Shunsui in *Zōho gedai kagami* (Enlarged mirror of literary titles, 1838), where an as yet unpublished adaptation of scholar and beauty fiction by Bakin is advertised and discussed. See also Nakamura Katsunori, "Kyokutei Bakin to ninjōbon," *Sōsho Edo bunko geppō* 36 (1995): 2–3.

73. Tamenaga Shunsui, *Shungyō Hachimangane* (Tokyo: Tōkyō fukyūsha, 1932), 32.

74. Hino Tatsuo, "Kaisetsu: 'Mono no aware o shiru' no setsu no raireki," in *Motoori Norinaga shū*, ed. Hino Tatsuo, Shinchō Nihon koten shūsei 60 (Tokyo: Shinchōsha, 1983), 505–51.

75. Maruyama Shigeru, *Shunsui ninjōbon no kenkyū* (Tokyo: Ōfūsha, 1978), 7–44.

76. See Mutō Motoaki, *Ninjōbon no sekai: Edo no "ada" ga tsumugu ren'ai monogatari* (Tokyo: Kasama shoin, 2014), chapter 3, for a discussion of the notion of "exposing emotion" (*ninjō o ugatsu*) in *kokkeibon* and later *ninjōbon*. Mutō argues that *ninjōbon* and *kokkeibon* are directly related.

77. Tamenaga, *Shunshoku umegoyomi*, 68.

78. Tamenaga, *Shunshoku umegoyomi*, 101–2.

79. Tamenaga, *Shunshoku umegoyomi*, 148–49.

80. The publisher of the first edition of *Shunshoku tatsumi no sono* is unknown. The illustrator was Utagawa Kuninao (1793–1854).

81. Tamenaga, *Shungyō Hachimangane*, 47–50.
82. Tamenaga, *Shunshoku umegoyomi*, 173. For the view that Shunsui here has Bakin in mind, see Jinbō Kazuya, *Tamenaga Shunsui no kenkyū* (Tokyo: Hakujitsusha, 1964), 101–2.
83. Tamenaga, *Shunshoku umegoyomi*, 237, and *Shunshoku tatsumi no sono*, in *Shunshoku umegoyomi*, ed. Nakamura Yukihiko, NKBT 64 (Tokyo: Iwanami shoten, 1971), 242. For Shunsui's awareness of Bakin, see also Nakamura Yukihiko, "Kaisetsu," in *Shunshoku umegoyomi*, 11–12.
84. See, for instance, Tamenaga, *Shunshoku umegoyomi*, 148.
85. On Bakin's and Seiken's critique, see Nakamura, "Kaisetsu," 24–25.
86. Kimura Mokurō, "Kokuji shōsetsu tsū," in *Zoku enseki jisshu*, ed. Iwamoto Kattōshi (Tokyo: Chūōkōronsha, 1980), 1:303.
87. Kimura, "Kokuji shōsetsu tsū," 299.
88. Peter F. Kornicki, *The Book in Japan: A Cultural History from the Beginnings to the Nineteenth Century* (Honolulu: University of Hawai'i Press, 2001), 344–45; Maeda Ai, "Tenpō kaikaku ni okeru sakusha to shoshi," in *Kindai dokusha no seiritsu* (Tokyo: Chikuma shobō, 1989), 18–24. According to the documents that Maeda cites, the censorship of the year 1842 to which Shunsui fell victim targeted, among other items, "erotic picture books" (*kōshoku ehon*). Obscenity remained a major censorship criterion in the modern system as well; see Jay Rubin, *Injurious to Public Morals: Writers and the Meiji State* (Seattle: University of Washington Press, 1984).
89. Kyokutei, *Hakkenden*, 8:309–14.
90. For a reading that highlights dialogic performance (*engi*) in Shunsui's writings, see Inoue Yasushi, *Ren'ai shōsetsu no tanjō: Romansu, shōhi, iki* (Tokyo: Kasama shoin, 2009), chapters 2–4. For a different reading of *Shunshoku umegoyomi* as melodrama, see Zwicker, *Practices*, chapter 2.
91. Tamenaga, *Shunshoku tatsumi no sono*, 369–70.

2. QUESTIONING THE IDEALIST NOVEL

1. Kimura Mokurō, "Kokuji shōsetsu tsū," in *Zoku enseki jisshu*, ed. Iwamoto Kattōshi (Tokyo: Chūōkōronsha, 1980), 1:293–306.
2. Kyokutei Bakin, *Kinsei mononohon Edo sakusha burui*, ed. Tokuda Takeshi (Tokyo: Iwanami shoten, 2014), 154. On Bakin's understanding of *yomihon*, see also Glynne Walley, *Good Dogs: Edification, Entertainment, and Kyokutei Bakin's Nansō Satomi hakkenden* (Ithaca, N.Y.: Cornell University East Asia Program, 2017), chapter 2.
3. This is the phonetic gloss Shōyō provides for *gokubi shōsetsu* 極美小説. See Tsubouchi Shōyō, "Aidiaru noberu no koto ni tsukite," in *Tsubouchi Shōyō kenkyū: Fu, bungakuron shoshutsu shiryō*, ed. Ishida Tadahiko (Fukuoka: Kyūshū daigaku shuppankai, 1988), 426–28.
4. My understanding of *kanzen chōaku* in *Hakkenden* here follows the excellent discussion in Walley, *Good Dogs*, chapter 4. The most comprehensive discussion of the concept historically is Hamada Keisuke, "'Kanzen chōaku' hoshi," in *Kinsei shōsetsu: Eii to yōshiki ni kansuru shiken* (Kyoto: Kyōto daigaku gakujutsu shuppankai, 1993), 397–438.

5. For the dates of publication and the publishers of *Hakkenden* over the course of the work's almost thirty years of serialization, see Thomas Glynne Walley, "'I Would Rather Be a Faithful Dog Than an Unrighteous Man': Virtue and Vice in Kyokutei Bakin's *Nansō Satomi hakkenden*" (PhD diss., Harvard University, 2009), 30–37.

6. *Hakkenden*'s positive ending was the conscious attempt to rewrite and correct the plot of *The Water Margin*, which Bakin and other critics perceived as morally deficient. On this aspect and Bakin's critical views of *The Water Margin*, see Walley, *Good Dogs*, chapter 4.

7. Bakin's commercial profit from *yomihon*, however, was lower than from the illustrated and more heavily entertaining *kusazōshi* and *gōkan*. Hamada Keisuke links this to the artistic and critical ambition that Bakin pursued in writing *yomihon*. See Hamada Keisuke, "Bakin o meguru shoshi, sakusha, dokusha no mondai," in *Kinsei shōsetsu*, 272–97.

8. Bakin's adaptation of the *Jinpingmei* was a *gōkan*, titled *Shinpen Kinpeibai* (*The Plum in the Golden Vase* newly edited, 1831–1847). The most comprehensive scholarship on this text is Kanda Masayuki, *Bakin to shomotsu: Denki sekai no teiryū* (Tokyo: Yagi shoten, 2011).

9. Walley, *Good Dogs*, 30.

10. For an insightful discussion of Bakin's playful adaptation of literary sources, see Walley, *Good Dogs*, chapter 3.

11. I have not been able to ascertain the third title Bakin cites.

12. Kyokutei Bakin, *Nansō Satomi hakkenden*, ed. Hamada Keisuke, vol. 10, Shinchō Nihon koten shūsei bekkan 10 (Tokyo: Shinchōsha, 2004), 260–61.

13. In the *Jinpingmei*, Ximen Qing dies as a result of his overindulgence in erotic desire and only Pan Jinlian dies at the hands of her husband's brother.

14. Kyokutei Bakin to Tonomura Jōsai, Tenpō 13/3/26 [April 18, 1830], in *Bakin shokan shūsei*, ed. Shibata Mitsuhiko and Kanda Masayuki (Tokyo: Yagi shoten, 2002), 1:287–89. For a helpful overview of Bakin's critical views on *Jinpingmei*, see Kawashima Yūko, "Edo jidai ni okeru *Kinpeibai* no juyō (2): Kyokutei Bakin no kijutsu o chūshin toshite," *Ryūkoku kiyō* 32, no. 2 (2011): 35–57.

15. Bakin was nonetheless fearful of the censorship that struck Shunsui and other authors in the early 1840s. See Maeda Ai, "Tenpō kaikaku ni okeru sakusha to shoshi," in *Kindai dokusha no seiritsu* (Tokyo: Chikuma shobō, 1989), 23.

16. Even earlier, during the Bunka period (1804–1818), Bakin wrote middle-sized (*chūhon*) *yomihon* that bore a strong affinity to scholar and beauty plots but often borrowed their material from theatrical, especially *jōruri*, sources. See Kigoshi Shunsuke, *Edo Ōsaka no shuppan ryūtsū to yomihon, ninjōbon* (Osaka: Seibundō, 2013), 168–87, who also discusses how Bakin strove to establish a distance from theatrical sources.

17. For an insightful discussion of this novel and its subversive political implications, see Kamei Hideo, "*Shōsetsu*" ron: "*Shōsetsu shinzui*" to kindai (Tokyo: Iwanami shoten, 1999), chapter 3. For Bakin's appropriation of *The Fortunate Union*, see also Ling Hon Lam, *The Spatiality of Emotion in Early Modern China: From Dreamscapes to Theatricality* (New York: Columbia University Press, 2018), chapter 4.

18. Uchida Roan, "*Hakkenden* yodan," in *Uchida Roan zenshū*, ed. Nomura Takashi (Tokyo: Yumani shobō, 1985), 4:449. Another similar episode that, according to

Roan, was loved by Meiji youth was the scene where the dog warrior Inumura Dai-kaku chastely resists the advances of his beautiful wife, Hinakinu.

19. Shino will marry the surrogate of his former fiancée, Hamaji, who carries the same name and is one of Satomi Yoshinari's daughters.

20. Ellen Widmer, *The Margins of Utopia: Shui-hu hou-chuan and the Literature of Ming Loyalism* (Cambridge, Mass.: Harvard University Council on East Asian Studies, 1987), chapter 5, discusses similar scholar and beauty motifs in the *Shuihu houzhuan* (*The Water Margin* continued). This was an early Qing-period martial novel and sequel to *The Water Margin* known to Bakin. His exposure to scholar and beauty motifs, however, derived from his direct acquaintance with the genre rather than through his reception of martial works like the *Shuihu houzhuan*.

21. Kyokutei Bakin to Ozu Keisō, Tenpō 11/1/8 [February 10, 1840], in *Bakin shokan shūsei*, 5:154. For the context, see Nakamura Katsunori, "Kyokutei Bakin to ninjōbon," *Sōsho Edo bunko geppō* 36 (1995): 1–5, and Kanda Masayuki, "Saishi kajin shōsetsu *Nidobai* to Bakin: Narabi ni Oda bunko-bon *Nidobai* no ichi," *Tōyō bunka* 96 (2006): 14–28.

22. Nakamura, "Kyokutei Bakin to ninjōbon," 3.

23. Mizuno Minoru, "Bakin bungaku no keisei," in *Edo shōsetsu ronsō* (Tokyo: Chūōkōronsha, 1974), 229.

24. Hattori Hitoshi, "Bakin to ninjō," in *Kyokutei Bakin no bungakuiki* (Tokyo: Wakakusa shobō, 1997), 31–32. Hattori and Mizuno are the only scholars to my knowledge to discuss the significance of *ninjō* in Bakin's works, but their concern is mostly with Bakin's usage of the term *ninjō* itself rather than the narrative and conceptual issues I examine.

25. The other important source of inspiration for Bakin's writing of *ninjō* was the theater, a topic that unfortunately lies beyond the scope of my study.

26. The Satomi clan was defeated at the historical Battle of Yūki (1441). *Hakkenden* starts with the scene of this battle and Yoshizane's subsequent search for a new territory, which he finds in the province of Awa. For a helpful guide through *Hakkenden*'s complex chronology, see Itasaka Noriko, "*Hakkenden* nenpyō," in *Kyokutei Bakin*, ed. Mizuno Minoru et al. (Tokyo: Shūeisha, 1980), 68–72; for a concise synopsis of the novel's plot, see Walley, *Good Dogs*, 375–96.

27. Kyokutei, *Hakkenden*, 1:157.

28. On the narrative function of the Buddhist principle of karmic cause and retribution (*inga ōhō*), see Tokuda Takeshi, "*Nansō Satomi hakkenden*: Ingaritsu no hatten," in *Iwanami kōza Nihon bungaku to bukkyō*, ed. Konno Tōru et al. (Tokyo: Iwanami shoten, 1994), 2:131–56.

29. Kyokutei, *Hakkenden*, 1:155.

30. Kyokutei, *Hakkenden*, 1:155. These are Tamazusa's own words, which she skillfully uses in her plea for pardon.

31. For scholars endorsing Bakin's discourse, see Ishikawa Hidemi, "Tamazusa juso no shatei," in *Fukkō suru Hakkenden*, ed. Suwa Haruo and Takada Mamoru (Tokyo: Bensei shuppan, 2008), 216–18, and Walley, *Good Dogs*, 242–44.

32. Kyokutei, *Hakkenden*, 1:299.

33. Kyokutei, *Hakkenden*, 1:299.

34. Kyokutei, *Hakkenden*, 1:323.

35. The dialogue comments on the early chapters of *Hakkenden* and Bakin's *yomihon Asaina shimameguri no ki* (A record of Asaina's island peregrinations, 1815–1858). For the passage I discuss, see Kyokutei Bakin, "Ken'i hyōbanki," in *Edo meibutsu hyōbanki shūsei*, ed. Nakano Mitsutoshi (Tokyo: Iwanami shoten, 1987), 352–55.

36. Chudai is the religious name of Kanamari Daisuke, who is an important unifying figure in *Hakkenden*. He becomes a monk after accidentally shooting Fusehime, to whom he had been betrothed. Through his wanderings as a monk he brings the scattered dog warriors together and serves as their spiritual father; his continuous prayers help accumulate the good karma that undoes Tamazusa's curse. But Daisuke's birth is also the product of an erotic transgression, which taints his virtue and reiterates *Hakkenden*'s leitmotif of the susceptibility of virtue to desire.

37. For the possible fictionality of "Ken'i hyōbanki," see Nakano Mitsutoshi, "Kaisetsu," in *Edo meibutsu hyōbanki shūsei*, 425–30.

38. The surname Obayuki has canine connotations through the proverb "Snow [*yuki*] is the aunt [*oba*] of a dog"; see Kyokutei, *Hakkenden*, 3:166–67 and 325.

39. For Awayuki Nashirō's crime of murder and licentiousness, see Kyokutei, *Hakkenden*, 4:312–13, 343. Note that virtuous protagonists who are receptive to illicit amorous feelings and desire also include the retainer Kanamari Takayoshi and the female fox, Masaki, the doppelgänger of the evil tanuki, Myōchin.

40. Hamada Keisuke, "*Hakkenden* no kōsō ni okeru tai-kanreisen no igi," in *Kinsei shōsetsu*, 357–67.

41. Kyokutei, *Hakkenden*, 7:228–29.

42. These are Lord Yoshinari's words; see Kyokutei, *Hakkenden*, 7:227.

43. Kyokutei, *Hakkenden*, 10:255.

44. Kyokutei, *Hakkenden*, 4:280–82. For another scene of reading from the *Taiheiki* involving erotic references, see Kyokutei, *Hakkenden*, 9:189–94.

45. Walley, *Good Dogs*, chapter 5, provides an insightful summary and discussion of the Tatsumi-Otoko episode, focusing in particular on the gender ambiguity of the woman Otoko, whose name literally means "man." Otoko's death scene establishes a connection between her and the tiger boy, which Walley reads as an indication of this gender ambiguity.

46. Kyokutei, *Hakkenden*, 10:142.

47. Tokuda Takeshi, "*Hakkenden* to Ienari jidai: 'Inbi' sairon," in *Nihon kinsei shōsetsu to Chūgoku shōsetsu* (Musashi Murayama: Seishōdō shoten, 1987), 715–63. Tokuda also interprets the tiger as an allusion to Ōshio Heihachirō's (1793–1837) popular revolt against bad shogunal policies in 1837. Similarly, Maeda Ai notes that, by writing Ikkyū's critique, Bakin briefly metamorphoses into a politically dangerous writer. See Maeda Ai, "*Hakkenden* no sekai: Yoru no aregorī," in *Bakumatsu ishinki no bungaku: Narushima Ryūhoku* (Tokyo: Chikuma shobō, 1989), 89.

48. For these references, see Takada Mamoru, *Kanpon "Hakkenden" no sekai* (Tokyo: Chikuma bungei bunko, 2005), 472–78.

49. Kyokutei, *Hakkenden*, 9:314–15.

50. Kyokutei, *Hakkenden*, 10:142–43.

51. Kyokutei, *Hakkenden*, 9:303.

52. Kyokutei, *Hakkenden*, 10:260.

53. Kyokutei, *Hakkenden*, 2:12.

54. Kyokutei, *Hakkenden*, 6:12.

55. For a discussion of *yomihon* readership that confirms Bakin's view, see Nakamura Yukihiko, "Yomihon no dokusha," in *Kinsei shōsetsushi no kenkyū* (Tokyo: Ōfūsha, 1961), 326.

56. Kyokutei, *Hakkenden*, 10:262–63.

57. For these critics, see David L. Rolston, *Traditional Chinese Fiction and Fiction Commentary: Reading and Writing Between the Lines* (Stanford, Calif.: Stanford University Press, 1997), chapters 1 and 2. See also chapter 5 for the attempt by Chinese critics to emancipate narrative fiction from the historiographical tradition.

58. Kamei, *"Shōsetsu" ron*, 103. For an overview of scholarly positions on *inbi*, see Walley, *Good Dogs*, chapter 3.

59. Hamada, "*Hakkenden* no kōsō," 361–67; Maeda, "*Hakkenden* no sekai," 89–91.

60. Kyokutei, *Hakkenden*, 12:425.

61. Kyokutei, *Hakkenden*, 12:427; see also 12:437–43. For the historical sources cited here, see Hamada Keisuke, "*Satomi hakkenden* to *Satomi gunki*," *Kinsei bungei* 42 (1985): 48–55.

62. Walley, *Good Dogs*, 344–46.

63. Kyokutei, *Hakkenden*, 1:253, 5:12, 11:11.

64. For the allegorically dense mirror imagery in traditional Buddhist discourse and Cao Xueqin's novel, see Anthony C. Yu, *Rereading the Stone: Desire and the Making of Fiction in* Dream of the Red Chamber (Princeton, N.J.: Princeton University Press, 1997), 137–51.

65. See the detailed discussion, based on evidence from Bakin's letters, in Kanda, "Saishi kajin shōsetsu *Nidobai* to Bakin," 23–27.

66. Bakin had probably read at least portions of *Hongloumeng* before attempting to reread the novel in the late 1830s for his *chūhon* adaptation, but Itō Sōhei voices doubts about his linguistic ability to comprehend the novel in nuanced depth. Especially its frequent dialogues in the Beijing dialect, according to Itō, were linguistically inaccessible to Bakin. See Itō Sōhei, "Nihon ni okeru *Kōrōmu* no ryūkō: Bakumatsu kara gendai made no shoshiteki sobyō," in *Chūgoku bungaku no hikaku bungakuteki kenkyū*, ed. Furuta Keiichi (Tokyo: Kyūko shoin, 1986), 460.

67. Tsubouchi Shōyō, *Shōsetsu shinzui*, in *Tsubouchi Shōyō shū*, ed. Nakamura Kan and Umezawa Nobuo, NKiBT 3 (Tokyo: Kadokawa shoten, 1974), 70.

3. TRANSLATING LOVE IN THE EARLY-MEIJI NOVEL

1. Iwamoto first refers only to the "period of the Fujiwara [regents]" (that is, the Heian period) but later includes the "feudal age" (*hōken no yo*) as well, a term used in reference to the Edo period. See Iwamoto Yoshiharu, "Fujin no chii," *Jogaku zasshi* 2 (1885): 24.

2. Iwamoto, "Fujin no chii," *Jogaku zasshi* 5 (1885): 83.

3. An early example of civilizational history is Taguchi Ukichi's *Nihon kaika shōshi* (A short civilizational history of Japan, 1877–1882). Miyazaki Koshoshi's (1874–1922) slightly later *Nihon jōkō no hensen* (Transformations of intimacy in Japan, 1887) provides a more elaborate version of Iwamoto's model of gender history. On the discourse of civilizational stages in Scottish enlightenment thought that influenced

discussions in Japan, see Albert M. Craig, *Civilization and Enlightenment: The Early Thought of Fukuzawa Yukichi* (Cambridge, Mass.: Harvard University Press, 2009), chapter 1. One example of a Scottish enlightenment treatise that, like Iwamoto's essay, investigates the "rank and condition of women" in connection to gender relations, sexuality, and love (including "passion") in various civilizational stages is John Millar's (1735–1801) *The Origin of the Distinction of Ranks* (1771). There was a broader discourse on women and civilizational development, though, and it is difficult to ascertain the exact source that might have influenced Iwamoto.

4. For a helpful discussion of "civilization and enlightenment" summarizing previous scholarship, see Douglas R. Howland, *Translating the West: Language and Political Reason in Nineteenth-Century Japan* (Honolulu: University of Hawai`i Press, 2002), chapter 2. See also David L. Howell, *Geographies of Identity in Nineteenth-Century Japan* (Berkeley: University of California Press, 2005), chapters 6–7; Craig, *Civilization and Enlightenment*.

5. On this aspect, see Sharon L. Sievers, *Flowers in Salt: The Beginnings of Feminist Consciousness in Modern Japan* (Stanford, Calif.: Stanford University Press, 1983), chapter 2; Rebecca L. Copeland, *Lost Leaves: Women Writers of Meiji Japan* (Honolulu: University of Hawai`i Press, 2000), 10–11.

6. The classical account of this dichotomy in Western love is Denis de Rougemont, *L'amour et l'Occident* (Paris: Plon, 1939). See also William M. Reddy, *The Making of Romantic Love: Longing and Sexuality in Europe, South Asia, and Japan, 900–1200 CE* (Chicago: University of Chicago Press, 2012), chapters 1–3.

7. For "passion," note the following contemporary definition in *Encyclopedia Britannica*, 7th ed. (1842), s.v. "emotion": "An internal motion or agitation of the mind, when it passeth away without desire, is denominated an emotion; when desire follows, the motion or agitation is denominated a passion. A fine face, for example, raises in us a pleasant feeling; if that feeling vanishes without producing any effect, it is in proper language an emotion; but if the feeling, by reiterated views of the object, becomes sufficiently strong to occasion desire, it loses its name of emotion, and acquires that of passion."

8. Higashi Kan'ichi, "Haishi shōsetsu no kashihon o kinzubeki no gi," *Tōkyō nichinichi shinbun*, March 4, 1876. For excellent overviews of the early-Meiji discourse on fiction and *ninjōbon*, see Wolfgang Schamoni, "Die Entwicklung der Romantheorie in der japanischen Aufklärungsperiode," *Nachrichten der Gesellschaft für Natur- und Völkerkunde Ostasiens/Hamburg* 118 (1975): 9–39; Yamada Shunji, "Ninjōbon no saisei made: Meiji shonen no ren'ai shōsetsu ni kansuru ichikōsatsu," *Nihon bungaku* 56, no. 10 (2007): 12–25. A still indispensible source on early-Meiji critical discourse is Yanagida Izumi, *Meiji shoki no bungaku shisō*, 2 vols. (Tokyo: Shunjūsha, 1965).

9. Translator's afterword to *Karyū shunwa*, published in 1879. See Niwa Jun'ichirō, trans., *Karyū shunwa*, in *Meiji hon'yaku bungaku shū*, ed. Kimura Ki, MBZ 7 (Tokyo: Chikuma shobō, 1972), 109.

10. Tsubouchi Shōyō, *Shōsetsu shinzui*, in *Tsubouchi Shōyō shū*, ed. Nakamura Kan and Umezawa Nobuo, NKiBT 3 (Tokyo: Kadokawa shoten, 1974), 68, 88.

11. Tsubouchi, *Shōsetsu shinzui*, 69.

12. The novel appeared in five fascicles published by Sakagami Hanshichi in Tokyo. "Ōshū kiji" is a so-called *tsunogaki* (literally, "horn writing"), a subtitle placed in

small letters on top of a work's main title. Here as for subsequent Meiji titles, I mention the *tsunogaki* only when referring to a work for the first time in a chapter.

13. Yanagida Izumi, *Meiji shoki hon'yaku bungaku no kenkyū* (Tokyo: Shunjūsha, 1961), 13. Niwa (later surname Oda) traveled to England twice in 1870–1874 and 1874–1877. He seems to have studied law in Edinburgh and London, but the facts of his life abroad remain controversial and to a great extent unknown. For the limited biographical material on Niwa, see Yanagida, *Meiji shoki hon'yaku bungaku*, 299–316, and Shōwa Joshi Daigaku Kindai Bungaku Kenkyūshitsu, ed., *Kindai bungaku kenkyū sōsho*, vol. 18 (Tokyo: Shōwa joshi daigaku kōyōkai, 1962), 307–59.

14. For the boom in translations following the publication of *Karyū shunwa*, see Taguma Itsuko, "Meiji hon'yaku bungaku nenpyō," in *Meiji hon'yaku bungaku shū*, 412–16. For adaptations and rewritings, see Hata Minoru, "Meiji shoki no ninjō shōsetsu: *Karyū shunwa* no nagare," *Komazawa kokubun* 29 (1992): 69–78.

15. Tsubouchi Shōyō, preface to *Gaisei shiden* [Chronicle of a patriot's life], in *Shōyō senshū: Bessatsu*, ed. Shōyō Kyōkai (Tokyo: Daiichi shobō, 1977), 2:445–48. Alongside *Karyū shunwa*, Shōyō favorably discusses *Seitō yodan: Shun'ōten* (A political digression: Orioles warbling in spring, 1884), Seki Naohiko's translation of Benjamin Disraeli's *Coningsby*, and Yano Ryūkei's political novel *Tēbe meishi: Keikoku bidan* (Heroes of Thebes: Beautiful tales of statesmanship, 1883–1884). *Karyū shunwa*, however, was the earliest title and produced the literary field that made later works like Seki's translation possible. For the continuous reception and reprintings of Edo *gesaku* works in Meiji, see Peter F. Kornicki, "The Survival of Tokugawa Fiction in the Meiji Period," *Harvard Journal of Asiatic Studies* 41, no. 2 (1981): 461–82. For Bakin in particular, see also Brian C. Dowdle, "Why Saikaku Was Memorable but Bakin Was Unforgettable," *Journal of Japanese Studies* 42, no. 1 (2016): 91–121.

16. Lydia H. Liu, *Translingual Practice: Literature, National Culture, and Translated Modernity—China, 1900–1937* (Stanford, Calif.: Stanford University Press, 1995), 1–42. The terms "host" and "guest" are Liu's.

17. Saeki Junko, *"Iro" to "ai" no hikaku bunkashi* (Tokyo: Iwanami shoten, 1998), chapter 1. See also Yanabu Akira, *Hon'yakugo seiritsu jijō* (Tokyo: Iwanami shoten, 1982), chapter 5.

18. For helpful overviews of these discussions, see Marnie S. Anderson, *A Place in Public: Women's Rights in Meiji Japan* (Cambridge, Mass.: Harvard University Asia Center, 2010), chapter 2; Nadja Kischka-Wellhäußer, *Frauenerziehung und Frauenbild im Umbruch: Ideale von Mädchenerziehung, Frauenrolle und weiblichen Lebensentwürfen in der frühen* Jogaku zasshi *(1885–1889)* (Munich: Iudicium Verlag, 2004), chapter 2; Sievers, *Flowers in Salt*, chapter 2.

19. Mori Arinori, "Saishōron," in *Meiji keimō shisō shū*, ed. Ōkubo Toshiaki, MBZ 3 (Tokyo: Chikuma shobō, 1967), 260–63. Translations for all *Meiroku zasshi* publications are available in William Reynolds Braisted, trans., *Meiroku zasshi: Journal of the Japanese Enlightenment* (Cambridge, Mass.: Harvard University Press, 1976).

20. Fukuzawa Yukichi, *Gakumon no susume*, in *Fukuzawa Yukichi zenshū*, ed. Keiō Gijuku (Tokyo: Iwanami shoten, 1959), 3:82. Fukuzawa makes a similar argument in his "Danjo dōsūron" ["The Equal Numbers of Men and Women"], in *Fukuzawa Yukichi zenshū*, 19:552. This essay was published in *Meiroku zasshi* in 1875. However, like the Meiji state, Fukuzawa also approved of prostitution as necessary for the

maintenance of order in a civilized society; see Douglas R. Howland, "The *Maria Luz* Incident: Personal Rights and International Justice for Chinese Coolies and Japanese Prostitutes," in *Gender and Law in the Japanese Imperium*, ed. Susan L. Burns and Barbara J. Brooks (Honolulu: University of Hawai'i Press, 2013), 35.

21. Anderson, *A Place in Public*, 61–64, discusses in detail the difference that Meiroku commentators made between the equality (*dōtō*) of men and women as marital partners and equal legal rights (*dōken*).

22. Nakamura Masanao, "Zenryō naru haha o tsukuru setsu," in *Meiji keimō shisō shū*, 301.

23. Tsuda Mamichi, "Jōyokuron" ["Desire"], in *Meiji keimō shisō shū*, 129–30.

24. Fukuzawa, *Gakumon no susume*, 78–79.

25. Ueno Chizuko, "Kaisetsu (3)," in *Fūzoku, sei*, ed. Ogi Shinzō et al., Nihon kindai shisō taikei 23 (Tokyo: Iwanami shoten, 1990), 520–21, lists sixteen *zōkakiron* titles for the years 1876–1889. On early-Meiji sexology, see also Christine L. Marran, *Poison Woman: Figuring Female Transgression in Modern Japanese Culture* (Minneapolis: University of Minnesota Press, 2007), chapter 1.

26. Jim Reichert, *In the Company of Men: Representations of Male-Male Sexuality in Meiji Literature* (Stanford, Calif.: Stanford University Press, 2006), 54.

27. Kawamura Kunimitsu, *Sekushuaritī no kindai* (Tokyo: Kōdansha, 1996), 61–66; Ueno, "Kaisetsu," 532–35.

28. *Chōya shinbun* [Chōya newspaper], October 4, 1880; cited from Yamada, "Ninjōbon no saisei made," 17. The article, titled "Ryūkō shoseki no nageki" (Lamenting the current craze for books), was authored by a certain Sōchikuan.

29. On Hattori Bushō's *Tōkyō shinshi*, see Maeda Ai, "Ōgai no Chūgoku shōsetsu shumi," in *Kindai dokusha no seiritsu* (Tokyo: Chikuma shobō, 1989), 86. The title of the abridged edition of Feng Menglong's *Qingshi leilüe* was *Jōshishō* (History of emotion in excerpts), published in 1878 by Shōzandō.

30. For a seminal discussion of the reading tastes of 1870s students and the young Ōgai, see Maeda, "Ōgai no Chūgoku shōsetsu shumi," 74–87. Masturbation over reading is an implicit theme in *Gan*.

31. Maeda Ai, "*Karyū shunwa* no ichi," *Meiji bungaku zenshū geppō* 71 (1972): 2.

32. Also note that *Karyū shunwa* was one of the first novels in Japan to be published in a Western-style movable-type cardboard-cover (*bōru hyōshi*) edition. Throughout the 1870s, only bureaucratic, educational, or legal texts had been published in this prestigious new format. The format underlines *Karyū shunwa*'s special status as a Western translation at a time when other popular literary works were available only as woodblock prints. By 1878, however, the price of Western-style cardboard-cover books had dropped, making them not cheap but still affordable to a broader reading public. See Kido Yūichi, "Meiji-ki 'bōru hyōshi-bon' no tanjō," in *Meiji no shuppan bunka*, ed. Kokubungaku Kenkyū Shiryōkan (Tokyo: Rinsen shoten, 2002), 24–26.

33. Niwa, *Karyū shunwa*, 3.

34. Wolfgang Schamoni, "Narushima Ryūhoku: Vorwort zu *Karyū shunwa*," hon'yaku—*Heidelberger Werkstattberichte zum Übersetzen Japanisch-Deutsch* 5 (2003): 32, makes the count. Schamoni also provides a carefully annotated German translation of the foreword.

35. Matthew Fraleigh, *Plucking Chrysanthemums: Narushima Ryūhoku and Sinitic Literary Traditions in Modern Japan* (Cambridge, Mass.: Harvard University Asia Center, 2016), 343; for the broader context, see chapters 6 and 7.

36. Ryūhoku's fame derived greatly from his own *jōshi* titled *Ryūkyō shinshi* (*New Chronicles of Yanagibashi*, 1859–1874), the satirical evocation of the Yanagibashi pleasure quarter; for a translation, see Matthew Fraleigh, trans., New Chronicles of Yanagibashi *and* Diary of a Journey to the West: *Narushima Ryūhoku Reports from Home and Abroad* (Ithaca, N.Y.: Cornell University East Asia Program, 2010). Ryūhoku's name alone probably evoked an elegant erotic flavor to many readers.

37. Niwa, *Karyū shunwa*, 109.

38. *Yomiuri shinbun*, November 6, 1878; quoted from Maeda, "*Karyū shunwa* no ichi," 1.

39. Franco Moretti, *The Way of the World: The Bildungsroman in European Culture* (London: Verso, 2000), 8–9.

40. Edward Bulwer-Lytton, *Alice, or the Mysteries* (London: Routledge, 1887), 362.

41. Similarly, John Pierre Mertz, *Novel Japan: Spaces of Nationhood in Early Meiji Narrative, 1870–88* (Ann Arbor: Center for Japanese Studies, University of Michigan, 2003), 109, argues that, in *Karyū shunwa*, Maltravers's attempt to educate Alice allegorically illustrates the possibility, envisioned by the Meirokusha intellectuals and other enlightenment reformers, of educating the lower classes and integrating them into the national project of civilization and enlightenment.

42. For an excellent discussion of the ideological implications of love in Rousseau's novel, see David J. Denby, *Sentimental Narrative and the Social Order in France, 1760–1820* (Cambridge: Cambridge University Press, 1994), chapter 3.

43. Anthony Giddens, *The Transformation of Intimacy: Sexuality, Love, and Eroticism in Modern Societies* (Stanford, Calif.: Stanford University Press, 1992), chapters 2 and 3.

44. In the 1840s preface to *Ernest Maltravers*, Bulwer-Lytton explicitly mentions Goethe's novel as his model; see Edward Bulwer-Lytton, *Ernest Maltravers* (London: Routledge, 1877), 8. He also dedicates his work to "the great German people."

45. For the very different literary format of early-Meiji adaptations of Western literature, see J. Scott Miller, *Adaptations of Western Literature in Meiji Japan* (New York: Palgrave, 2001).

46. Niwa, *Karyū shunwa*, 6.

47. Kimura Ki, "Kaidai," in *Meiji hon'yaku bungaku shū*, 396. Niwa writes *shushin o isshō su* 朱唇ヲ一甞ス. 朱唇 is glossed *akai kuchibiru* (red lips) and 甞 is glossed *name* (to taste). In Bulwer-Lytton's novel, Ernest Maltravers says, "I should sleep well if I could get one kiss from those coral lips" (19).

48. Niwa, *Karyū shunwa*, 14. In the English novel, Maltravers declares, "Alice, dear Alice, I love thee" (45).

49. For this definition of passion in the European literary tradition, see Niklas Luhmann, *Liebe als Passion: Zur Codierung von Intimität* (Frankfurt/Main: Suhrkamp Verlag, 1994).

50. Bulwer-Lytton, *Ernest Maltravers*, 31.

51. For these references, see Yamamoto Yoshiaki, "'Ānesuto Marutorabāzu' 'Arisu' ron: *Karyū shunwa* no gensho no sakuhin sekai to wa nani ka?" *Nihon kindai bungaku* 31 (1984): 1–13.

52. The free association of men and women as the epitome of civilized gender relations became an important catchphrase in 1880s enlightenment reform discourse. See the influential essays by Fukuzawa Yukichi and Iwamoto Yoshiharu, both titled "Danjo kōsairon" (On the association of men and women) and published in the journals *Jiji shinpō* (1886) and *Jogaku zasshi* (1888), respectively; for an English translation of Fukuzawa's essay, see Kiyooka Eiichi, trans., *Fukuzawa Yukichi on Japanese Women: Selected Works* (Tokyo: University of Tokyo Press, 1988), 103–27.

53. Niwa, *Karyū shunwa*, 10.

54. I do not argue that Maltravers's passion was not titillating for British readers as well, but the English novel more clearly articulates the enlightenment implications of this passion.

55. Several *ninjōbon* protagonists were heirs of wealthy families, such as Bairi in Shunsui's *Harutsugedori*. Tanjirō in *Shunshoku umegoyomi* turns out to be the scion of a powerful daimyo house.

56. Niwa, *Karyū shunwa*, 11.

57. Bulwer-Lytton, *Ernest Maltravers*, 33–34. For Bulwer-Lytton's Byronism, see James L. Campbell Sr., *Edward Bulwer-Lytton* (Boston: Twayne, 1986), chapter 2.

58. The English novel refers to her mostly as Madame de Ventadour or Valerie.

59. Niwa, *Karyū shunwa*, 24.

60. Niwa, *Karyū shunwa*, 25–26.

61. Note, however, that such a stylistic and thematic mixture was reminiscent of Chinese scholar and beauty fiction. For a reading that touches on *Karyū shunwa* within a genealogy of Meiji "scholar and beauty" literature (but without discussing the Chinese genre in detail), see Chiba Shunji, *Erisu no ekubo: Mori Ōgai e no kokoromi* (Tokyo: Ozawa shoten, 1997), chapters 1 and 2.

62. Niwa, *Karyū shunwa*, 27.

63. Bulwer-Lytton, *Ernest Maltravers*, 105.

64. Niwa, *Karyū shunwa*, 28. Another key term in Ventadour's discourse that Niwa here translates as *ri* is "virtue."

65. Niwa, *Karyū shunwa*, 28. For an insightful discussion of *Karyū shunwa* that highlights the narrative connection between the control of passion and the discourse on ambition, see Takahashi Osamu, "*Karyū shunwa* no shikō suru sekai," *Nihon kindai bungaku* 31 (1984): 14–27.

66. For translations of typical *Eisai shinshi* essays, see Earl H. Kinmonth, *The Self-Made Man in Meiji Japanese Thought: From Samurai to Salary Man* (Berkeley: University of California Press, 1981), chapter 2. On early-Meiji *risshin shusse* discourse, see also Maeda Ai, "Meiji risshin shusse shugi no keifu: *Saigoku risshihen* kara *Kisei* made," in *Kindai dokusha no seiritsu*, 88–107; Takeuchi Yō, *Risshin shusse shugi: Kindai Nihon no roman to yokubō* (Kyoto: Sekai shisōsha, 2005).

67. For an insightful study on the theme in the later Meiji novel, see Timothy J. Van Compernolle, *Struggling Upward: Worldly Success and the Japanese Novel* (Cambridge, Mass.: Harvard University Asia Center, 2016).

68. Maeno Michiko, "Meiji shoki hon'yaku shōsetsu *Ōshū kiji: Karyū shunwa* ni okeru ren'ai to kekkon," in *Ronshū ibunka toshite no Nihon: Kokusai shinpojiumu "Ibunka toshite no Nihon" kinen ronbun shū*, ed. Nagoya Daigaku Daigakuin Kokusai Gengo

Bunka Kenkyūka (Nagoya: Nagoya daigaku daigakuin kokusai gengo bunka kenkyūka, 2009), 158.

69. Niwa, *Karyū shunwa*, 28.

70. Tsubouchi Shōyō, *Imotose kagami*, in *Tsubouchi Shōyō shū*, ed. Inagaki Tatsurō, MBZ 16 (Tokyo: Chikuma shobō, 1969), 188. On Japanese feudal customs, see 212.

71. Niwa, *Karyū shunwa*, 68–69.

72. Niwa, *Karyū shunwa*, 84. As noted earlier, both *Shunshoku umegoyomi* and *Hakkenden* ended on such a marriage.

73. For a similar reason, marriage was a major trope of social integration in the bildungsroman, especially in the Anglo-German tradition that served as Bulwer-Lytton's model; see Moretti, *Way of the World*, 7–8.

74. Niwa, *Karyū shunwa*, 87, 91.

75. On the life and writings of Kikutei Kōsui (Satō Kuratarō), see Yanagida Izumi, *Seiji shōsetsu kenkyū* (Tokyo: Shunjūsha, 1967), 1:208–26.

76. The novel appeared in the same movable-type cardboard-cover (*bōru hyōshi*) format as *Karyū shunwa*.

77. Kikutei Kōsui, *Seiro nikki*, in *Meiji meisaku shū*, ed. Tanikawa Keiichi et al., SNKBTM 30 (Tokyo: Iwanami shoten, 2009), 15. For the establishment of the elementary-school system in the wake of the promulgation of the Fundamental Code of Education (Gakusei) in 1872, see Brian Platt, *Burning and Building: Schooling and State Formation in Japan, 1750–1890* (Cambridge, Mass.: Harvard University Asia Center, 2004), chapters 3 and 4. Kikutei himself was an elementary-school teacher in his native Oita prefecture after undergoing professional training in the prefectural normal school (*shihan gakkō*), the nationwide institution established by the Meiji state for elementary-teacher training; see Yanagida, *Seiji shōsetsu kenkyū*, 1:222.

78. For a representative text of this discourse, see Iwamoto Yoshiharu's essay "Kon'inron" (On marriage), published in *Jogaku zasshi* in 1891. The Meirokusha publications of the 1870s did not yet discuss the freedom of marriage.

79. *Analects* 16:7. Quoted from Confucius, *The Analects (Lun yü)*, trans. D. C. Lau (London: Penguin Books, 1979), 140. Kikutei cites only the first of the three items discussed by Confucius.

80. Kikutei Kōsui, preface to *Ensai shunwa* (Tokyo: Shunzandō, 1882).

81. Kikutei, *Seiro nikki*, 41–42; another potentially erotic scene directly follows Kikuo's declaration of his love to Take (22).

82. Kikutei, *Seiro nikki*, 41.

83. Kikutei, *Seiro nikki*, 134–35. The stepmother also arranges for the annulment of Take's previous marriage.

84. The political ending of *Seiro nikki* was probably motivated by Kikutei's relationship with the famous political journalist Yano Ryūkei (1850–1931), whose widely read political novel *Keikoku bidan* had just appeared. Ryūkei was, like Kikutei, from the town of Saeki in Kyushu and acted as Kikutei's mentor, procuring him a position with his *Yūbin hōchi* newspaper in Tokyo. See Yanagida, *Seiji shōsetsu kenkyū*, 1:222–23. In 1895, Kikutei published an expanded version of *Seiro nikki* that covered Kikuo's political activity in Tokyo.

85. Isobe Atsushi, *Shuppan bunka no Meiji zenki: Tōkyō haishi shuppansha to sono shūhen* (Tokyo: Perikansha, 2012), 72.

86. Quoted from Isobe, *Shuppan bunka no Meiji zenki*, 72.
87. Isobe persuasively argues that *Seiro nikki*'s narration of Kikuo and Take's separation was modeled on Shino and Hamaji's farewell scene in *Hakkenden*, extending even to the illustrations. See Isobe, *Shuppan bunka no Meiji zenki*, 85–106.

4. HISTORICIZING LITERARY REFORM

1. For this discursive appropriation of *Shōsetsu shinzui* as the origin of modern Japanese literature, see Atsuko Ueda, *Concealment of Politics, Politics of Concealment: The Production of "Literature" in Meiji Japan* (Stanford, Calif.: Stanford University Press, 2007), chapter 6.
2. For charts with numbers, see Seki Ryōichi, *Shōyō, Ōgai: Kōshō to shiron* (Tokyo: Yūseidō shuppan, 1971), 83–84, 93. References to Bakin and *Hakkenden* in particular greatly outnumber those to other writers and works, even Shunsui's.
3. Yanagida Izumi, *Wakaki Tsubouchi Shōyō* (Tokyo: Nihon tosho sentā, 1990), provides detailed documentation of Shōyō's early biography and study curriculum. On the development of the university curriculum, especially for the Japanese and Chinese classics, see Michael C. Brownstein, "From *Kokugaku* to *Kokubungaku*: Canon-Formation in the Meiji Period," *Harvard Journal of Asiatic Studies* 47, no. 2 (1987): 435–60.
4. Yanagida, *Wakaki Tsubouchi Shōyō*, 88.
5. Yanagida Izumi, *Seiji shōsetsu kenkyū* (Tokyo: Shunjūsha, 1968), 2:4.
6. I have been unable to find biographical information on this individual, and my reading of the name 丹乙馬 is tentative.
7. Takata Sanae, *Hanpō mukashibanashi* [Hanpō's old tales], Meiji Taishō bungaku kaisō shūsei 6 (Tokyo: Nihon tosho sentā, 1983), 45–47.
8. Takata, *Hanpō mukashibanashi*, 48.
9. Tanaka Shōhei (1862–1945) later became an eminent physicist and musicologist.
10. Tsubouchi Shōyō, "Kaioku mandan," in *Shōyō senshū*, ed. Shōyō Kyōkai (Tokyo: Daiichi shobō, 1977), 12:343.
11. However, only slightly later (in 1887), Aeba Kōson (1855–1922) translated Poe's stories "The Black Cat" and "The Murders in the Rue Morgue" into Japanese. See Satoru Saito, *Detective Fiction and the Rise of the Japanese Novel, 1880–1930* (Cambridge, Mass.: Harvard University Asia Center, 2012), 46.
12. On lending libraries (*kashihon'ya*) in Meiji, see Peter F. Kornicki, "The Publisher's Go-Between: *Kashihonya* in the Meiji Period," *Modern Asian Studies* 14, no. 2 (1980): 331–44; on the Daisō lending library, see Andrew L. Markus, "The Daisō Lending Library of Nagoya, 1767–1899," *Gest Library Journal* 3, no. 3 (1989): 5–34.
13. Tsubouchi Shōyō, "Shinkyū katoki no kaisō" [Recollections of the transition between the new and old age, 1925], in *Shōyō senshū*, ed. Shōyō Kyōkai (Tokyo: Daiichi shobō, 1977), 12:325.
14. Alexandre Dumas's (1802–1870) novels were popular in the early 1880s, especially among supporters of the People's Rights Movement. See my later discussion in this chapter.
15. Tsubouchi Shōyō, preface to *Gaisei shiden* [Chronicle of a patriot's life], in *Shōyō senshū: Bessatsu*, ed. Shōyō Kyōkai (Tokyo: Daiichi shobō, 1977), 2:448.

16. Shōyō also produced translations of Shakespeare's historical play *Julius Caesar* and of Walter Scott's narrative poem *The Lady of the Lake* (1810). Both translations were published in 1884.
17. Quoted from Shōyō Kyōkai, ed., foreword to *Shōyō senshū: Bessatsu*, 2:2.
18. Tsubouchi Shōyō, trans., *Shunpū jōwa*, in *Tsubouchi Shōyō Futabatei Shimei shū*, ed. Aoki Toshihiro and Togawa Shinsuke, SNKBTM 18 (Tokyo: Iwanami shoten, 2002), 63.
19. For this assessment, see also Honma Hisao, *Tsubouchi Shōyō: Hito to sono geijutsu* (Tokyo: Nihon tosho sentā, 1993), 92.
20. This plot had an affinity to *Hakkenden*'s Shino-Hamaji episode that was probably not lost on contemporary readers. Hamaji's adopted parents, like Rushi's father, are "small-minded" and resent Shino's father, who is a true warrior like Edogaru's father. But the filial Shino, unlike Edogaru, leaves his fiancée to fulfill his father's wish. His loyalty lets him give up romance, whereas Edogaru's inability to control his passion leads to the downfall of his house and his death.
21. The term "passion" does not appear in Shōyō's unfinished translation, but it is a key word in the later chapters of Scott's novel. Shōyō was clearly aware of the term.
22. Iwamoto Yoshiharu, "Fujin no chii," *Jogaku zasshi* 2 (1885): 23.
23. Tsubouchi, preface to *Gaisei shiden*, 457–58.
24. In the English novel, the passage is in book 1, chapter 11.
25. For both quotes, see Edward Bulwer-Lytton, *Rienzi, the Last of the Roman Tribunes* (Leipzig: Tauchnitz, 1842), 93.
26. Bulwer-Lytton, *Rienzi*, 93–94.
27. Tsubouchi, *Gaisei shiden*, 576.
28. Tsubouchi Shōyō, *Tōsei shosei katagi*, in *Tsubouchi Shōyō shū*, ed. Nakamura Kan and Umezawa Nobuo, NKiBT 3 (Tokyo: Kadokawa shoten, 1974), 358.
29. Tsubouchi, preface to *Gaisei shiden*, 447. Shōyō also mentions Yano Ryūkei's political novel *Keikoku bidan* as "excellent material to awaken the deluded dreams of our degenerated novelists." The novel was a fictionalized rewriting of English-language historical accounts about the reinstatement of Theban democracy against Spartan oligarchic oppression in fourth-century BCE Greece. In the first edition of *Shōsetsu shinzui*, Shōyō also referred to *Keikoku bidan* alongside *Shun'ōten* as examples of political fiction (*seiji shōsetsu*), but he elided this reference from subsequent editions. The reason was probably that *Keikoku bidan*'s focus on *ninjō* was too minor in comparison with the political plot. However, the type of love depicted in *Keikoku bidan* (for instance, in chapter 9), highlighting the partners' mutual support, is very similar to that in *Gaisei shiden*. On Shōyō's shifting views of *Keikoku bidan*, but not with regard to *ninjō*, see Ochi Haruo, "*Meiji seiji shōsetsu shū* kaisetsu," in *Meiji seiji shōsetsu shū*, ed. Ochi Haruo, NKiBT 2 (Tokyo: Kadokawa shoten, 1974), 34–35.
30. Shōyō's critique here probably targets the radical political fiction associated with the Liberal Party and contemporary serial (*tsuzukimono*) fiction—works by authors like Kanagaki Robun (1829–1894) and Sansantei Arindo (1832–1902) that were serialized in the newly emerging popular medium of the so-called small newspapers (*koshinbun*) and attracted an ever-increasing reading public. For Shōyō's view of *tsuzukimono* fiction, see Saito, *Detective Fiction*, 18–20.

237

4. HISTORICIZING LITERARY REFORM

31. *Shōsetsu shinzui* was first published in nine fascicles by Shōgetsudō between September 1885 and April 1886.
32. For useful background information and a summary in English, see J. Thomas Rimer, "Hegel in Tokyo: Ernest Fenollosa and His 1882 Lecture on the Truth of Art," in *Japanese Hermeneutics: Current Debates on Aesthetics and Interpretation*, ed. Michael F. Marra (Honolulu: University of Hawai'i Press, 2002), 97–108.
33. Tsubouchi Shōyō, *Shōsetsu shinzui*, in *Tsubouchi Shōyō shū*, 43–44. See also Ōuchi Seiran, "*Dai Nihon bijutsu shinpō shogen*," in *Dai Nihon bijutsu shinpō*, Kindai bijutsu zasshi sōsho 1 (Tokyo: Yumani shobō, 1990), 1:3.
34. Tsubouchi, *Shōsetsu shinzui*, 45.
35. Tsubouchi, *Shōsetsu shinzui*, 82.
36. Tsubouchi, *Shōsetsu shinzui*, 79–82.
37. Tsubouchi, *Shōsetsu shinzui*, 68–78. For an insightful discussion of Shōyō's notion of making visible hidden emotions in connection to the modern narrative paradigm of detective fiction, see Saito, *Detective Fiction*, chapter 1.
38. The title of the Japanese translation was "Shūji oyobi ni kabun." For a detailed study, see Sugaya Hiromi, *Shūji oyobi kabun no kenkyū* (Tokyo: Kyōiku shuppan sentā, 1978).
39. William Chambers and Robert Chambers, eds., *Chambers's Information for the People* (Philadelphia: Lippincott, 1867), 2:750; italics added. Chambers's text was inspired by Alexander Bain's (1818–1903) earlier rhetorical treatise *English Composition and Rhetoric* (1866). See Massimiliano Tomasi, *Rhetoric in Modern Japan: Western Influences on the Development of Narrative and Oratorical Style* (Honolulu: University of Hawai'i Press, 2004), chapter 4, and Ojima Kenji, "*Shōsetsu shinzui to Bein* [*sic*] no shūjisho: Sono moshashugi to risōshugi," *Kokubungaku kenkyū* 42 (1970): 22–33.
40. Tsubouchi Shōyō, *Haishika ryakuden narabi ni hihyō* [Short biographies and critiques of (late-Edo) novelists], in *Tsubouchi Shōyō Futabatei Shimei shū*, 148, and *Tōsei shosei katagi*, 432. The relevant sections of both texts were written in 1886. Shōyō's awareness of the term "realist" probably derived from discussions with Futabatei Shimei (1864–1909), whom he met for the first time early in 1886; see Marleigh Grayer Ryan, *Japan's First Modern Novel: Ukigumo of Futabatei Shimei* (New York: Columbia University Press, 1967), chapter 2. The term does not appear in *Shōsetsu shinzui*, which started serialization in September 1885. For the emergence of "truth," "reality," and "realism" as new critical concepts in Japanese discourse on the *shōsetsu*, see Tomi Suzuki, *Narrating the Self: Fictions of Japanese Modernity* (Stanford, Calif.: Stanford University Press, 1996), 19–26.
41. Yamada Shunji, "*Nansō Satomi hakkenden* to iu kagami: Tsubouchi Shōyō, moshasetsu no seiritsu," *Bungei to hihyō* 6, no. 9 (1989): 31–46. Karatani Kōjin presents a similar argument, although not with regard to *Shōsetsu shinzui*, about modern realism as a liberation of the visual field from the "figurality" of premodern representation; *Origins of Modern Japanese Literature*, trans. Brett de Bary et al. (Durham, N.C.: Duke University Press, 1993), chapters 1 and 2.
42. Maeda Ai, "Mō hitotsu no *Shōsetsu shinzui*: Shikakuteki sekai no seiritsu," in *Kindai dokusha no seiritsu* (Tokyo: Chikuma shobō, 1989), 349–63, and "*Shōsetsu shinzui* no riarizumu to wa nani ka," in *Kindai dokusha no seiritsu*, 364–71. Maeda also links Shōyō's realism to the new technology of movable-type printing. In a different essay,

however, he notes that Shōyō's *mosha* should not be understood in the modern sense of realism (*shajitsu*) but as close in meaning to the same term that Edo-period painters used to sign their paintings, meaning "so-and-so painted this." See Maeda, "Kindai bungaku to katsujiteki sekai," in *Kindai dokusha no seiritsu*, 329. For a more recent argument about Shōyō's realism in connection to modern technology and media, see Seth Jacobowitz, *Writing Technology in Meiji Japan: A Media History of Modern Japanese Literature and Visual Culture* (Cambridge, Mass.: Harvard University Asia Center, 2015), chapter 8.

43. Ueda, *Concealment of Politics*, chapter 6. Ueda critiques the traditional view of Shōyō's notion of *mosha* as mimetic realism. Another important recent attempt to historicize Shōyō's critical notions, both in connection with traditional Japanese literary discourse and contemporary Western sources, is Kamei Hideo, *"Shōsetsu" ron: "Shōsetsu shinzui" to kindai* (Tokyo: Iwanami shoten, 1999). Kamei's study, however, leaves out a discussion of *ninjō*.

44. Tsubouchi, *Shōsetsu shinzui*, 70–71.

45. Tsubouchi, *Shōsetsu shinzui*, 159; Tsubouchi, *Haishika ryakuden*, 139.

46. Tsubouchi, *Shōsetsu shinzui*, 87.

47. From a slightly different perspective, Tomi Suzuki has called this contradiction the novel's "aporia" in *Shōsetsu shinzui*. See Tomi Suzuki, "*The Tale of Genji*, National Literature, Language, and Modernism," in *Envisioning* The Tale of Genji: *Media, Gender, and Cultural Production*, ed. Haruo Shirane (New York: Columbia University Press, 2008), 246–47.

48. Tsubouchi, *Shōsetsu shinzui*, 88.

49. Tsubouchi, *Shōsetsu shinzui*, 69.

50. Peter Kornicki also discusses the affinity of Shōyō's use of the term *ninjō* to the meanings it had in earlier literary discourse and genres, including *ninjōbon*, but not in reference to contemporary civilizational concerns. His study is an important early critique of traditional scholarship viewing Shōyō's *ninjō* and *mosha* as simply synonymous with modern psychology and realism. See Peter F. Kornicki, *The Reform of Fiction in Meiji Japan* (London: Ithaca Press, 1982), 26–34.

51. This view was probably also informed by psychological knowledge taught at the university. Ochi Haruo notes that the scholar Toyama Masakazu (1848–1900) used *jōyoku* as a translation for "passion" in his 1880–1881 psychology lectures at the University of Tokyo. Shōyō probably attended these lectures as a student. See Ochi Haruo, "*Shōsetsu shinzui* no botai," in *Tsubouchi Shōyō, Futabatei Shimei*, ed. Nihon Bungaku Kenkyū Shiryō Kankōkai, NBKSS (Tokyo: Yūseidō, 1979), 2.

52. Shōyō differentiates between the novel's "direct benefit" (*chokusetsu no rieki*) of giving readers aesthetic pleasure and its "indirect benefits" (*kansetsu no hieki*) of didactic instruction. Two other indirect benefits that he discusses are the novel's ability to complement official history (*seishi*)—a traditional idea deriving from the notion of the novel as "unofficial history"—and to serve as a stylistic guide for writing; see Tsubouchi, *Shōsetsu shinzui*, 82–97.

53. Tsubouchi, *Shōsetsu shinzui*, 84–86. Shōyō's argument here is directly inspired by Bakin, who compares the novel to the sweetness of a candy that helps uneducated readers—"women and children"—digest the otherwise unpalatable moral teachings of the Confucian classics; see Kyokutei Bakin, *Nansō Satomi hakkenden*, ed. Hamada Keisuke, vol. 2, Shinchō Nihon koten shūsei bekkan 2 (Tokyo: Shinchōsha: 2003), 12.

54. Tsubouchi, *Shōsetsu shinzui*, 83. The section corresponding to Shōyō's summary in Morley's original essay is as follows: "If a novel has any use at all apart from the idlest diversion and time-killing, it must be as a repertory of vivid texts, by which I certainly do not mean merely texts of morals, pointing only to the right and wrong of conduct, though this is the first standard, but those reflections also which lead people to work out for themselves notions of what is graceful and seemly, to teach themselves a more exquisite intellectual sensibility, and to enlarge their own scope of affection and intensity of passion. These are the rightful fruits of that pleasure which is the first aim of the novel-reader" (John Morley, "George Eliot's Novels," *Macmillan's Magazine* 14 [1866]: 273). Note that Matsumura Masaie, "Tsubouchi Shōyō to Igirisu no shōsetsuka-tachi: *Shōsetsu shinzui* no seiritsu o megutte," in *Hikaku bungaku o manabu hito no tame ni*, ed. Matsumura Masaie (Kyoto: Sekai shisō sha, 1995), 37–58, only recently identified Morley's essay as the source for Shōyō's quote.

55. Tsubouchi, *Shōsetsu shinzui*, 80.

56. This is because civilized readers are more amenable to self-reflection induced by realist depiction than to the crude didacticism offered by works like *Hakkenden*.

57. Tsubouchi, preface to *Gaisei shiden*, 451–52.

58. Here I fully agree with Seki, *Shōyō, Ōgai*, 154–57.

59. Tsubouchi, *Shōsetsu shinzui*, 89–90.

60. For these terms, see Tsubouchi, *Shōsetsu shinzui*, 42.

61. Stylistically, Shōyō also envisions the artistic novel as an updated version of the "mixed elegant and colloquial style" (*gazoku setchūtai*) of Bakin's *yomihon*, which appeals to him because of its great adaptability to a broad spectrum of subjects: refined and vulgar, high-class and low-class, beautiful and sublime. But Shōyō also sees Bakin's stylistic mastery as inimitable and urges novelists to develop their own mixed style. See Tsubouchi, *Shōsetsu shinzui*, 107–29; for an effective summary of Shōyō's views on literary style, see Tomi Suzuki, "The Tale of Genji," 248–49, 278n10.

62. These "incidents" were named after the places where they took place. They involved, in the case of the Fukushima and Chichibu incidents, protests of local farmers against harsh taxation practices, but also, as in the Kabasan Incident, attempted terrorist attacks against members of the central government. In all the incidents, members of the Liberal Party were involved. For useful overviews, see Roger W. Bowen, *Rebellion and Democracy in Meiji Japan: A Study of Commoners in the Popular Rights Movement* (Berkeley: University of California Press, 1980), chapter 1; Stephen Vlastos, "Opposition Movements in Early Meiji, 1868–1885," in *The Cambridge History of Japan, Volume 5: The Nineteenth Century*, ed. Marius B. Jansen (Cambridge: Cambridge University Press, 1989), 367–431.

63. A vivid account of this moment from the perspective of a young male intellectual is Tokutomi Roka's (1868–1927) semiautobiographical novel *Omoide no ki* (Record of remembrance, 1900–1901). For an English translation, see Kenjirō Tokutomi, *Footprints in the Snow: A Novel of Meiji Japan*, trans. Kenneth Strong (New York: Pegasus, 1970).

64. For political songs, see Maeda Ai, "Tobu uta: Minken kayō to enka," in *Genkei no Meiji* (Tokyo: Chikuma shobō, 1989), 56–67; for the novel, see Yamada Shunji, "Seiji shōsetsu no ichi: Shōsetsu no shakaiteki ninchi to iu bunmyaku kara," in *Seiji shōsetsu shū 1*, ed. Yamada Shunji and Rinbara Sumio, SNKBTM 16 (Tokyo: Iwanami shoten, 2003), 539–56.

65. "Waga kuni ni jiyū no shushi o hanshoku suru ichishudan wa haishi gikyoku nado no tagui o kairyō suru ni ari," in KBHT, vol.1, ed. Yoshida Seiichi and Asai Kiyoshi (Tokyo: Kadokawa shoten, 1971), 17. The essay was published in the pro-Liberal Party newspaper *Nihon rikken seitō shinbun* (Japan constitutional party newspaper) in 1883.

66. Sakurada Momoe's *Nishi no umi chishio no saarashi* (Small storms of blood in the western sea, 1882) and Miyazaki Muryū's *Furansu kakumeiki: Jiyū no kachidoki* (Record of the French revolution: A battle cry of liberty, 1882–1883) were partial translations of Alexandre Dumas's novels *Mémoires d'un médicin: Joseph Balsamo* (*Memoirs of a Physician*, 1846–1848) and *Ange Pitou* (1851), respectively, both focusing on the French Revolution.

67. See in particular Miyazaki Muryū's novel *Kyomutō jitsudenki: Kishūshū* (A truthful record of the anarchist party: Wailing spirits, 1884–1885), an adaptation of Sergey Stepnyak's (1851–1895) *Underground Russia* (1882).

68. Ueda, *Concealment of Politics*, chapter 3.

69. For Bakin's reception among People's Rights activists, see Maeda Ai, "Bakin to Tōkoku: 'Kyō' o megutte," in *Genkei no Meiji*, 347–60. On the communal recitation of *Hakkenden* and political novels through which publicly shared political sentiments could be produced, see Maeda Ai, "Ondoku kara mokudoku e: Kindai dokusha no seiritsu," in *Kindai dokusha no seiritsu*, 122–50, and Ueda, *Concealment of Politics*, 64–68.

70. Ueda, *Concealment of Politics*, 59–60, sees *Shōsetsu shinzui*'s key rhetorical movement in the rejection of Bakin's *kanzen chōaku*. She accordingly argues that key concepts in Shōyō's treatise like *ninjō* and *mosha* are only negatively defined, through what she calls a semantic chain of negation, against *kanzen chōaku*.

71. For a nuanced discussion of the ideological differences between both parties, see Kyu Hyun Kim, *The Age of Visions and Arguments: Parliamentarianism and the National Public Sphere in Early Meiji Japan* (Cambridge, Mass.: Harvard University Asia Center, 2007), 408–12. Kim also notes that, although some "radicals" in the Liberal Party "leaned toward insurrectionary 'direct action,'" "the overall character of the party was in many ways far less 'ideological' than that of the Progressive [Reform] Party" (412). The revolutionary ideology was therefore not necessarily characteristic of the Liberal Party as a whole.

72. For a discussion of Shiran's writings in this context, see Ochi Haruo, "Seiji shōsetsu ni okeru 'noberu' no imi: *Setchūbai* to *Gaimu daijin*," *Nihon kindai bungaku* 1 (1964): 3.

73. Sakazaki Shiran [Mui Shinjin], "Nihon jōshi no kairyō o nozomu" [Envisioning the reform of the Japanese love story], *Jiyū no tomoshibi* 343 (1885). See also Shiran's similar essay "Shōsetsu haishi no honbun o ronzu" [On the true role of the novel, 1885], in KBHT, 1:23–25. This essay was also published in *Jiyū no tomoshibi*.

74. *Kajin no kigū*'s author was Tōkai Sanshi (Shiba Shirō, 1852–1922). For the affinity of *Kajin no kigū* to *Karyū shunwa*, see Kimura Ki, "Kaidai," in *Meiji hon'yaku bungaku shū*, ed. Kimura Ki, MBZ 7 (Tokyo: Chikuma shobō, 1972), 396. For a stimulating reading of *Kajin no kigū* in English, see Atsuko Sakaki, "*Kajin no kigū*: The Meiji Political Novel and the Boundaries of Literature," *Monumenta Nipponica* 55, no. 1 (2000): 83–108.

75. *Jōkai haran*'s author was Toda Kindō (1850–1890).

76. See Kunino's speech in Suehiro Tetchō, *Setchūbai*, in *Seiji shōsetsu shū* 1, 352–68.

77. Suehiro, *Setchūbai*, 506.
78. Christopher L. Hill, *National History and the World of Nations: Capital, State, and the Rhetoric of History in Japan, France, and the United States* (Durham, N.C.: Duke University Press, 2008), 169.
79. Tsubouchi Shōyō, "*Setchūbai* (shōsetsu) no hihyō" [Critique of the novel *Setchūbai*], in *Tsubouchi Shōyō kenkyū: Fu, bungakuron shoshutsu shiryō*, ed. Ishida Tadahiko (Fukuoka: Kyūshū daigaku shuppankai, 1988), 382; see also "*Setchūbai* kahen no hihyō" [Critique of the second part of *Setchūbai*], in *Tsubouchi Shōyō kenkyū*, 384–86. Both critiques appeared in *Gakugei zasshi* (Arts and sciences journal).
80. For a detailed discussion of the reception of Disraeli's novels in Meiji Japan, see Peter F. Kornicki, "Disraeli and the Meiji Novel," *Harvard Journal of Asiatic Studies* 44, no. 1 (1984): 29–55, and Yanagida, *Seiji shōsetsu kenkyū*, 2:121–217. For a more recent discussion of Disraeli and the political novel as a "world genre" with an impact on both China and Japan, see Catherine Vance Yeh, *The Chinese Political Novel: Migration of a World Genre* (Cambridge, Mass.: Harvard University Asia Center, 2015).
81. Tsubouchi Shōyō, "Shōsetsu o ronjite *Shosei katagi* no shui ni oyobu" [On the novel and primary intent of *Shosei katagi*], in *Shōsetsu shinzui*, ed. Munakata Kazushige (Tokyo: Iwanami shoten, 2010), 214.
82. Tsubouchi, "Shōsetsu o ronjite," 214.
83. Tsubouchi, "Shōsetsu o ronjite," 216.
84. Tsubouchi, preface to *Tōsei shosei katagi*, 332. Shōyō points out that the adjective (*keiyōji*) "political" merely qualifies a specific type of novel but not the novel as such. The only reference to political fiction (*seiji shōsetsu*) in *Shōsetsu shinzui* is in the section "The Types of the Novel" (Shōsetsu no shurui), where Shōyō lists the genre as one among other types. The single example for political fiction he cites is the translation *Shun'ōten*. See Tsubouchi, *Shōsetsu shinzui*, 81.
85. An excellent study of this historical and discursive space is Kim, *Age of Visions and Arguments*.
86. On the emergence of the *seinen* ideal, see Kimura Naoe, *Seinen no tanjō: Meiji Nihon ni okeru seijiteki jissen no tenkan* (Tokyo: Shin'yōsha, 1998); Jim Reichert, *In the Company of Men: Representations of Male-Male Sexuality in Meiji Literature* (Stanford, Calif.: Stanford University Press, 2006), 140–44.
87. Tokutomi Sohō, "Kinrai ryūkō no seiji shōsetsu o hyōsu" [A critique of the recently hailed political novels, 1887], in *Kirisuto-sha hyōron shū*, ed. Yabu Teiko, Yoshida Masanobu, and Izuhara Takatoshi, SNKBTM 26 (Tokyo: Iwanami shoten, 2002), 195–206, and "Hi-ren'ai" [Against love, 1891], in *Kirisuto-sha hyōron shū*, 244–49. Both essays were published in *Kokumin no tomo*.

5. THE NOVEL'S FAILURE

1. The reference is to Zhang Zhupo (1670–1698), who wrote a famous commentary on the *Jinpingmei*. For more detailed background, see David L. Rolston, ed., *How to Read the Chinese Novel* (Princeton, N.J.: Princeton University Press, 1990), chapter 4.
2. Tsubouchi Shōyō, *Imotose kagami*, in *Tsubouchi Shōyō shū*, ed. Inagaki Tatsurō, MBZ 16 (Tokyo: Chikuma shobō, 1969), 194–95.

3. For the traditional Chinese discourse on the novel as a "sweet" but "highly toxic" drug, see Judith T. Zeitlin, "Xiaoshuo," in *The Novel*, ed. Franco Moretti (Princeton, N.J.: Princeton University Press, 2006), 1:256.

4. The framing of the scene during the "gloomy season of the fifth-month rains" alludes to Tamakazura's reading of tales and Genji's critical discussion of narrative fiction in the "Fireflies" chapter of *The Tale of Genji*.

5. Another reason that Shōyō's narrator provides is Misawa's lack of experience in reading novels.

6. Tsubouchi Shōyō, *Tōsei shosei katagi*, in *Tsubouchi Shōyō shū*, ed. Nakamura Kan and Umezawa Nobuo, NKiBT 3 (Tokyo: Kadokawa shoten, 1974), 342.

7. *Tōsei shosei katagi* was first published in seventeen fascicles by Banseidō between June 1885 and January 1886.

8. *Kokkeibon* usually consisted of plotless scenes involving various character types and their dialogue reproducing contemporary speech.

9. Important scenes of this romance do not take place in the pleasure quarter, including the novel's famous opening scene that shows the lovers' reencounter at a cherry blossom viewing party. However, that Tanoji is a geisha belonging to a courtesan house and Komachida her customer indicates the *ninjōbon*-inspired quality of their relationship.

10. Critical discussions have also connected this subplot to the *kusazōshi* (picture books). Since its narrative, however, is not image-based as traditional *kusazōshi* were, I discuss it only in connection to the *yomihon*. In the Meiji period, *shizoku* was the designation for the status group of members of the former warrior (samurai) class.

11. On the transitional status of *Tōsei shosei katagi*, see, for example, Yamada Shunji, "*Nansō Satomi hakkenden* to iu kagami: Tsubouchi Shōyō, moshasetsu no seiritsu," *Bungei to hihyō* 6, no. 9 (1989): 42. For a seminal discussion of the novel's awareness of Edo- and Meiji-period *gesaku* works, see Maeda Ai, "Gesaku bungaku to *Tōsei shosei katagi*," in *Kindai dokusha no seiritsu* (Tokyo: Chikuma shobō, 1989), 372–86.

12. Tsubouchi, *Tōsei shosei katagi*, 358–59; Iwamoto Yoshiharu, "Fujin no chii," *Jogaku zasshi* 2 (1885): 22–25. Iwamoto's essay had appeared slightly earlier than Shōyō's novel in August 1885.

13. As noted earlier, Shōyō similarly defines idealism as a "propensity of wanting to realize things that cannot be realized in the world." In a seminal essay that defined the subsequent understanding of the term in literary scholarship, Ochi Haruo argued that Shōyō denigrates idealism as the students' (and his own) youthful licentiousness and fancifulness that the novel seeks to overcome by a new orientation toward reason and reality (*genjitsu*). However, this perspective on the term is problematic because it does not include its metacritical and civilizational implications such as the reference to *Rienzi* and high-class love. See Ochi Haruo, "*Shosei katagi* no seishun," in *Tsubouchi Shōyō, Futabatei Shimei*, ed. Nihon Bungaku Kenkyū Shiryō Kankōkai, NBKSS (Tokyo: Yūseidō, 1979), 38–48.

14. Tsubouchi, *Tōsei shosei katagi*, 341.

15. Tsubouchi, *Tōsei shosei katagi*, 342.

16. Tsubouchi, *Tōsei shosei katagi*, 336. Shōyō writes the term "ideal," a katakana gloss, with the characters *kakūteki no* (fictional).

243

5. THE NOVEL'S FAILURE

17. For a discussion of this stigma, see Tsubouchi, *Tōsei shosei katagi*, 387. Shōyō himself married a former courtesan, named Katō Sen, in October 1886. His marriage certainly forms the biographical backdrop for his novels *Tōsei shosei katagi* and *Imotose kagami*. On Shōyō's marriage, see Wada Shigejirō, "Shōyō *Imotose kagami* shiron," *Ritsumeikan bungaku* 152 (1958): 1–13, and Yanagida Izumi, "Shōyō sensei to josei," *Meiji Taishō bungaku kenkyū* 16 (1955): 64–70.

18. Ironically, student-teacher relationships became a privileged site in later Meiji literature for probing the ambiguous line between enlightened gender notions (including spiritual love) and licentious eroticization; see, for instance, Tayama Katai's (1871–1930) much later novel *Futon* (*The Quilt*, 1907).

19. For Shōyō's awareness of contemporary discourses of nervous disease, see Asano Masamichi, "Imōto, chichi, 'hōyūtachi': *Ichidoku santan: Tōsei shosei katagi* ni okeru 'jōyoku' no hensei," *Nihon bungaku* 57, no. 12 (2008): 24–36.

20. For a different reading that sees in Komachida's inactivity a strategic elision of the political and the production of the "alienated intellectual" as a politically neutral figure whose interiority is predicated on "love," see Atsuko Ueda, *Concealment of Politics, Politics of Concealment: The Production of "Literature" in Meiji Japan* (Stanford, Calif.: Stanford University Press, 2007), chapter 5, esp. 137–41.

21. Tsubouchi, *Tōsei shosei katagi*, 331–32. To underline his point, Shōyō makes reference to the depiction of prostitutes and thieves in Charles Dickens's novels.

22. Tsubouchi, *Tōsei shosei katagi*, 222.

23. Iwamoto Yoshiharu, "Danjo kōsairon," in *Kirisuto-sha hyōron shū*, ed. Yabu Teiko, Yoshida Masanobu, and Izuhara Takatoshi, SNKBTM 26 (Tokyo: Iwanami shoten, 2002), 121.

24. Tsubouchi, *Tōsei shosei katagi*, 252–53. A similar metacritical reflection occurs in a discussion about prophetic dreams. Although the students, spokesmen of civilization and enlightenment, denounce such dreams as opposed to psychology and reason, the novel proves true a dream of Tanoji's father, which presages that his daughter is alive; see 299–301.

25. Tsubouchi Shōyō, *Shōsetsu shinzui*, in *Tsubouchi Shōyō shū*, ed. Nakamura Kan and Umezawa Nobuo, NKiBT 3 (Tokyo: Kadokawa shoten, 1974), 55. Shōyō's notion of "romance" was inspired by Walter Scott's "Essay on Romance," which appeared as the supplement to the *Encyclopedia Britannica* of 1824.

26. Ochi, "*Shosei katagi* no seishun," 42–45. Ochi argues that Shōyō had to revert to this format after his initial aim to write the "students' transformation" failed. I would push Ochi's point even further and argue that the *yomihon* subplot, by making Komachida's civilized marriage possible, is the only (and admittedly contorted) way to "fictionally" write a "transformation of students" after its realist representation has become impossible.

27. Tsubouchi, *Tōsei shosei katagi*, 431–32.

28. Tsubouchi Shōyō, "Shōsetsu o ronjite *Shosei katagi* no shui ni oyobu" [On the novel and primary intent of *Shosei katagi*], in *Shōsetsu shinzui*, ed. Munakata Kazushige (Tokyo: Iwanami shoten, 2010), 216.

29. Jim Reichert, *In the Company of Men: Representations of Male-Male Sexuality in Meiji Literature* (Stanford, Calif.: Stanford University Press, 2006), chapter 3, convincingly shows that the student Kiriyama Benroku in *Tōsei shosei katagi* is associated with both political violence and male-male sexuality. He argues that *Shōsetsu*

shinzui and *Tōsei shosei katagi* promote civilizational progress by institutionalizing compulsory male heterosexuality and marginalizing male-male sexuality, which they stigmatize as uncivilized. I agree with Reichert's argument, but it is important to note that Shōyō also includes most manifestations of male-female love and sexuality under the negative label of "effete customs."

30. Takata Sanae, "*Tōsei shosei katagi* no hihyō," in KBHT, vol. 1, ed. Yoshida Seiichi and Asai Kiyoshi (Tokyo: Kadokawa shoten, 1971), 330–32.

31. *Imotose kagami* was first published in thirteen fascicles by Kaishin Shooku between December 1885 and September 1886.

32. Tsubouchi, *Imotose kagami*, 164.

33. The dialogue, for instance, often reproduces vernacular speech as in a *ninjōbon*, but each illocution is newly indented, thus more strongly producing the graphic effect of a Western novel. Moreover, rather than focusing on static dialogue-centered scenes, *Imotose kagami* presents a coherent plot-driven narration that mostly does away with unlikely coincidences reminiscent of what Shōyō labeled as romance.

34. Ishibashi Ningetsu, "*Imotose kagami* o yomu" [Reading *Imotose kagami*], in *Yamada Bimyō, Ishibashi Ningetsu, Takase Bun'en shū*, ed. Fukuda Kiyoto, MBZ 23 (Tokyo: Chikuma shobō, 1971), 255.

35. Iwamoto Yoshiharu, "Kon'inron," in *Jogaku zasshi, Bungakukai shū*, ed. Sasabuchi Tomoichi, MBZ 32 (Tokyo: Chikuma shobō, 1973), 31–34, 39. Ishibashi, "*Imotose kagami* o yomu," 256–57, points out that Oyuki, given her education, should not have let herself be forced. He sees this as an inconsistency in Shōyō's presentation of the material.

36. Tsubouchi, *Imotose kagami*, 212.

37. Iwamoto, "Danjo kōsairon," 138–39.

38. Tsubouchi, *Imotose kagami*, 195.

39. Tsubouchi, *Imotose kagami*, 191.

40. Tsubouchi, *Imotose kagami*, 195.

41. The work was published in June 1886 by Hino Shōten. On the intertextual connections between *Kyō waranbe* and *Imotose kagami*, see also Asano Masamichi, "*Shinmigaki: Imotose kagami* no shūjiteki, soshite seijiteki-shakaiteki jigen: *Fūkai: Kyō waranbe* to no hikaku ni oite," *Kokugo kokubun kenkyū* 136 (2009): 43–55.

42. See Shōyō's quote in Shōyō Kyōkai, ed., foreword to *Shōyō senshū: Bessatsu* (Tokyo: Daiichi shobō, 1977), 1:2. This quote also provides allegorical readings of all involved figures and incidents in *Kyō waranbe*.

43. The profligacy of Misawa's father can be seen as an oblique reference to the sexual escapades of the governing Meiji oligarchy, whose sex scandals were explored by contemporary journalism and *gesaku* works. For these materials and Shōyō's interest in them, see Maeda, "Gesaku bungaku," 373–74, and Maeda Ai, "Mishima Michitsune to Rokumeikan jidai," in *Genkei no Meiji* (Tokyo: Chikuma shobō, 1989), 79–98.

44. Tsubouchi, *Imotose kagami*, 209.

45. Eavesdropping is an important motif in the novel and the origin of misunderstandings and false rumors. Shōyō's narrator qualifies the practice as uncivilized and characteristic of Japan, but not the West; see Tsubouchi, *Imotose kagami*, 241–42. Much prior scholarship on *Imotose kagami* has been concerned with the motif's narratological implications. See in particular Maeda Ai, "Meiji no hyōgen shisō to buntai: Shōsetsu no 'katari' o megutte," in *Kindai dokusha no seiritsu*, 444–53;

245

5. THE NOVEL'S FAILURE

Takahashi Osamu, "*Shinmigaki: Imotose kagami* ron: *Karyū shunwa* o jiku toshite," *Jōchi daigaku kokubungaku ronshū* 18 (1985): 113–16; and Satoru Saito, *Detective Fiction and the Rise of the Japanese Novel, 1880–1930* (Cambridge, Mass.: Harvard University Asia Center, 2012), chapter 1.

46. Tsubouchi, *Imotose kagami*, 227.

47. *Mirai no yume* appeared in ten successive fascicles published by Banseidō, the publisher of *Tōsei shosei katagi*. For one of the rare critical discussions of this novel, see Yanagida Izumi, *Seiji shōsetsu kenkyū* (Tokyo: Shunjūsha, 1968), 2:45–57.

48. Appendix to Tsubouchi Shōyō, *Tōsei shosei katagi* (Tokyo: Banseidō, 1886), 2:11.

49. On the renegotiation of the unequal treaties and the connected public debates, see Kenneth B. Pyle, *The New Generation in Meiji Japan: Problems of Cultural Identity, 1885–1895* (Stanford, Calif.: Stanford University Press, 1969), chapter 5; Kyu Hyun Kim, *The Age of Visions and Arguments: Parliamentarianism and the National Public Sphere in Early Meiji Japan* (Cambridge, Mass.: Harvard University Asia Center, 2007), chapter 11. The years 1887 and 1888 witnessed the publication of 101 and 122 political novels, respectively; only 27 and 52 titles were published in 1886 and 1889, respectively. For these numbers, see Hiraoka Toshio, *Nihon kindai bungaku no shuppatsu* (Tokyo: Hanawa shobō, 1992), 58. Hiraoka's count is based on Yanagida Izumi's exhaustive list of titles of political fiction in the appendix to *Seiji shōsetsu kenkyū*, vol. 3, titled "Seiji shōsetsu nenpyō."

50. Tsubouchi Shōyō, *Mirai no yume*, in *Shōyō senshū: Bessatsu*, ed. Shōyō Kyōkai (Tokyo: Daiichi shobō, 1977), 1:579, 617, 693.

51. *Setchūbai* presents the Reform Party struggle for a democratic public sphere from a future perspective of national success and prosperity. For a discussion of *Setchūbai's* futurity, see Christopher L. Hill, *National History and the World of Nations: Capital, State, and the Rhetoric of History in Japan, France, and the United States* (Durham, N.C.: Duke University Press, 2008), chapter 5. On the "future record" as a genre of political fiction, see Kyoko Kurita, "Meiji Japan's Y23 Crisis and the Discovery of the Future: Suehiro Tetchō's *Nijūsan-nen mirai-ki*," *Harvard Journal of Asiatic Studies* 60, no. 1 (2000): 5–43.

52. Tsubouchi Shōyō, "Miraiki ni ruisuru shōsetsu," in *Tsubouchi Shōyō kenkyū: Fu, bungakuron shoshutsu shiryō*, ed. Ishida Tadahiko (Fukuoka: Kyūshū daigaku shuppankai, 1988), 420–21.

53. The essay appeared in the journal *Shakai no kenshō* (Social phenomena) in April 1888.

54. Tsubouchi Shōyō, "Aidiaru noberu no koto ni tsukite," in *Tsubouchi Shōyō kenkyū*, 426.

55. Tsubouchi, "Aidiaru noberu," 428.

56. On Sudō Nansui, see Yanagida, *Seiji shōsetsu kenkyū*, 2:218–318.

57. Tsubouchi Shōyō, *Saikun*, in *Tsubouchi Shōyō Futabatei Shimei shū*, ed. Aoki Toshihiro and Togawa Shinsuke, SNKBTM 18 (Tokyo: Iwanami shoten, 2002), 1–57. Another similar experiment was the unfinished novel *Shōsetsu: Gaimu daijin* (A novel: Minister of foreign affairs, 1888), which satirically illustrates, among other elements, the shortcomings of the superficially enlightened upper-class Rokumeikan society, including the debauchery of educated young women. For a reprint, see Shōyō Kenkyūkai, ed., *Honkoku to kenkyū: Tsubouchi Shōyō Shōsetsu: Gaimu daijin* (Tokyo: Sōbunsha, 1994), 141–326.

58. For an assessment in this vein, see Marleigh Grayer Ryan, *The Development of Realism in the Fiction of Tsubouchi Shōyō* (Seattle: University of Washington Press, 1975), 113.
59. Iwamoto Yoshiharu, "*Saikun,*" *Jogaku zasshi* 144 (1889): 10–11.
60. For a discussion of Shōyō's diary entries and self-doubts, see Aoki Toshihiro, "'Kyūaku zensho' no jidai," in *Tsubouchi Shōyō Futabatei Shimei shū*, 499–500.
61. For these terms, see Tsubouchi Shōyō, "Azusa miko" [Catalpa-bow shaman, 1891], in *Shōyō senshū*, ed. Shōyō Kyōkai (Tokyo: Daiichi shobō, 1977), 8:160, 169. The essay was published in the *Yomiuri shinbun*. For a helpful discussion of these terms in the broader context of the "debate over submerged ideals," see Yamanouchi Shōshi, "Shōyō ni okeru botsurisō ron no keisei: Bungei riron toshite no realism [*sic*] ron no mondai o chūshin toshite," in *Tsubouchi Shōyō, Futabatei Shimei*, 74–89.
62. Tsubouchi, "Azusa-miko," 168.
63. Tsubouchi Shōyō, "*Makubesu hyōshaku* no shogen" [Preface to *Commentary of Macbeth*, 1891], in *Tsubouchi Shōyō shū*, NKiBT 3, 182. The essay was published in the journal *Waseda bungaku* (Waseda literature).
64. Tsubouchi Shōyō, "Soko shirazu no mizuumi," in *Tsubouchi Shōyō shū*, MBZ 16, 279–82. The essay was published in the *Yomiuri shinbun*.
65. Tsubouchi Shōyō, "Botsurisō no gogi o benzu" [On the meaning of submerged ideals, 1892], in *Tsubouchi Shōyō shū*, NKiBT 3, 192. The essay was published in *Waseda bungaku*.
66. Ōgai criticizes Shōyō's essays for ignoring the transcendental "a priori ideas" (*senten no risō*) on which phenomenal reality, including works of art and literature, is predicated. Influenced by German idealism, Ōgai's use of the term *risō* as the equivalent for the German *Idee* differs significantly from Shōyō's understanding of "ideal." See, for instance, Mori Ōgai, "Waseda bungaku no botsurisō" [The submerged ideals of *Waseda bungaku*, 1891], in KBHT, 1:196. For a similar misunderstanding in later criticism, see Kubota Yoshitarō, "Botsurisō ronsō o megutte: Mōruton to Harutoman," in *Tsubouchi Shōyō, Futabatei Shimei*, 105.
67. Tsubouchi, "*Makubesu hyōshaku* no shogen," 186.

6. *NINJŌ* AND THE LATE-MEIJI NOVEL

1. Sōseki's cat narrator calls his own writing an attempt at *shaseibun*. See Natsume Sōseki, *Wagahai wa neko de aru*, in *Sōseki zenshū*, vol. 1, ed. Takemori Ten'yū and Andō Fumihito (Tokyo: Iwanami shoten, 1993), 183.
2. Natsume Sōseki, "Shaseibun," in *Sōseki zenshū*, vol. 16, ed. Komori Yōichi (Tokyo: Iwanami shoten, 1995), 50–55.
3. For Sōseki's *shaseibun* as a literary form of resistance (*teikō*) to the novel, see Karatani Kōjin, "Sōseki to janru," in *Zōho Sōseki ron shūsei* (Tokyo: Heibonsha, 2001), 227–68, and "Sōseki to 'bun,'" in *Zōho Sōseki ron shūsei*, 269–300. Karatani discusses Sōseki's experimentation with diverse genres and writing styles (*bun*) as a challenge to the increasingly unified aesthetics of *genbun itchi* (unification of the spoken and written languages) especially in the contemporary naturalist novel. See also James A. Fujii, *Complicit Fictions: The Subject in the Modern Japanese Prose Narrative* (Berkeley: University of California Press, 1993), chapter 4.

4. Hiraoka Toshio, *Nihon kindai bungaku no shuppatsu* (Tokyo: Hanawa shobō, 1992), chapter 3.

5. Although not primarily with regard to *Ukigumo*, Karatani Kōjin's argument about the interdependence between what he defines as the speech-centered phonocentricism of the *genbun itchi* style and the production of interiority in Meiji literary texts has been particularly influential. See Karatani Kōjin, *Origins of Modern Japanese Literature*, trans. Brett de Bary et al. (Durham, N.C.: Duke University Press, 1993), chapters 1 and 2. More recently, Indra A. Levy, *Sirens of the Western Shore: The Westernesque Femme Fatale, Translation, and Vernacular Style in Modern Japanese Literature* (New York: Columbia University Press, 2006), has complicated this view by highlighting the role of Western translation and exoticism in Futabatei's and other authors' experimentation with *genbun itchi*.

6. For an incisive discussion of this novel, see Rebecca L. Copeland, *Lost Leaves: Women Writers of Meiji Japan* (Honolulu: University of Hawai'i Press, 2000), chapter 2. For an English translation, see Miyake Kaho, *Warbler in the Grove*, trans. Rebecca L. Copeland, in *The Modern Murasaki: Writing by Women of Meiji Japan*, ed. Rebecca L. Copeland and Melek Ortabasi (New York: Columbia University Press, 2006), 73–125.

7. Despite his later confrontation with Shōyō over the notion of "submerged ideals," Ōgai largely endorsed Shōyō's critical ideas, partly translating them into the terms of German philosopher Rudolf von Gottschall (1823–1909), whose aesthetic criticism he had read during his stay in Germany in the late 1880s. In his most important early critical essay "Ima no shoka no shōsetsuron o yomite" [Reading contemporary discussions on the novel, 1889], in *Ōgai zenshū* (Tokyo: Iwanami shoten, 1973), 22:65–82, Ōgai agrees with the idea that the novel should focus on *ninjō* and *setai*—or, in Gottschall's terms, "human life" (*jinsei*). But not unlike Shōyō, he also states that the novel must contain an "idealist" element concerned with "beauty" to avoid a vulgar realism merely depicting "licentiousness" (*in'yoku*). For Ōgai's reception of Shōyō through the eyes of Gottschall, see Kobori Keiichirō, *Wakaki hi no Mori Ōgai* (Tokyo: Tōkyō daigaku shuppankai, 1973), 414–21, and Richard John Bowring, *Mori Ōgai and the Modernization of Japanese Culture* (Cambridge: Cambridge University Press, 1979), 63–87.

8. Christopher Hill, "Mori Ōgai's Resentful Narrator: Trauma and the National Subject in 'The Dancing Girl,'" *positions* 10, no. 2 (2002): 365–97, reads the protagonist's resentment as a "symptom" produced by the traumatic process of his subjection to the nation. He defines *Maihime* as a "national allegory" narrating the production of national subjecthood. However, the hero's resistance to his subjection, epitomized by his love, also produces a subjectivity defined by individual freedom. Ultimately, both freedom and subjection to the nation, two contradictory ideological orientations inherent in the bildungsroman, are two sides of the same coin. See also Tomiko Yoda, "First-Person Narration and Citizen-Subject: The Modernity of Ōgai's 'The Dancing Girl,'" *Journal of Asian Studies* 65, no. 2 (2006): 277–306.

9. A careful study of this appropriation is Peter F. Kornicki, *The Reform of Fiction in Meiji Japan* (London: Ithaca Press, 1982), chapters 4–6.

10. Ozaki Kōyō, *Iro zange*, in *Ozaki Kōyō shū*, ed. Suda Chisato and Matsumura Tomomi, SNKBTM 19 (Tokyo: Iwanami shoten, 2003), 6.

248

11. Ken K. Ito, *An Age of Melodrama: Family, Gender, and Social Hierarchy in the Turn-of-the-Century Japanese Novel* (Stanford, Calif.: Stanford University Press, 2008). Shincho hyakushu (One hundred new works), published by Yoshioka Shosekiten, was an influential series of recently published *shōsetsu*. A preface by Shōyō started the series, and its first volume was Kōyō's *Iro zange*. My own use of the term "melodrama" here is rather broad, indicating the tearful or sentimental quality of a literary work.

12. Carol Gluck, *Japan's Modern Myths: Ideology in the Late Meiji Period* (Princeton, N.J.: Princeton University Press, 1985), 27–29.

13. See, for instance, Doppo's story "Kyūshi" (A miserable death, 1907). On these developments, see also the pertinent remarks in Suzuki Sadami, *Nihon no "bungaku" gainen* (Tokyo: Sakuhinsha, 1998), 234.

14. These novels were serialized in the *Kokumin shinbun* (The nation's newspaper) and *Yomiuri shinbun*, respectively. For incisive readings of them as melodrama, see Jonathan E. Zwicker, *Practices of the Sentimental Imagination: Melodrama, the Novel, and the Social Imaginary in Nineteenth-Century Japan* (Cambridge, Mass.: Harvard University Asia Center, 2006), chapter 4, and Ito, *An Age of Melodrama*, chapters 1 and 2.

15. Natsume Sōseki, *Kusamakura*, in *Sōseki zenshū*, vol. 3, ed. Imanishi Junkichi and Izuhara Takatoshi (Tokyo: Iwanami shoten, 1994), 10.

16. For premodern notions of *bungaku*, see Suzuki, *Nihon no "bungaku" gainen*, 65–124.

17. See especially the debate surrounding the notion of the "extreme decline of literature" (*bungaku gokusui*) in the early 1890s. For excellent overviews, see Togawa Shinsuke, "Bungaku gokusuiron zengo," *Bungaku* 44, no. 6 (1976): 757–73; Wolfgang Schamoni, *Kitamura Tōkoku: Die frühen Jahre; von der "Politik" zur "Literatur"* (Wiesbaden: Steiner Verlag, 1983), chapter 5; Hiraoka, *Nihon kindai bungaku no shuppatsu*, 222–37; Tomi Suzuki, *Narrating the Self: Fictions of Japanese Modernity* (Stanford, Calif.: Stanford University Press, 1996), 25–26. For the relevant sources, see KBHT, vol. 1, ed. Yoshida Seiichi and Asai Kiyoshi (Tokyo: Kadokawa shoten, 1971), 89–130.

18. "Bungaku sekai no kinkyō," in KBHT, 1:98. The essay was published in the *Chōya shinbun*.

19. Aeba Kōson was one of the authors whose works, included in the Shincho hyakushu series, thematized *ninjō* in the wake of Shōyō's reform.

20. Kitamura Tōkoku [Hototogisu], "Tōsei bungaku no ushio moyō" [Currents in contemporary literature], in KBHT, 1:90–91. See also the carefully annotated German translation in Schamoni, *Kitamura Tōkoku*, 190–96. The essay was published in *Jogaku zasshi*.

21. See Iwamoto Yoshiharu, "Shōsetsuka no chakugan" [The novelist's main focus, 1889], in *Kirisuto-sha hyōron shū*, ed. Yabu Teiko, Yoshida Masanobu, and Izuhara Takatoshi, SNKBTM 26 (Tokyo: Iwanami shoten, 2002), 180. In another essay, Iwamoto encouraged especially female novelists to depict other emotions than love; see Iwamoto Yoshiharu, "Joryū shōsetsuka no honshoku" [The duty of female novelists, 1889], in *Kirisuto-sha hyōron shū*, 172. Both essays were published in *Jogaku zasshi*. Iwamoto's wife, Wakamatsu Shizuko (1864–1896), accordingly translated Frances Hodgson Burnett's (1849–1924) novel *Little Lord Fauntleroy* (1885) depicting

the emotions between parents and children; for a detailed discussion, see Copeland, *Lost Leaves*, chapter 3.

22. Uchida Roan, "Seiji shōsetsu o tsukure yo" [Write political novels!, 1898], in *Kindai
hyōron shū 1*, ed. Kawazoe Kunimoto et al., NKiBT 57 (Tokyo: Kadokawa shoten,
1972), 147–56. The essay was published in *Dainihon* (The greater Japan).

23. Tokutomi Sohō, "Shin Nihon no shijin" [The poet of a new Japan, 1888], in *Kirisuto-
sha hyōron shū*, 222. The essay was published in *Kokumin no tomo*.

24. See, for example, Kitamura Tōkoku, "Naibu seimei ron" [On the inner life, 1893], in
Kirisuto-sha hyōron shū, 300–312. The essay was published in the journal *Bungakukai* (The literary world).

25. Kitamura Tōkoku, "Ensei shika to josei," in *Jinsei ni ai-wataru to wa nan no ii zo*,
ed. Oketani Hideaki (Tokyo: Ōbunsha, 1979), 82.

26. Kitamura, "Ensei shika to josei," 84.

27. On this continuum, see Schamoni, *Kitamura Tōkoku*, 167–68. Suzuki, *Narrating the
Self*, 36, also notes that the Western authors whom critics like Tōkoku and other
Christian intellectuals were drawn to as exemplary "poets"—Byron, Shelley, Word-
sworth, Carlyle, and Emerson—were patriotic, political activists, highlighting the
continuity between literature and its social mission.

28. Mikami Sanji and Takatsu Kuwasaburō, *Nihon bungakushi* [History of Japanese lit-
erature] (Tokyo: Nihon tosho sentā, 1999), 1:13. For a discussion of this work and
other 1890s literary histories, see Tomi Suzuki, "Gender and Genre: Modern Literary Histories and Women's Diary Literature," in *Inventing the Classics: Modernity,
National Identity, and Japanese Literature*, ed. Haruo Shirane and Tomi Suzuki
(Stanford, Calif.: Stanford University Press, 2000), 73–83; see also Suzuki, *Nihon no
"bungaku" gainen*, 218–23.

29. This broader definition reflected the traditional use of the term "literature" in the
West and became institutionalized beginning in the late 1870s through the estab-
lishment of Western academic disciplines at the University of Tokyo. See Suzuki,
"Gender and Genre," 76.

30. Mikami and Takatsu, *Nihon bungakushi*, 1:14.

31. Mikami and Takatsu, *Nihon bungakushi*, 1:3. The authors here point to a welcome
recent "flourishing of novels."

32. The romantic movement centered around the journal *Bungakukai*, which shaped
the intellectual discourse of the 1890s and influenced major authors like Shimazaki Tōson (1872–1943) and Tayama Katai. See Michael C. Brownstein, "*Jogaku
zasshi* and the Founding of *Bungakukai*," *Monumenta Nipponica* 35, no. 3 (1980),
319–36. On Tōson's early romantic poetry, see Michael K. Bourdaghs, *The Dawn
That Never Comes: Shimazaki Tōson and Japanese Nationalism* (New York: Columbia University Press, 2003), 4–12.

33. Fujioka Sakutarō, *Kokubungaku zenshi: Heianchō-hen* [Complete history of Japanese literature: The Heian court], ed. Akiyama Ken et al. (Tokyo: Heibonsha, 1971),
1:45–46. On Fujioka's project, see Suzuki, "Gender and Genre," 80–83, and Tomiko
Yoda, *Gender and National Literature: Heian Texts in the Constructions of Japanese
Modernity* (Durham, N.C.: Duke University Press, 2004), chapter 2.

34. See, for instance, Takayama Chogyū, "Bunmei hihyōka toshite no bungakusha" [The
literary author as cultural critic, 1901], in *Kindai hyōron shū 1*, 158–71. The essay was
published in the popular magazine *Taiyō* (The sun).

35. Takayama Chogyū, "Biteki seikatsu o ronzu" [On the aesthetic life, 1901], in *Kindai hyōron shū 1*, 180–81. The essay was published in *Taiyō*.
36. Takayama, "Bunmei hihyōka," 158, 165, 171.
37. For a helpful overview of these discourses, see Suzuki, *Narrating the Self*, 79–88.
38. Nagai Kafū, *Jigoku no hana*, in *Kafū zenshū*, ed. Inagaki Tatsurō, Takemori Ten'yū, and Nakajima Kunihiko (Tokyo: Iwanami shoten, 1993), 2:221. The terms "dark" and "animalistic" (*dōbutsuteki*) are key words in Kafū's discourse.
39. For a reading of *shaseibun* as realism, see Etō Jun, *Riarizumu no genryū* (Tokyo: Kawade shobō shinsha, 1989), chapter 1. On *shaseibun* and *genbun itchi*, see Yamamoto Masahide, *Genbun itchi no rekishi ronkō: Zokuhen* (Tokyo: Ōfūsha, 1981), 466–87.
40. Masaoka Shiki, "Jojibun," in *Masaoka Shiki shū*, ed. Matsui Toshihiko, NKiBT 16 (Tokyo: Kadokawa shoten, 1972), 362. The essay was serialized in the weekly supplement to the newspaper *Nihon* (*Nihon furoku shūhō*) from January to March 1900.
41. Masaoka, "Jojibun," 367.
42. On this discourse, see Siu-kit Wong, "Ch'ing in Chinese Literary Criticism" (PhD diss., Oxford University, 1969); Nakamura Yukihiko, *Kinsei bungei shichōkō* (Tokyo: Iwanami shoten, 1975), 133–44.
43. On nature and seasonality in *waka* and traditional Japanese literature, see Haruo Shirane, *Japan and the Culture of the Four Seasons: Nature, Literature, and the Arts* (New York: Columbia University Press, 2012).
44. On topicality in haiku, both seasonal and human, see Haruo Shirane, *Traces of Dreams: Landscape, Cultural Memory, and the Poetry of Bashō* (Stanford, Calif.: Stanford University Press, 1998).
45. *Wagahai wa neko de aru* was serialized in the haiku journal *Hototogisu* (Cuckoo). Other *shaseibun* experiments by Sōseki include *Jitensha nikki* (Bicycle diary, 1903) and *Rondon shōsoku* (Letters from London, 1901), both published in *Hototogisu*. Another important novel-length *shaseibun* work was *Botchan*, also published in *Hototogisu* in 1906.
46. On this aspect, see Daniel Poch, "Ethics of Emotion in Nineteenth-Century Japanese Literature: Shunsui, Bakin, the Political Novel, Shōyō, Sōseki" (PhD diss., Columbia University, 2014), chapter 4.
47. *Kusamakura* was first published in the journal *Shinshōsetsu* (New novel) in September 1906.
48. The fact that *Kusamakura*'s narrator is a painter in the Western style is a veiled reference to the discourse of Shiki, who discussed the idea of *shasei* with reference to Western oil painting. On this aspect, see Mark Morris, "Buson and Shiki: Part Two," *Harvard Journal of Asiatic Studies* 45, no. 1 (1985): 273–88.
49. Natsume, *Kusamakura*, 8. For an excellent recent translation, see Natsume Sōseki, *Kusamakura*, trans. Meredith McKinney (New York: Penguin Books, 2008).
50. Natsume, *Kusamakura*, 12–13.
51. On the physicality of the body and its movements, see Ōtsu Chisako, "Hadō suru setsuna: *Kusamakura* ron," in *Botchan, Kusamakura*, ed. Kataoka Yutaka and Komori Yōichi (Tokyo: Ōfūsha, 1990), 269–82. See also with regard to the body as a site of "subconscious" movement and resistance, Ubukata Tomoko, *Seishin bunseki izen: Muishiki no Nihon kindai bungaku* (Tokyo: Kanrin shobō, 2009), 100–19.

52. Sōseki derived this idea from Masaoka Shiki, who developed a similar notion of objectivity in *shasei* as a way to distance frightening emotions—in Shiki's case, concretely the fear of death in the face of his incurable tuberculosis. For discussions that touch on this aspect, see Karatani Kōjin, "Shi to shi: Shiki kara Sōseki e," in *Zōho Sōseki ron shūsei*, 335–39, and Komori Yōichi, *Shiki to Sōseki: Yūjō ga hagukunda shajitsu no kindai* (Tokyo: Shūeisha, 2016), chapter 6.

53. Note the gendering of the poetic quotes, with Nami reciting a *waka* and the narrator English and Sinitic poetry. Both, however, participate in haiku composition, and the fact that Nami playfully corrects his poems in chapter 4 can be seen as a challenge to the gender hierarchy. For a reading that points out Nami's "feminist resistance to male narrative authority," see Atsuko Sakaki, *Recontextualizing Texts: Narrative Performance in Modern Japanese Fiction* (Cambridge, Mass.: Harvard University Asia Center, 1999), chapter 3.

54. Natsume, *Kusamakura*, 36.

55. Natsume, *Kusamakura*, 49–50. The verses quoted by Sōseki form two stanzas of three verses each in Meredith's novel; see George Meredith, *The Shaving of Shagpat: An Arabian Entertainment* (London: Constable, 1914), 30. I quote the poem from Sōseki's text.

56. Natsume Sōseki, *Bungakuron*, ed. Kamei Shunsuke (Tokyo: Iwanami shoten, 2007), 2:207.

57. Natsume, *Bungakuron*, 1:31. For a discussion of F and f, see Komori Yōichi, *Sōseki ron: 21-seiki o ikinuku tame ni* (Tokyo: Iwanami shoten, 2010), 311–22. *Bungakuron* was first published in book form in 1907 by Ōkura Shoten. For a partial English translation, see Natsume Sōseki, *Theory of Literature and Other Critical Writings*, ed. Michael K. Bourdaghs, Atsuko Ueda, and Joseph A. Murphy (New York: Columbia University Press, 2009). For a valuable discussion of *Bungakuron*'s textual history and relevant critical issues, see the editors' introduction to that volume. See also the special issues in *Japan Forum* 20, no. 1 (2008), and *Bungaku* 13, no. 3 (2012).

58. Thomas LaMarre, "Expanded Empiricism: Natsume Sōseki with William James," *Japan Forum* 20, no. 1 (2008): 47–77; Joseph A. Murphy, "Separation of Cognition and Affect in *Bungakuron*," *Japan Forum* 20, no. 1 (2008): 103–26. Sōseki's quantitative model and his notion that literature should appeal to the reader's emotions were not unprecedented in Japan. Similar ideas can be found in earlier Meiji-period rhetorical treatises, which were equally informed by nineteenth-century anglophone psychology. For a discussion that touches on this, see Massimiliano Tomasi, *Rhetoric in Modern Japan: Western Influences on the Development of Narrative and Oratorical Style* (Honolulu: University of Hawai`i Press, 2004), chapters 4 and 5.

59. Natsume, *Bungakuron*, 2:187.

60. Natsume, *Bungakuron*, 1:140.

61. Natsume, *Bungakuron*, 2:13–191.

62. Bai Juyi, "Changhenge," in *Hakushi monjū* vol. 2, part 2, ed. Okamura Shigeru, Shinshaku kanbun taikei 117 (Tokyo: Meiji shoin, 2007), 815. Yang Guifei (716–756) was a Chinese palace lady and femme fatale who monopolized the affection of the Tang emperor Xuanzong (685–762; r. 712–756) and, according to official historiography, accelerated the downfall of the dynasty. Sōseki cites only the second verse of the Chinese original (omitting the character 春), paraphrasing the first one. See Natsume, *Bungakuron*, 2:83.

63. To illustrate the additory emotional effect, Sōseki employs the mathematical formula "f + f' = 2f, or 2f'." See Natsume, *Bungakuron*, 2:94.

64. Natsume, *Bungakuron*, 2:84–85.

65. Natsume, *Bungakuron*, 2:189.

66. Natsume, *Bungakuron*, 2:190.

67. *Sōsakuka no taido* was first presented as a talk in February 1908.

68. Sōseki also labels the two stances the "objective" (*kyakkanteki*) and "subjective" (*shukanteki*) attitudes, respectively.

69. Natsume Sōseki, "Sōsakuka no taido," in *Sōseki zenshū*, vol. 16, ed. Komori Yōichi (Tokyo: Iwanami shoten, 1995), 185–206

70. Natsume, "Sōsakuka no taido," 203–4.

71. Natsume, "Sōsakuka no taido," 213–14.

72. Natsume, *Kusamakura*, 78.

73. Natsume, *Kusamakura*, 79–80. In *Kusamakura*, the poem is presented as a genuine production of the narrator, but it was actually composed by Sōseki earlier, in March 1898, while he was teaching in Kumamoto. In later editions of Sōseki's works, the poem became anthologized under the title "Sitting Quietly on a Spring Day" (Shunjitsu seiza). For a carefully annotated edition, see Natsume Sōseki, *Kanshi*, in *Sōseki zenshū*, vol. 18, ed. Ikkai Tomoyoshi (Tokyo: Iwanami shoten, 1995), 201–4.

74. Natsume Sōseki, "Eikoku shijin no tenchi sansen ni taisuru kannen," in *Sōseki zenshū*, vol. 13, ed. Yamanouchi Hisaaki (Tokyo: Iwanami shoten, 1995), 23. Sōseki also uses the term "naturalism" (*shizenshugi*) synonymously with "romanticism." The term here refers to the orientation toward nature in the eighteenth-century English poets discussed in the essay.

75. Natsume, "Eikoku shijin," 46–47.

76. See Michele Marra, *The Aesthetics of Discontent: Politics and Reclusion in Medieval Japanese Literature* (Honolulu: University of Hawai'i Press, 1991).

77. Natsume, *Kanshi*, 198–201. For a recent translation, see Xiaohui Zhang, "The Pursuit of the Dao: Natsume Sōseki and His *Kanshi* of 1916," *Journal of Chinese Literature and Culture* 5, no. 1 (2018): 153. I am grateful to one of my anonymous reviewers for pointing out this reference.

78. Natsume, *Kanshi*, 200.

79. For this poetry, see Matthew Fraleigh, "Songs of the Righteous Spirit: 'Men of High Purpose' and Their Chinese Poetry in Modern Japan," *Harvard Journal of Asiatic Studies* 69, no. 1 (2009): 109–71. Another, more recent potential context for this imagery would be the People's Rights Movement, in which Sōseki, however, does not seem to have been involved.

80. Natsume, *Kusamakura*, 152; see also Natsume, *Kanshi*, 194–98. The poem is untitled in *Kusamakura*; the title "Spring Mood" (Shunkyō) was added in later collections of Sōseki's works.

81. For the narrator's age, see Natsume, *Kusamakura*, 4. The notions of "free and easy wandering" (Ch. *xiaoyao*, Jp. *shōyō*) and dispassionately following the "transformation of things" (Ch. *wuhua*, Jp. *bukka*) were central ideas in the early Daoist classic *Zhuangzi*. See Burton Watson, trans., *Zhuangzi: Basic Writings* (New York: Columbia University Press, 2003), 23, 44.

82. Natsume, *Kusamakura*, 10. The narrator cites the following famous couplet from Tao Yuanming's poem "Drinking Wine" (Yinjiu): "I picked a chrysanthemum by

the eastern hedge, off in the distance gazed on south mountain." Quoted from Stephen Owen, *An Anthology of Chinese Literature: Beginnings to 1911* (New York: Norton, 1996), 316.

83. For a recent attempt to theorize the concept of *bun* in Japan, see Kōno Kimiko and Wiebke Denecke, eds., *Nihon ni okeru "bun" to "bungaku"* (Tokyo: Bensei shuppan, 2013).

EPILOGUE

1. On this discourse, see Atsuko Ueda, *Concealment of Politics, Politics of Concealment: The Production of "Literature" in Meiji Japan* (Stanford, Calif.: Stanford University Press, 2007), chapter 6.

2. For the rhetoric of unadorned depiction (*rokotsu naru byōsha*) or flat depiction (*heimen byōsha*) in contemporary naturalist discourse, see Tayama Katai, "Rokotsu naru byōsha" [1904], in *Kindai hyōron shū 1*, ed. Kawazoe Kunimoto et al., NKiBT 57 (Tokyo: Kadokawa shoten, 1972), 198–203. This rhetoric became particularly powerful in later discourses on the so-called I-novel (*shishōsetsu*), which predicated the novel's realism on the unadorned depiction of the author's own, often "ugly," inner emotions and desires.

3. Ikuta Chōkō, *Meiji jidai bunpan* (Tokyo: Hakubunkan, 1907), 67–68. I owe knowledge of this reference to Ueda, *Concealment of Politics*, 150, where the same passage is cited. The translation here is mine.

4. For in-depth discussions of Katai's work, see Tomi Suzuki, *Narrating the Self: Fictions of Japanese Modernity* (Stanford, Calif.: Stanford University Press, 1996), chapter 4; Indra Levy, *Sirens of the Western Shore: The Westernesque Femme Fatale, Translation, and Vernacular Style in Modern Japanese Literature* (New York: Columbia University Press, 2006), chapters 3–5; Satoru Saito, *Detective Fiction and the Rise of the Japanese Novel, 1880–1930* (Cambridge, Mass.: Harvard University Asia Center, 2012), chapter 3.

5. Suzuki, *Narrating the Self*, 42–47. The most detailed source is still Yamamoto Masahide, *Kindai buntai hassei no shiteki kenkyū* (Tokyo: Iwanami shoten, 1965).

BIBLIOGRAPHY

Anderson, Marnie S. *A Place in Public: Women's Rights in Meiji Japan*. Cambridge, Mass.: Harvard University Asia Center, 2010.

Andō Tameakira. *Shika shichiron*. In *Hihyō shūsei Genji monogatari*, ed. Akiyama Ken et al., 1:204–30. Tokyo: Yumani shobō, 1999.

Aoki Toshihiro. "'Kyūaku zensho' no jidai." In *Tsubouchi Shōyō Futabatei Shimei shū*, ed. Aoki Toshihiro and Togawa Shinsuke, 491–502. SNKBTM 18. Tokyo: Iwanami shoten, 2002.

Asano Masamichi. "Imōto, chichi, 'hōyūtachi': *Ichidoku santan: Tōsei shosei katagi* ni okeru 'jōyoku' no hensei." *Nihon bungaku* 57, no. 12 (2008): 24–36.

——. "*Shinmigaki: Imotose kagami* no shūjiteki, soshite seijiteki-shakaiteki jigen: *Fūkai: Kyō waranbe* to no hikaku ni oite." *Kokugo kokubun kenkyū* 136 (2009): 43–55.

Atherton, David. "Valences of Vengeance: The Moral Imagination of Early Modern Japanese Vendetta Fiction." PhD diss., Columbia University, 2013.

Bai Juyi. "Changhenge." In *Hakushi monjū*, vol. 2, part 2, ed. Okamura Shigeru, 809–33. Shinshaku kanbun taikei 117. Tokyo: Meiji shoin, 2007.

Bourdaghs, Michael K. *The Dawn That Never Comes: Shimazaki Tōson and Japanese Nationalism*. New York: Columbia University Press, 2003.

Bowen, Roger W. *Rebellion and Democracy in Meiji Japan: A Study of Commoners in the Popular Rights Movement*. Berkeley: University of California Press, 1980.

Bowring, Richard John. *Mori Ōgai and the Modernization of Japanese Culture*. Cambridge: Cambridge University Press, 1979.

Braisted, William Reynolds, trans. *Meiroku zasshi: Journal of the Japanese Enlightenment*. Cambridge, Mass.: Harvard University Press, 1976.

Brooks, Peter. *The Melodramatic Imagination: Balzac, Henry James, Melodrama, and the Mode of Excess*. New Haven, Conn.: Yale University Press, 1995.

Brownstein, Michael C. "From *Kokugaku* to *Kokubungaku*: Canon-Formation in the Meiji Period." *Harvard Journal of Asiatic Studies* 47, no. 2 (1987): 435–60.
——. "*Jogaku Zasshi* and the Founding of *Bungakukai*." *Monumenta Nipponica* 35, no. 3 (1980): 319–36.
Bulwer-Lytton, Edward. *Alice, or the Mysteries*. London: Routledge, 1887.
——. *Ernest Maltravers*. London: Routledge, 1877.
——. *Rienzi, the Last of the Roman Tribunes*. Leipzig: Tauchnitz, 1842.
"Bungaku sekai no kinkyō." In KBHT, vol. 1, ed. Yoshida Seiichi and Asai Kiyoshi, 98–99. Tokyo: Kadokawa shoten, 1971.
Caddeau, Patrick W. *Appraising* Genji: *Literary Criticism and Cultural Anxiety in the Age of the Last Samurai*. Albany: State University of New York Press, 2006.
Campbell, James L., Sr. *Edward Bulwer-Lytton*. Boston: Twayne, 1986.
Chambers, William, and Robert Chambers, eds. *Chambers's Information for the People*. 2 vols. Philadelphia: Lippincott, 1867.
Chan, Wing-tsit. *A Source Book in Chinese Philosophy*. Princeton, N.J.: Princeton University Press, 1963.
Chiba Shunji. *Erisu no ekubo: Mori Ōgai e no kokoromi*. Tokyo: Ozawa shoten, 1997.
Confucius. *The Analects (Lun yü)*. Trans. D. C. Lau. London: Penguin Books, 1979.
Copeland, Rebecca L. *Lost Leaves: Women Writers of Meiji Japan*. Honolulu: University of Hawai`i Press, 2000.
Craig, Albert M. *Civilization and Enlightenment: The Early Thought of Fukuzawa Yukichi*. Cambridge, Mass.: Harvard University Press, 2009.
Davis, John Francis, trans. *The Fortunate Union: A Romance*. 2 vols. London: Oriental Translation Fund, 1829.
Denby, David J. *Sentimental Narrative and the Social Order in France, 1760–1820*. Cambridge: Cambridge University Press, 1994.
Dowdle, Brian C. "Why Saikaku Was Memorable but Bakin Was Unforgettable." *Journal of Japanese Studies* 42, no. 1 (2016): 91–121.
Emmerich, Michael. *The Tale of Genji: Translation, Canonization, and World Literature*. New York: Columbia University Press, 2013.
Etō Jun. *Riarizumu no genryū*. Tokyo: Kawade shobō shinsha, 1989.
Fleming, William D. "Strange Tales from Edo: *Liaozhai zhiyi* in Early Modern Japan." *Sino-Japanese Studies* 20 (2013): 75–115.
——. "The World Beyond the Walls: Morishima Chūryō (1756–1810) and the Development of Late Edo Fiction." PhD diss., Harvard University, 2011.
Flueckiger, Peter. *Imagining Harmony: Poetry, Empathy, and Community in Mid-Tokugawa Confucianism and Nativism*. Stanford, Calif.: Stanford University Press, 2011.
Foucault, Michel. *Histoire de la sexualité*. 3 vols. Paris: Gallimard, 1976–1984.
Fraleigh, Matthew, trans. New Chronicles of Yanagibashi *and* Diary of a Journey to the West: *Narushima Ryūhoku Reports from Home and Abroad*. Ithaca, N.Y.: Cornell University East Asia Program, 2010.
——. *Plucking Chrysanthemums: Narushima Ryūhoku and Sinitic Literary Traditions in Modern Japan*. Cambridge, Mass.: Harvard University Asia Center, 2016.
——. "Songs of the Righteous Spirit: 'Men of High Purpose' and Their Chinese Poetry in Modern Japan." *Harvard Journal of Asiatic Studies* 69, no. 1 (2009): 109–71.

Fujii, James A. *Complicit Fictions: The Subject in the Modern Japanese Prose Narrative.* Berkeley: University of California Press, 1993.

Fujioka Sakutarō. *Kokubungaku zenshi: Heianchō-hen.* 2 vols. Ed. Akiyama Ken et al. Tokyo: Heibonsha, 1971.

Fukuchi Ōchi. "Bunron." In *Fukuchi Ōchi shū,* ed. Yanagida Izumi, 344–45. MBZ 11. Tokyo: Chikuma shobō, 1966.

——. "Nihon bungaku no fushin o tanzu." In *Fukuchi Ōchi shū,* ed. Yanagida Izumi, 342–43. MBZ 11. Tokyo: Chikuma shobō, 1966.

Fukuzawa Yukichi. "Danjo dōsūron." In *Fukuzawa Yukichi zenshū,* ed. Keiō Gijuku, 19:552. Tokyo: Iwanami shoten, 1962.

——. *Gakumon no susume.* In *Fukuzawa Yukichi zenshū,* ed. Keiō Gijuku, 3:21–144. Tokyo: Iwanami shoten, 1959.

Giddens, Anthony. *The Transformation of Intimacy: Sexuality, Love, and Eroticism in Modern Societies.* Stanford, Calif.: Stanford University Press, 1992.

Gluck, Carol. *Japan's Modern Myths: Ideology in the Late Meiji Period.* Princeton, N.J.: Princeton University Press, 1985.

Graham, A. C. *Studies in Chinese Philosophy and Philosophical Literature.* Albany: State University of New York Press, 1990.

Habermas, Jürgen. *Strukturwandel der Öffentlichkeit: Untersuchungen zu einer Kategorie der bürgerlichen Gesellschaft.* Frankfurt/Main: Suhrkamp Verlag, 1990.

Hamada Keisuke. "Bakin o meguru shoshi, sakusha, dokusha no mondai." In *Kinsei shōsetsu: Eii to yōshiki ni kansuru shiken,* 272–97. Kyoto: Kyōto daigaku gakujutsu shuppankai, 1993.

——. "*Hakkenden* no kōsō ni okeru tai-kanreisen no igi." In *Kinsei shōsetsu: Eii to yōshiki ni kansuru shiken,* 357–67. Kyoto: Kyōto daigaku gakujutsu shuppankai, 1993.

——. "'Kanzen chōaku' hoshi." In *Kinsei shōsetsu: Eii to yōshiki ni kansuru shiken,* 397–438. Kyoto: Kyōto daigaku gakujutsu shuppankai, 1993.

——. "*Satomi hakkenden* to *Satomi gunki.*" *Kinsei bungei* 42 (1985): 48–55.

Hansen, Chad. "Qing (Emotions) 情 in Pre-Buddhist Chinese Thought." In *Emotions in Asian Thought: A Dialogue in Comparative Philosophy,* ed. Joel Marks and Roger T. Ames, 181–211. Albany: State University of New York Press, 1995.

Harper, Thomas J. "Motoori Norinaga's Criticism of the *Genji monogatari*: A Study of the Background and Critical Content of His *Genji monogatari tama no ogushi.*" PhD diss., University of Michigan, 1971.

Harper, Thomas, and Haruo Shirane, eds. *Reading The Tale of Genji: Sources from the First Millennium.* New York: Columbia University Press, 2015.

Hartmann, Nan Ma. "From Translation to Adaptation: Chinese Language Texts and Early Modern Japanese Literature." PhD diss., Columbia University, 2014.

Hata Minoru. "Meiji shoki no ninjō shōsetsu: *Karyū shunwa* no nagare." *Komazawa kokubun* 29 (1992): 69–78.

Hattori Hitoshi. "Bakin to ninjō." In *Kyokutei Bakin no bungakuiki,* 8–32. Tokyo: Wakakusa shobō, 1997.

Hedberg, William C. "Reclaiming the Margins: Seita Tansō's *Suikoden hihyōkai* and the Poetics of Cross-Cultural Influence." *International Journal of Asian Studies* 12, no. 2 (2015): 193–215.

——. "Separating the Word and the Way: Suyama Nantō's *Chūgi Suikodenkai* and Edo-Period Vernacular Philology." *Journal of Japanese Studies* 41, no. 2 (2015): 347–71.

Hessney, Richard C. "Beautiful, Talented, and Brave: Seventeenth-Century Chinese Scholar-Beauty Romances." PhD diss., Columbia University, 1979.

Hill, Christopher L. "Mori Ōgai's Resentful Narrator: Trauma and the National Subject in 'The Dancing Girl.'" *positions* 10, no. 2 (2002): 365–97.

——. *National History and the World of Nations: Capital, State, and the Rhetoric of History in Japan, France, and the United States*. Durham, N.C.: Duke University Press, 2008.

Hino Tatsuo. "Kaisetsu: 'Mono no aware o shiru' no setsu no raireki." In *Motoori Norinaga shū*, ed. Hino Tatsuo, 505–51. Shinchō Nihon koten shūsei 60. Tokyo: Shinchōsha, 1983.

Hiraoka Toshio. *Nihon kindai bungaku no shuppatsu*. Tokyo: Hanawa shobō, 1992.

Honma Hisao. *Tsubouchi Shōyō: Hito to sono geijutsu*. Tokyo: Nihon tosho sentā, 1993.

Howell, David L. *Geographies of Identity in Nineteenth-Century Japan*. Berkeley: University of California Press, 2005.

Howland, Douglas R. "The *Maria Luz* Incident: Personal Rights and International Justice for Chinese Coolies and Japanese Prostitutes." In *Gender and Law in the Japanese Imperium*, ed. Susan L. Burns and Barbara J. Brooks, 21–47. Honolulu: University of Hawai'i Press, 2013.

——. *Translating the West: Language and Political Reason in Nineteenth-Century Japan*. Honolulu: University of Hawai'i Press, 2002.

Hozumi Ikan. "Chikamatsu no gensetsu: *Naniwa miyage* hottanshō." In *Chikamatsu jōruri shū*, vol. 2, ed. Shuzui Kenji and Ōkubo Tadakuni, 355–59. NKBT 50. Tokyo: Iwanami shoten, 1959.

Huang, Martin W. *Desire and Fictional Narrative in Late Imperial China*. Cambridge, Mass.: Harvard University Asia Center, 2001.

——. "Sentiments of Desire: Thoughts on the Cult of Qing in Ming-Qing Literature." *Chinese Literature* 20 (1998): 153–84.

Ihara Saikaku. *The Great Mirror of Male Love*. Trans. Paul Gordon Schalow. Stanford, Calif.: Stanford University Press, 1990.

Ikuta Chōkō. *Meiji jidai bunpan*. Tokyo: Hakubunkan, 1907.

Inoue Yasushi. *Ren'ai shōsetsu no tanjō: Romansu, shōhi, iki*. Tokyo: Kasama shoin, 2009.

Ishibashi Ningetsu. "*Imotose kagami* o yomu." In *Yamada Bimyō, Ishibashi Ningetsu, Takase Bun'en shū*, ed. Fukuda Kiyoto, 255–59. MBZ 23. Tokyo: Chikuma shobō, 1971.

Ishikawa Hidemi. "Tamazusa juso no shatei." In *Fukkō suru Hakkenden*, ed. Suwa Haruo and Takada Mamoru, 199–227. Tokyo: Bensei shuppan, 2008.

Isobe Atsushi. *Shuppan bunka no Meiji zenki: Tōkyō haishi shuppansha to sono shūhen*. Tokyo: Perikansha, 2012.

Itasaka Noriko. "*Hakkenden* nenpyō." In *Kyokutei Bakin*, ed. Mizuno Minoru et al., 68–72. Tokyo: Shūeisha, 1980.

Itō Baiu. *Kenbun dansō*. Ed. Kamei Nobuaki. Tokyo: Iwanami shoten, 1940.

Itō Jinsai. *Dōjimon*. In *Kinsei shisōka bunshū*, ed. Ienaga Saburō et al., 25–291. NKBT 97. Tokyo: Iwanami shoten, 1966.

259

BIBLIOGRAPHY

——. *Kogaku sensei bunshū.* In *Itō Jinsai Itō Tōgai*, ed. Yoshikawa Kōjirō and Shimizu Shigeru, 169–295. Nihon shisō taikei 33. Tokyo: Iwanami shoten, 1971.

Ito, Ken K. *An Age of Melodrama: Family, Gender, and Social Hierarchy in the Turn-of-the-Century Japanese Novel.* Stanford, Calif.: Stanford University Press, 2008.

Itō Sōhei. "Nihon ni okeru *Kōrōmu* no ryūkō: Bakumatsu kara gendai made no shoshiteki sobyō." In *Chūgoku bungaku no hikaku bungakuteki kenkyū*, ed. Furuta Keiichi, 449–95. Tokyo: Kyūko shoin, 1986.

Iwamoto Yoshiharu. "Danjo kōsairon." In *Kirisuto-sha hyōron shū*, ed. Yabu Teiko, Yoshida Masanobu, and Izuhara Takatoshi, 101–53. SNKBTM 26. Tokyo: Iwanami shoten, 2002.

——. "Fujin no chii." *Jogaku zasshi* 2, 3, 5 (1885): 22–25, 41–43, 81–84.

——. "Joryū shōsetsuka no honshoku." In *Kirisuto-sha hyōron shū*, ed. Yabu Teiko, Yoshida Masanobu, and Izuhara Takatoshi, 164–72. SNKBTM 26. Tokyo: Iwanami shoten, 2002.

——. "Kon'inron." In *Jogaku zasshi, Bungakukai shū*, ed. Sasabuchi Tomoichi, 31–39. MBZ 32. Tokyo: Chikuma shobō, 1973.

—— [Shinobu]. "Saikun." *Jogaku zasshi* 144 (1889): 10–11.

——. "Shōsetsuka no chakugan." In *Kirisuto-sha hyōron shū*, ed. Yabu Teiko, Yoshida Masanobu, and Izuhara Takatoshi, 173–80. SNKBTM 26. Tokyo: Iwanami shoten, 2002.

Jacobowitz, Seth. *Writing Technology in Meiji Japan: A Media History of Modern Japanese Literature and Visual Culture.* Cambridge, Mass.: Harvard University Asia Center, 2015.

Jinbō Kazuya. *Tamenaga Shunsui no kenkyū.* Tokyo: Hakujitsusha, 1964.

Kamei Hideo. *"Shōsetsu" ron: "Shōsetsu shinzui" to kindai.* Tokyo: Iwanami shoten, 1999.

Kanda Masayuki. *Bakin to shomotsu: Denki sekai no teiryū.* Tokyo: Yagi shoten, 2011.

——. "Saishi kajin shōsetsu *Nidobai* to Bakin: Narabi ni Oda bunko-bon *Nidobai* no ichi." *Tōyō bunka* 96 (2006): 14–28.

Karatani Kōjin. *Origins of Modern Japanese Literature.* Trans. Brett de Bary et al. Durham, N.C.: Duke University Press, 1993.

——. "Shi to shi: Shiki kara Sōseki e." In *Zōho Sōseki ron shūsei*, 303–57. Tokyo: Heibonsha, 2001.

——. "Sōseki to 'bun.'" In *Zōho Sōseki ron shūsei*, 269–300. Tokyo: Heibonsha, 2001.

——. "Sōseki to janru." In *Zōho Sōseki ron shūsei*, 227–68. Tokyo: Heibonsha, 2001.

Katsube Seigyo. *Sentō zuihitsu.* 5 vols. Manuscript. Tokyo: National Diet Library, n.d. http://dl.ndl.go.jp/info:ndljp/pid/2566455?tocOpened=1.

Kawamura Kunimitsu. *Sekushuaritī no kindai.* Tokyo: Kōdansha, 1996.

Kawashima Yūko. "Edo jidai ni okeru *Kinpeibai* no juyō (1): Jisho, zuihitsu, sharebon o chūshin toshite." *Ryūkoku kiyō* 32, no. 1 (2010): 1–20.

——. "Edo jidai ni okeru *Kinpeibai* no juyō (2): Kyokutei Bakin no kijutsu o chūshin toshite." *Ryūkoku kiyō* 32, no. 2 (2011): 35–57.

Kido Yūichi. "Meiji-ki 'bōru hyōshi-bon' no tanjō." In *Meiji no shuppan bunka*, ed. Kokubungaku Kenkyū Shiryōkan, 1–30. Tokyo: Rinsen shoten, 2002.

Kigoshi Shunsuke. *Edo Ōsaka no shuppan ryūtsū to yomihon, ninjōbon.* Osaka: Seibundō, 2013.

Kikutei Kōsui. [*Geppyō kigū:*] *Ensai shunwa*. Tokyo: Shunzandō, 1882.

——. [*Sanpū hiu:*] *Seiro nikki*. In *Meiji meisaku shū*, ed. Tanikawa Keiichi et al., 1–139. SNKBTM 30. Tokyo: Iwanami shoten, 2009.

Kim, Kyu Hyun. *The Age of Visions and Arguments: Parliamentarianism and the National Public Sphere in Early Meiji Japan*. Cambridge, Mass.: Harvard University Asia Center, 2007.

Kimura Ki. "Kaidai." In *Meiji hon'yaku bungaku shū*, ed. Kimura Ki, 395–410. MBZ 7. Tokyo: Chikuma shobō, 1972.

Kimura Mokurō. "Kokuji shōsetsu tsū." In *Zoku enseki jisshu*, ed. Iwamoto Kattōshi, 1:293–306. Tokyo: Chūōkōronsha, 1980.

Kimura Naoe. *Seinen no tanjō: Meiji Nihon ni okeru seijiteki jissen no tenkan*. Tokyo: Shin'yōsha, 1998.

Kinmonth, Earl H. *The Self-Made Man in Meiji Japanese Thought: From Samurai to Salary Man*. Berkeley: University of California Press, 1981.

Kischka-Wellhäußer, Nadja. *Frauenerziehung und Frauenbild im Umbruch: Ideale von Mädchenerziehung, Frauenrolle und weiblichen Lebensentwürfen in der frühen Jogaku zasshi (1885–1889)*. Munich: Iudicium Verlag, 2004.

Kitamura Tōkoku. "Ensei shika to josei." In *Jinsei ni ai-wataru to wa nan no ii zo*, ed. Oketani Hideaki, 82–93. Tokyo: Ōbunsha, 1979.

——. "Naibu seimei ron." In *Kirisuto-sha hyōron shū*, ed. Yabu Teiko, Yoshida Masanobu, and Izuhara Takatoshi, 300–312. SNKBTM 26. Tokyo: Iwanami shoten, 2002.

—— [Hototogisu]. "Tōsei bungaku no ushio moyō." In KBHT, vol. 1, ed. Yoshida Seiichi and Asai Kiyoshi, 90–92. Tokyo: Kadokawa shoten, 1971.

Kiyooka, Eiichi, trans. *Fukuzawa Yukichi on Japanese Women: Selected Works*. Tokyo: University of Tokyo Press, 1988.

Ko, Dorothy. *Teachers of the Inner Chambers: Women and Culture in Seventeenth-Century China*. Stanford, Calif.: Stanford University Press, 1994.

——. "Thinking About Copulating: An Early-Qing Confucian Thinker's Problem with Emotion and Words." In *Remapping China: Fissures in Historical Terrain*, ed. Gail Hershatter et al., 59–76. Stanford, Calif.: Stanford University Press, 1996.

Kobori Keiichirō. *Wakaki hi no Mori Ōgai*. Tokyo: Tōkyō daigaku shuppankai, 1973.

Komori Yōichi. *Shiki to Sōseki: Yūjō ga hagukunda shajitsu no kindai*. Tokyo: Shūeisha, 2016.

——. *Sōseki ron: 21-seiki o ikinuku tame ni*. Tokyo: Iwanami shoten, 2010.

Kōno Kimiko and Wiebke Denecke, eds. *Nihon ni okeru "bun" to "bungaku."* Tokyo: Bensei shuppan, 2013.

Kornicki, Peter F. *The Book in Japan: A Cultural History from the Beginnings to the Nineteenth Century*. Honolulu: University of Hawai`i Press, 2001.

——. "Disraeli and the Meiji Novel." *Harvard Journal of Asiatic Studies* 44, no. 1 (1984): 29–55.

——. "The Publisher's Go-Between: *Kashihonya* in the Meiji Period." *Modern Asian Studies* 14, no. 2 (1980): 331–44.

——. *The Reform of Fiction in Meiji Japan*. London: Ithaca Press, 1982.

——. "The Survival of Tokugawa Fiction in the Meiji Period." *Harvard Journal of Asiatic Studies* 41, no. 2 (1981): 461–82.

Kubota Yoshitarō. "Botsurisō ronsō o megutte: Mōruton to Harutoman." In *Tsubou-chi Shōyō, Futabatei Shimei*, ed. Nihon Bungaku Kenkyū Shiryō Kankōkai, 97–105. NBKSS. Tokyo: Yūseidō, 1979.

Kurita, Kyoko. "Meiji Japan's Y23 Crisis and the Discovery of the Future: Suehiro Tetchō's *Nijūsan-nen mirai-ki*." *Harvard Journal of Asiatic Studies* 60, no. 1 (2000): 5–43.

Kyokutei Bakin. "Ken'i hyōbanki." In *Edo meibutsu hyōbanki shūsei*, ed. Nakano Mitsu-toshi, 335–69. Tokyo: Iwanami shoten, 1987.

——. *Kinsei mononohon Edo sakusha burui*. Ed. Tokuda Takeshi. Tokyo: Iwanami shoten, 2014.

——. *Nansō Satomi hakkenden*. 12 vols. Ed. Hamada Keisuke. Shinchō Nihon koten shūsei bekkan. Tokyo: Shinchōsha: 2003–2004.

Lam, Ling Hon. *The Spatiality of Emotion in Early Modern China: From Dreamscapes to Theatricality*. New York: Columbia University Press, 2018.

LaMarre, Thomas. "Expanded Empiricism: Natsume Sōseki with William James." *Japan Forum* 20, no. 1 (2008): 47–77.

Langer, Sara. "Sentimental Fictions: A Study of Gender Politics in Selected Writings of Hanasanjin (1790–1858)." PhD diss., Indiana University, 2002.

Lean, Eugenia. *Public Passions: The Trial of Shi Jianqiao and the Rise of Popular Sym-pathy in Republican China*. Berkeley: University of California Press, 2007.

Lee, Haiyan. "All the Feelings That Are Fit to Print: The Community of Sentiment and the Literary Public Sphere in China, 1900–1918." *Modern China* 27, no. 3 (2001): 291–327.

——. *Revolution of the Heart: A Genealogy of Love in China, 1900–1950*. Stanford, Calif.: Stanford University Press, 2007.

Legge, James, trans. *Li Chi, Book of Rites: An Encyclopedia of Ancient Ceremonial Usages, Religious Creeds, and Social Institutions*. 2 vols. Edited with an introduction and study guide by Ch'u Chai and Winberg Chai. New York: University Books, 1967.

Levy, Indra A. *Sirens of the Western Shore: The Westernesque Femme Fatale, Transla-tion, and Vernacular Style in Modern Japanese Literature*. New York: Columbia Uni-versity Press, 2006.

——, ed. *Translation in Modern Japan*. New York: Routledge, 2011.

Li, Wai-yee. *Enchantment and Disenchantment: Love and Illusion in Chinese Literature*. Princeton, N.J.: Princeton University Press, 1993.

Liu, Lydia H. *Translingual Practice: Literature, National Culture, and Translated Modernity—China, 1900–1937*. Stanford, Calif.: Stanford University Press, 1995.

Luhmann, Niklas. *Liebe als Passion: Zur Codierung von Intimität*. Frankfurt/Main: Suhrkamp Verlag, 1994.

Maeda Ai. "Bakin to Tōkoku: 'Kyō' o megutte." In *Genkei no Meiji*, 347–60. Tokyo: Chi-kuma shobō, 1989.

——. "Gesaku bungaku to *Tōsei shosei katagi*." In *Kindai dokusha no seiritsu*, 372–86. Tokyo: Chikuma shobō, 1989.

——. "*Hakkenden* no sekai: Yoru no aregorī." In *Bakumatsu ishinki no bungaku: Narushima Ryūhoku*, 66–91. Tokyo: Chikuma shobō, 1989.

——. "*Karyū shunwa* no ichi." *Meiji bungaku zenshū geppō* 71 (1972): 1–2.

——. "Kindai bungaku to katsujiteki sekai." In *Kindai dokusha no seiritsu*, 329–48. Tokyo: Chikuma shobō, 1989.

262

BIBLIOGRAPHY

——. "Meiji no hyōgen shisō to buntai: Shōsetsu no 'katari' o megutte." In *Kindai dokusha no seiritsu*, 444–53. Tokyo: Chikuma shobō, 1989.
——. "Meiji risshin shusse shugi no keifu: *Saigoku risshihen* kara *Kisei* made." In *Kindai dokusha no seiritsu*, 88–107. Tokyo: Chikuma shobō, 1989.
——. "Mishima Michitsune to Rokumeikan jidai." In *Genkei no Meiji*, 79–98. Tokyo: Chikuma shobō, 1989.
——. "Mō hitotsu no *Shōsetsu shinzui*: Shikakuteki sekai no seiritsu." In *Kindai dokusha no seiritsu*, 349–63. Tokyo: Chikuma shobō, 1989.
——. "Ōgai no Chūgoku shōsetsu shumi." In *Kindai dokusha no seiritsu*, 74–87. Tokyo: Chikuma shobō, 1989.
——. "Ondoku kara mokudoku e: Kindai dokusha no seiritsu." In *Kindai dokusha no seiritsu*, 122–50. Tokyo: Chikuma shobō, 1989.
——. "*Shōsetsu shinzui* no riarizumu to wa nani ka." In *Kindai dokusha no seiritsu*, 364–71. Tokyo: Chikuma shobō, 1989.
——. "Tenpō kaikaku ni okeru sakusha to shoshi." In *Kindai dokusha no seiritsu*, 17–43. Tokyo: Chikuma shobō, 1989.
——. "Tobu uta: Minken kayō to enka." In *Genkei no Meiji*, 56–67. Tokyo: Chikuma shobō, 1989.
Maeno Michiko. "Meiji shoki hon'yaku shōsetsu *Ōshū kiji: Karyū shunwa* ni okeru ren'ai to kekkon." In *Ronshū ibunka toshite no Nihon: Kokusai shinpojiumu "Ibunka toshite no Nihon" kinen ronbun shū*, ed. Nagoya Daigaku Daigakuin Kokusai Gengo Bunka Kenkyūka, 153–62. Nagoya: Nagoya daigaku daigakuin kokusai gengo bunka kenkyūka, 2009.
Marceau, Lawrence E. "*Ninjō* and the Affective Value of Literature at the Kogidō Academy." *Sino-Japanese Studies* 9, no. 1 (1996): 47–55.
Markus, Andrew L. "The Daisō Lending Library of Nagoya, 1767–1899." *Gest Library Journal* 3, no. 3 (1989): 5–34.
——. "Kimura Mokurō (1774–1856) and His *Kokuji shōsetsu tsū* (1849)." *Journal of Japanese Studies* 26, no. 2 (2000): 341–70.
Marra, Michele. *The Aesthetics of Discontent: Politics and Reclusion in Medieval Japanese Literature*. Honolulu: University of Hawai'i Press, 1991.
Marran, Christine L. *Poison Woman: Figuring Female Transgression in Modern Japanese Culture*. Minneapolis: University of Minnesota Press, 2007.
Maruyama Masao. *Nihon seiji shisōshi kenkyū*. Tokyo: Tōkyō daigaku shuppankai, 2014.
——. *Studies in the Intellectual History of Tokugawa Japan*. Trans. Mikiso Hane. Princeton, N.J.: Princeton University Press, 1974.
Maruyama Shigeru. *Shunsui ninjōbon no kenkyū*. Tokyo: Ōfūsha, 1978.
Masaoka Shiki. "Jojibun." In *Masaoka Shiki shū*, ed. Matsui Toshihiko, 361–69. NKiBT 16. Tokyo: Kadokawa shoten, 1972.
Matsumura Masaie. "Tsubouchi Shōyō to Igirisu no shōsetsuka-tachi: *Shōsetsu shinzui* no seiritsu o megutte." In *Hikaku bungaku o manabu hito no tame ni*, ed. Matsumura Masaie, 37–58. Kyoto: Sekai shisō sha, 1995.
McMahon, Keith. *Misers, Shrews, and Polygamists: Sexuality and Male-Female Relations in Eighteenth-Century Chinese Fiction*. Durham, N.C.: Duke University Press, 1995.
McMullen, James. *Idealism, Protest, and The Tale of Genji: The Confucianism of Kumazawa Banzan (1619–91)*. Oxford: Oxford University Press, 1999.

Meredith, George. *The Shaving of Shagpat: An Arabian Entertainment*. London: Constable, 1914.

Mertz, John Pierre. *Novel Japan: Spaces of Nationhood in Early Meiji Narrative, 1870–88*. Ann Arbor: Center for Japanese Studies, University of Michigan, 2003.

Metzger, Thomas A. *Escape from Predicament: Neo-Confucianism and China's Evolving Political Culture*. New York: Columbia University Press, 1977.

Mikami Sanji and Takatsu Kuwasaburō. *Nihon bungakushi*. 2 vols. Tokyo: Nihon tosho sentā, 1999.

Miller, J. Scott. *Adaptations of Western Literature in Meiji Japan*. New York: Palgrave, 2001.

Minamoto Ryōen. *Giri to ninjō: Nihonteki shinjō no ichikōsatsu*. Tokyo: Chūōkōronsha, 2013.

Miyake Kaho. *Warbler in the Grove*. Trans. Rebecca L. Copeland. In *The Modern Murasaki: Writing by Women of Meiji Japan*, ed. Rebecca L. Copeland and Melek Ortabasi, 73–125. New York: Columbia University Press, 2006.

Mizuno Minoru. "Bakin bungaku no keisei." In *Edo shōsetsu ronsō*, 217–32. Tokyo: Chūōkōronsha, 1974.

Moretti, Franco. *The Way of the World: The Bildungsroman in European Culture*. London: Verso, 2000.

Mori Arinori. "Saishōron." In *Meiji keimō shisō shū*, ed. Ōkubo Toshiaki, 260–63. MBZ 3. Tokyo: Chikuma shobō, 1967.

Mori Ōgai. "Ima no shoka no shōsetsuron o yomite." In *Ōgai zenshū*, 22:65–82. Tokyo: Iwanami shoten, 1973.

——. "Waseda bungaku no botsurisō." In KBHT, vol. 1, ed. Yoshida Seiichi and Asai Kiyoshi, 193–99. Tokyo: Kadokawa shoten, 1971.

Morikawa, Takemitsu. *Liebessemantik und Sozialstruktur: Transformationen in Japan von 1600 bis 1920*. Bielefeld: transcript Verlag, 2015.

Morley, John. "George Eliot's Novels." *Macmillan's Magazine* 14 (1866): 272–79.

Morris, Mark. "Buson and Shiki: Part Two." *Harvard Journal of Asiatic Studies* 45, no. 1 (1985): 255–321.

Motoori Norinaga. *Genji monogatari tama no ogushi*. In *Motoori Norinaga zenshū*, ed. Ōno Susumu and Ōkubo Tadashi, 4:169–523. Tokyo: Chikuma shobō, 1969.

Mowry, Hua-yuan Li, trans. *Chinese Love Stories from Ch'ing-shih*. Hamden, Conn.: Archon Books, 1983.

Murasaki Shikibu. *Genji monogatari*. Ed. Yanai Shigeshi et al. SNKBT 19–23. Tokyo: Iwanami shoten, 1993–1997.

Murphy, Joseph A. "Separation of Cognition and Affect in *Bungakuron*." *Japan Forum* 20, no. 1 (2008): 103–26.

Mutō Motoaki. *Ninjōbon no sekai: Edo no "ada" ga tsumugu ren'ai monogatari*. Tokyo: Kasama shoin, 2014.

Nagai Kafū. *Jigoku no hana*. In *Kafū zenshū*, ed. Inagaki Tatsurō, Takemori Ten'yū, and Nakajima Kunihiko, 2:105–222. Tokyo: Iwanami shoten, 1993.

Nakamura Katsunori. "Kyokutei Bakin to ninjōbon." *Sōsho Edo bunko geppō* 36 (1995): 1–5.

Nakamura Masanao. "Zenryō naru haha o tsukuru setsu." In *Meiji keimō shisō shū*, ed. Ōkubo Toshiaki, 300–302. MBZ 3. Tokyo: Chikuma shobō, 1967.

Nakamura Yukihiko. "Kaisetsu." In *Shunshoku umegoyomi*, ed. Nakamura Yukihiko, 4–34. NKBT 64. Tokyo: Iwanami shoten, 1971.

——. *Kinsei bungei shichōkō.* Tokyo: Iwanami shoten, 1975.

——. "Ninjōbon to chūhongata yomihon." In *Kinsei shōsetsu yōshiki shikō,* 459–78. Tokyo: Chūōkōronsha, 1982.

——. "Yomihon no dokusha." In *Kinsei shōsetsushi no kenkyū,* 314–33. Tokyo: Ōfūsha, 1961.

Nakano Mitsutoshi. "Kaisetsu." In *Edo meibutsu hyōbanki shūsei,* ed. Nakano Mitsutoshi, 397–432. Tokyo: Iwanami shoten, 1987.

Natsume Sōseki. *Bungakuron.* 2 vols. Ed. Kamei Shunsuke. Tokyo: Iwanami shoten, 2007.

——. "Eikoku shijin no tenchi sansen ni taisuru kannen." In *Sōseki zenshū,* vol. 13, ed. Yamanouchi Hisaaki, 21–60. Tokyo: Iwanami shoten, 1995.

——. *Kanshi.* In *Sōseki zenshū,* vol. 18, ed. Ikkai Tomoyoshi. Tokyo: Iwanami shoten, 1995.

——. *Kusamakura.* In *Sōseki zenshū,* vol. 3, ed. Imanishi Junkichi and Izuhara Takatoshi, 1–171. Tokyo: Iwanami shoten, 1994.

——. *Kusamakura.* Trans. Meredith McKinney. New York: Penguin Books, 2008.

——. "Shaseibun." In *Sōseki zenshū,* vol. 16, ed. Komori Yōichi, 48–56. Tokyo: Iwanami shoten, 1995.

——. "Sōsakuka no taido." In *Sōseki zenshū,* vol. 16, ed. Komori Yōichi, 161–250. Tokyo: Iwanami shoten, 1995.

——. *Theory of Literature and Other Critical Writings.* Ed. Michael K. Bourdaghs, Atsuko Ueda, and Joseph A. Murphy. New York: Columbia University Press, 2009.

——. *Wagahai wa neko de aru.* In *Sōseki zenshū,* vol. 1, ed. Takemori Ten'yū and Andō Fumihito. Tokyo: Iwanami shoten, 1993.

Niwa Jun'ichirō, trans. [*Ōshū kiji:*] *Karyū shunwa.* In *Meiji hon'yaku bungaku shū,* ed. Kimura Ki, 3–109. MBZ 7. Tokyo: Chikuma shobō, 1972.

Ōba Osamu. *Edo jidai ni okeru Chūgoku bunka juyō no kenkyū.* Kyoto: Dōhōsha shuppan, 1984.

——. *Edo jidai ni okeru tōsen mochiwatarisho no kenkyū.* Suita: Kansai daigaku tōzai gakujutsu kenkyūjo, 1967.

Ochi Haruo. "*Meiji seiji shōsetsu shū* kaisetsu." In *Meiji seiji shōsetsu shū,* ed. Ochi Haruo, 8–45. NKiBT 2. Tokyo: Kadokawa shoten, 1974.

——. "Seiji shōsetsu ni okeru 'noberu' no imi: *Setchūbai* to *Gaimu daijin.*" *Nihon kindai bungaku* 1 (1964): 1–14.

——. "*Shosei katagi* no seishun." In *Tsubouchi Shōyō, Futabatei Shimei,* ed. Nihon Bungaku Kenkyū Shiryō Kankōkai, 38–48. NBKSS. Tokyo: Yūseidō, 1979.

——. "*Shōsetsu shinzui* no botai." In *Tsubouchi Shōyō, Futabatei Shimei,* ed. Nihon Bungaku Kenkyū Shiryō Kankōkai, 1–12. NBKSS. Tokyo: Yūseidō, 1979.

Ojima Kenji. "*Shōsetsu shinzui* to Bein [*sic*] no shūjisho: Sono moshashugi to risōshugi." *Kokubungaku kenkyū* 42 (1970): 22–33.

Ōtsu Chisako. "Hadō suru setsuna: *Kusamakura* ron." In *Botchan, Kusamakura,* ed. Kataoka Yutaka and Komori Yōichi, 269–82. Tokyo: Ōfūsha, 1990.

Ōuchi Seiran. "*Dai Nihon bijutsu shinpō* shogen." In *Dai Nihon bijutsu shinpō,* 1:3–4. Kindai bijutsu zasshi sōsho 1. Tokyo: Yumani shobō, 1990.

Owen, Stephen. *An Anthology of Chinese Literature: Beginnings to 1911.* New York: Norton, 1996.

——. *Readings in Chinese Literary Thought.* Cambridge, Mass.: Harvard University Council on East Asian Studies, 1992.

Ozaki Kōyō. [*Ninin bikuni:*] *Iro zange.* In *Ozaki Kōyō shū*, ed. Suda Chisato and Matsumura Tomomi, 1–64. SNKBTM 19. Tokyo: Iwanami shoten, 2003.

Pastreich, Emanuel. *The Observable Mundane: Vernacular Chinese and the Emergence of a Literary Discourse on Popular Narrative in Edo Japan.* Seoul: Seoul National University Press, 2011.

Pflugfelder, Gregory M. *Cartographies of Desire: Male-Male Sexuality in Japanese Discourse, 1600–1950.* Berkeley: University of California Press, 1999.

Pincus, Leslie. *Authenticating Culture in Imperial Japan: Kuki Shūzō and the Rise of National Aesthetics.* Berkeley: University of California Press, 1996.

Plaks, Andrew H. *The Four Masterworks of the Ming Novel: Ssu ta ch'i-shu.* Princeton, N.J.: Princeton University Press, 1987.

Platt, Brian. *Burning and Building: Schooling and State Formation in Japan, 1750–1890.* Cambridge, Mass.: Harvard University Asia Center, 2004.

Poch, Daniel. "Ethics of Emotion in Nineteenth-Century Japanese Literature: Shunsui, Bakin, the Political Novel, Shōyō, Sōseki." PhD diss., Columbia University, 2014.

Pyle, Kenneth B. *The New Generation in Meiji Japan: Problems of Cultural Identity, 1885–1895.* Stanford, Calif.: Stanford University Press, 1969.

Reddy, William M. *The Making of Romantic Love: Longing and Sexuality in Europe, South Asia, and Japan, 900–1200 CE.* Chicago: University of Chicago Press, 2012.

Reichert, Jim. *In the Company of Men: Representations of Male-Male Sexuality in Meiji Literature.* Stanford, Calif.: Stanford University Press, 2006.

Rimer, J. Thomas. "Hegel in Tokyo: Ernest Fenollosa and His 1882 Lecture on the Truth of Art." In *Japanese Hermeneutics: Current Debates on Aesthetics and Interpretation*, ed. Michael F. Marra, 97–108. Honolulu: University of Hawai'i Press, 2002.

Rolston, David L., ed. *How to Read the Chinese Novel.* Princeton, N.J.: Princeton University Press, 1990.

——. *Traditional Chinese Fiction and Fiction Commentary: Reading and Writing Between the Lines.* Stanford, Calif.: Stanford University Press, 1997.

Rosenwein, Barbara H. *Emotional Communities in the Early Middle Ages.* Ithaca, N.Y.: Cornell University Press, 2006.

——. *Generations of Feeling: A History of Emotions, 600–1700.* Cambridge: Cambridge University Press, 2016.

——. "Worrying about Emotions in History." *American Historical Review* 107, no. 3 (2002): 821–45.

Rougemont, Denis de. *L'amour et l'Occident.* Paris: Plon, 1939.

Rowley, Gillian Gaye. *Yosano Akiko and The Tale of Genji.* Ann Arbor: Center for Japanese Studies, University of Michigan, 2000.

Rubin, Jay. *Injurious to Public Morals: Writers and the Meiji State.* Seattle: University of Washington Press, 1984.

Ryan, Marleigh Grayer. *The Development of Realism in the Fiction of Tsubouchi Shōyō.* Seattle: University of Washington Press, 1975.

——. *Japan's First Modern Novel: Ukigumo of Futabatei Shimei.* New York: Columbia University Press, 1967.

Saeki Junko. *"Ai" to "sei" no bunkashi.* Tokyo: Kadokawa gakugei shuppan, 2008.

——. *"Iro" to "ai" no hikaku bunkashi.* Tokyo: Iwanami shoten, 1998.

Saito, Satoru. *Detective Fiction and the Rise of the Japanese Novel, 1880–1930.* Cambridge, Mass.: Harvard University Asia Center, 2012.

Sakaki, Atsuko. "*Kajin no kigū*: The Meiji Political Novel and the Boundaries of Literature." *Monumenta Nipponica* 55, no. 1 (2000): 83–108.

——. *Recontextualizing Texts: Narrative Performance in Modern Japanese Fiction.* Cambridge, Mass.: Harvard University Asia Center, 1999.

Sakazaki Shiran [Mui Shinjin]. "Nihon jōshi no kairyō o nozomu." *Jiyū no tomoshibi* 342, 343 (1885), unpaginated.

——. "Shōsetsu haishi no honbun o ronzu." In KBHT, vol. 1, ed. Yoshida Seiichi and Asai Kiyoshi, 23–25. Tokyo: Kadokawa shoten, 1971.

Santangelo, Paolo. "The Cult of Love in Some Texts of Ming and Qing Literature." *East and West* 50, no. 1/4 (2000): 439–99.

Schamoni, Wolfgang. "Die Entwicklung der Romantheorie in der japanischen Aufklärungsperiode." *Nachrichten der Gesellschaft für Natur- und Völkerkunde Ostasiens/Hamburg* 118 (1975): 9–39.

——. *Kitamura Tōkoku: Die frühen Jahre; von der "Politik" zur "Literatur."* Wiesbaden: Steiner Verlag, 1983.

——. "Narushima Ryūhoku: Vorwort zu *Karyū shunwa.*" *hon'yaku—Heidelberger Werkstattberichte zum Übersetzen Japanisch-Deutsch* 5 (2003): 20–33.

Seki Ryōichi. *Shōyō, Ōgai: Kōshō to shiron.* Tokyo: Yūseidō shuppan, 1971.

Senuma Shigeki. "Shinri bungaku no hatten to sono kisū." In *Bungei hyōron shū*, ed. Honma Hisao, 145–54. Gendai Nihon bungaku taikei 96. Tokyo: Chikuma shobō, 1973.

Shibata Mitsuhiko and Kanda Masayuki, eds. *Bakin shokan shūsei.* 6 vols. Tokyo: Yagi shoten, 2002–2003.

Shikitei Sanba. *Ukiyoburo.* Ed. Nakamura Michio. NKBT 63. Tokyo: Iwanami shoten, 1957.

Shimazaki, Satoko. *Edo Kabuki in Transition: From the Worlds of the Samurai to the Vengeful Female Ghost.* New York: Columbia University Press, 2016.

Shirane, Haruo, ed. *Early Modern Japanese Literature: An Anthology, 1600–1900.* New York: Columbia University Press, 2002.

——. *Japan and the Culture of the Four Seasons: Nature, Literature, and the Arts.* New York: Columbia University Press, 2012.

——. *Traces of Dreams: Landscape, Cultural Memory, and the Poetry of Bashō.* Stanford, Calif.: Stanford University Press, 1998.

Shirane, Haruo, and Tomi Suzuki, eds. *Inventing the Classics: Modernity, National Identity, and Japanese Literature.* Stanford, Calif.: Stanford University Press, 2000.

Shōwa Joshi Daigaku Kindai Bungaku Kenkyūshitsu, ed. *Kindai bungaku kenkyū sōsho.* Vol. 18. Tokyo: Shōwa joshi daigaku kōyōkai, 1962.

Shōyō Kyōkai, ed. Foreword to vol. 1 of *Shōyō senshū: Bessatsu*, ed. Shōyō Kyōkai, 1–3. Tokyo: Daiichi shobō, 1977.

——, ed. Foreword to vol. 2 of *Shōyō senshū: Bessatsu*, ed. Shōyō Kyōkai, 1–6. Tokyo: Daiichi shobō, 1977.

Sievers, Sharon L. *Flowers in Salt: The Beginnings of Feminist Consciousness in Modern Japan.* Stanford, Calif.: Stanford University Press, 1983.

Stanley, Amy. *Selling Women: Prostitution, Markets, and the Household in Early Modern Japan.* Berkeley: University of California Press, 2012.

Suehiro Tetchō. *Seiji shōsetsu: Setchūbai.* In *Seiji shōsetsu shū 1*, ed. Yamada Shunji and Rinbara Sumio, 327–506. SNKBTM 16. Tokyo: Iwanami shoten, 2003.

Sugaya Hiromi. *Shūji oyobi kabun no kenkyū*. Tokyo: Kyōiku shuppan sentā, 1978.

Suzuki Sadami. *Nihon no "bungaku" gainen*. Tokyo: Sakuhinsha, 1998.

Suzuki, Tomi. "Gender and Genre: Modern Literary Histories and Women's Diary Literature." In *Inventing the Classics: Modernity, National Identity, and Japanese Literature*, ed. Haruo Shirane and Tomi Suzuki, 71–95. Stanford, Calif.: Stanford University Press, 2000.

———. *Narrating the Self: Fictions of Japanese Modernity*. Stanford, Calif.: Stanford University Press, 1996.

———. "*The Tale of Genji*, National Literature, Language, and Modernism." In *Envisioning* The Tale of Genji: *Media, Gender, and Cultural Production*, ed. Haruo Shirane, 243–87. New York: Columbia University Press, 2008.

Taguchi Ukichi. *Nihon kaika shōshi*. In *Taguchi Teiken shū*, ed. Ōkubo Toshiaki, 3–69. MBZ 14. Tokyo: Chikuma shobō, 1977.

Taguma Itsuko. "Meiji hon'yaku bungaku nenpyō." In *Meiji hon'yaku bungaku shū*, ed. Kimura Ki, 411–35. MBZ 7. Tokyo: Chikuma shobō, 1972.

Takada Mamoru. *Kanpon "Hakkenden" no sekai*. Tokyo: Chikuma bungei bunko, 2005.

Takahashi Osamu. "*Karyū shunwa* no shikō suru sekai." *Nihon kindai bungaku* 31 (1984): 14–27.

———. "*Shinmigaki: Imotose kagami* ron: *Karyū shunwa* o jiku toshite." *Jōchi daigaku kokubungaku ronshū* 18 (1985): 101–25.

Takata Sanae. *Hanpō mukashibanashi*. Meiji Taishō bungaku kaisō shūsei 6. Tokyo: Nihon tosho sentā, 1983.

———. "*Tōsei shosei katagi* no hihyō." In KBHT, vol. 1, ed. Yoshida Seiichi and Asai Kiyoshi, 327–38. Tokyo: Kadokawa shoten, 1971.

Takayama Chogyū. "Biteki seikatsu o ronzu." In *Kindai hyōron shū 1*, ed. Kawazoe Kunimoto et al., 172–83. NKiBT 57. Tokyo: Kadokawa shoten, 1972.

———. "Bunmei hihyōka toshite no bungakusha." In *Kindai hyōron shū 1*, ed. Kawazoe Kunimoto et al., 158–71. NKiBT 57. Tokyo: Kadokawa shoten, 1972.

Takeuchi Yō. *Risshin shusse shugi: Kindai Nihon no roman to yokubō*. Kyoto: Sekai shisō sha, 2005.

Tamenaga Shunsui. *Harutsugedori*. In *Sharebon, kokkeibon, ninjōbon*, ed. Nakano Mitsutoshi, Jinbō Kazuya, and Maeda Ai, 371–598. SNKBZ 80. Tokyo: Shōgakukan, 2000.

———. *Shungyō Hachimangane*. Tokyo: Tōkyō fukyūsha, 1932.

———. *Shunshoku tatsumi no sono*. In *Shunshoku umegoyomi*, ed. Nakamura Yukihiko, 239–439. NKBT 64. Tokyo: Iwanami shoten, 1971.

———. *Shunshoku umegoyomi*. In *Shunshoku umegoyomi*, ed. Nakamura Yukihiko, 41–238. NKBT 64. Tokyo: Iwanami shoten, 1971.

Tayama Katai. *Jūemon no saigo*. In *Tayama Katai shū*, ed. Sōma Tsuneo, 53–121. NKiBT 19. Tokyo: Kadokawa shoten, 1972.

———. "Rokotsu naru byōsha." In *Kindai hyōron shū 1*, ed. Kawazoe Kunimoto et al., 198–203. NKiBT 57. Tokyo: Kadokawa shoten, 1972.

Toda Kindō. [*Minken engi:*] *Jōkai haran*. In *Seiji shōsetsu shū 1*, ed. Yamada Shunji and Rinbara Sumio, 1–25. SNKBTM 16. Tokyo: Iwanami shoten, 2003.

Togawa Shinsuke. "Bungaku gokusuiron zengo." *Bungaku* 44, no. 6 (1976): 757–73.

Tokuda Takeshi. "*Hakkenden* to Ienari jidai: 'Inbi' sairon." In *Nihon kinsei shōsetsu to Chūgoku shōsetsu*, 715–63. Musashi Murayama: Seishōdō shoten, 1987.

———. "*Nansō Satomi hakkenden:* Ingaritsu no hatten." In *Iwanami kōza Nihon bungaku to bukkyō,* ed. Konno Tōru et al., 2:131–56. Tokyo: Iwanami shoten, 1994.

———. *Nihon kinsei shōsetsu to Chūgoku shōsetsu.* Musashi Murayama: Seishōdō shoten, 1987.

Tokutomi, Kenjirō. *Footprints in the Snow: A Novel of Meiji Japan.* Trans. Kenneth Strong. New York: Pegasus, 1970.

Tokutomi Sohō. "Hi-ren'ai." In *Kirisuto-sha hyōron shū,* ed. Yabu Teiko, Yoshida Masanobu, and Izuhara Takatoshi, 244–49. SNKBTM 26. Tokyo: Iwanami shoten, 2002.

———. "Kinrai ryūkō no seiji shōsetsu o hyōsu." In *Kirisuto-sha hyōron shū,* ed. Yabu Teiko, Yoshida Masanobu, and Izuhara Takatoshi, 195–206. SNKBTM 26. Tokyo: Iwanami shoten, 2002.

———. "Shin Nihon no shijin." In *Kirisuto-sha hyōron shū,* ed. Yabu Teiko, Yoshida Masanobu, and Izuhara Takatoshi, 221–33. SNKBTM 26. Tokyo: Iwanami shoten, 2002.

Tomasi, Massimiliano. *Rhetoric in Modern Japan: Western Influences on the Development of Narrative and Oratorical Style.* Honolulu: University of Hawai`i Press, 2004.

Tsubouchi Shōyō. "Aidiaru noberu no koto ni tsukite." In *Tsubouchi Shōyō kenkyū: Fu, bungakuron shoshutsu shiryō,* ed. Ishida Tadahiko, 426–28. Fukuoka: Kyūshū daigaku shuppankai, 1988.

———. "Azusa-miko." In *Shōyō senshū,* ed. Shōyō Kyōkai, 8:143–82. Tokyo: Daiichi shobō, 1977.

———. "Botsurisō no gogi o benzu." In *Tsubouchi Shōyō shū,* ed. Nakamura Kan and Umezawa Nobuo, 189–93. NKiBT 3. Tokyo: Kadokawa shoten, 1974.

———. "[Bunkai meisho:] Soko shirazu no mizuumi." In *Tsubouchi Shōyō shū,* ed. Inagaki Tatsurō, 279–82. MBZ 16. Tokyo: Chikuma shobō, 1969.

———. [*Fūkai:*] *Kyō waranbe.* In *Tsubouchi Shōyō shū,* ed. Inagaki Tatsurō, 258–78. MBZ 16. Tokyo: Chikuma shobō, 1969.

———. *Haishika ryakuden narabi ni hihyō.* In *Tsubouchi Shōyō Futabatei Shimei shū,* ed. Aoki Toshihiro and Togawa Shinsuke, 133–96. SNKBTM 18. Tokyo: Iwanami shoten, 2002.

———. [*Ichidoku santan:*] *Tōsei shosei katagi.* Tokyo: Banseidō, 1886.

———. [*Ichidoku santan:*] *Tōsei shosei katagi.* In *Tsubouchi Shōyō shū,* ed. Nakamura Kan and Umezawa Nobuo, 221–433. NKiBT 3. Tokyo: Kadokawa shoten, 1974.

———, trans. [*Kaikan hifun:*] *Gaisei shiden.* In *Shōyō senshū: Bessatsu,* ed. Shōyō Kyōkai, 2:441–656. Tokyo: Daiichi shobō, 1977.

———. "Kaioku mandan." In *Shōyō senshū,* ed. Shōyō Kyōkai, 12:341–72. Tokyo: Daiichi shobō, 1977.

———. "Makubesu hyōshaku no shogen." In *Tsubouchi Shōyō shū,* ed. Nakamura Kan and Umezawa Nobuo, 179–87. NKiBT 3. Tokyo: Kadokawa shoten, 1974.

———. "Miraiki ni ruisuru shōsetsu." In *Tsubouchi Shōyō kenkyū: Fu, bungakuron shoshutsu shiryō,* ed. Ishida Tadahiko, 417–21. Fukuoka: Kyūshū daigaku shuppankai, 1988.

———. [*Naichi zakkyo:*] *Mirai no yume.* In *Shōyō senshū: Bessatsu,* ed. Shōyō Kyōkai, 1:549–721. Tokyo: Daiichi shobō, 1977.

———. *Saikun.* In *Tsubouchi Shōyō Futabatei Shimei shū,* ed. Aoki Toshihiro and Togawa Shinsuke, 1–57. SNKBTM 18. Tokyo: Iwanami shoten, 2002.

269

BIBLIOGRAPHY

——. "*Setchūbai* kahen no hihyō." In *Tsubouchi Shōyō kenkyū: Fu, bungakuron shoshutsu shiryō*, ed. Ishida Tadahiko, 384–86. Fukuoka: Kyūshū daigaku shuppankai, 1988.

——. "*Setchūbai* (shōsetsu) no hihyō." In *Tsubouchi Shōyō kenkyū: Fu, bungakuron shoshutsu shiryō*, ed. Ishida Tadahiko, 381–84. Fukuoka: Kyūshū daigaku shuppankai, 1988.

——. "Shinkyū katoki no kaisō." In *Shōyō senshū*, ed. Shōyō Kyōkai, 12:319–39. Tokyo: Daiichi shobō, 1977.

——. [*Shinmigaki:*] *Imotose kagami*. In *Tsubouchi Shōyō shū*, ed. Inagaki Tatsurō, 164–248. MBZ 16. Tokyo: Chikuma shobō, 1969.

——. [*Shōsetsu:*] *Gaimu daijin*. In *Honkoku to kenkyū: Tsubouchi Shōyō Shōsetsu: Gaimu daijin*, ed. Shōyō Kenkyūkai, 141–326. Tokyo: Sōbunsha, 1994.

——. "Shōsetsu o ronjite *Shosei katagi* no shui ni oyobu." In *Shōsetsu shinzui*, ed. Munakata Kazushige, 213–17. Tokyo: Iwanami shoten, 2010.

——. *Shōsetsu shinzui*. In *Tsubouchi Shōyō shū*, ed. Nakamura Kan and Umezawa Nobuo, 39–165. NKiBT 3. Tokyo: Kadokawa shoten, 1974.

——, trans. *Shunpū jōwa*. In *Tsubouchi Shōyō Futabatei Shimei shū*, ed. Aoki Toshihiro and Togawa Shinsuke, 59–132. SNKBTM 18. Tokyo: Iwanami shoten, 2002

Tsuda Mamichi. "Jōyokuron." In *Meiji keimō shisō shū*, ed. Ōkubo Toshiaki, 129–30. MBZ 3. Tokyo: Chikuma shobō, 1967.

Tuck, Robert. *Idly Scribbling Rhymers: Poetry, Print, and Community in Nineteenth-Century Japan*. New York: Columbia University Press, 2018.

Ubukata Tomoko. *Seishin bunseki izen: Muishiki no Nihon kindai bungaku*. Tokyo: Kanrin shobō, 2009.

Uchida Roan. "*Hakkenden* yodan." In *Uchida Roan zenshū*, ed. Nomura Takashi, 4:447–79. Tokyo: Yumani shobō, 1985.

——. "Seiji shōsetsu o tsukure yo." In *Kindai hyōron shū 1*, ed. Kawazoe Kunimoto et al., 147–56. NKiBT 57. Tokyo: Kadokawa shoten, 1972.

Ueda, Atsuko. *Concealment of Politics, Politics of Concealment: The Production of "Literature" in Meiji Japan*. Stanford, Calif.: Stanford University Press, 2007.

Ueno Chizuko. "Kaisetsu (3)." In *Fūzoku, sei*, ed. Ogi Shinzō et al., 505–50. Nihon kindai shisō taikei 23. Tokyo: Iwanami shoten, 1990.

Van Compernolle, Timothy J. *Struggling Upward: Worldly Success and the Japanese Novel*. Cambridge, Mass.: Harvard University Asia Center, 2016.

Van Zoeren, Steven. *Poetry and Personality: Reading, Exegesis, and Hermeneutics in Traditional China*. Stanford, Calif.: Stanford University Press, 1991.

Vincent, J. Keith. *Two-Timing Modernity: Homosocial Narrative in Modern Japanese Fiction*. Cambridge, Mass.: Harvard University Asia Center, 2012.

Vitiello, Giovanni. *The Libertine's Friend: Homosexuality and Masculinity in Late Imperial China*. Chicago: University of Chicago Press, 2011.

Vlastos, Stephen. "Opposition Movements in Early Meiji, 1868–1885." In *The Cambridge History of Japan, Volume 5: The Nineteenth Century*, ed. Marius B. Jansen, 367–431. Cambridge: Cambridge University Press, 1989.

Wada Shigejirō. "Shōyō *Imotose kagami* shiron." *Ritsumeikan bungaku* 152 (1958): 1–13.

"Waga kuni ni jiyū no shushi o hanshoku suru ichishudan wa haishi gikyoku nado no tagui o kairyō suru ni ari." In KBHT, vol. 1, ed. Yoshida Seiichi and Asai Kiyoshi, 15–19. Tokyo: Kadokawa shoten, 1971.

Walley, Glynne. *Good Dogs: Edification, Entertainment, and Kyokutei Bakin's* Nansō Satomi hakkenden. Ithaca, N.Y.: Cornell University East Asia Program, 2017.

——. "'I Would Rather Be a Faithful Dog Than an Unrighteous Man': Virtue and Vice in Kyokutei Bakin's *Nansō Satomi hakkenden*." PhD diss., Harvard University, 2009.

Watson, Burton, trans. *The Lotus Sutra*. New York: Columbia University Press, 1993.

——, trans. *Zhuangzi: Basic Writings*. New York: Columbia University Press, 2003.

Widmer, Ellen. *The Margins of Utopia: Shui-hu hou-chuan and the Literature of Ming Loyalism*. Cambridge, Mass.: Harvard University Council on East Asian Studies, 1987.

Williams, Raymond. *Marxism and Literature*. Oxford: Oxford University Press, 1977.

Wong, Siu-kit. "Ch'ing in Chinese Literary Criticism." PhD diss., Oxford University, 1969.

Wu, Cuncun. *Homoerotic Sensibilities in Late Imperial China*. London: RoutledgeCurzon, 2004.

Yamada Shunji. "*Nansō Satomi hakkenden* to iu kagami: Tsubouchi Shōyō, moshasetsu no seiritsu." *Bungei to hihyō* 6, no. 9 (1989): 31–46.

——. "Ninjōbon no saisei made: Meiji shonen no ren'ai shōsetsu ni kansuru ichikōsatsu." *Nihon bungaku* 56, no. 10 (2007): 12–25.

——. "Seiji shōsetsu no ichi: Shōsetsu no shakaiteki ninchi to iu bunmyaku kara." In *Seiji shōsetsu shū 1*, ed. Yamada Shunji and Rinbara Sumio, 539–56. SNKBTM 16. Tokyo: Iwanami shoten, 2003.

Yamamoto Masahide. *Genbun itchi no rekishi ronkō: Zokuhen*. Tokyo: Ōfūsha, 1981.

——. *Kindai buntai hassei no shiteki kenkyū*. Tokyo: Iwanami shoten, 1965.

Yamamoto Yoshiaki. "'Ānesuto Marutorabāzu' 'Arisu' ron: *Karyū shunwa* no gensho no sakuhin sekai to wa nani ka?" *Nihon kindai bungaku* 31 (1984): 1–13.

Yamanouchi Shōshi. "Shōyō ni okeru botsurisō ron no keisei: Bungei riron toshite no realism [*sic*] ron no mondai o chūshin toshite." In *Tsubouchi Shōyō, Futabatei Shimei*, ed. Nihon Bungaku Kenkyū Shiryō Kankōkai, 74–89. NBKSS. Tokyo: Yūseidō, 1979.

Yan Xiaomei. "Nihon ni okeru saishi kajin shōsetsu no juyō ni tsuite: Torai saishi kajin shōsetsu mokuroku." In *Yomihon kenkyū shinshū*, ed. Yomihon Kenkyū no Kai, 4:124–44. Tokyo: Kanrin shobō, 2003.

Yanabu Akira. *Hon'yakugo seiritsu jijō*. Tokyo: Iwanami shoten, 1982.

Yanagida Izumi. *Meiji shoki hon'yaku bungaku no kenkyū*. Tokyo: Shunjūsha, 1961.

——. *Meiji shoki no bungaku shisō*. 2 vols. Tokyo: Shunjūsha, 1965.

——. *Seiji shōsetsu kenkyū*. 3 vols. Tokyo: Shunjūsha, 1967–1968.

——. "Shōyō sensei to josei." *Meiji Taishō bungaku kenkyū* 16 (1955): 64–70.

——. *Wakaki Tsubouchi Shōyō*. Tokyo: Nihon tosho sentā, 1990.

Yano Ryūkei. [*Tēbe meishi:*] *Keikoku bidan (zenpen)*. In *Meiji seiji shōsetsu shū*, ed. Ochi Haruo, 161–320. NKiBT 2. Tokyo: Kadokawa shoten, 1974.

Yeh, Catherine Vance. *The Chinese Political Novel: Migration of a World Genre*. Cambridge, Mass.: Harvard University Asia Center, 2015.

Yoda, Tomiko. "First-Person Narration and Citizen-Subject: The Modernity of Ōgai's 'The Dancing Girl.'" *Journal of Asian Studies* 65, no. 2 (2006): 277–306.

——. *Gender and National Literature: Heian Texts in the Constructions of Japanese Modernity*. Durham, N.C.: Duke University Press, 2004.

Yu, Anthony C. *Rereading the Stone: Desire and the Making of Fiction in* Dream of the Red Chamber. Princeton, N.J.: Princeton University Press, 1997.

Zeitlin, Judith T. "Shared Dreams: The Story of the Three Wives' Commentary on *The Peony Pavilion.*" *Harvard Journal of Asiatic Studies* 54, no. 1 (1994): 127–79.

——. "Xiaoshuo." In *The Novel*, ed. Franco Moretti, 1:249–61. Princeton, N.J.: Princeton University Press, 2006.

Zhang, Xiaohui. "The Pursuit of the Dao: Natsume Sōseki and His *Kanshi* of 1916." *Journal of Chinese Literature and Culture* 5, no. 1 (2018): 148–78.

Zwicker, Jonathan E. *Practices of the Sentimental Imagination: Melodrama, the Novel, and the Social Imaginary in Nineteenth-Century Japan.* Cambridge, Mass.: Harvard University Asia Center, 2006.

INDEX

285

INDEX

poetry: ambiguity in, 33, 35; classical vs. vernacular, 36; and desire, 30, 34, 47; didacticism in, 30, 31–32, 35–36, 38, 41; and emotional distance, 191, 192–95; English, 192, 199, 206, 251n53; eremitic, 203; *haikai*, 45–46, 47; martial, 205; nature in, 190, 196; neo-Confucianism on, 33; *ninjō* in, 3, 11, 17, 21, 35, 190; politics in, 203–6; and private subjectivity, 17; Sinitic (*kanshi*), 30, 38, 41, 181, 185, 190, 192, 195, 196, 199, 201–8, 220n29, 251n53; and Sōseki, 24, 190, 197–98, 199, 206; *waka* (classical Japanese), 31, 37, 38, 45, 46, 47, 51, 190, 193, 196, 199, 217n1, 251n53. *See also* haiku; *Shijing*

politics: and Confucianism, 204; democratic, 17, 22, 93, 102, 109, 112, 122, 140, 142, 143, 147, 161, 165, 166, 170, 236n29; and didacticism, 140–47, 148; and literary reform, 140–47; and new literature concept, 186; and *ninjō*, 139–47; parliamentarian, 95, 112, 143; participation in, 110–11, 112, 113, 142, 144, 147; in poetry, 203–6; and *Seiro nikki*, 114, 117; and violence, 140, 145–47, 161, 239n62, 243n29; and Western literature, 131, 141, 249n27. *See also* Constitutional Reform Party; fiction, political; Liberal Party; National Diet; People's Rights Movement; utopia, political

private vs. public spheres, 16–18, 43, 216n29

prostitution, 95, 104, 108, 153–54, 164, 166–68, 214n12, 230n20, 243n17

psychology, Western, 18, 216n33, 238n50

publishing, commercial, 42, 100, 101, 225n7; of *gesaku*, 6, 8, 9, 48, 50, 55, 85, 230n15; for mass audience, 4, 6, 20–21, 48, 49, 58, 184, 216n29; and movable type, 231n32, 234n76, 237n42

qing (emotion), 218n15, 219n23; Chinese cult of, 21, 41–48

Qing dynasty (China), 5, 8, 41

Qingshi leilüe (History of emotion in encyclopedic categories; Feng Menglong), 98, 231n29

readers: of English literature, 124–26, 149–52, 174, 233n54; and *Imotose kagami*, 151, 166; of *Jinpingmei*, 98, 150; of *Karyū shunwa*, 94–101, 119; and literary reform, 124; Meiji, 94, 98–99, 100, 101; of novels, 94, 98–99, 151–52, 184, 238n53; and politics, 140, 142; and *Seiro nikki*, 118; Shōyō on, 138, 139; tears of, 13, 179–80, 184; women as, 37, 53, 55, 65, 81; of *zōkakiron* genre, 97–98

realism (*mosha; shajitsu*): aporia between idealism and, 23, 137, 139, 141, 142, 148, 149–75, 180, 190, 238n47, 242n13, 247n7; bourgeois psychological, 216n33; civilized, 148, 152; and didacticism, 122, 137–39, 142–47, 157, 166, 239n56, 240n70; and emotions and customs, 139, 141, 142, 148, 154, 157–58; and enlightenment discourse, 148, 152, 153; and *Kusamakura*, 207, 208; and licentiousness, 152, 175, 199; and literary reform, 121, 216n33; method of (*shjitsuhō*), 196; *mosha* as unrelated to, 238nn42–43, 238n50; and *ninjō*, 11, 18, 120, 212; in the novel, 3, 133–39, 180, 210; and political fiction, 141, 142, 146, 186; psychological, 182; vs. romanticism, 195–201; and *shaseibun*, 189–90; Shōyō on, 18, 120, 122, 132–39, 149–75, 210–11, 237nn40–42; Sōseki on, 180, 181, 199; universal, 174–75

"Record of Music" (Yueji), 32–33, 34

Record of Rites (Liji), 12, 218n13

"Reed-Choked House" (Asaji ga yado; Ueda Akinari), 49

Reichert, Jim, 97, 243n29

Revolution of the Heart (Haiyan Lee), 19

"Rhetoric and Belles Lettres" (Chambers), 134

Richardson, Samuel, 171, 198, 216n29

"Shaseibun" (On sketch prose; Natsume Sōseki), 179, 184, 190, 197, 199
Shaving of Shagpat, The: An Arabian Entertainment (Meredith), 193, 251n55
Shijing (Classic of Poetry), 30–34, 38–41, 52, 82, 219n24; desire in, 34, 47; didacticism in, 31–32, 41; and Genji, 36, 38; "Great Preface" (Daxu) to, 31–32, 33, 34, 218nn9–12, 219n23; and Mao school of exegesis, 31–32, 40; and ninjōbon, 57, 58
Shikitei Sanba, 214n14
Shimazaki, Satoko, 217n37
Shimazaki Tōson, 249n32
shin (truth), 75–80, 134–35
Shincho hyakushu (One hundred new works) series (Yoshioka Shosekiten), 183, 248n11, 248n19
Shinjū ten no Amijima (jōruri play; Love Suicides at Amijima; Chikamatsu Monzaemon), 39–40
Shinmigaki: Imotose kagami (Newly polished: Mirror of marriage; Tsubouchi Shōyō), 111, 149–52, 162–69, 172; eavesdropping in, 167, 244n45; on novel as morphine, 1, 29, 86, 150, 151, 166
Shinpen Kinpeibai (The Plum in the Golden Vase newly edited; Kyokutei Bakin), 45, 225n8
Shōsetsu: Gaimu daijin (A novel: Minister of foreign affairs; unfinished; Tsubouchi Shōyō), 245n57
Shōsetsu shinzui (The Essence of the Novel; Tsubouchi Shōyō), 118, 132–39; and Bakin, 6, 9, 10, 23, 133, 135–39, 141–42, 148; and Imotose kagami, 150, 151, 166, 167; and literary reform, 10–11, 120–48; and Mirai no yume, 170; on ninjō, 1–2, 91, 97, 100, 133, 136–37; and political fiction, 141–47, 236n29; preface to, 132; on realism, 18, 132–39, 152, 210–11; and Tōsei shosei katagi, 154, 156, 157, 158, 159; and Western literature, 8, 125, 127
Shuihu houzhuan (The Water Margin continued), 226n20

Shungyō Hachimangane (The Hachiman Shrine bell at spring dawn; Tamenaga Shunsui), 51
"Shunjitsu seiza" (Sitting Quietly on a Spring Day poem; Natsume Sōseki), 252n73
Shun'ōten. See Seitō yodan: Shun'ōten
Shunpū jōwa (Spring breeze love tale; trans. Bride of Lammermoor; unfinished; Tsubouchi Shōyō), 113, 127–28, 131
Shunshoku (Spring colors) series (Tamenaga Shunsui), 50, 51
Shunshoku tatsumi no sono (Spring: color southeast garden; Tamenaga Shunsui), 54, 56
Shunshoku umegoyomi (Spring-Color Plum Calendar; Tamenaga Shunsui), 21, 50–57, 65; and Karyū shunwa, 100, 106; licentiousness vs. chastity in, 7, 30–31, 51, 54, 55, 57, 91, 168; and literary reform, 121
Shunsui. See Tamenaga Shunsui
Sinitic, literary, 97, 98, 100, 109, 116, 118, 127, 220n29, 222n55. See also Chinese vernacular language; Japanese literary style; poetry
Sino-Japanese War, 184, 211
social class: and education, 232n41; and egalitarian love, 103, 104–5; in English literature, 128; and freedom, 116, 165; in Karyū shunwa, 110, 111; and politics, 142, 144, 146, 147; in Tōsei shosei katagi, 158
socialism, 141
social order: and control of passion, 108–13; and cult of qing, 42; vs. freedom, 93, 101; and Genji, 40–41; in Hakkenden, 62; and marriage, 111–12, 113; and ninjō, 1–5, 8, 13, 17, 18–19, 20, 23, 209; and poetry, 36; in political fiction, 141; in Western novels, 93
"Song of Everlasting Sorrow" (Changhenge; Bai Juyi), 197–98
Sorai school (Ogyū Sorai), 38
Sorekara (And Then; Natsume Sōseki), 208